I0815784

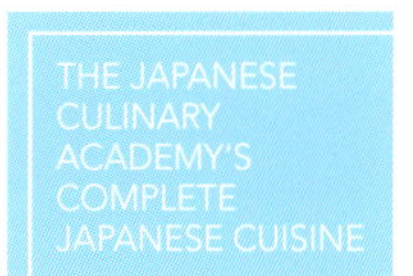

MUKOITA II

Cutting Techniques

—Seafood, Poultry, and Vegetables

THE JAPANESE CULINARY ACADEMY'S COMPLETE JAPANESE CUISINE

MUKOITA 

Cutting Techniques

Seafood, Poultry, and Vegetables

JAPANESE CULINARY ACADEMY

C O N T E N T S

DISCLAIMER: All procedures described herein should be mastered under the guidance of a professional chef. The advice and strategies contained herein are based on the assumption of professional training and familiarity with the basics of Japanese cuisine. Neither the publisher, nor authors, nor editor shall be liable for any damages, special, incidental, or consequential, to health, reputation, or enterprise, resulting from reference to the content described herein.

Published by
Japanese Culinary Academy
office@culinary-academy.jp
https://culinary-academy.jp/
#305 Eiwa Oike Bldg. 436 Sasayacho,
Nakagyo-ku, Kyoto-shi, Kyoto 604-8187,
Japan

Distributed in the United States and Canada by Kodansha USA Publishing, LLC.

Previously published by Shuhari Initiative Ltd.
2025 edition by Japanese Culinary Academy
Editorial supervision of both original and 2025 editions by the Japanese Culinary Academy

Published 2025
Printed in Japan

30 29 28 27 26 25 10 9 8 7 6 5 4 3 2 1

ISBN 978-4-911188-07-1

The jacket features the work of Yoshioka Sachio (1946–2019), the fifth generation of a lineage of Kyoto master dyers. Yoshioka was known for the finesse of his traditional vegetable dyeing techniques. The jacket of this volume displays *ai*, the deep blue of indigo that is thought to be one of the oldest of dyes, and is familiar overseas as "Japan blue."

NOTE: Japanese names in this book are given in traditional order, surname first.

PREFACE

MURATA Yoshihiro

Honorary Chairman, Japanese Culinary Academy

This second volume of *Mukoita* explains the techniques of carving fish and shellfish, poultry, and vegetables, illustrated with detailed photographs. As in the previous volume, it also presents comprehensive information needed by a chef about the types and uses of the knives for performing the techniques, and about the bone structure of fish and fowl.

Work in the kitchen of a Japanese restaurant is generally handled by specialists who take charge of simmered dishes, grilled dishes, and so forth, and function as a team. The *mukoita* position in this team (*ita* means "board"; *mukoita* connotes "facing" or "before the cutting board") handles mainly the sashimi and other dishes that contain raw fish. The *mukoita* chef not only possesses the highly skilled arts of cutting sashimi but is in charge of evaluating, storing, and appropriately distributing the fish as needed by the other members of the team. The *mukoita* will decide, for example, based on the parts and condition of the fish, that the upper fillets (*uwami*) will be used for sashimi and the lower fillets (*shitami*) for grilled dishes and will exercise judgment based on a wide variety of criteria about how to arrange the sashimi for serving depending on the degree to which it has been matured and other factors. As the person who orchestrates everything in the kitchen, the *mukoita* chef doubles as the head chef in many restaurants. Although the scaling and gutting of fish (*mizu-arai*) is ordinarily the job of chefs in training, those steps are included here for each topic in order to assure understanding of the entire preparation process.

Mukoita I explained cutting techniques, particularly for sashimi, for the major fish frequently served in Japanese restaurants—sea bream, flounder, devil stinger, and so on. This book, *Mukoita II*, takes up long fish like eel (*unagi*) and smaller fish such as horse mackerel (*aji*) and sardines, shrimp, squid, octopus, and shellfish. Among these is pike conger (*hamo*), which is in demand especially in the summertime when few other types of fish are at their best. In the days when distribution routes for fresh fish were not as well developed as they are today, particularly in land-locked Kyoto, where the main source of protein was freshwater fish, the vigorous pike conger that could survive shipment inland was highly prized among seawater fish. Today it is a hallmark summer ingredient served throughout the country for parboiled (*otoshi*) or grilled dishes, soups, and other preparations.

Though a popular delicacy, pike conger's numerous and extremely fine bones branching like pine needles (*nikukankotsu*) present special difficulties and cannot be easily removed, even with fish-bone tweezers. Any dish prepared with *hamo* flesh just as it is would offer little more than inedible mouthfuls of bones. The technique of *honekiri*—scoring the flesh to sever the fine bones, leaving them in situ but making them palatable—was devised to overcome that problem. After removing the spine and the central bones, the flesh is scored at 1.2-to-1.3-mm intervals, severing the small bones so that they may be easily chewed. The process is somewhat painstaking but distills the wisdom of chefs in finding ways to make a valuable fish into an enjoyable dish. This book explains the *honekiri* method based on a transparent specimen diagram of the *hamo* bone structure (pp. 72–73), making it clear how chefs deal with the small bones spread throughout the fish. Also included are transparent specimen diagrams for horse mackerel, sardines, eel, and quail. We hope these diagrams will increase understanding of the cutting techniques introduced.

In addition to shrimp, squid, crab, octopus, and shellfish, the book covers carving techniques for chicken, duck, and quail. In Japan, where it was taboo to eat four-legged animal meat for many centuries until modern times, the most common meat consumed was fowl. Particularly in Kyoto, it was customary for shops that sold freshwater fish to also stock quail (*uzura*) or thrush (*tsugumi*), and they were ingredients of household cooking also. While the household food culture of earlier times has changed considerably in Japan, older traditions are passed down in professionally prepared cuisine. Consumption of meat has greatly increased just in the past 20 years, and traditional Japanese-style restaurants today sometimes serve beef, but the meat used most often in *washoku* recipes is fowl.

This book also details the major techniques for cutting vegetables. In addition to preparation of vegetables for cooking or salads, there are also special ways of peeling and creating decorative garnishes to add a sense of the season and enhance the presentation of dishes. The decorative curlicues called *yori*, which evoke the image of waves on a beach, are a garnish for sashimi. Recently, use of sprouts and similar ingredients signals a greater emphasis not only on presenting a beautiful dish but enhancing the tastes it offers.

Cutting comes first in the list of the "five techniques" that are central to Japanese cuisine, along with grilling, simmering, steaming, and deep-frying, and when the ingredients of a dish are eaten raw, how they are cut is essential to enjoyment. The way foods are cut has been a particular focus of attention historically and culturally, with emphasis on displaying respect for the victuals received through the bounty of nature. Slices of sashimi, as with other ingredients, are cut in bite-sized pieces, based on the wisdom that the opening of the mouth is about 3 centimeters and that the volume of the mouth is about the same for most people. Cutting ingredients into shapes that are easy to eat is a form of consideration for others, but chefs also know that the quality of flavor of foods depends on how they are cut.

Even outside Japan, chefs are increasingly using Japanese kitchen knives. Although different cuisines may focus on different aspects of food preparation—Japan emphasizing cutting, France the application of heat, and so on—each has much to learn from the others. We hope that this book will allow chefs to acquire new ideas and knowledge about cutting techniques and that it will help open up new pages for the advancement of Japanese cuisine.

Basic Cutting Techniques

In Japanese cuisine, which prizes not only flavor but appearance, well-sharpened knives and skilled cutting techniques are crucial. This chapter explains the types of knives used, their uses and maintenance, as well as the basics of cutting techniques to be mastered by chefs.

The Hygiene for Food Eaten Raw

In Japanese cuisine, which often features ingredients prepared without heating or cooking, proper hygiene in the kitchen is particularly important. The hygienic practices not only of suppliers all along the food supply chain but of individual restaurants should give high priority to the principles of hazard analysis and critical control points (HACCP), the international management system for food quality control. HACCP provides for analysis of possible hazards that might occur along the path from food production to consumption and identifies essential points for control and monitoring. Japan has its own Food Sanitation Act, which spells out regulations and other measures relevant to food safety from the viewpoint of public health. HACCP similarly aims to protect consumers of food, but in contrast to such conventional regulations, which focus mainly on culinary professionals and kitchen conditions such as cooking tools, or counters and cutting boards, its system offers broad, overall guidelines ranging widely from sanitation during food production and distribution to the washing and handling of ingredients in the kitchen, as well as refrigeration temperatures, shelf life, and other considerations for safe consumption.

Good judgment regarding the quality of food ingredients and the temperature at which they are kept is crucial, of course, but those engaged in cooking must also practice the fundamental principles of good hygiene. They must maintain careful track of food quality and temperature, keep their hands clean, and be scrupulous about their personal care as well, including hair, fingernails, and clothing. Thorough attention to all of these things, no matter how basic, is the first step to introducing HACCP.

The professional chef is constantly conscious of the following three key principles for a safe and healthy kitchen:

Safe Handling of Food

Seafood, meat, and vegetables carry all sorts of bacteria at the time of purchase. The best way to safeguard food and the kitchen is to always select fresh ingredients, wash them carefully in plenty of clean water, place them in clean containers, and keep them in refrigeration of at least 46°F (8°C). Those handling ingredients and preparing food should make it a habit to thoroughly wash their hands with soap, not only before cooking, but after contact with different ingredients as well as after activities outside the kitchen.

Keeping Bacteria at Bay

Take care to keep all foodstuffs at the proper temperature. With raw ingredients, especially, care should be taken to store them at around 40°F (4°C) and not leave them at room temperature. Foods left standing after being made ready to eat are prime sites for the propagation of bacteria and so should be served as soon after preparation as possible.

Clean and Disinfect

Bacteria on meat, eggs, etc. can be killed by sufficient application of heat. Kitchen cloths, dishcloths, cutting boards, knives, and other utensils will harbor bacteria if not carefully disinfected. Especially after contact with meat, fish, eggs, etc. they should be thoroughly washed with detergent and sterilized by either chlorination or boiling water.

Putting these three principles into practice translates into not only personal cleanliness but good health and fitness. The conscientious chef, moreover, will be aware of the temperature in the kitchen and in the storage of ingredients and be careful to judge whether they are safe to be eaten raw or should be prepared by heating instead. Sensitivity to even the slightest concern about spoilage will protect kitchen and customers from food poisoning.

The pursuit of good flavor and the safety of food may seem quite different things, but the professional chef will always have food safety in mind in the creation of fine cuisine.

The eyes of fish are one indication of freshness, as in this example of striped mackerel (*shima-aji*). The eyes of fresh fish are round and clear in color. Clouded and bloodshot eyes signal that freshness has passed.

Knives in the Japanese Kitchen

The kitchen knife, the *hocho*, is the most important tool in Japanese cookery. The word *hocho* (Ch. *paoding*) is said to come from the name of a legendary court cook, Pao Ding, described in the ancient Chinese philosophical treatise *Zhuangzi*. Later, the story goes, his name was applied to knives for preparing fish, meat, and vegetables. Great value is accorded to the *hocho*, to the extent that it is often likened to the "soul" of a chef, and much can be known about a chef's abilities simply by looking at his knives. Particularly in Japanese cuisine, where cutting skills are paramount, knives must answer to the demand for razor sharpness and nuanced control. Western knives are typically steel or stainless steel and double-ground, that is to say sharpened on both sides of the blade. By contrast, most Japanese knives have a single-ground blade in one of two types: *hon-yaki*, which is 100 percent high-carbon steel, and *kasumi* (also *awase*), or high-carbon steel forged onto soft iron. *Hon-yaki*, a high-end product crafted of the same material as traditional Japanese swords, boasts a sharp edge that keeps well, but because of its hardness takes longer to hone. The more commonly available *kasumi* consists of a high-carbon steel edge to perform the actual cutting jacketed onto a body of soft iron. It cuts well and is more affordable and easier to maintain than *hon-yaki*, but suffers in terms of edge retention. Whereas double-ground Western knives are made mainly to cleave food, dividing it left and right, single-ground Japanese *hocho* are efficiently designed to slice foods thinly without crushing the delicate tissue. The back side of the blade is curved to keep food from sticking, further enhancing cutting capability.

The three major kinds of *hocho* are *usuba*, *yanagiba* (*sashimibocho*), and *deba* (pp. 14–17); together these will serve most tasks in Japanese cooking. There is a varied array of other knives for custom purposes, including the *ai-deba*, which is made lighter than a *deba* for use on smaller foods, *honekiri* knives used for preparing pike conger, knives for filleting eel, and many more.

BLADE CROSS SECTION

hon-yaki **(single-forged steel)**

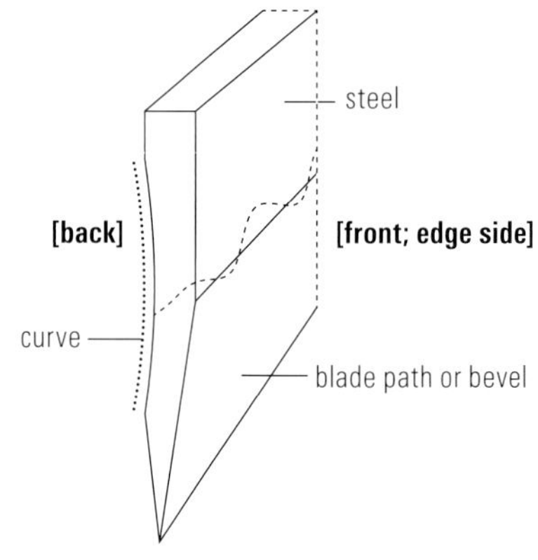

kasumi **(steel-jacketed soft iron)**

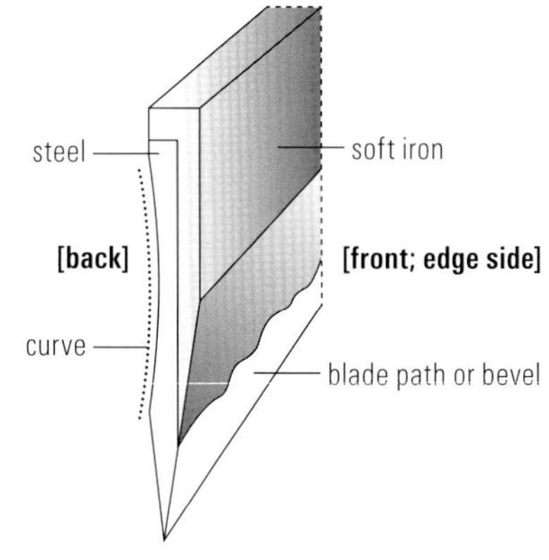

Parts of a *Hocho*

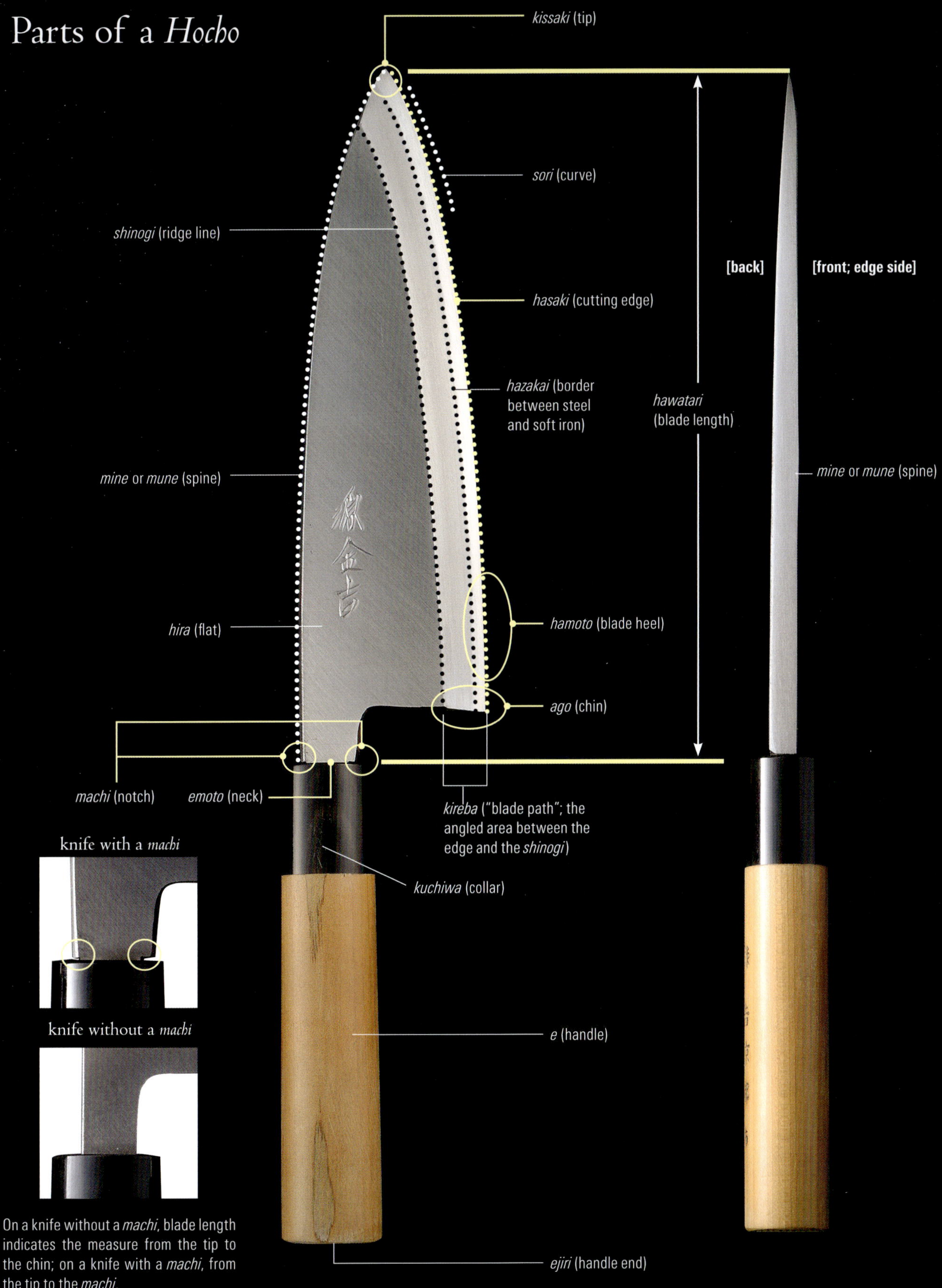

On a knife without a *machi*, blade length indicates the measure from the tip to the chin; on a knife with a *machi*, from the tip to the *machi*.

Types of *Hocho*

usuba *yanagiba* *deba: shomi-deba* *deba: ai-deba* *honekiri: hamokiribocho*

Shown here are three basic types of *hocho*—*usuba*, *yanagiba*, and *deba*. *Deba* knives are further classified into *shomi-deba* ("true" *deba*; also *hon-deba*) and *ai-deba* depending on the thickness of the blade. Each type of knife is available in varied blade lengths—e.g., five *sun* five *bu* (167 millimeters), six *sun* (approx. 180 millimeters), and so on. There are also many knives for specific purposes, among them being *hamokiri* knives used to sever the tiny bones of pike conger as well as *unagibocho* for eel and *kaiwari* knives for shellfish, as shown here.

Uses of *Hocho*

Hocho come in many different shapes, sizes, edges, and thicknesses tailored to their purpose and the foods they are to cut.

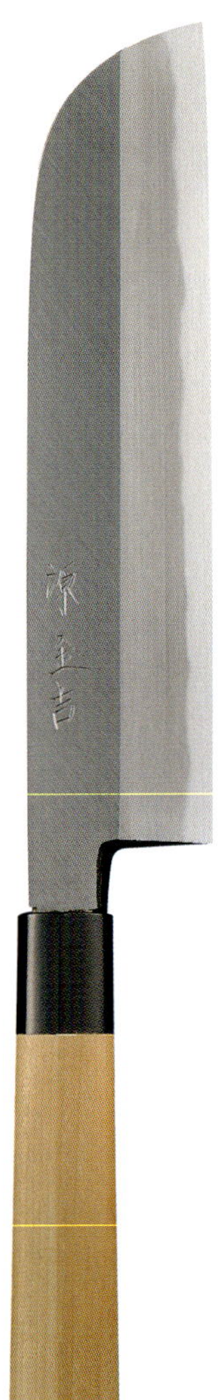

Usuba

Usuba knives from the Kansai (Kyoto-Osaka) area have a rounded head, for which they are also known as *kamagata* ("sickle-shaped"; see left). *Usuba* from Kanto (Tokyo and its environs) have square top corners. Primarily for use with vegetables, *usuba* are equipped with a thin blade that offers little resistance and is suited to skinning or to fine work such as *katsuramuki* rotary peeling and decorative cutting. Slicing is done using the entire length of the blade; mincing or julienning, the area from the tip to about the middle; and peeling, the heel. To cut straight on thick foods, direct the force toward the front (side facing right) of the blade. In terms of orientation, the front (*omote*) side of the blade is called the "outside" while the back (*ura*) side is the "inside."

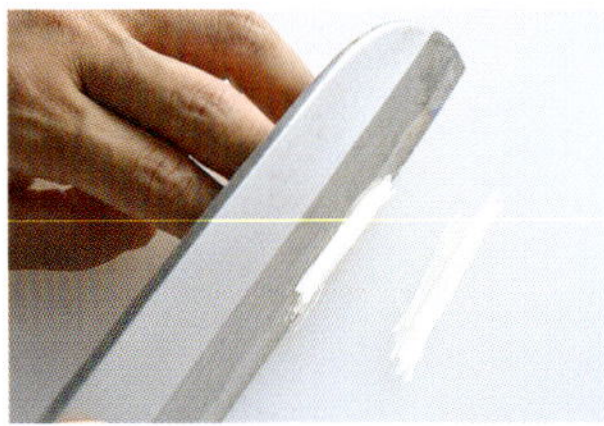

Yanagiba

Yanagiba knives are named for their likeness to the tapered leaves of the willow (*yanagi*). They are also called sashimi knives after their purpose, although in the Kanto area the *takohiki*, another *hocho* characterized by a blade of uniform width from heel to tip, is sometimes used to make sashimi. The long blade of the *yanagiba* slices as it is pulled, without crushing the tissue; its thinness minimizes resistance, ensuring a clean cut surface. Aside from sashimi, the *yanagiba* can be used to fillet meat as well as small fish with soft bones.

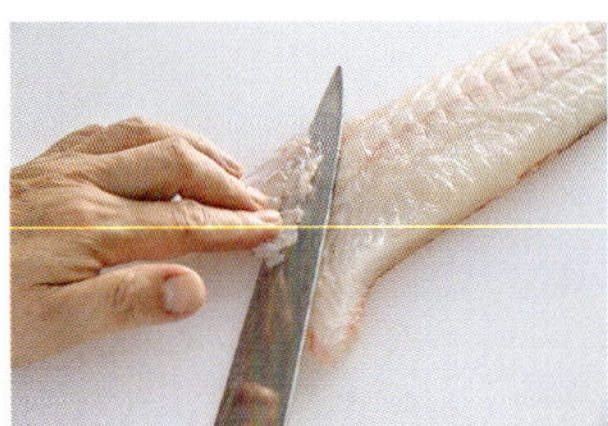

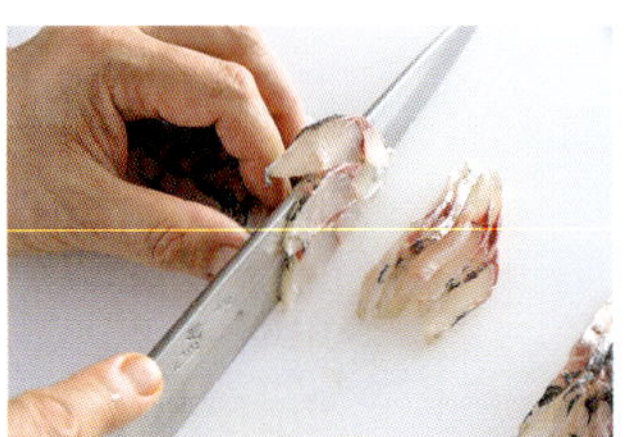

Deba

The hefty blade of the *deba* knife is designed to fillet fish and meat and to cut through tough bones. The blade is made extra thick along the spine to support greater pressure, in contrast to the tip, which is kept thinner for more precision work. Chopping bones and other hard materials is done with the part from the heel to the center of the blade, and filleting with the top half from the center to the tip. A range of knife dimensions accommodates foods of different sizes and thicknesses.

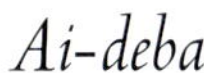

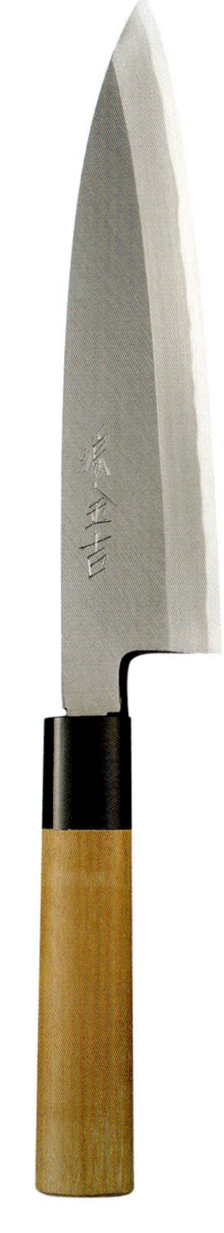

Ai-deba

Ai-deba knives are somewhat narrower in width than *deba* knives. Lighter and easier to handle, they are excellent for skinning or slicing fish but not as well suited for chopping through things like large bones. To cut hard objects using an *ai-deba*, place the edge against the surface and drive the blade in by pushing on the spine with the left hand.

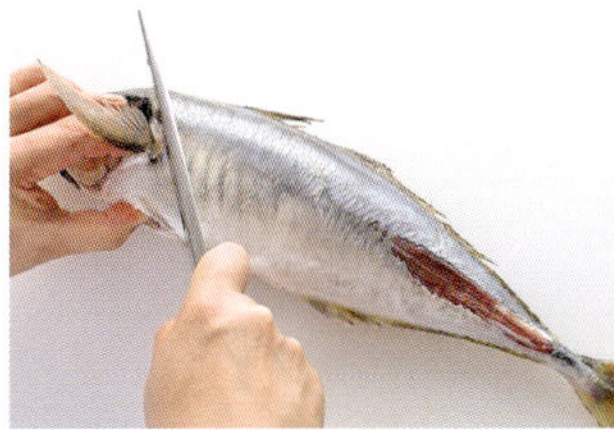

Honekiri (hamokiribocho)

Pike conger (*hamo*) fillets have many fine bones (see pp. 72–73), skillful removal with fish-bone tweezers of which is extremely difficult. To make the fish palatable, the fillet and bones are finely scored, using this long-bladed, thick-spined *honekiri* knife. The knife's weight helps cleanly cut through the fine bones.

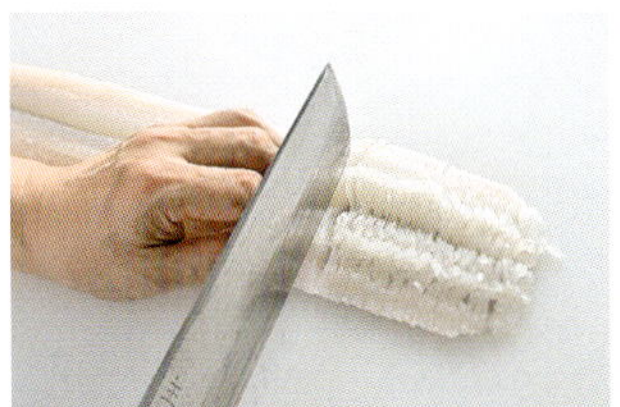

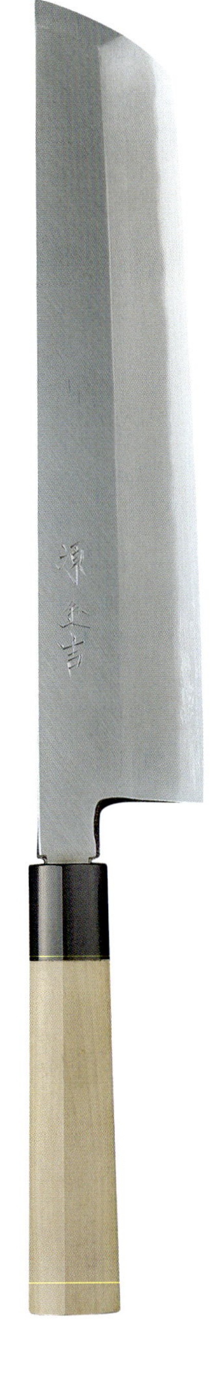

Kaiwari (kaimuki)

Kaiwari (clam) knives are for removing the flesh of shellfish. They are used for other styles of cooking as well. They come in various shapes and sizes depending on whether used for abalone, oysters, scallops, etc. The knife tip is used to pry bivalves apart or to remove adductor muscles and hinge ligaments.

Unagibocho

Unagibocho knives vary in type according to traditional styles of carving eel: *Kyo-wari*, *Edo-wari*, and *Osaka-wari*. This book introduces the *Kyo-wari* knife for opening the eel from the belly and the *Edo-wari* from the back. *Unagibocho* is also used to fillet conger eel (*anago*).

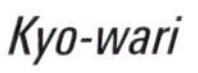

Kyo-wari

Edo-wari

Kyo-wari (for opening from the belly)

This *bocho*, used to slice open the eel from the belly, looks like a hatchet with a short blade and rounded end. The blade is held by the spine of the knife.

Edo-wari (for opening from the back)

This *bocho* is used to slice open the eel from the back. It has a triangular tip with a sharply pointed edge. After splitting open the back, it is also used to cut the flesh and remove the fins, so the blade is rather long among eel knives. The wooden handle is short to easily fit in the hand.

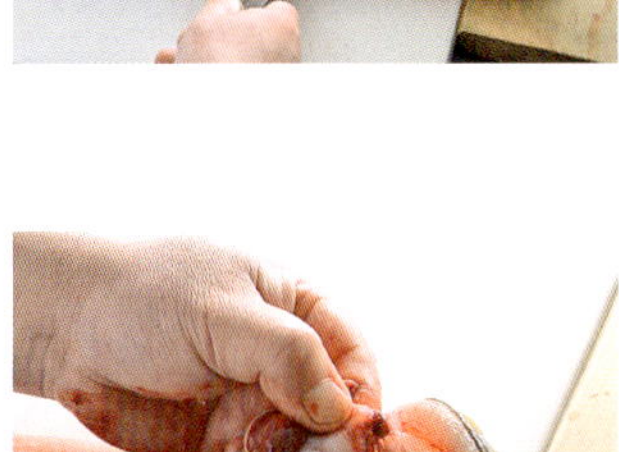

Me-uchi

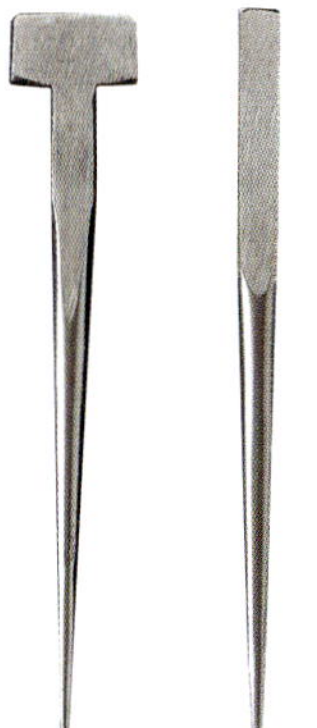

The headed nail functions to anchor a long, narrow fish like an eel (*unagi*) or a pike conger (*hamo*) to the cutting board. Its point is driven in at the edge of the fish's eye to hold the fish in place.

Posture and Grip

When using a *hocho*, it is important to stand at a proper distance from the cutting board (*manaita*) and maintain correct posture to facilitate smooth movement. A correct hold is the key to skillful manipulation. Some chefs wear tall *geta* clogs in the kitchen in order to adjust their height in relation to the board and also to make it easier to serve food to customers sitting across from them at a counter.

In the most basic technique, the knife is inserted perpendicularly into the food; the illustration here shows this basic stance. Depending on where the cut is to be made, adjust your own position by pulling your right foot backward or forward.

NOTE: The directions given in this book are intended for handling of right-handed knives. For handling of left-handed knives, reverse the directions given. (The chef at right is photographed without an apron to better show the position of his feet.)

Basic Posture

- Stand at an angle from the cutting board. Set your feet shoulder-width apart, pulling your right foot half a step backward so that the blade can be positioned to enter perpendicularly when making a cut.
- Place the cutting board at the height of your navel and hold the knife perpendicular to the board.
- Keep your body at about a fist's length (approximately 10 cm or 4 in.) away from the board.
- Incline yourself slightly forward and direct your gaze to the inside (back) of the blade.

Hand position

- Hold the food in place by curling your left hand over it into a light fist as though cupping an egg inside.
- Rest the first knuckle of your left middle or index finger against the flat of the knife and shift the hand away from the blade as you cut.

Basic Grip

Regardless of type, all *hocho* are held in basically the same way. Mastering the correct grip is essential to cutting precisely and efficiently with minimum force.

Usuba

Mincing

With the *hocho* spine-side up, take the area near the heel of the blade between your thumb and index finger; lightly wrap your other fingers around the handle. Firmly gripping with the thumb and index finger helps stabilize the blade, making this the optimum hold for mincing and skinning vegetables.

Peeling

For *katsuramuki* rotary peeling or decorative cutting, hold the *hocho* as described at left but with the blade held horizontal to the surface to be peeled, as shown.

Yanagiba

Start by holding as you would an *usuba* knife. When filleting fish, extend the index finger over the spine; this allows you to sense the blade all the way to the tip and also stabilizes the knife, ensuring smooth, straight slicing.

Deba

Filleting fish

Start by holding as you would an *usuba* knife. Place your index finger along the spine as with the *yanagiba* but further forward, pushing your fist up near the root of the blade. This stabilizes the center of gravity and makes it easier to work while filleting fish and meat.

Chopping

Hold the handle lightly near the end. Grasping the end helps exert more force on the heel—which is heavier compared with the rest of the blade—thus imparting the power necessary to cut through tough bones or chop flesh finely.

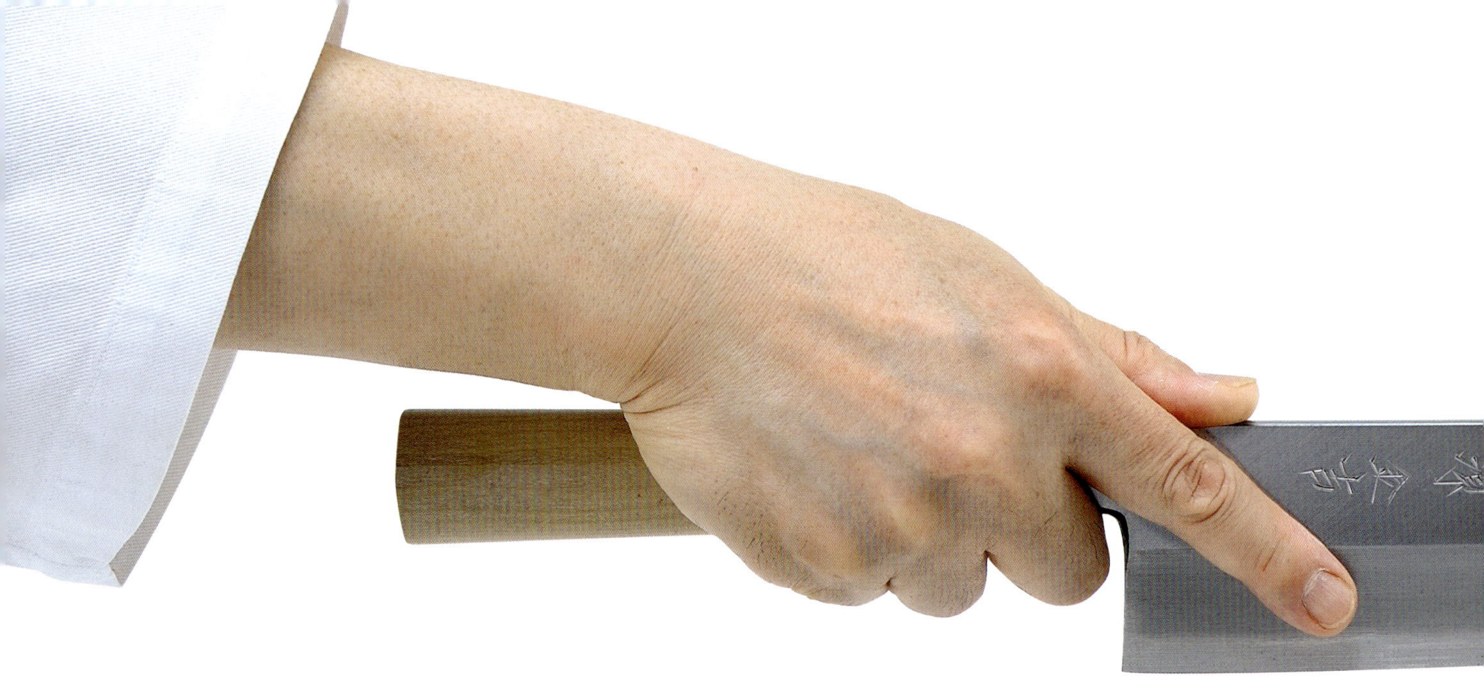

Honekiri (*hamokiribocho*)

Grip when severing fine bones

Hold the knife with your right thumb on the spine and index finger on the flat, thereby steadying the angle of the blade. This helps to keep the movement of the arm smooth as well as utilize the weight of the knife. When severing the fine bones, place the head-end of the fillet to the right, tilt the knife slightly toward the tail-end side, and make incisions leaving the skin layer uncut (see p. 81).

Unagibocho

Kyo-wari (for opening from the belly)

The blade is very short, so the grip extends from the handle over part of the back of the blade. Place your thumb on the back side of the blade and grip the spine, applying force directly for filleting the fish.

Grip for belly bone removal

When removing belly bones of a long fish, place your thumb on the back side of blade and your index finger on the spine of the blade. Set the blade horizontally and insert it between the belly bone and flesh to scrape off the bones (see p. 80).

Edo-wari (for opening from the back)

Grip for opening from the back

To open the nailed eel from its back, hold the knife with the index finger placed on the spine and slice the eel with the cutting edge.

Grip for spine and central bone removal

After slicing the eel open, place your thumb on the back side of blade, hold the handle lightly, and remove the belly bones.

Knife Maintenance

The cutting performance of a chef's knives is considered key to the quality of the cuisine. A knife should be sharpened until its edge is perfectly smooth. Three grades of whetstones (*toishi*) are available for sharpening—*arato* (coarse), *nakato* (fine), and *shiageto* (finishing)—each with its own purpose. Here we explain the sharpening process with the *shiageto* whetstone, which is used for daily knife care.

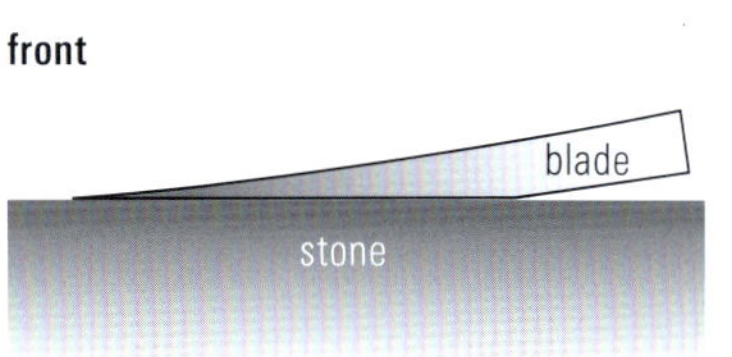

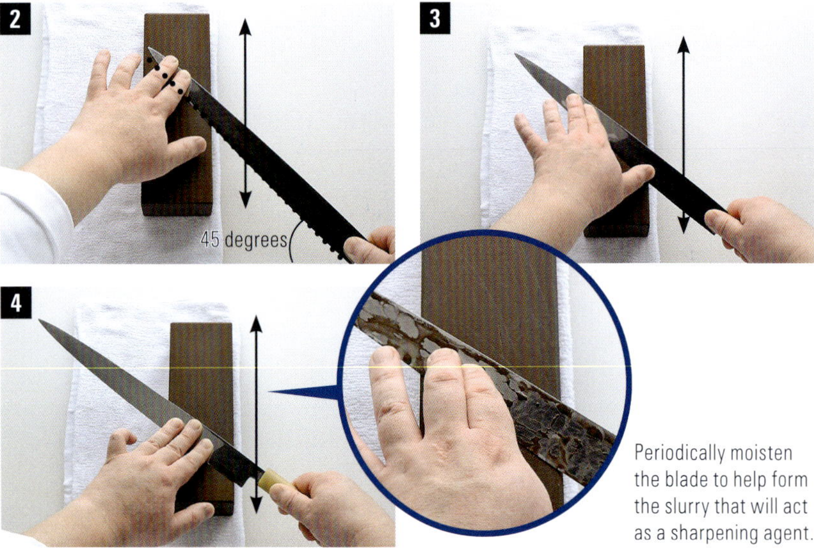

Periodically moisten the blade to help form the slurry that will act as a sharpening agent.

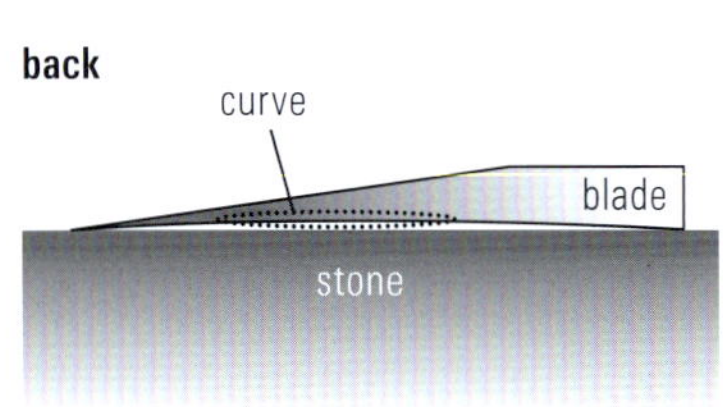

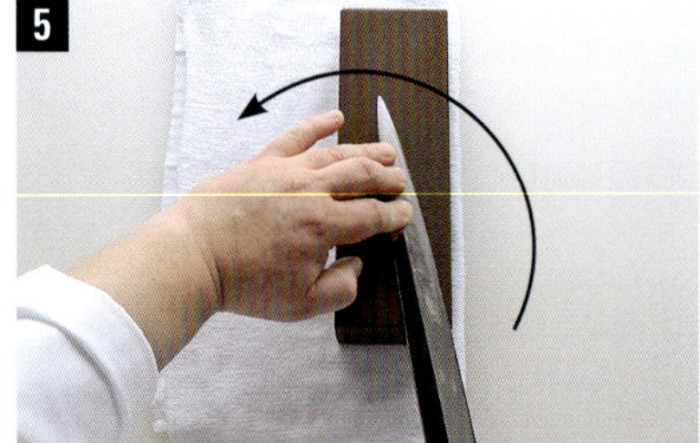

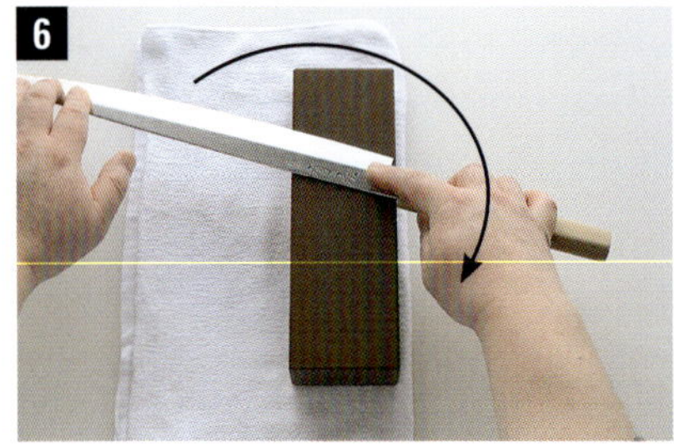

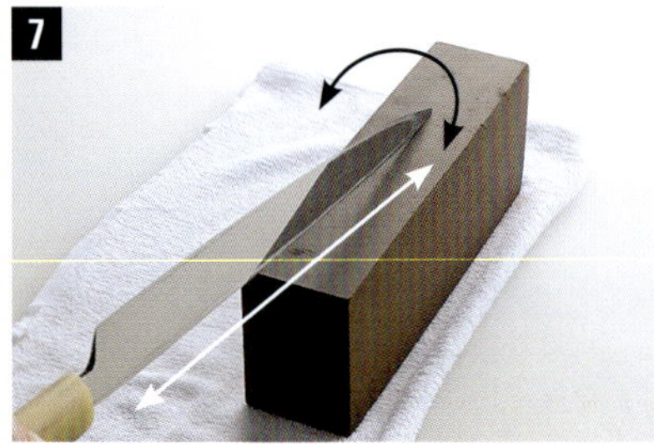

Sharpening

1. Soak the whetstone in water for about an hour beforehand, because the friction of whetting a blade on a dry surface may cause the edge to chip. Giving the stone plenty of water also allows this water to mix with the grit that shaves off against the blade, forming a slurry that acts as a sharpening agent.
2. Place a damp, well-wrung-out towel under the stone, both to prevent the stone from drying out and to hold it in place. Lay the stone on the towel with the shortest side facing you at a distance of about one fist. Start working on the beveled side of the blade (the front) from the tip end, keeping it at a 45-degree angle from the vertical axis and holding down with the fingers so that the bevel of the blade fits flush against the stone.
3. As you slide the blade across the stone, grasp the handle firmly with your right hand and with the fingers of your left hand press down on the blade (be careful not to press too hard and injure yourself).
4. Whet the upper part of the blade about ten times, then the middle part ten times, and finally the lower part ten times. For long knives such as the *yanagiba*, work a quarter of the length at a time, ten times each.
5. Turn the blade over to work the back side. Be careful not to sharpen this side too much, since doing so will reduce the back curve (see p. 12). Run the blade gently over the stone, circling it around to the left as you move from tip to heel.
6. Once you have made a semicircle, reverse the process and rotate the blade back down toward the right. Flip the knife over and sharpen the front again three more times, sprinkling water as you go to wash away the slurry.
7. Roll the stone over on its side and slide the knife tip and spine straight against it, back and forth. Then slide the spine back and forth again while tipping to either side (this restores the bevel on the spine that was flattened out when it was first rubbed). Knives are sharpened several times a day, as needed, maintaining the blade, the tip of the spine, and tip of the blade, for best performance.

A polisher made from a rolled-up old dishcloth bound with kite string. A regular dishcloth or sponge may also be used.

Polishing

1. After the blade has been sharpened, it needs to be polished. Place the knife on a cutting board, front side up. Apply cleansing agent to a dishcloth and polish the blade from the heel toward the tip. Scrub hard to completely remove the slurry caught deep in the fine scratches on the blade.
2. Repeat step 1 on the back side.
3. Repeat again along the spine.
4. To polish the wood of the handle, switch to cleansing agent and a scrubbing brush. (Do not polish the collar, since it may scratch.)
5. Finally, clean the base of the blade near the handle using a sanding block or other solid abrasive.
6. Rub to remove dirt and rust.
7. Be sure to remove all soiling thoroughly to prevent rusting of the blade above the collar.

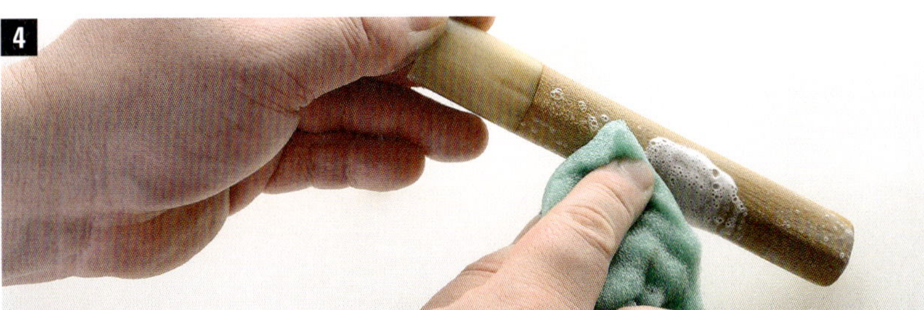

Fish and Fowl Anatomy for Chefs

Fish

Fish can be categorized according to shape, habitat, the way they swim, and other factors. The diagrams here show the bone structures for several of the fish for which carving procedures are explained in this book. Since the methods for cutting fish are fairly uniform for fish of a similar shape, a good grasp of the fish's bone structure is the best way to understand the correct procedure for carving. Oval fish are the most common; they include sea bream, sea bass, salmon, horse mackerel, and sardine. In the diagrams, reddish purple indicates hard bones and blue soft bones. For the bone structure of pike conger, see pages 72–73.

Very long fish (eel-type)

Eel (*unagi*), conger eel (*anago*)

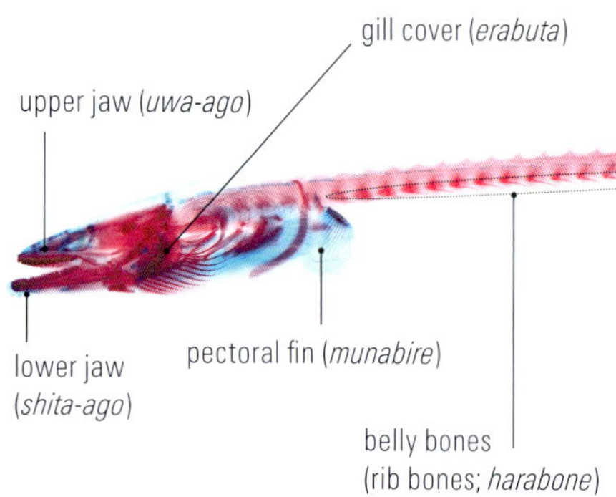

Oval fish (symmetrical)

Horse mackerel (*aji*)

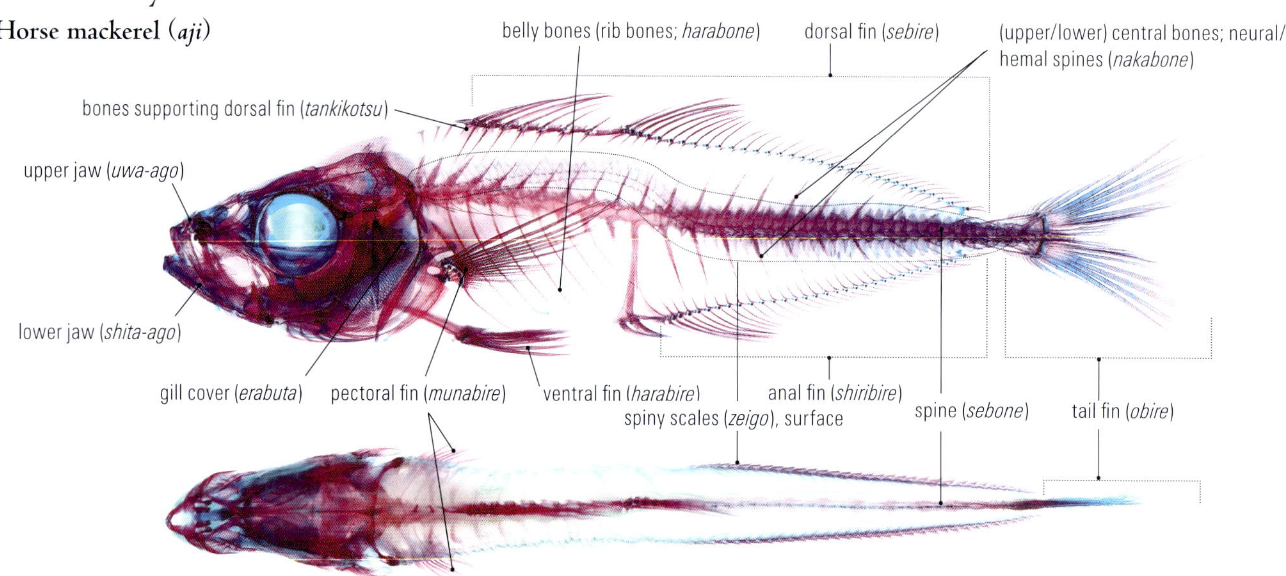

Sardine (*iwashi*)

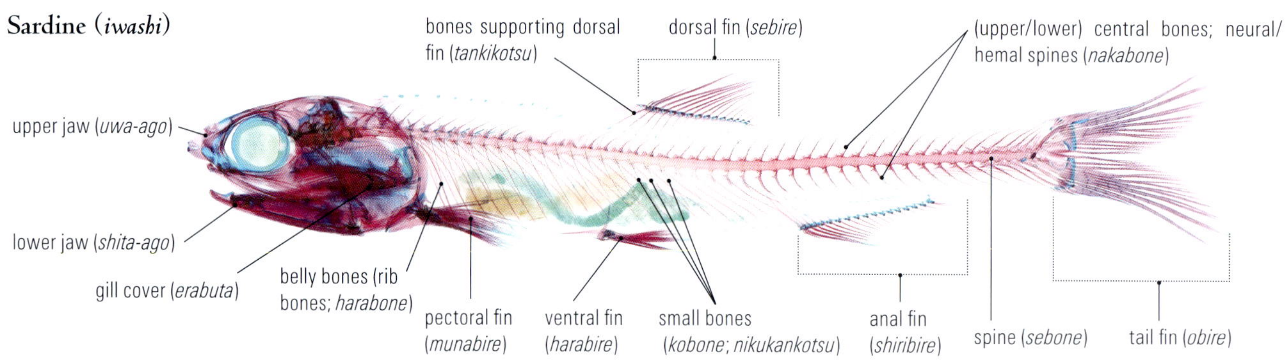

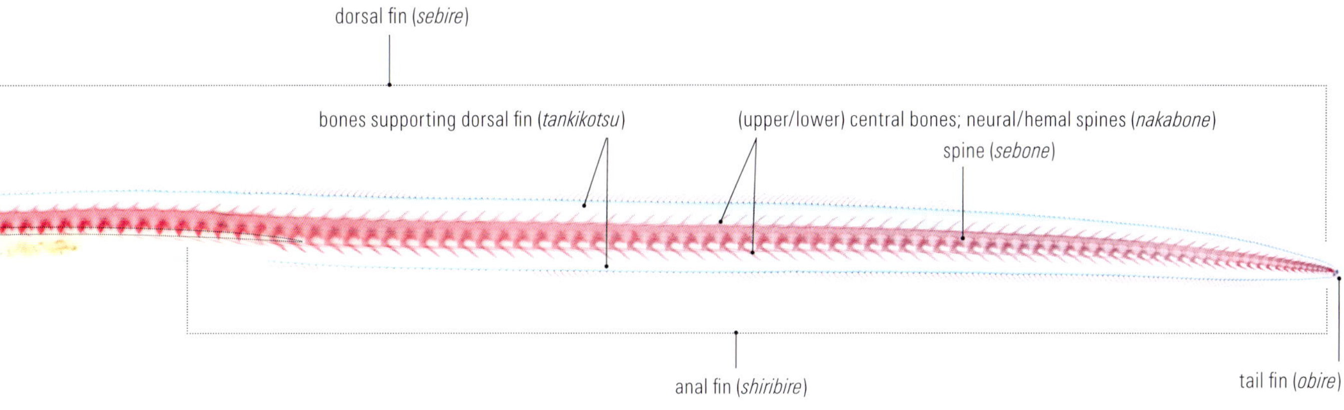

Fowl

Birds, or fowl, are rare among animals in that they are bipedal walkers like humans and their lower limbs are very well developed. Their bone structure is light and strong, suitable for flying. The diagrams here show the bone structure for quail, the carving procedures for which are explained in this book. The generally mature birds used for cooking consist largely of hard bones, but the example shown here is of a young bird, whose bones are mainly soft. The soft bones are indicated in blue.

Quail (*uzura*)

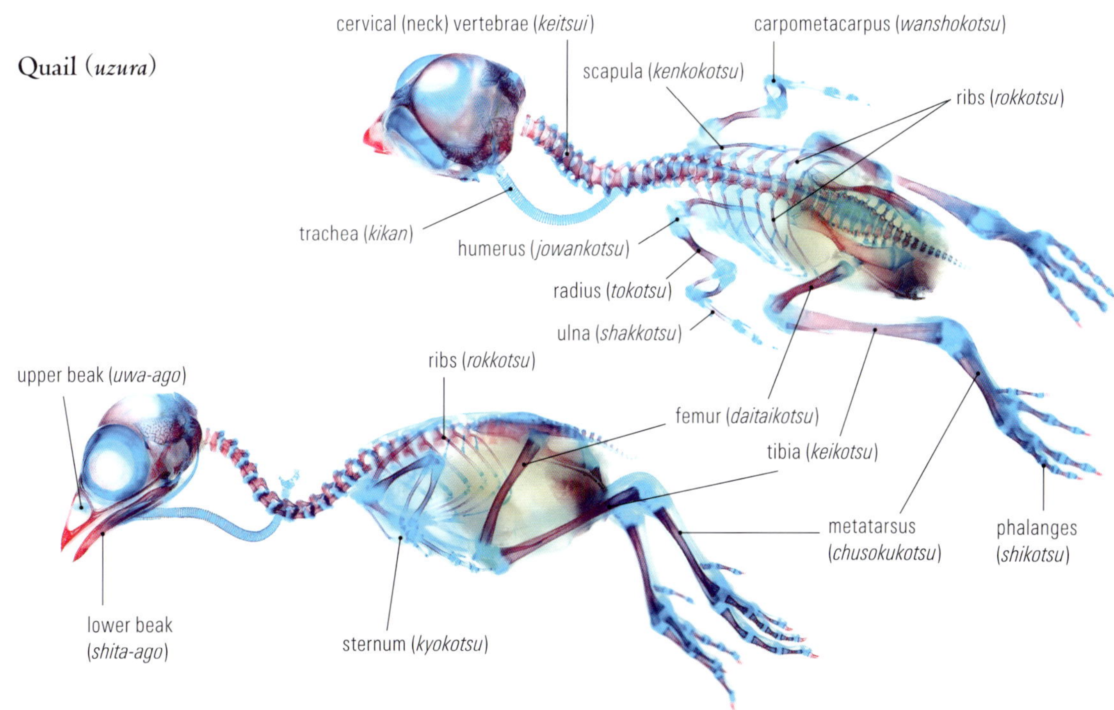

Chapter 1

Filleting Small Fish and Long Fish

Small fish like horse mackerel (*aji*) may be filleted in three pieces (*sanmai oroshi*) as well as by the variant *daimyo-oroshi* technique, which leaves more flesh on the bones. Small fish with soft and fragile flesh, such as sardines, are filleted by hand (*tebiraki*; see pp. 41–43).

Eel, pike conger, and other long fish are slippery; they need to be secured to the cutting board before filleting with special knives, which are described on pp. 18–19. Regional traditions and preferred methods of preparation may indicate opening eel and conger eel from the belly or from the dorsal side. Both techniques are shown here.

Aji
HORSE MACKEREL

Trachurus japonicus

What is commonly called "*aji*" refers to *ma-aji* ("true" horse mackerel), a species in the family Carangidae (order Perciformes). Recognizable for the row of hard spiny scales (*zeigo*) along its sides, *aji* is found all around Japan's coasts. The type of *aji* that migrates along the coasts has a slender body with a blackish back. The type that is not migratory inhabits shallow sea beds; it has a yellowish back, a smaller head, and plumper torso. Migratory *aji* are caught and marketed in much larger quantities than the yellow-backed mackerel, called *ki-aji* ("yellow horse mackerel"). The latter carry more fat, are tastier, and are sold at higher prices.

The sign of freshness in the case of migratory mackerel is a cobalt-blue hue over the whole body; for yellow mackerel, a lustrous gold. Small *aji* are usually flash-frozen in ice or killed upon capture, both methods being called *nojime*. The larger, high-priced *seki-aji* mackerel are spiked and the blood drained (*ikejime*).

Horse mackerel is in season in summer when at their fattiest. They are prepared in various ways—sashimi, chopped sashimi (*tataki*), salt grilled (*shio-yaki*), deep-fried, and so on. As the harvest is generally abundant and the price relatively low, horse mackerel, along with sardines, are fish frequently found on the dinner table.

CUTTING HORSE MACKEREL INTO THREE PIECES
(*Sanmai oroshi*)

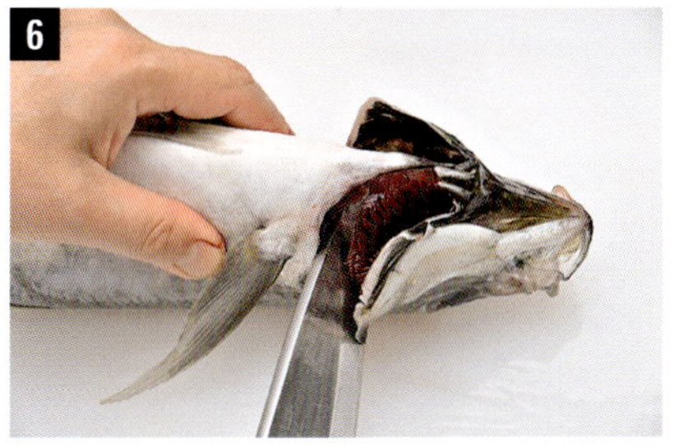

Preparation

1 Removing the spiny scales (steps **1**–**3**). With the head to the left and the belly facing you, grasp the fish lightly with the left hand, hold the *ai-deba* knife horizontally, and start cutting beneath the spiny scales from the tail end.

2 Moving the knife in a sawing motion, cut in the direction of the head to slice off the hard scales.

3 Remove the hard scales as shown. Do the same on the other side.

4 Holding the head with the left hand and placing the knife blade vertical to the spine, scrape off the scales in tail-to-head strokes. Remove the scales near the fins and remaining tiny scales with the tip of the blade. Take care not to cut the skin or damage the fins. Follow the same procedure on the other side. Wash off all the scales in running water and blot dry with a cloth.

5 Place the fish with the head to the right, belly side up. Open the gill covers with your fingers; insert the tip of the knife, blade facing right (*sakasabocho*), and sever the attachment of the gills, i.e., the base of the collar (*kama*), the area between the gill cover and pectoral fin.

6 Insert the knife at the center of the lower jaw and pull the blade toward you to sever the base of the gills.

7 With the left hand placed lightly along the dorsal side of the fish (as shown), and the blade facing left, cut the fish down the center of the ventral side from the lower jaw toward the tail, as far back as the ventral fins.

8 Reverse the direction of the blade and cut from the anal vent up to the ventral fins to meet the incision made in step **7**.

9 Holding the belly cavity open with the left hand, blade facing the head, cut away the membranes covering the internal organs.

10 Pull out the internal organs.

11 With the tip of the knife, cut the white membrane (air bladder) away from the spine. Take care not to cut the flesh.

12 Under running water, use a *sasara* (p. 246) bamboo brush (or equivalent stiff-bristled brush) to clean out blood and remaining bits of the organs. Blot dry both the inner cavity and the outside of the fish with a cloth.

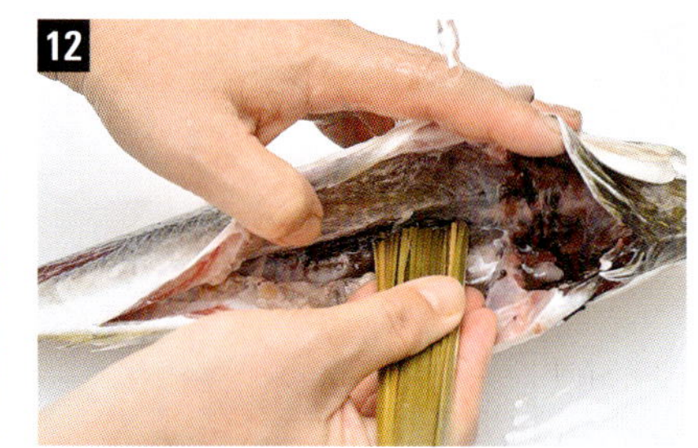

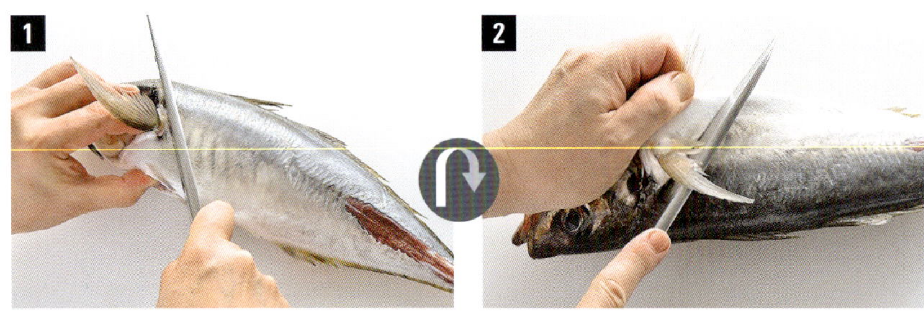

Cutting into three pieces

1 Place the head to the upper left as shown and the belly facing you. Lift the pectoral fin with the left hand and insert the knife diagonally from the base of the pectoral fin to the base of the ventral fin.

2 Turn the fish over so that the head is on the left with the dorsal side facing you. With the left hand, lift the *kama* collar together with the ventral fin. Lowering the angle of the knife, place the blade on the fish at the base of the pectoral fin as shown. Push the knife in once, cutting toward the belly side, and then pull it toward the dorsal side, that is, cutting toward you.

3 Pulling the knife toward the dorsal side, cut where the head and the spine are connected to remove the head (*tasuki-otoshi* technique).

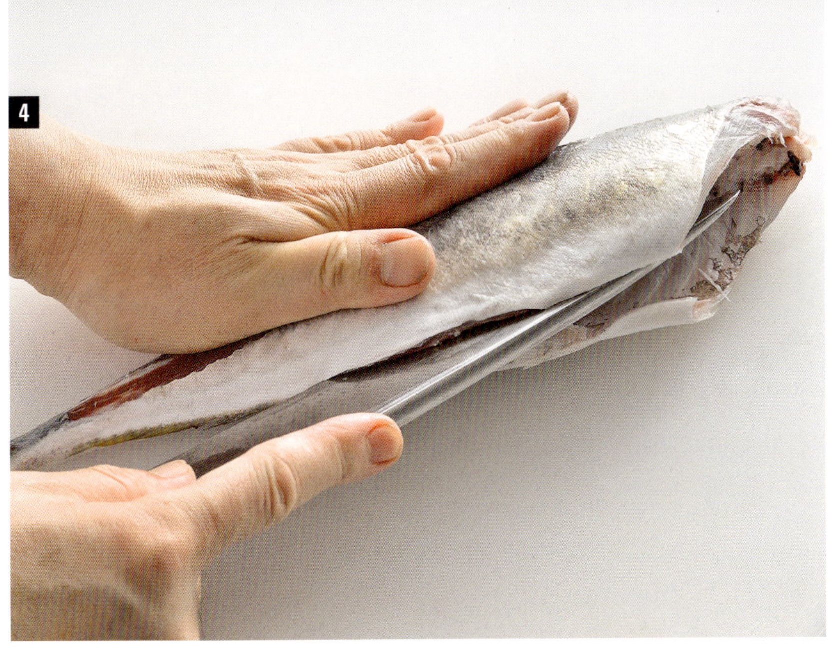

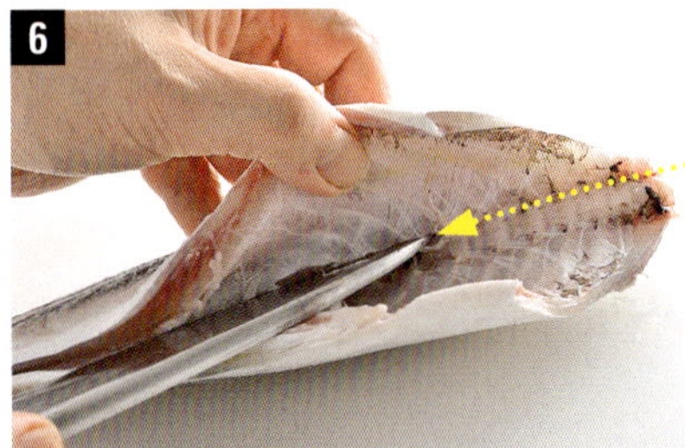

4 Cutting the lower fillet (*shitami*) (steps **4**–**8**). Place the fish with the head end to the upper right and the belly facing you. Steady the body lightly on the dorsal side with the left hand, insert the blade over the ventral fin and cut in over the central bones until the knife reaches the spine.

5 Keeping the knife horizontal, draw the tip of the knife over the central bones, cutting to the base of the tail.

6 With the left hand, lift the flesh and cut in further (indicated by the arrow) along the central bones.

7 Holding the flesh open, cut back to the base of the spine. Draw the knife through the flesh in several passes, checking the location of the spine with each pass and cutting all the way to the tail.

8 Cut entirely through the flesh over the dorsal fin and, while lifting the flesh with the left hand, slide the knife over the spine and open the fish back to the tail, separating the upper and lower fillets.

9 The lower fillet cut away.

to next page

from previous page

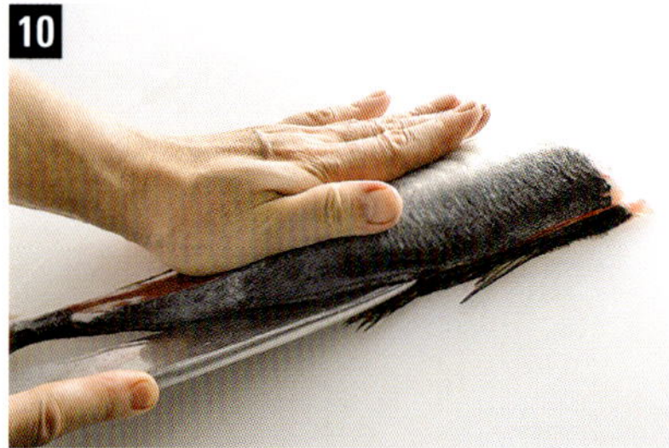

10 Cutting the upper fillet (*uwami*). Place the fish at a slight angle, head end to the right and the dorsal side facing you. Steady the fish lightly with the left hand as shown and insert the knife just over the dorsal fin.

11 Lifting the flesh with the left hand and sliding the knife over the central bones, cut back to the tail.

12 Reverse the direction of the fish, placing the head end to the left and the belly toward you at a slight angle. Steady the fish lightly with the left hand as shown and insert the knife just over the anal fin.

13 Lifting the flesh with the left hand, cut in the direction of the head end, sliding the knife over the central bones to open the fish.

14 Continue lifting the flesh with the left hand and cut in to the edge of the spine.

15 Steadying the fish lightly with the left hand, reverse the knife to face right and cut back, sliding the tip of the knife over the central bones to the base of the tail (but not severing central bones from the tail).

16 Change the direction of the knife to face left and, holding the fish lightly at the base of the tail, run the knife over the spine toward the head, completely separating the flesh from the bones. Finally, cut the fillet away from the base of the tail.

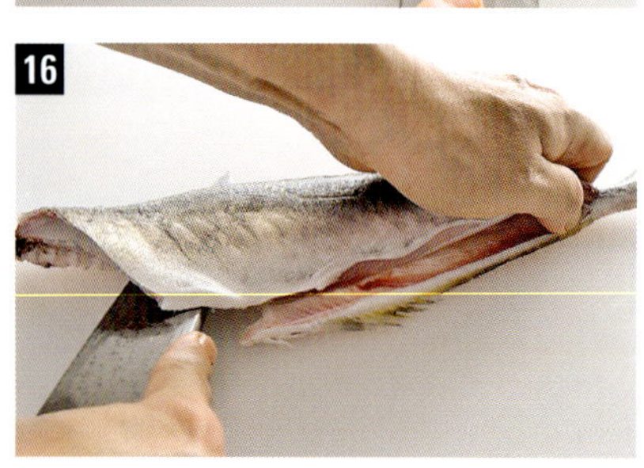

horse mackerel cut into three pieces

to next page

from previous page

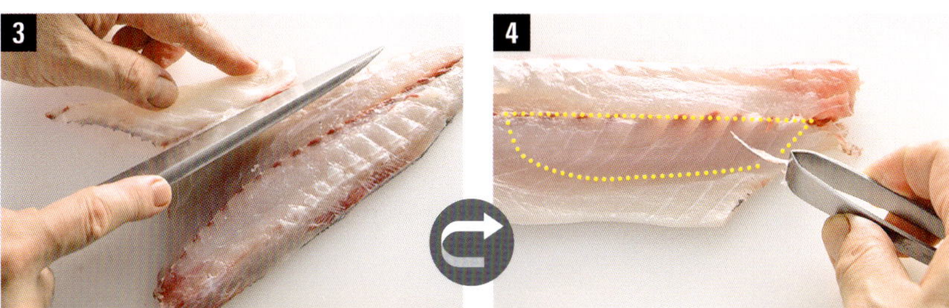

Removing the belly bones and the skin

1 Place the upper fillet with the head end away from you and the belly side facing you. Holding the knife blade to the right (*sakasabocho*), insert the tip of the knife as shown and cut along the inner edge of the belly bones.

2 Reverse the direction of the fish (dorsal side facing you), and, while steadying the belly bones with the left hand, insert the knife into the incision made in step **1**.

3 Drawing the knife toward you so as to leave as little flesh on the bones as possible, cut off the bones in a scooping motion. Where the flesh on the belly membrane is thin, raise the angle of the blade and cut through the base of the flesh to remove the belly bones with the ventral fin left intact on the bones.

4 Remove bones remaining in the fillet with bone tweezers.

5 Change to a *yanagiba* knife. Place the fillet with the head end to the right, skin side up. Make an incision from the head end beneath the skin and pull the skin back from the flesh about 3 cm (1¼ in.).

6 Place the head end to the left, skin side down. Reversing the direction of the knife (*sakasabocho*), insert the knife into the incision made in step **5** and, while pulling on the skin with the left hand, slide the knife toward the tail end (to the right) between the skin and the flesh.

7 At the tip of the fillet, separate flesh and skin.

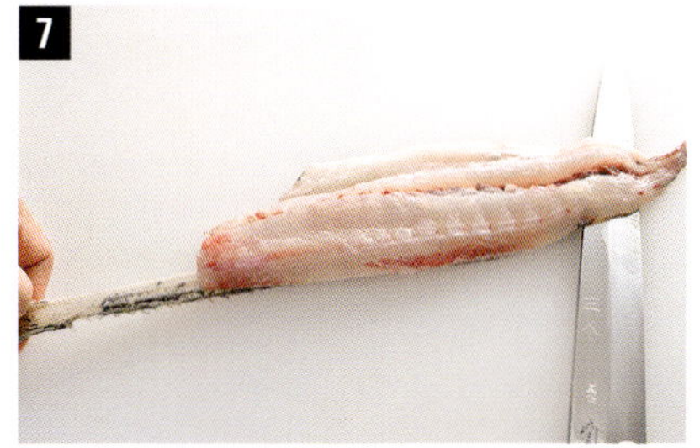

skin removed from the fillet

Horse Mackerel *Tataki*

Aji Tataki

Tataki is the method of chopping thin slices of fish into small pieces as well as the name of this style of dish. The *tataki* style derives from the way fisherfolk prepare fish and is most commonly made with horse mackerel. The recipe here calls for cutting the flesh in small pieces, rather than chopping finely, and tossing them with aromatic ingredients.

Serves 4

120 g (4 oz.) horse mackerel fillet with skin removed

2 *shiso* leaves

1 *myoga*

12 stalks of *asatsuki*

1 tsp. grated ginger

10 g (1/3 oz.) shoyu jelly (see below)

15 g (1/2 oz.) *nagaimo* yam

4 *shiso* flowerets

Shoyu jelly (yields about 430 g or 14 oz.)

Scant 1 cup shoyu

Scant 1/2 cup de-alcoholized sake

Scant 1/2 cup mirin

35 g pearl agar

Prepare the shoyu jelly. Mix all ingredients and cool in the refrigerator until jelled. Press the jelly through a sieve (*uragoshi*).

1. Use fillet that has been skinned. With the skin side up, steady the flesh with the left hand and cut into 4–5 mm (about 1/4 in.)-wide strips from the right side. Stack the slices and cut them in two.
2. Stack the *shiso* leaves and cut into thin strips from the right side (see p. 222). Cut the *myoga* bud in two lengthwise, stack the halves, and slice using the "small-end cut" (*koguchigiri*) technique (see p. 229). Prepare the *asatsuki* by the small-end cut technique as well. Place the chopped *shiso*, *myoga*, chives, and grated ginger on top of the horse mackerel and toss the ingredients gently with chopsticks to mingle them.
3. Shape the preparation by placing in a cylindrical mold such as shown.
4. Spread a layer of the shoyu jelly in the serving dish and place the molded ingredients on top. Garnish with a crown of finely diced *nagaimo* yam, *shiso* flowerets, and topped by a sprinkling of *asatsuki*.

Horse Mackerel *Tataki*

nagaimo yam
shiso leaves
myoga
shiso flowerets
asatsuki
grated ginger
shoyu jelly

Chives, ginger, and other aromatics counteract any briny tastes to bring out the best flavor of the fish.

Hegi-zukuri

The *hegi-zukuri* technique involves slicing fish in a motion as if shaving off slices over the end of the block. The knife is inserted into the block at a low angle and then raised to complete the slice. This technique is used for thin slicing of sea bream, flounder, and other white-fleshed fish that are firm in texture, but mackerel flesh is quite soft, so it is best to cut fairly thick slices.

1 Place the fillet with the head end facing at an angle upward to the left. With the blade at a slightly low angle (as shown), cut in at a thickness of about 5 mm (¼ in.).

2 Cut along the grain of the flesh.

Horse Mackerel Sashimi

radish *ken*
red bud *shiso*
shiso flowerets
grated ginger

Iwashi

SARDINE

Sardinops melanostictus

Iwashi (sardine) is the common name for *ma-iwashi* ("true" sardine) and *urume iwashi* (big-eye sardine) of the herring family of Clupeidae (order Clupeiformes) and *katakuchi iwashi* (anchovy) in the family Engraulidae (the same order). They are an important food fish not only in Japan but in many other countries and regions facing the sea. They are agile swimmers, traveling in schools that migrate along the coasts. They have elongated bodies dark blue on the back and silvery white on the belly.

Sardines have long played a central role in Japanese fishery. Their plentiful supply and relatively low price make *iwashi* a popular and much-favored fish. When fresh, the flesh is excellent as sashimi, and sardines are also commonly grilled or deep-fried as well as simmered and used in numerous kinds of dishes. Widely available processed products include sardines pickled in fermented rice bran (*nukazuke*), sardines pickled in vinegar (*suzuke*), *gyosho* sauce made by fermenting salted sardines, dried sardines (*niboshi*), and *shirasu* and *chirimen-jako* made by boiling and drying sardine fry. Sardines carry the most fat and are especially tasty in autumn and winter but are marketed all year round.

The *ma-iwashi* species are dotted with black spots on the sides and grow to become the biggest sardines, some as long as 30 centimeters. The *urume iwashi* are recognizable for their large, teary-looking eyes, and the *katakuchi iwashi* for their small size, long upper jaw, and receding lower jaw.

FILLETING SARDINE BY HAND (*Tebiraki*)

Small fish like sardines, which have fine bones and soft flesh that is easily crushed if cut with a knife, are generally filleted by hand (*tebiraki*). After cutting away the head and removing the organs, the flesh is separated from the bones with the fingers. Almost all of the bones can be removed by hand.

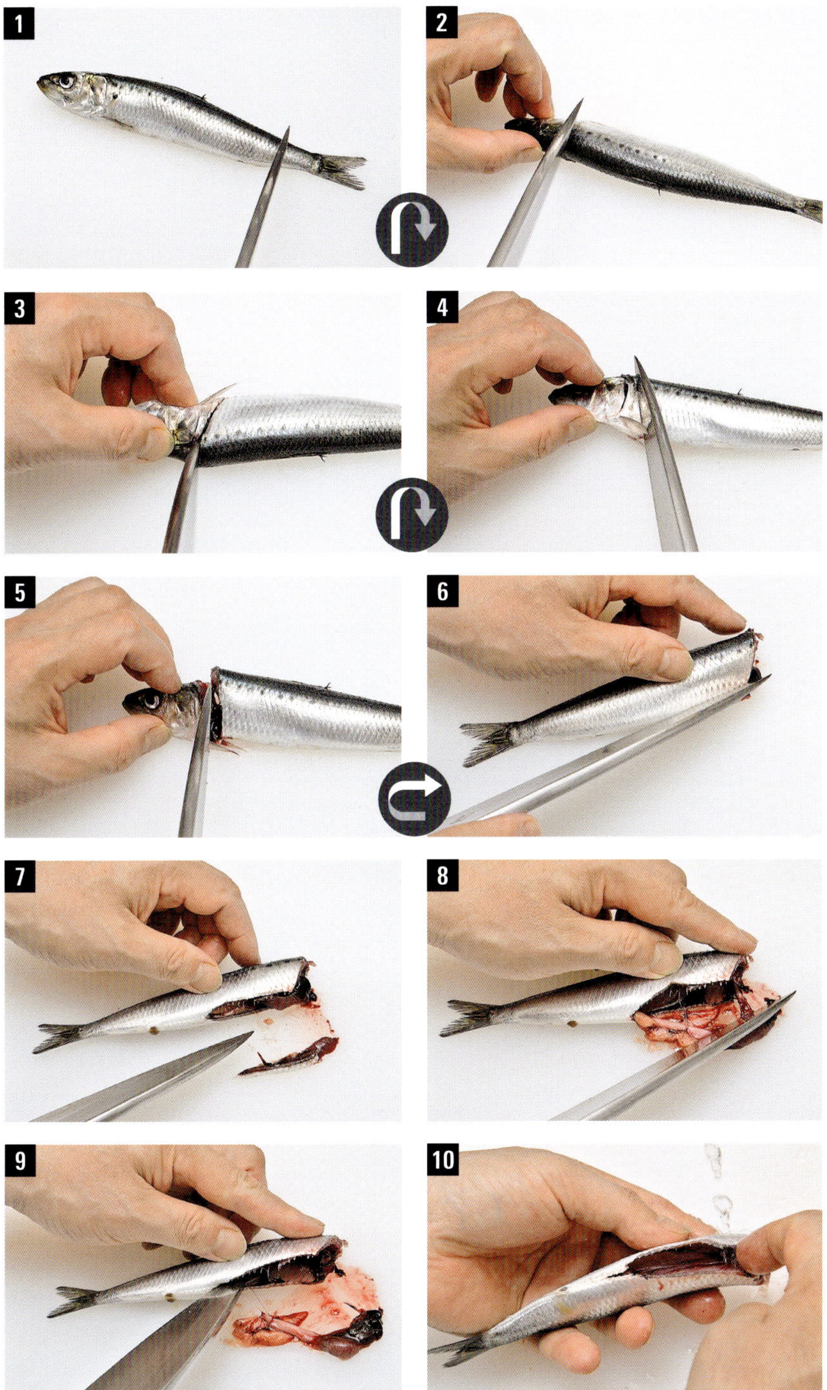

Preparation

1 The scales of sardines fall away almost entirely in the course of shipment, but remove any remaining scales by running the blade of an *ai-deba* knife lightly along the fish from tail toward the head.

2–**3** Place the fish, head facing left and dorsal side facing you, at a slight angle as shown, insert the knife at a slight angle under the pectoral fin, and cut down about halfway through the fish, as shown.

4 With the head to the left, turn the belly side to face you. Place the knife under the pectoral fin at an angle, as in steps **2** and **3** above.

5 Cut down and remove the head.

6 Place the fish with the tail to the left and belly toward you. Insert the knife at the cut (head-end) edge of the belly.

7 Cut off the edge of the belly, severing the ends of the belly bones. (This creates an opening for removal of the organs as well as removes the belly bones.)

8 Insert the tip of the knife in the opening and clear out the internal organs.

9 Using the tip of the knife, make a small, 1-cm (½-in.) incision in the direction of the anal vent (as shown) to facilitate cleaning of the cavity.

10 Clean the inner cavity in running water, using the fingers. Blot dry with a cloth.

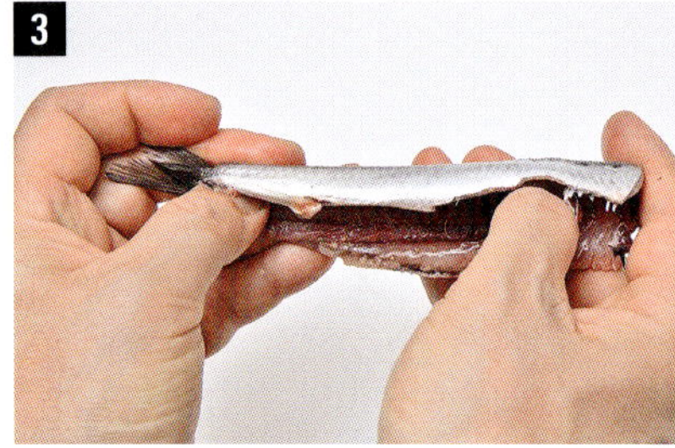

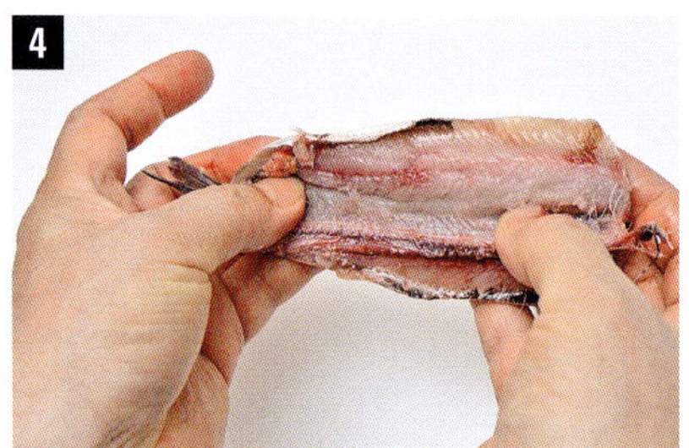

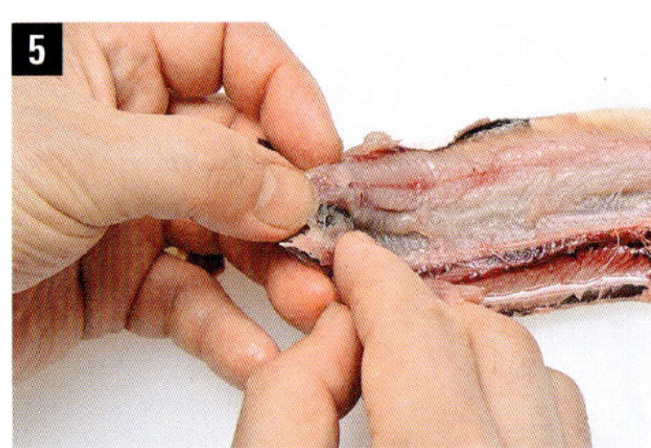

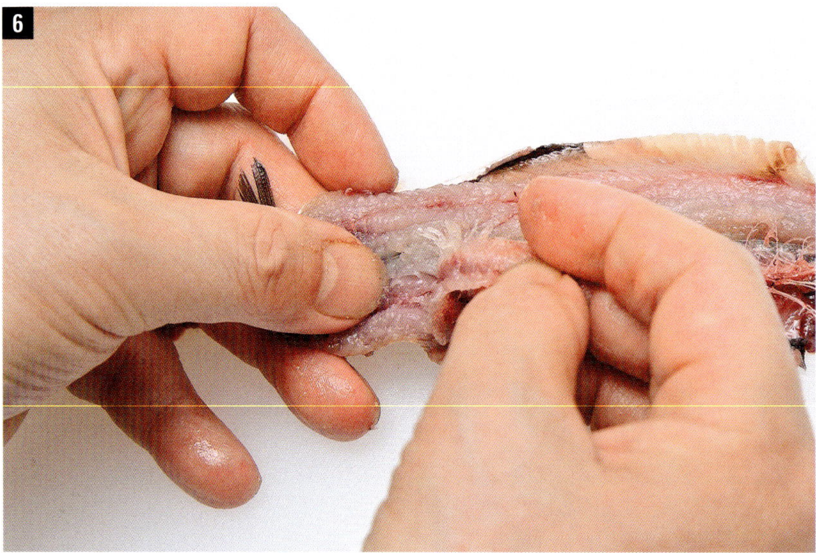

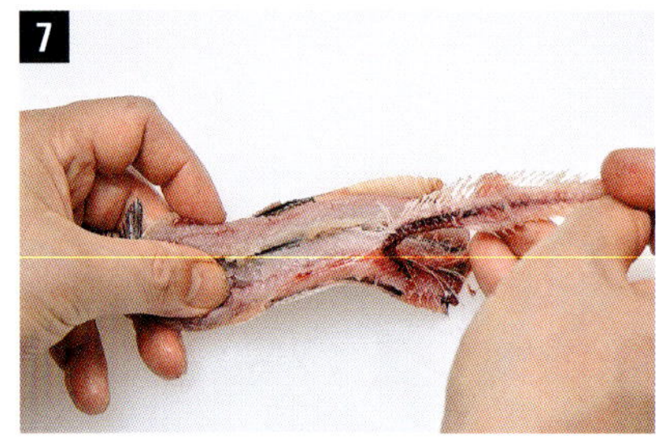

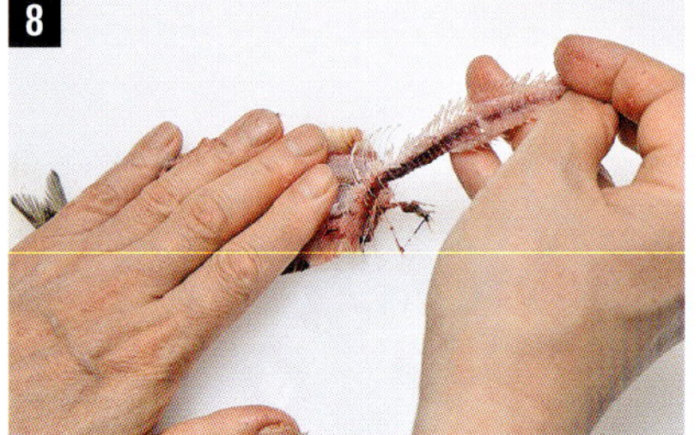

Removing the spine, central bones, and belly bones

1. Holding the fish with the tail to the left and belly facing you, insert both thumbs into the inner cavity, at the same time pressing with the other fingers against the dorsal side.
2. With the thumbs in the cavity, feel for the spine. Move the left thumb toward the tail, separating the soft flesh from the spine.
3. When the flesh has been separated with the left thumb as far as the tail, move the right thumb toward the head, separating the remaining flesh from the spine.
4. Open the cavity, spreading out the flesh above and below the thumbs.
5. Break off the spine at the base of the tail.
6. Hold the tail area with the left hand and remove the spine from the flesh by pulling it toward the head end.
7. Filleting by hand allows removal of the belly bones together with the central bones.
8. Steadying the flesh with the left hand, pull the spine, central bones, and belly bones away entirely.

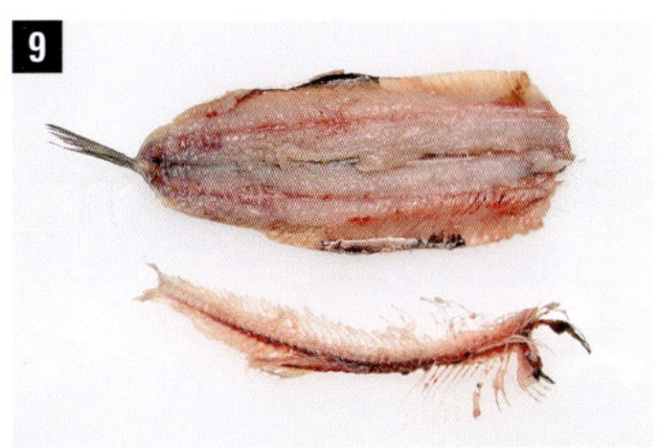

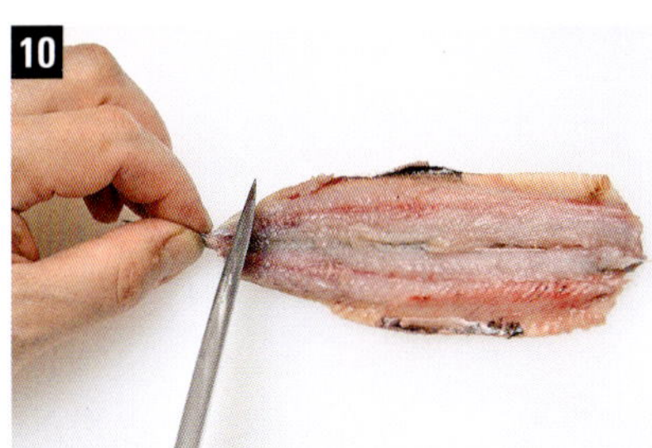

9 The filleted flesh separated from the spine, central bones, and belly bones.

10 Cut off the tail at its base.

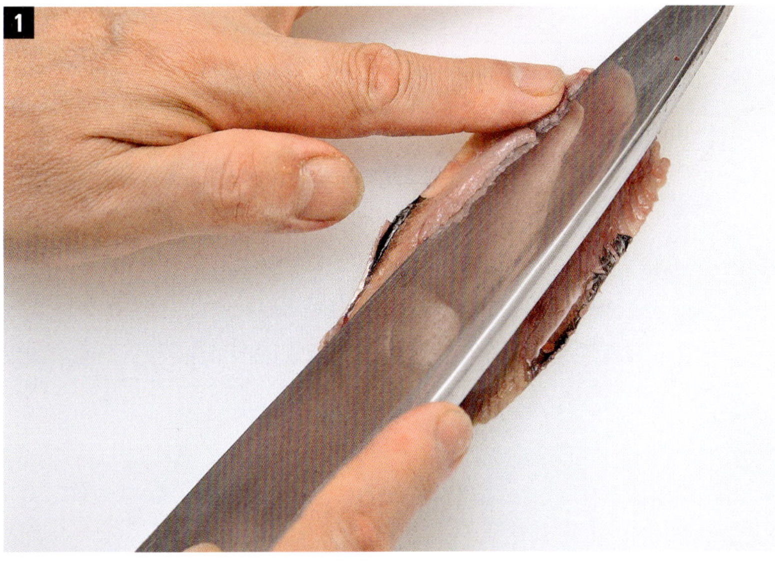

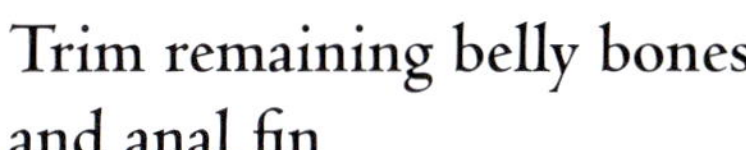

Trim remaining belly bones and anal fin

1 Place the filleted fish with the head end away from you, skin side down. Lift the remaining belly bones by inserting the knife beneath them.

2 Cut away the belly bones remaining along the edge of the fillet.

3 Cut off the belly bones holding the anal fin.

4 Place the head end facing you and trim off the remaining belly bones and ventral fin.

5 Completed fillet after belly bones and ventral fins have been removed. The fillet is now ready for deep frying or other preparations.

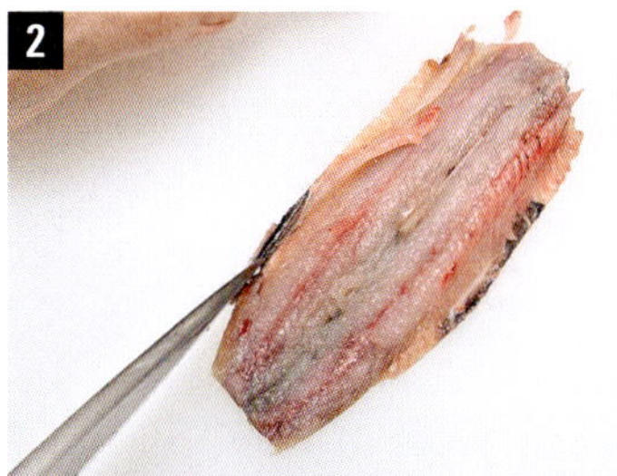

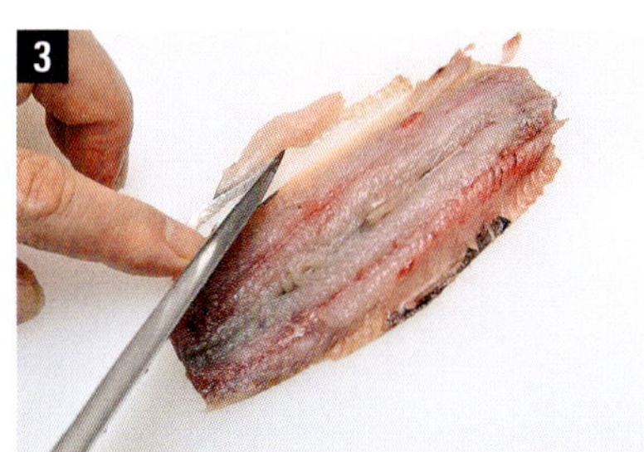

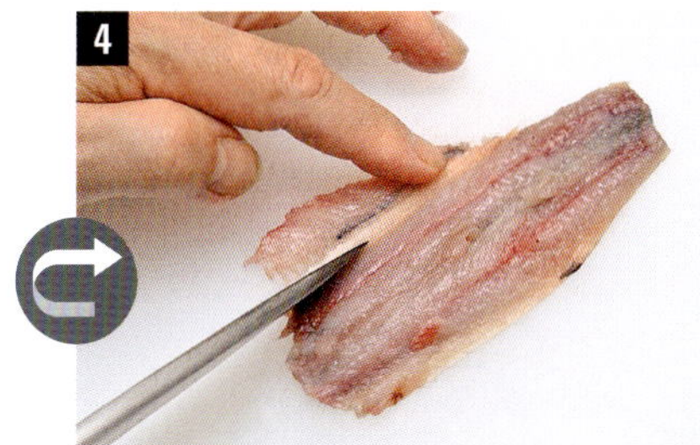

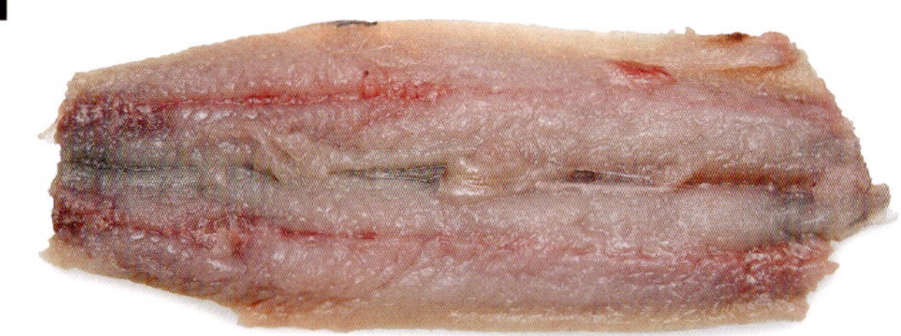

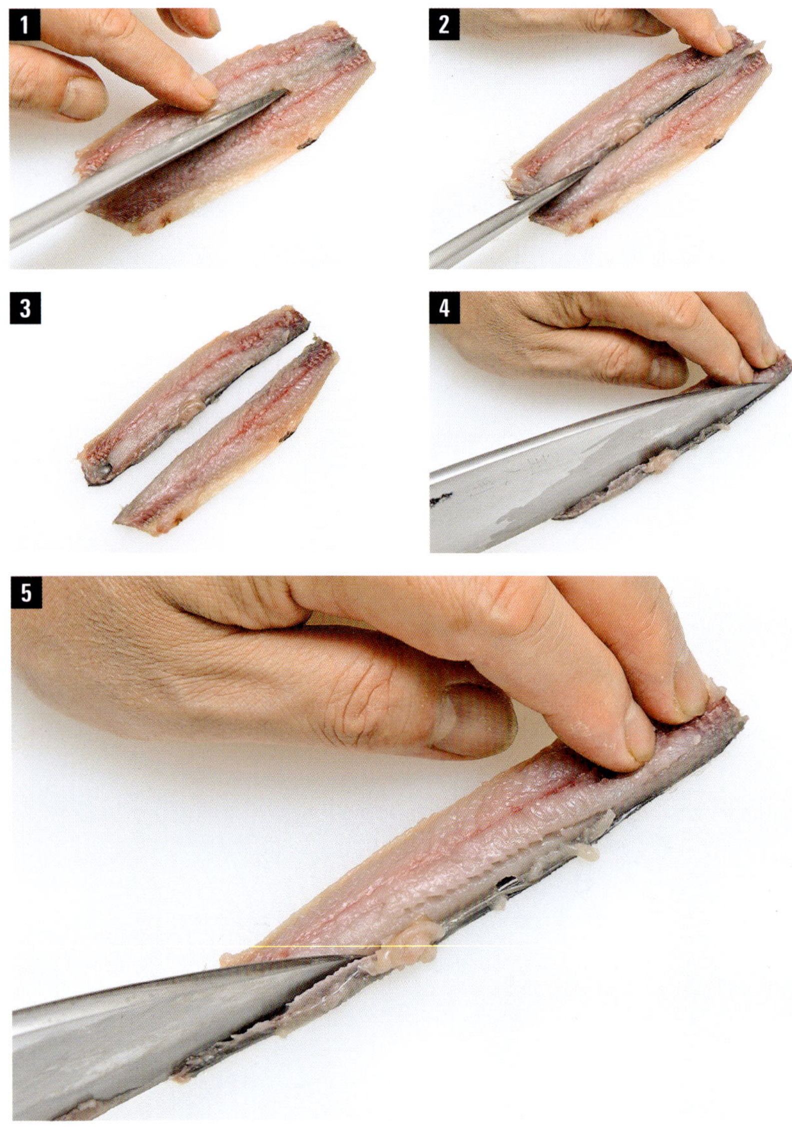

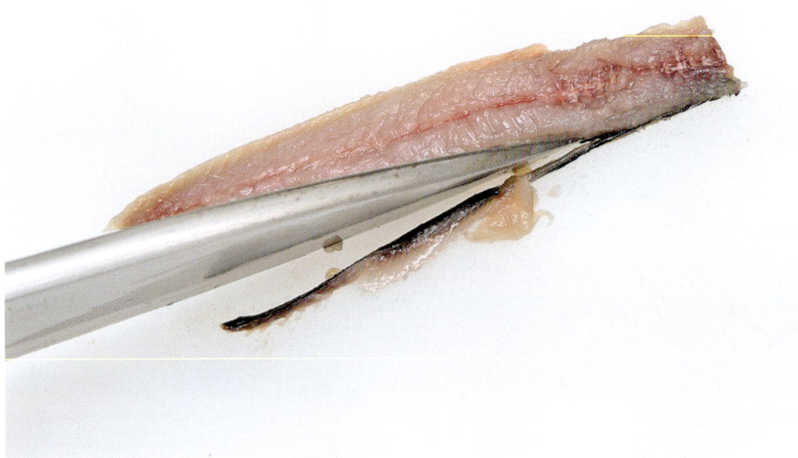

Dividing the fillet in two and removing the dorsal fin and small bones

1. Place the fillet skin side down with the head end toward you. Place the knife along the center of the flesh at the position of the dorsal fin.
2. Draw the knife toward you, cutting apart the upper half of the fish. Reverse the fish end to end and cut the lower half, dividing the fillet into two.
3. The fillet cut in two.
4. Place the knife along the dorsal side of each half.
5. Draw the knife toward you to cut off the dorsal fin and small bones remaining in the flesh (*tankikotsu*, see p. 28)
6. If parts of the dorsal fin and small bones remain on the other half, trim likewise.

Sardine "Sleeve-Shaped" Sushi

Iwashi Kosode-zushi

Kosode-zushi, or "sleeve-shaped" sushi, so named because of the cross-section shape of a cut piece, is a small, mold-pressed sushi. It is made with mackerel, sardines, sea bream, or other fish that has been salted and then marinated in vinegar.

Sardine "Sleeve-Shaped" Sushi

sushi rice
shiso leaves
toasted sesame
shiroita kombu
pickled ginger (*gari*)

1

2

Marinate

1. Lightly sprinkle two sardine fillet pieces with salt (1.5 percent by weight) and allow to sit for one hour.
2. Prepare *ama-zu* (see p. 245) consisting of equal parts rice vinegar, water, and sugar. Marinate sardine fillets with the flesh side facing down for 10 to 15 minutes. For sushi rice, see page 245.

Anago

CONGER EEL

Conger myriaster

More than 30 types of conger eel, a subdivision of the family Congridae (order Anguilliformes), are found in the world. The word *anago* usually refers to *ma-anago* (white-spotted conger or *Conger myriaster*), which is the tastiest of the conger eels and is in ample supply in Japan. The white-spotted conger's long body has no ventral fins or scales, and a regular line of white dots runs horizontally along its sides. Males are larger than females, the former reaching about 90 centimeters and the latter about 40–50 centimeters. The surface of the body is covered with a viscous substance that should be removed before cooking to eliminate the fishy taste. *Anago* is carved while alive since the gills are easily torn after death. As with *unagi* (eel), *anago* is generally opened from the back in the Kanto region (Tokyo included) and from the belly in the Kansai (Kyoto–Osaka) region, and the knives used also differ (see p. 19). Opening from the back is well suited to grilled dishes, since less of its luscious fat will drip away during grilling. Opening from the belly is best for simmered dishes as well as for the *shiramushi* method of steaming after grilling, because the flesh is less likely to break apart.

Anago tastes the best in summer from June to August. Rich in vitamin A, DHA, and other nutrients, it contains ample fat, but the amount of fat is about half that of *unagi* (eel), giving it a lighter texture. *Anago* is a standard ingredient for tempura and sushi; simmered *anago* (*ni-anago*) is favored in the Kanto region and grilled *anago* (*yaki-anago*) in the Kansai region. *Noresore*, conger eel fry, are transparent and mildly sticky and a springtime delicacy enjoyed for their chewy texture and sweetness as a vinegared dish (*sunomono*), a sushi ingredient, and the like.

CARVING CONGER EEL

Opening from the back (*Sebiraki*)

1

2

3

4

5

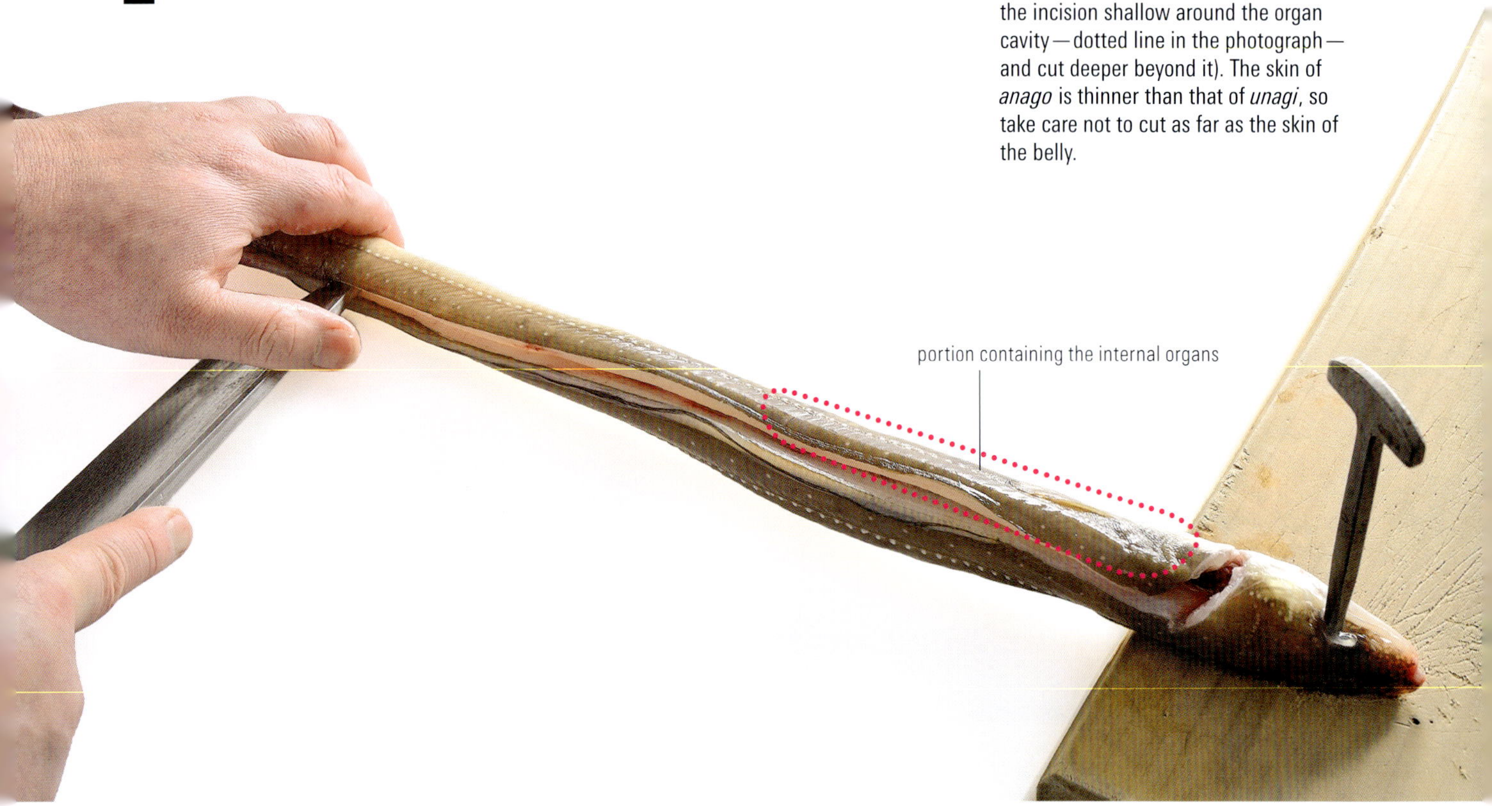

portion containing the internal organs

Opening from the back and removing internal organs

1. Use the *Edo-wari unagibocho* knife (for opening from the back; see p. 19). Place the head to the right, dorsal side toward you. Pin the head to the cutting board with a *me-uchi* spike (place the spike close to the hard bone encircling the eye for best results).
2. Strike the spike with the spine of the knife to firmly secure the eel to the board.
3. Insert the knife beneath the gill flap until it strikes the spine.
4. Draw the tip of the knife along the spine.
5. Holding the body firmly with the left hand and, laying the blade flat, cut the conger eel open along the spine back to the tail (damage to the internal organs can cause bitterness to seep into the flesh, so keep the incision shallow around the organ cavity—dotted line in the photograph—and cut deeper beyond it). The skin of *anago* is thinner than that of *unagi*, so take care not to cut as far as the skin of the belly.

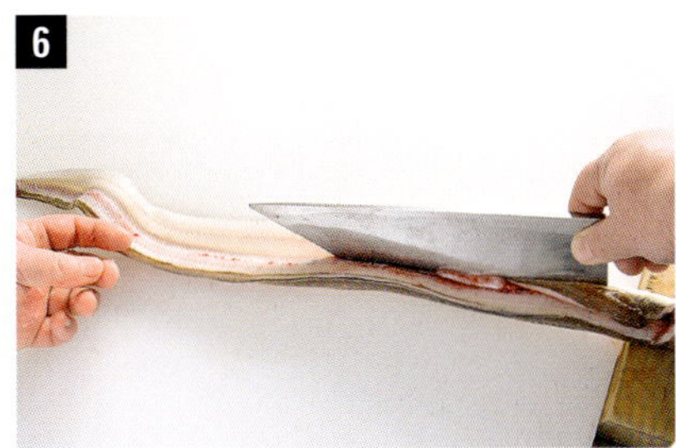

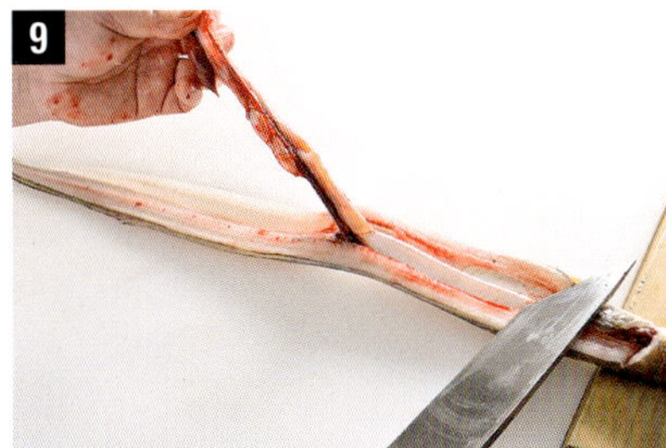

6 Draw the knife toward the tail again to completely open the flesh (taking care not to cut the skin).

7 Insert the knife at the side of the internal organs (*kimo*).

8 With the left hand, lift out the internal organs and cut them off at the base.

9 Steadying the flesh with the knife as shown, pull out and detach the internal organs.

Removing the spine, central bones, head, tail fin, dorsal fin, and anal fin

1 From the head end, cut in under the spine from the base of the head, drawing up the end of the spine.

2 Insert the knife in the cut made in step **1** and cut toward the tail as if to peel it away from the flesh. At the tail, cut to detach the spine.

3 Scrape the edge of the knife over the flesh to remove blood and debris.

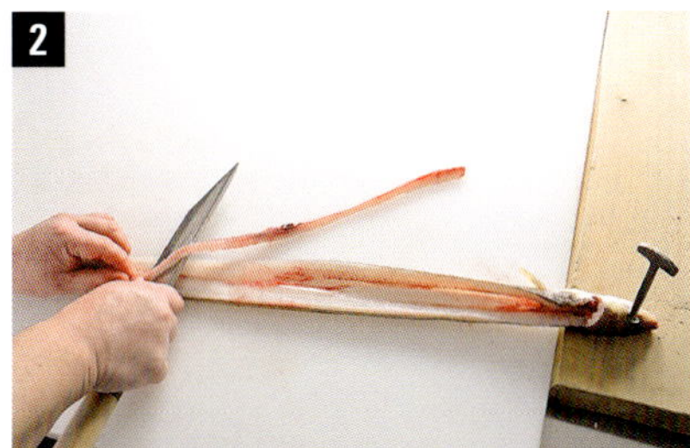

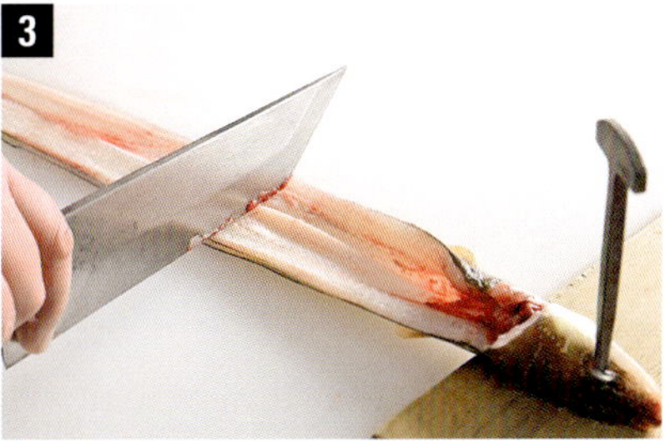

4 Cut away the head at the base of the jaw.

5 To detach the tail and dorsal fins, make a diagonal cut at the base of the tail and detach the tail fin, then pull out the tail fin and, with the tip of the knife inserted at about a 45-degree angle, cut away the long dorsal fin, as shown.

6 Cut toward the head end and cut away the entire dorsal fin.

7 Close the opened flesh and place with the head end to the right and the back to the far side.

8 Remove the remnants of the tail fin and the anal fin. Make a diagonal cut at the end of the remnant of the tail fin.

9 As in steps **5** and **6**, pull out the end of the tail while cutting away the anal fin.

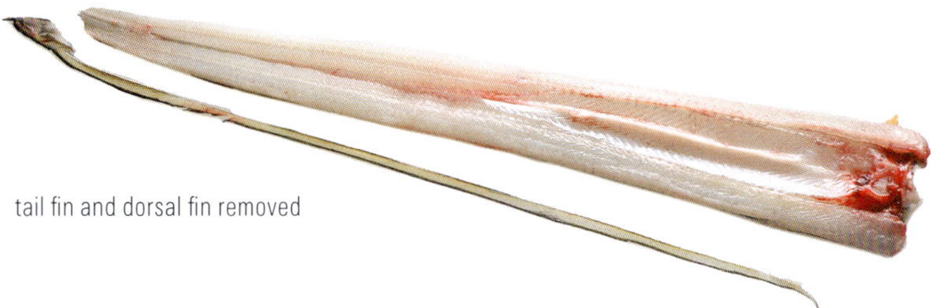

tail fin and dorsal fin removed

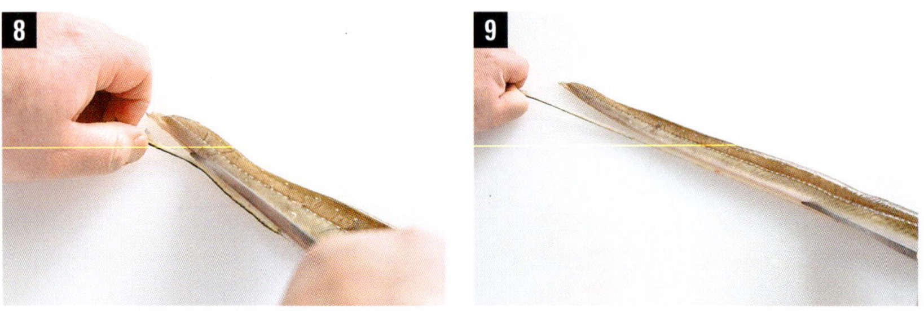

anal fin and remnant of the tail fin removed

Preparation

1. Place the conger on the board skin-side up. Pour boiling water over the flesh (this tightens the flesh and makes it easier to remove the belly bones).
2. When the surface turns white, plunge into ice water (*shimofuri*). Chill well; if left hot, the skin will discolor. It is not necessary to wipe off excess moisture.
3. Use the *deba* knife. With the skin-side up and the head end placed to the upper left, scrape off the remaining viscous substance with the spine of the knife. The substance retains a fishy smell, so it is best removed thoroughly.
4. Place with the head to the right, skin side up. With a diagonal cut, remove the lower corner with the pectoral fin.
5. Remove the upper corner with the opposite pectoral fin with a similar diagonal cut.
6. Lift up the end of the strip of the belly bones remaining on the flesh and, placing the knife under them, scoop them off while pulling the strip with the left hand.

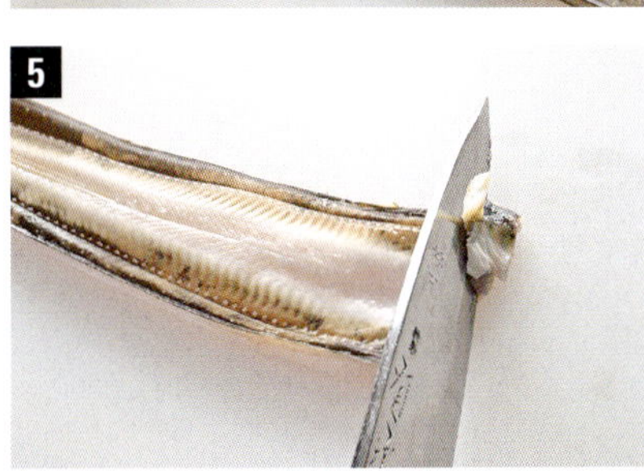

flesh with the pectoral fins removed

Opening from the belly (*Harabiraki*)

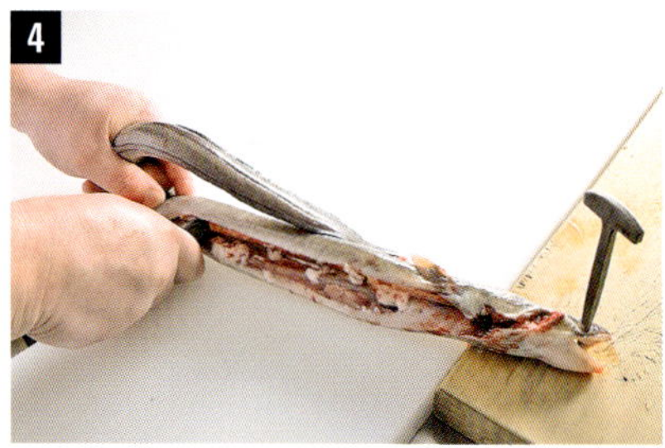

Opening from the belly and removing internal organs

1. Use the *Kyo-wari unagibocho* knife (for opening from the belly; see p. 19). Place the head and belly facing you. Pin the head to the cutting board with a *me-uchi* spike (place the spike close to the hard bone encircling the eye for best results).
2. Strike the spike with the spine of the knife to firmly secure the conger eel to the board.
3. Fold the eel over on itself and insert the knife at the gill cover. (Because there are no bones in the belly, it is difficult to steady the eel. Folding the eel in this way and pressing down on the board makes it easier to carve).
4. Laying the blade flat and with the knuckles of the hand gripping the knife against the cutting board, open the eel along the spine, and back to the tail.
5. When the cut reaches the tail, spread the flesh open.
6. Insert the knife at the side of the internal organs (*kimo*). With the left hand, lift out the internal organs and cut at the base.

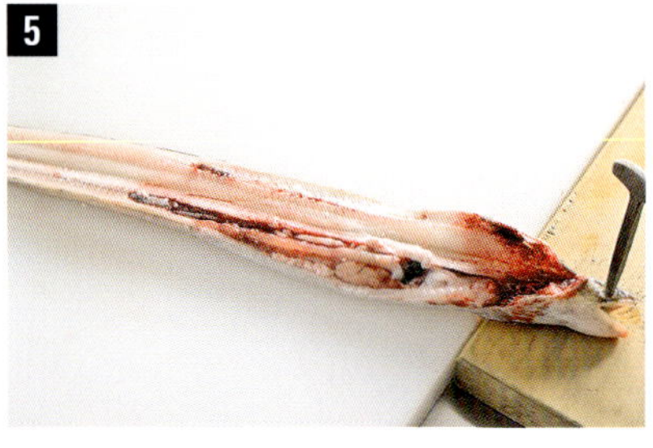

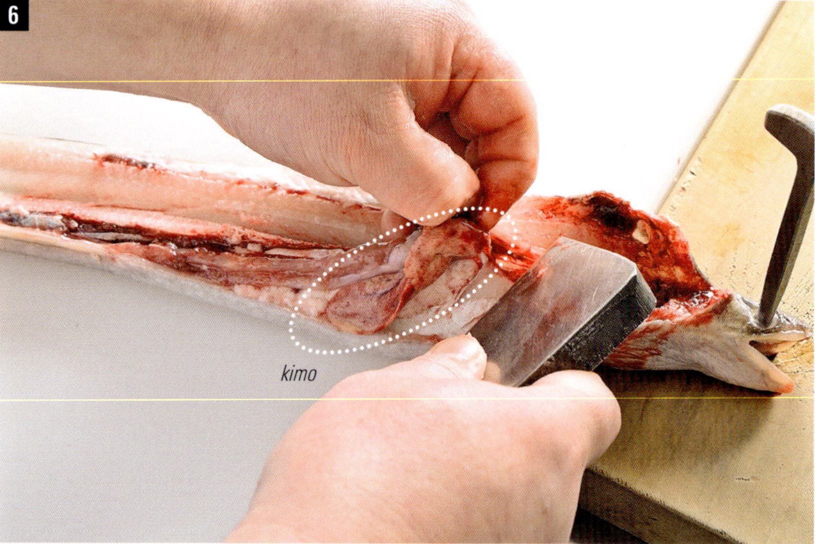

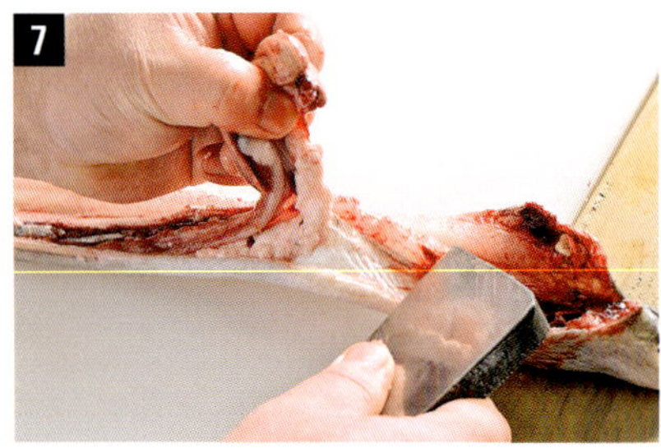

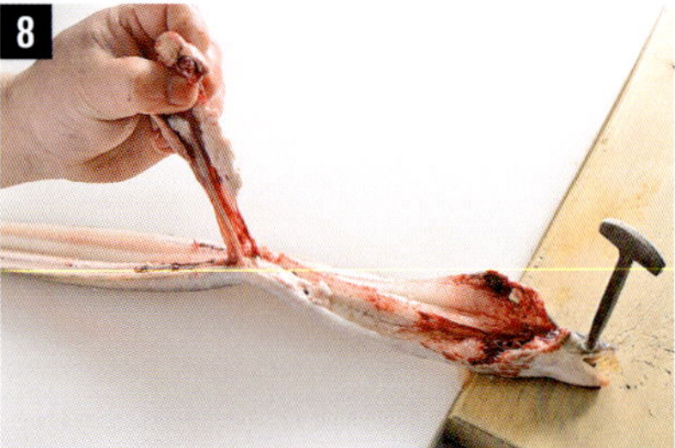

7. Steadying the flesh with the knife as shown, pull out the internal organs.
8. When they are pulled to the center, remove the knife and pull away the organs by hand.

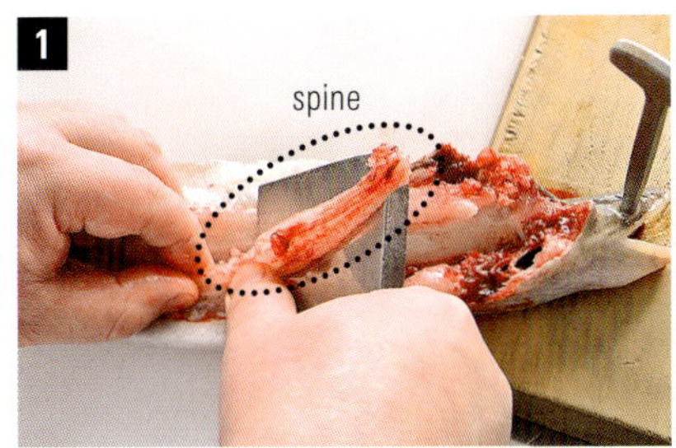

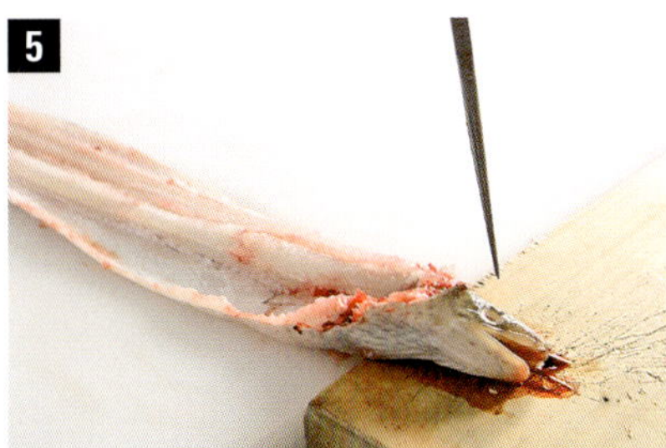

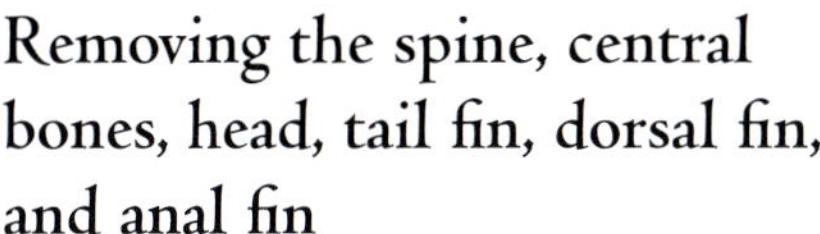

Removing the spine, central bones, head, tail fin, dorsal fin, and anal fin

1. Under the lower jaw, insert the knife beneath the spine and central bones and cut off the spine at its base near the head. With the knife at a low angle, insert it under the spine and remove it in a series of shaving motions.
2. Draw the knife toward the tail as if to shave off the spine. Cut the spine away from the flesh at the tail.
3. The flesh with the spine removed.
4. Scrape the edge of the knife over the flesh to remove blood and debris.
5. Withdraw the *me-uchi* spike.
6. Remove the tail fin and the dorsal fin. Close the flesh of the just-opened eel and place it with the dorsal side facing you. Cut on the diagonal from the tail to the base of the dorsal fin to remove the dorsal fin. Pulling the tail fin with the left hand, insert the tip of the knife at a 45-degree angle and start cutting the dorsal fin from the body.
7. Continue cutting in the direction of the head and remove the fin.

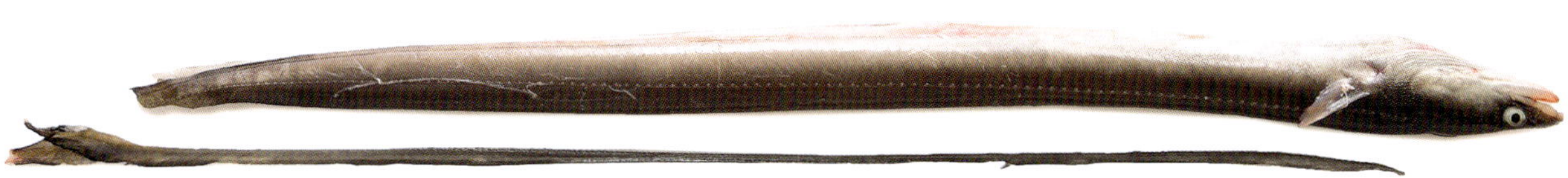

tail and dorsal fin removed

8 Open the body and place with the head to the right, as shown.

9 Remove the remnant of the tail fin and the anal fin. At the end of the tail fin on the belly side, make a diagonal incision.

10 Pulling the tail fin with the left hand, and with the tip of the knife inserted at about a 45-degree angle, cut away the anal fin.

remnants of the tail fin and anal fin removed

Preparation

1 With the skin side up, place the eel with the head end toward you. Pour boiling water over the flesh (this tightens the flesh and makes it easier to remove the belly bones).

2 When the surface turns white, plunge into ice water (*shimofuri*). Chill well; if left hot, the skin will discolor. It is not necessary to wipe off excess moisture.

3 Use the *deba* knife. With the skin-side up, hold the head with the left hand and scrape off the remaining viscous substance with the spine of the knife.

4 Turn the flesh over and place with the head to the right. Cut diagonally under the pectoral fin on one side.

5 Cut diagonally, leaving the pectoral fin attached to the head.

6 Cut similarly at the edge of the pectoral fin on the opposite side.

7 With the knife, shave off any belly bones remaining on the flesh.

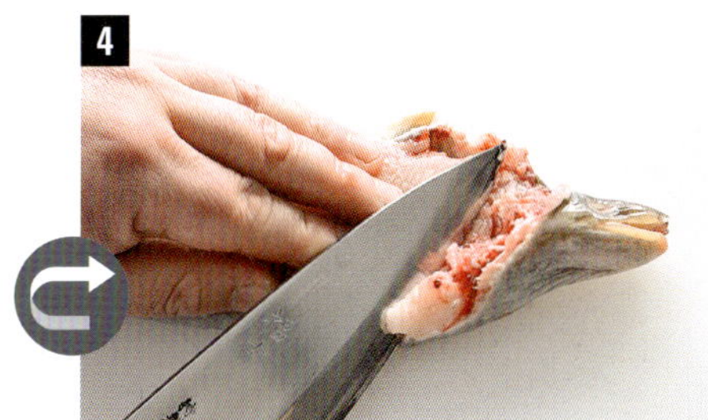

head and pectoral fins removed

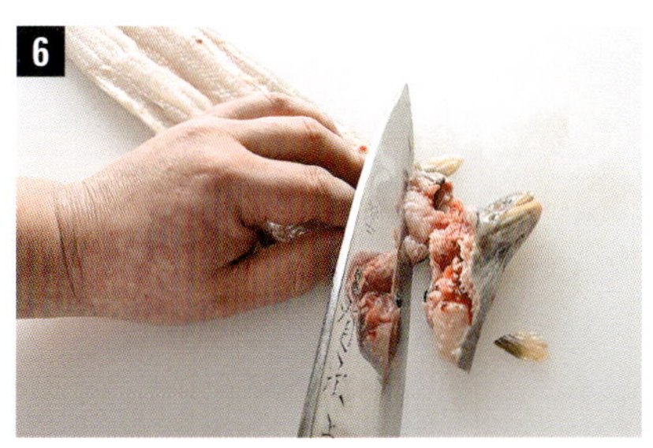

Usu-zukuri

With its translucent and chewy texture, *anago* is well suited to thin-sliced sashimi. Served with spicy grated daikon (*aka-oroshi*), sliced *negi* long onion (*arai-negi*), and *pon-zu* (see p. 245) sauce, the flavor is light but rich in umami.

1

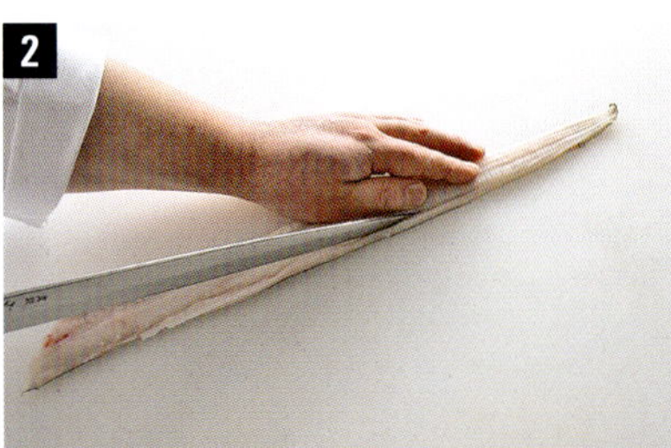
2

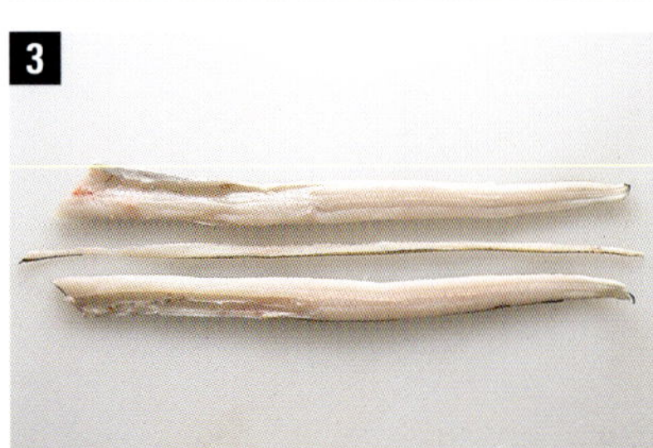
3

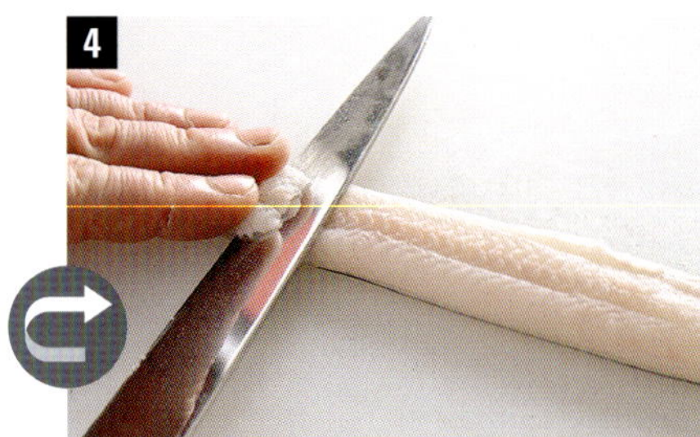
4

5

1. Use a *yanagiba* knife. Place the conger eel opened from the belly flesh-side up with the head end toward you. Cut into two along the center line.
2. Cut away any of the remaining support bones of the dorsal fin (*tankikotsu*), because these are unpleasant to chew.
3. Strips prepared for slicing sashimi and the strip containing the dorsal fin support bones.
4. Place a strip with the head end to the right. Pressing the end of the strip lightly with the left hand, cut in with the knife nearly horizontal.
5. Cutting from close to the tail, cut 3-to-4-mm (about ⅛ in.)-thick slices.

Thin-sliced Conger Eel sashimi

aka-oroshi *arai-negi*

Simmered Conger Eel Sushi *Ni-anago Nigiri*

Nigiri-zushi made with simmered *anago* is a sushi standard that allows you to savor the melts-in-your-mouth texture. *Nitsume* sauce is brushed over the freshly cooked *anago* and peppercorns (*mi-zansho*) are added to the sushi rice (see p. 245) as an accent.

Nitsume Sauce **yields about 3.5 kg (8 lbs.)**

1.5 L (1.6 qt.) de-alcoholized sake

2 L (2.1 qt.) de-alcoholized mirin

Generous 4 cups *koikuchi* shoyu

Scant ⅔ cup *tamari* shoyu

150 g (5 oz.) glucose syrup (*mizuame*)

500 g (generous 1 lb.) granulated sugar

Heat the de-alcoholized sake and mirin in a pot, then add the *koikuchi* and *tamari* shoyu. While bringing gently to a boil, add the glucose syrup and sugar and stir until it dissolves.

Simmered Conger Eel Sushi

pickled ginger (*gari*)

Unagi

EEL

Anguilla japonica

Eel belongs to the family Anguillidae (order Anguilliformes), of which 18 species are found around the world. Members of this family found in Japan are *Nihon unagi* (Japanese eel; *Anguilla japonica*) and *o-unagi* (giant eel; *Anguilla marmorata*). Of these the *Nihon unagi* is widely available on the market. *Unagi* usually grow to 40 to 50 centimeters, some reaching 1 meter. Adult *unagi* live in freshwater rivers and lakes and return to the ocean to spawn; their incubation period is spent in the ocean.

Like the *anago* conger eel, *unagi* have a tube-like body without ventral fins, and the long dorsal, tail, and anal fins form a continuous fringe. The back is dark bluish-brown and the belly white. Rudimentary scales are buried in the skin, and the surface is slimy.

Unagi are either fished in the wild or farmed, but catches of wild eel in Japan have greatly decreased, making them very high priced. *Unagi* is an old-time favorite, and its high nutritional value made it established custom to eat eel at the height of summer when the high heat and humidity sap one's body energies. Wild *unagi* are tastiest from late autumn to early winter, during which time the flesh carries ample fat. The most popular methods of cooking are grilling with a sweet sauce (*kabayaki*) and grilling without any seasoning (*shira-yaki*).

Like *anago*, *unagi* are opened either from the back or the belly. Opening from the back prevents the valuable fat of the eel from dripping away during grilling, with the result that the meat is tender and mild. Opening from the belly gives the flesh volume and thickness so that it is not easily broken during preparation. Which method is chosen depends on the type of dish. Using the knife indicated (p. 19), it is best to fillet the *unagi* quickly while alive.

Opening from the back (*Sebiraki*)

Opening from the back and removing internal organs

1. Use the *Edo-wari unagibocho* knife (for opening from the back; see p. 19). Grasp the eel behind the head and insert the knife over the neck; cut down until the knife strikes the spine.
2. Turn the head to the right, with the dorsal side toward you. Insert the *me-uchi* spike under the jaw about one 1 cm (½ in.) between the mouth and neck, as shown.
3. Strike the spike with the spine of the knife to firmly secure the eel to the board.
4. With the knife at a low angle, insert the tip in the incision made in step 1.

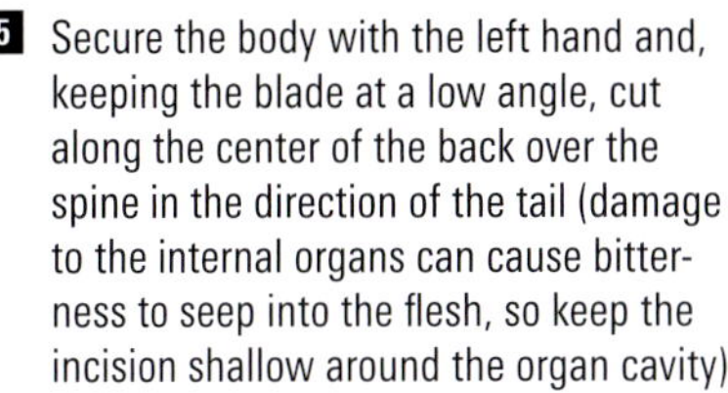

5. Secure the body with the left hand and, keeping the blade at a low angle, cut along the center of the back over the spine in the direction of the tail (damage to the internal organs can cause bitterness to seep into the flesh, so keep the incision shallow around the organ cavity).
6. Continue cutting all the way to the tail.
7. At the tail, cut through.
8. Insert the knife at the side of the internal organs (below the heart), lift up the internal organs with the left hand and sever the connections to the body.
9. Steadying the flesh with the knife as shown, pull out and detach the internal organs.
10. Cut the connections of the intestine and anal vent to detach the organs.

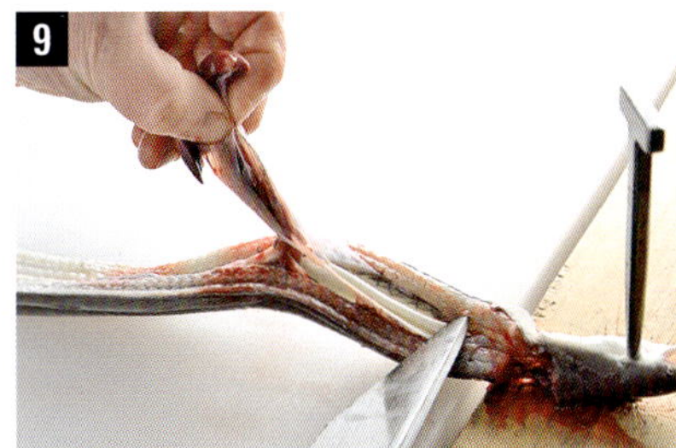

Removing the spine and central bones

1 Readjust your grip on the knife, as explained on p. 25. Insert the knife below the jaw and cut off the tissue attaching the base of the spine to the flesh.

2 From the cut made in step **1**, insert the knife at the base of the spine at the head end and, sliding the knife toward you, cut away the spine in sliding motions toward the tail.

3 Keep cutting toward the tail to detach the spine, as shown.

4 At the tail end, cut the spine from the tail.

5 The spine and central bones detached.

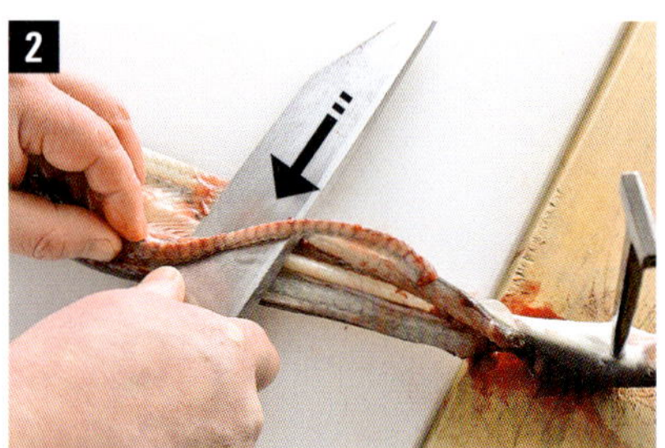

Removing the head, tail fin, dorsal fin, and anal fin

1. Adjust your grip on the knife, extending the index finger along the spine. Cut off the head at the back of the jaw.
2. Place the eel skin side down with the head end to the right.
3. Make a diagonal cut at the base of the tail and detach the tail fin.

4–5. Pull out the tail fin and, with the tip of the knife inserted at about a 45-degree angle, cut away the dorsal fin, as shown.

6. The tail fin and dorsal fin removed.

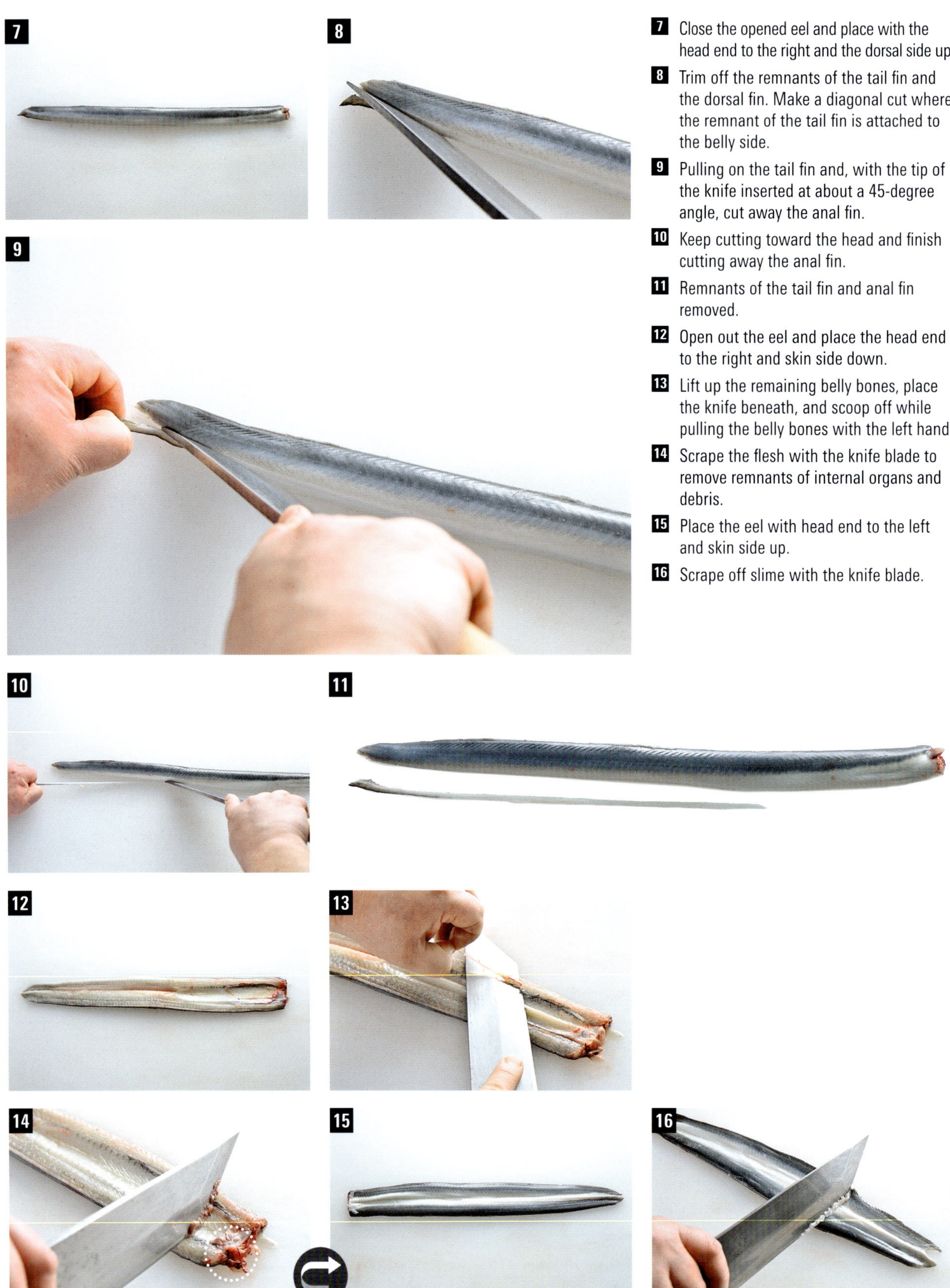

7 Close the opened eel and place with the head end to the right and the dorsal side up.

8 Trim off the remnants of the tail fin and the dorsal fin. Make a diagonal cut where the remnant of the tail fin is attached to the belly side.

9 Pulling on the tail fin and, with the tip of the knife inserted at about a 45-degree angle, cut away the anal fin.

10 Keep cutting toward the head and finish cutting away the anal fin.

11 Remnants of the tail fin and anal fin removed.

12 Open out the eel and place the head end to the right and skin side down.

13 Lift up the remaining belly bones, place the knife beneath, and scoop off while pulling the belly bones with the left hand.

14 Scrape the flesh with the knife blade to remove remnants of internal organs and debris.

15 Place the eel with head end to the left and skin side up.

16 Scrape off slime with the knife blade.

Opening from the belly (*Harabiraki*)

1

2

3

4

5

Opening from the belly and removing internal organs

1. Use the *Kyo-wari unagibocho* knife (for opening from the belly; see p. 19). Place the eel with the head to the right and the belly side facing up. Grasping the slippery eel firmly with the left hand, pin the head below the jaw with a *me-uchi* spike.
2. Strike the spike with the spine of the knife to firmly secure the eel to the board.
3. Pressing the eel to the board with the left hand, twist to bring the belly side facing you. With the knife horizontal, insert the tip between the spike and the pectoral fin, cutting into the gill cover and under the jaw. Open the eel with the knife sliding over the central bones, moving toward the tail.
4. Keeping the knife at a low angle and the eel pressed against the board, cut over the central bones toward the tail, open the belly, leaving the dorsal skin uncut.
5. Continue opening the eel's belly, sensing the position of the knife with the index finger or middle finger of the left hand held against the back of the eel, adjust the position of the tip of the blade (in this way you can open the whole eel from head to tail).

6

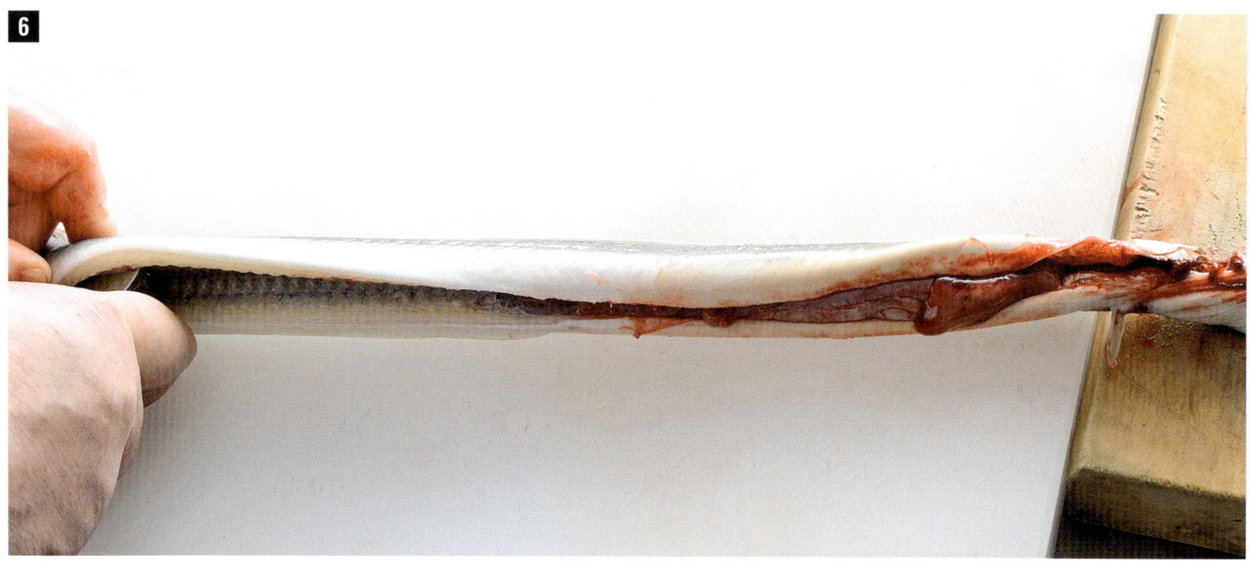

7

6 When the cut reaches the tail, open the flesh.

7 Steadying the flesh with the knife as shown, cut the connection between the gills and internal organs and pull out the internal organs.

8 Continue pulling the internal organs with the left hand.

9 Cut the connection between the intestine and anal vent to detach the internal organs. Remove the organs for use in *unagi kimo* soup or grilled *kimo*.

8

9

Removing the spine and central bones; removing slime

1 Insert the knife under the jaw and detach the spine at the head end.

2 With the knife at a low angle, insert it under the spine, moving toward the tail while lifting the spine and bones away from the flesh.

3 Continue toward the tail, slicing off the bones.

4 At the tail, cut the spine off and detach.

5 The spine and central bones removed.

6 Remove the *me-uchi* spike

7 Place the eel head to the left, skin side up.

8 Grasping the head with the left hand, scrape off the slime with the blade of the knife.

1

2

3

4

5

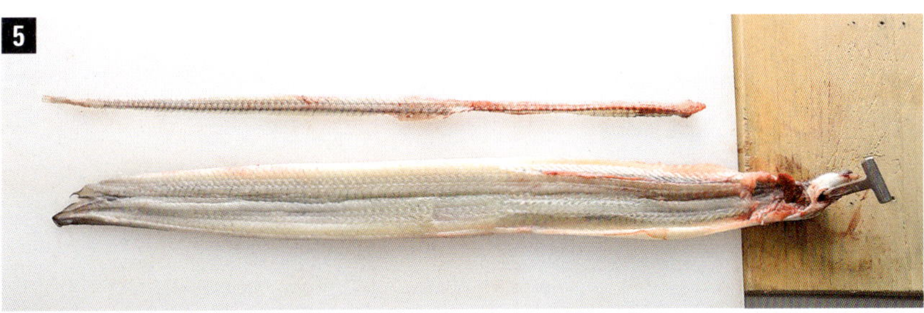

6

7

8

Sauce Grilled Eel *Unagi Kabayaki*

Opening eel from the back is best suited when grilling because it helps prevent excessive loss of fat. The addition of well-grilled eel bones in making the grilling sauce (p. 244) enhances the aroma and flavor of this dish.

Sauce Grilled Eel

hana sansho
grated daikon
sansho powder

Grilled Eel

Unagi Shira-yaki

Eel opened from the belly is best suited when steaming, resulting in a fluffy, thick texture. Grilling without sauce (*shira-yaki*) after steaming removes excess fat for a lighter taste. *Sansho* pepper and grated daikon bring out the savory flavor of *unagi*.

Grilled Eel

grated daikon
wasabi
warijoyu (see p. 244)

Hamo

PIKE CONGER

Muraenesox cinereus

A member of the family Muraenesocidae (order Anguilliformes), the *hamo* species of pike conger prefers temperate oceans and inhabits the coastal seas along central and southern Japan. Its approximately 1-meter-long bodies have no scales. Like *unagi* and *anago*, it lacks ventral fins and has a continuous fringe formed by the dorsal, anal, and tail fins. Chefs handle pike conger with special care to avoid its dagger-like teeth, which can inflict serious injury. *Hamo* flesh is filled with fine, long, and hard intermuscular bones. The *honekiri* (see p. 81) technique of severing the bones makes possible its preparation for tasty and palatable dishes of various kinds.

Hamo has been popular since olden times mainly in the Kansai region (western Japan centering around Osaka and Kyoto), notably in Kyoto, where the famous Gion Festival celebrated in the city in July is also known as the Hamo Matsuri, the Pike Conger Festival. Eating the fish thus plays an important cultural role as a signature event of summer. Although rather high in fat, *hamo* has a light, refreshing taste, making it an indispensable ingredient of summer dishes. In season around the end of the rainy weather of June and July as the fish puts on ample fat, the saying goes that "The *hamo* nourished by the rains of early summer (*tsuyu*) are especially tasty." Around September, toward the end of their spawning period, *hamo* slim down, but those caught in late autumn are fatty again, with a deeper flavor, and the bodies assume a golden color. This *kin hamo*, or golden pike conger, is also in great demand.

In summer, when they are fattiest, the flesh is usually scalded (*yubiki*) or grilled. Autumn *hamo* with a moderate amount of fat goes very well with *matsutake* mushrooms, a combination favored in seasonal terms as the matching of "out-going pike conger (*nagori-no-hamo*) and in-coming mushrooms (*hashiri-no-matsutake*)."

PIKE CONGER SKELETAL STRUCTURE

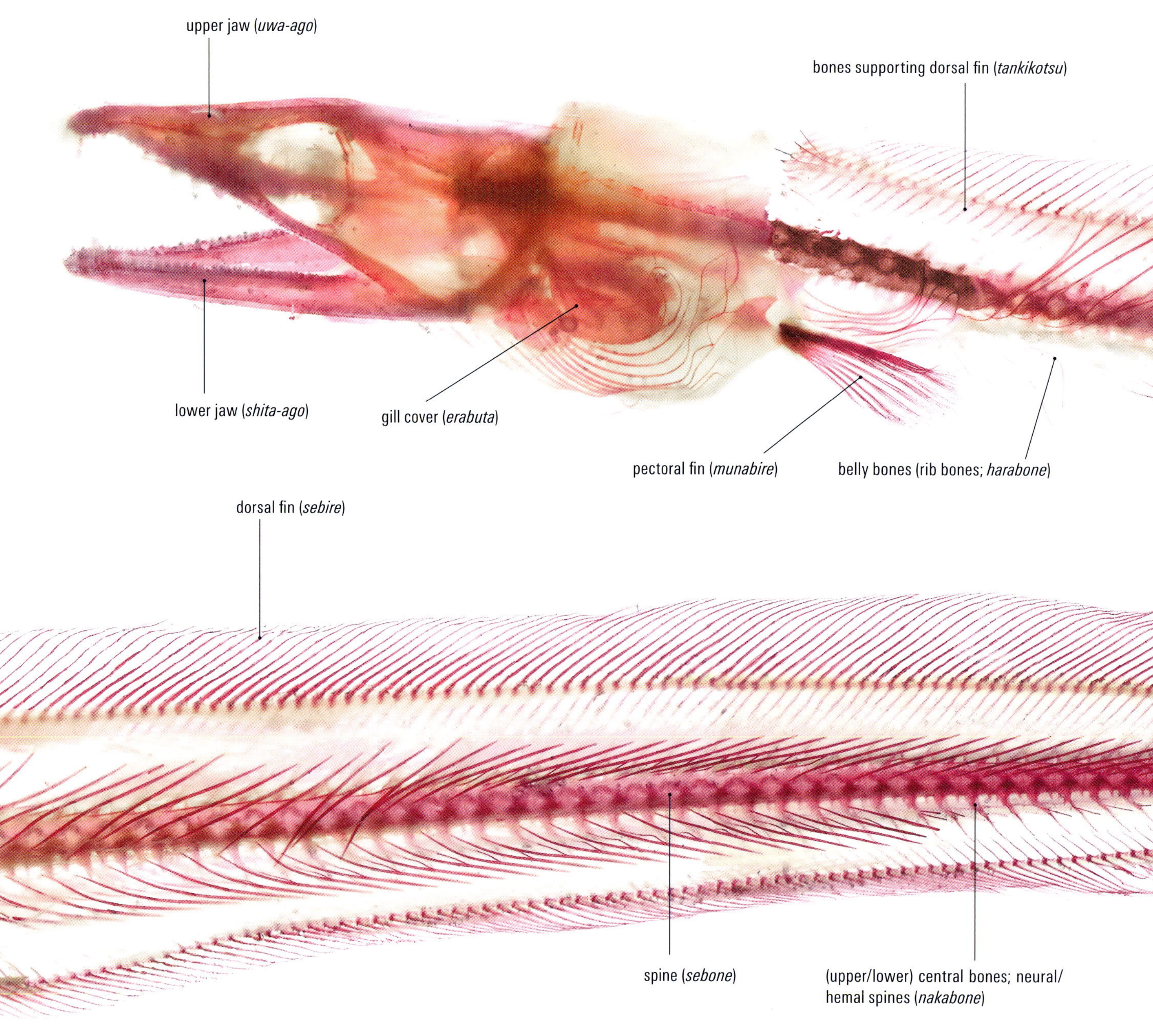

The skeletal structure of pike conger is very similar to the eel (see p. 28–29). The elongated jaw is filled with well-developed teeth and chefs must beware of its powerful bite. The skeleton is distinguished by the large number of small bones embedded in the flesh immediately beneath the skin. These small bones, called intermuscular bones (*nikukankotsu*) are not connected to the spine but suspended in the flesh apart from the central bones. These bones are likewise present in eel and conger eel, in sardines and herring. In such fish, these bones are fine and soft, so they can be dealt with fairly easily in cooking, but the intermuscular bones of *hamo* are not only hard and strong but splayed like pine needles firmly embedded in the flesh. The *honekiri* method of handling these bones in preparation of *hamo* cuisine is explained on page 81.

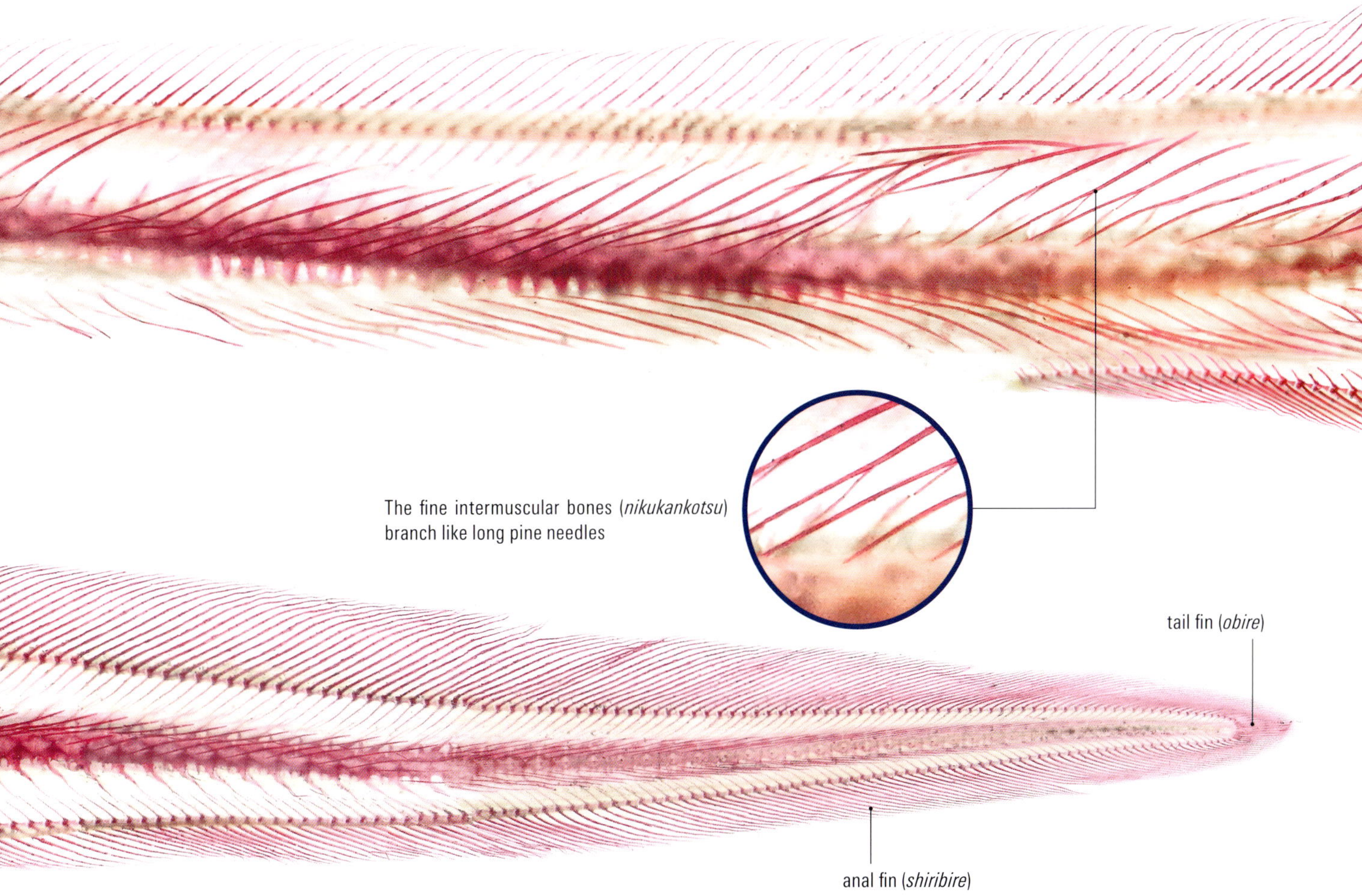

SPIKING PIKE CONGER

Pike conger should be carved after *ikejime* spiking. Spiking, performed by passing a wire through the central nerve of the pike conger, delays the process of rigor mortis.

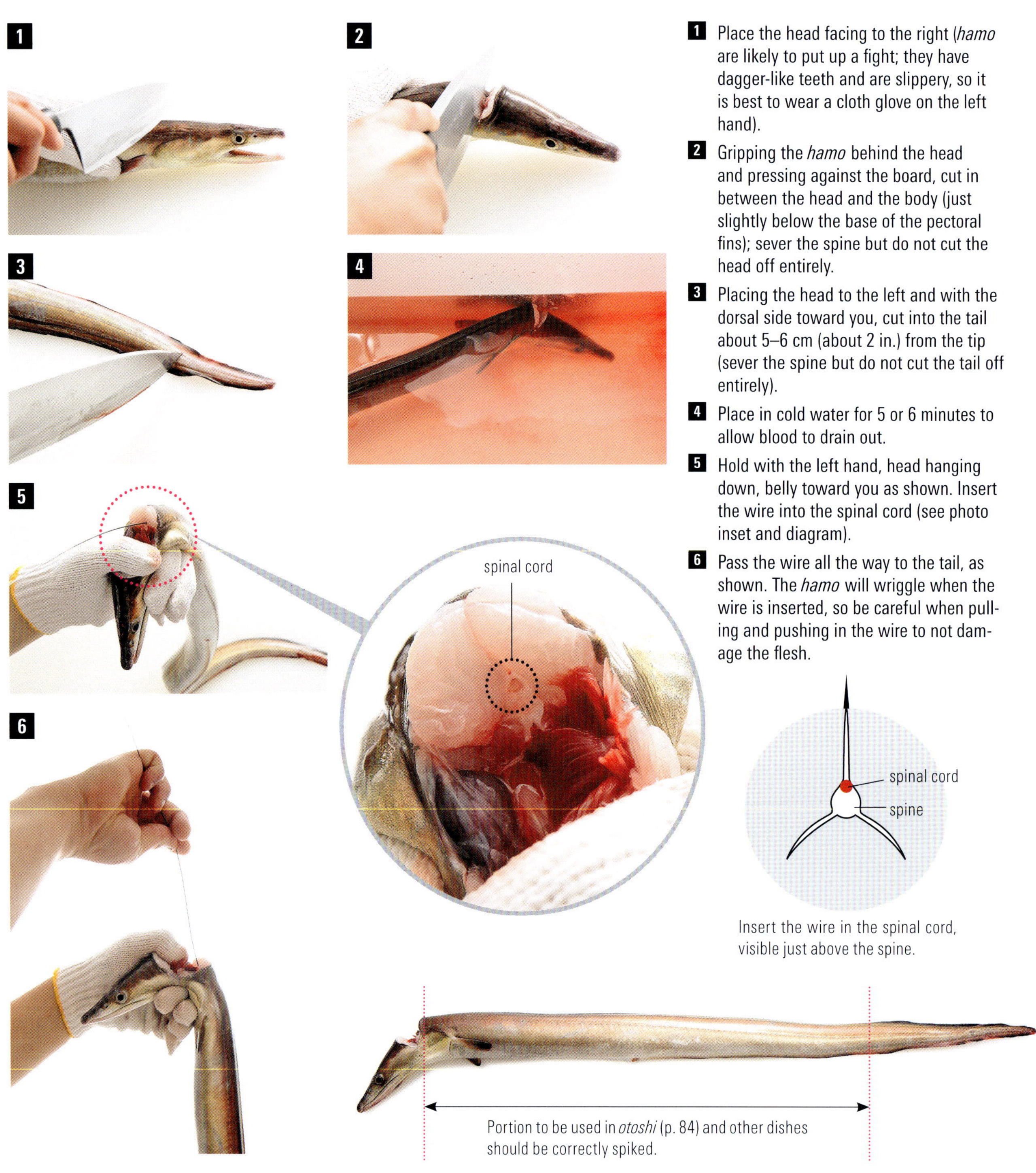

Insert the wire in the spinal cord, visible just above the spine.

Portion to be used in *otoshi* (p. 84) and other dishes should be correctly spiked.

1 Place the head facing to the right (*hamo* are likely to put up a fight; they have dagger-like teeth and are slippery, so it is best to wear a cloth glove on the left hand).

2 Gripping the *hamo* behind the head and pressing against the board, cut in between the head and the body (just slightly below the base of the pectoral fins); sever the spine but do not cut the head off entirely.

3 Placing the head to the left and with the dorsal side toward you, cut into the tail about 5–6 cm (about 2 in.) from the tip (sever the spine but do not cut the tail off entirely).

4 Place in cold water for 5 or 6 minutes to allow blood to drain out.

5 Hold with the left hand, head hanging down, belly toward you as shown. Insert the wire into the spinal cord (see photo inset and diagram).

6 Pass the wire all the way to the tail, as shown. The *hamo* will wriggle when the wire is inserted, so be careful when pulling and pushing in the wire to not damage the flesh.

CARVING PIKE CONGER

Removing the internal organs

1 Lay the spiked *hamo* with head to the left and belly facing you. Holding the head with the left hand, scrape the surface of the skin with the blade of the *deba* knife, in strokes moving in the direction of the tail, to remove the slime.

2 Place the head to the right and belly facing you. With the knife blade facing right (*sakasabocho*), make an incision from the anal vent with the tip of the knife.

3 Continue the incision along the center of the belly toward the head.

4 *Hamo* can bite even after being killed, so cut through the lower jaw.

5 Cut through from vent through jaw. Once the jaw is cut through, the internal organs are visible.

6 Insert the knife again at the anal vent.

7 *Hamo* have internal organs as far as the area near the tail, so insert the knife at the anal vent and cut the membranes that attach the internal organs at the tail end.

8–**9** Lift the flesh with the left hand and, from the incision made in step **7**, cut on toward the tail until the internal organs are visible (take care not to damage the organs), then pull out the organs with the tip of the knife.

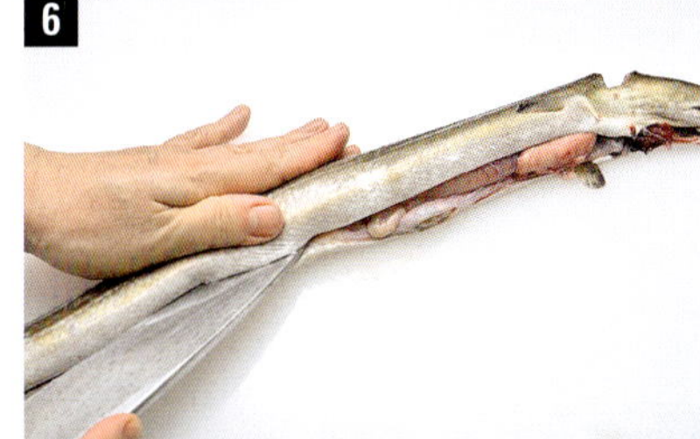

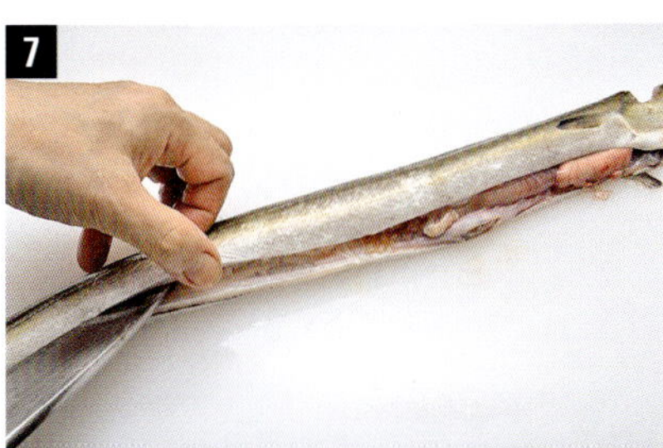

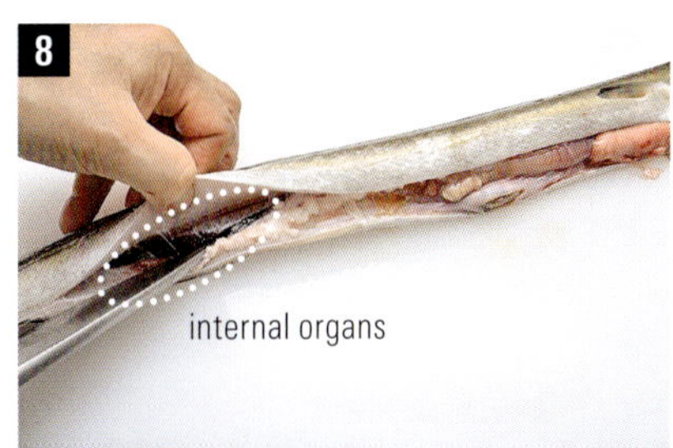

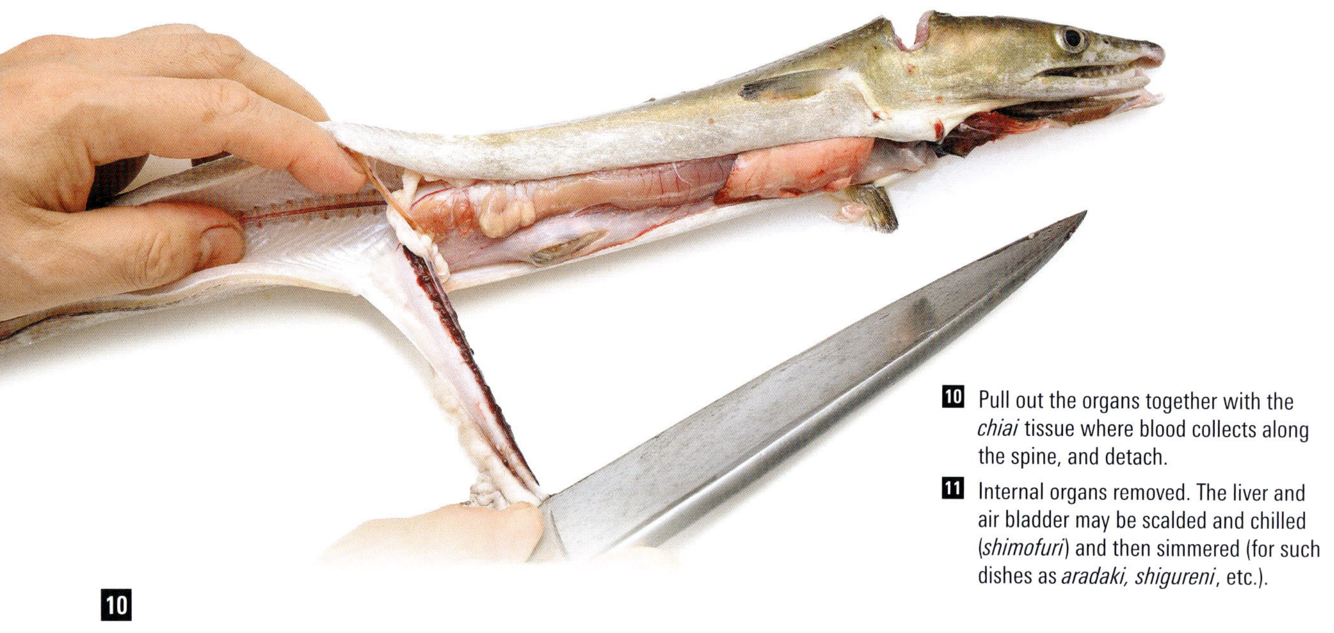

10 Pull out the organs together with the *chiai* tissue where blood collects along the spine, and detach.

11 Internal organs removed. The liver and air bladder may be scalded and chilled (*shimofuri*) and then simmered (for such dishes as *aradaki, shigureni*, etc.).

10

11

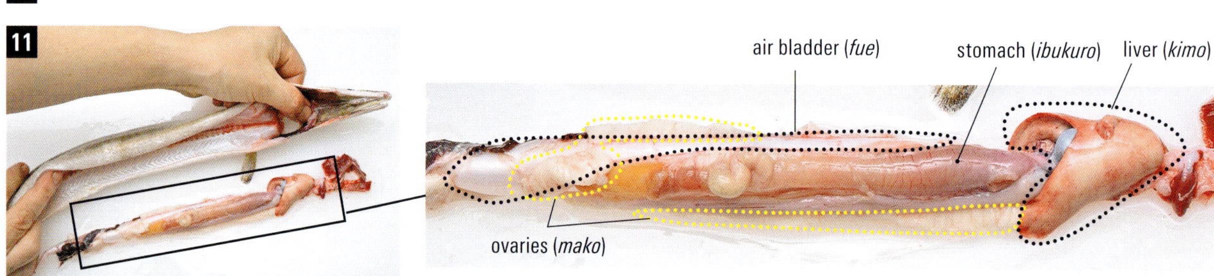

1

Open from the belly

1 Placing the head to the right and the belly toward you, grasp the neck firmly and insert the *me-uchi* at the edge of the eye (place the spike close to the hard bone encircling the eye for best results).

2 Strike the spike with the spine of the knife to firmly secure the *hamo* to the board.

3 Insert the knife in the belly from the lower jaw and, with the knife held at a low angle, open the *hamo* by sliding the knife over the central bones toward the tail.

4 Open the body and confirm that the knife has cut through beyond the spine.

2

3

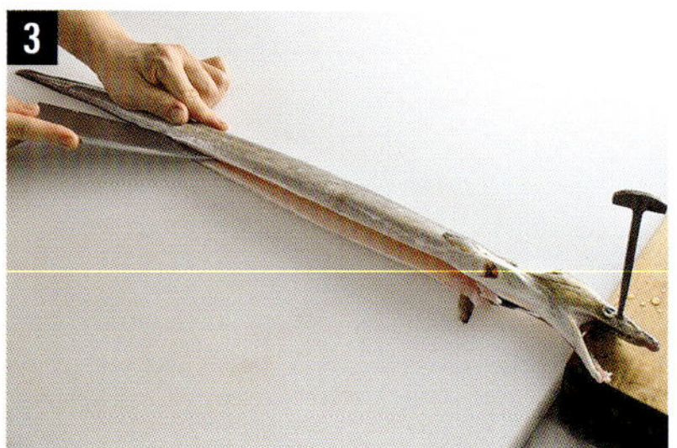

4

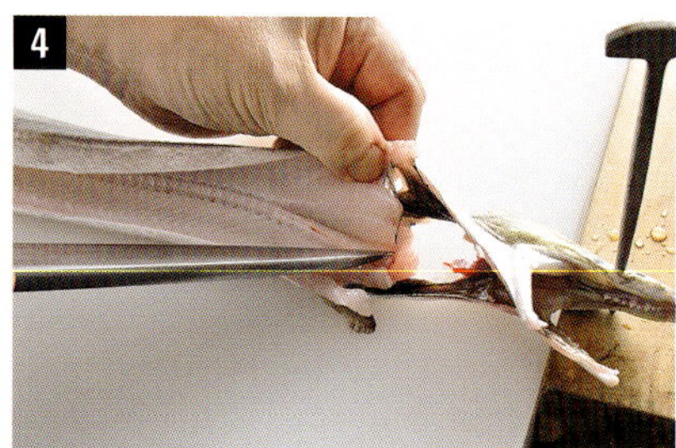

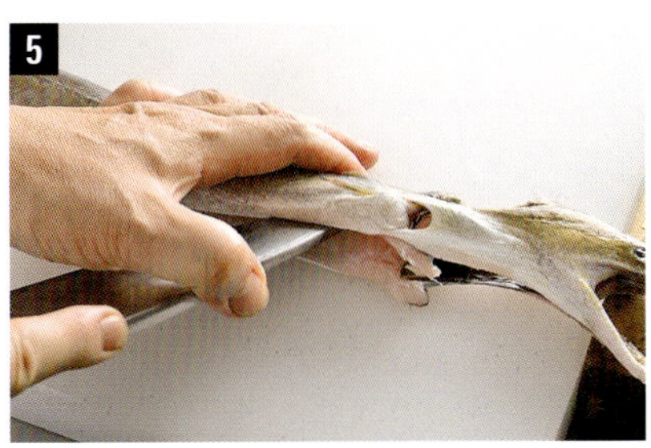

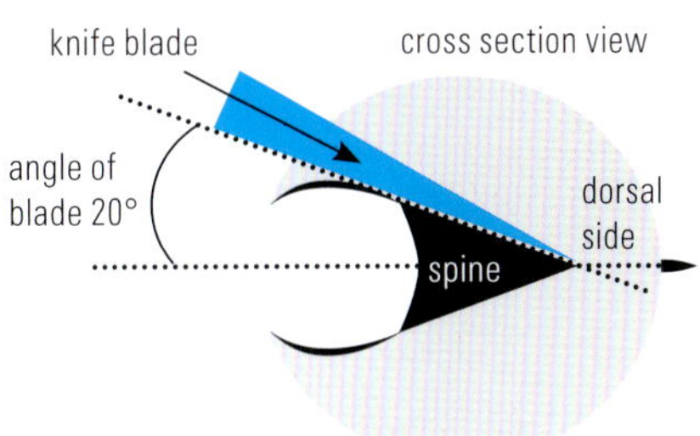

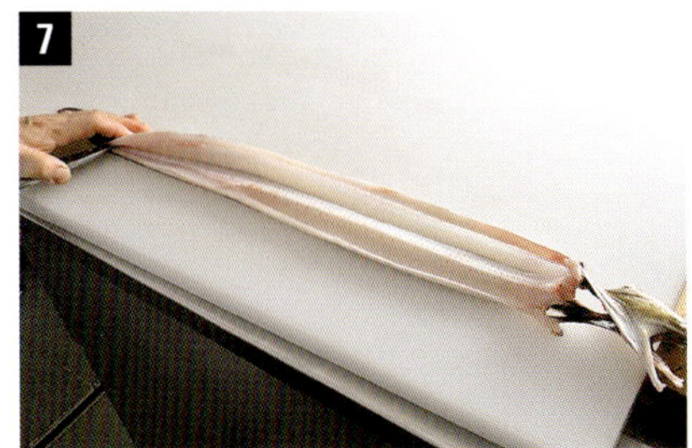

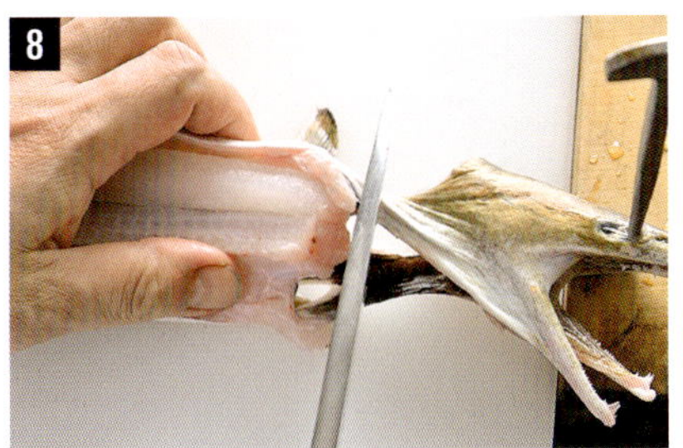

5 Holding the flesh firmly with the left hand as shown, detach the tissue connecting the spine to the central bones and cut open further.

6 The *hamo* spine is triangular in cross section (as shown in the diagram). Start at an angle of about 20 degrees at the top of the spine to align the knife with the contour of the spine and lay the knife flat at the point where the anal fin begins. This will make it easier to insert the blade and less flesh will remain on the bones.

7 Continue cutting toward the tail, opening up the flesh.

8 When opened to the tail, cut the body away from the head.

9 The *hamo* with head removed, body opened.

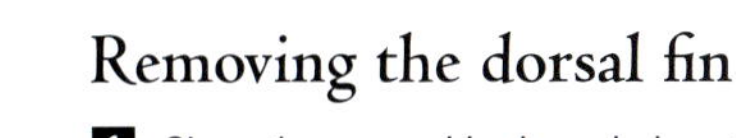

Removing the dorsal fin

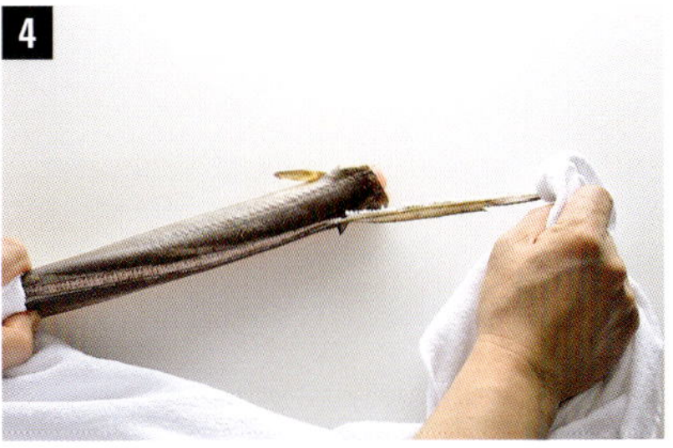

1 Close the opened body and place the tail to the left, dorsal side facing you. Make a shallow cut at the edge of the dorsal fin about 10 cm (4 in.) from the tail in order to cut away part of the dorsal fin.

2 Grasping the tail firmly with the left hand (it may be best to wrap the tail with a towel to prevent the hand from slipping).

3 Grasp the detached part of the dorsal fin with the right hand and detach it, pulling it toward the head end (again, it may be best to hold the tail in a towel).

4 Pull out the bones supporting the dorsal fin (*tankikotsu*; see p. 72) along with the fin and detach at the end.

5 The *hamo* body with the dorsal fin removed (in some cases the dorsal fin is removed before opening the body).

Removing the anal fin, the spine, central bones

1. Place the flesh with the skin side up and tail to the right. Insert the knife, held at a low angle, at the edge of the anal fin.
2. Continue cutting along the anal fin and cut it off along with the bones supporting the fin (*tankikotsu*).
3. Insert the knife again along the incision made in step 1, and, sliding the knife over the central bones toward the head end, detach them from the flesh.
4. Lift up the flesh, checking that the incision goes in as far as the spine, and continue cutting.
5. Holding up the flesh, continue cutting, sliding the knife over the central bones toward the head end,
6. Reverse the body, placing the head end to the right and the skin side down. Grasping the spine with the left hand and laying the knife flat beneath the central bones, separate the spine and central bones from the flesh in a continuous motion in the direction of the tail.

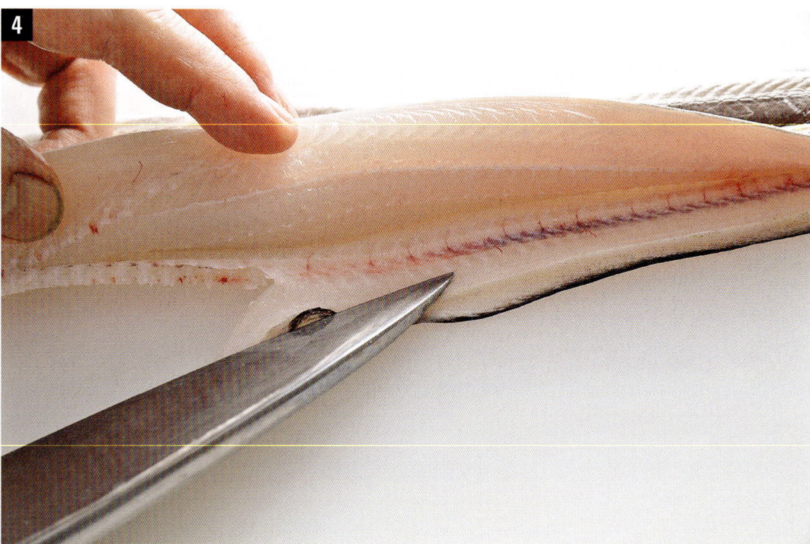

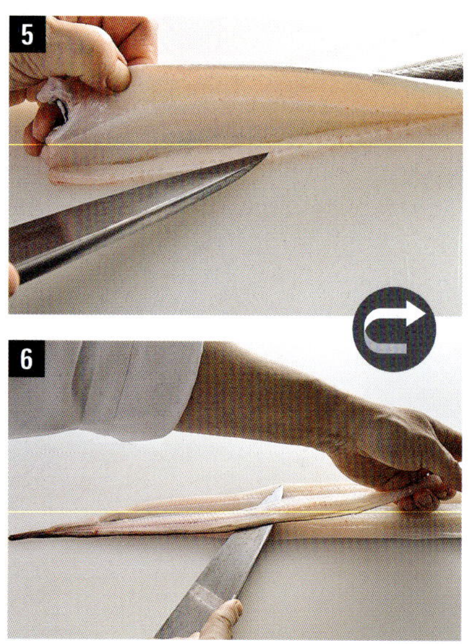

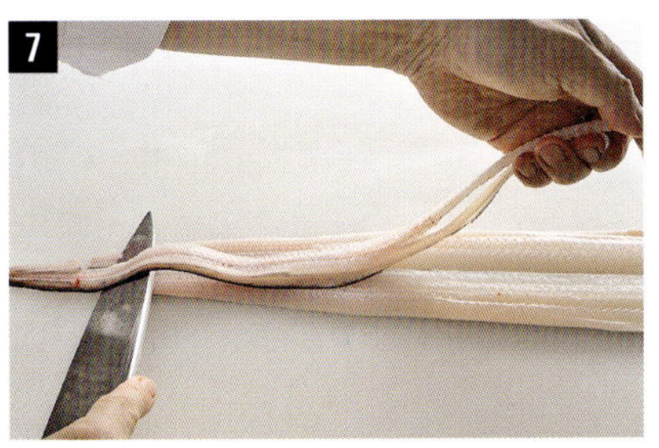

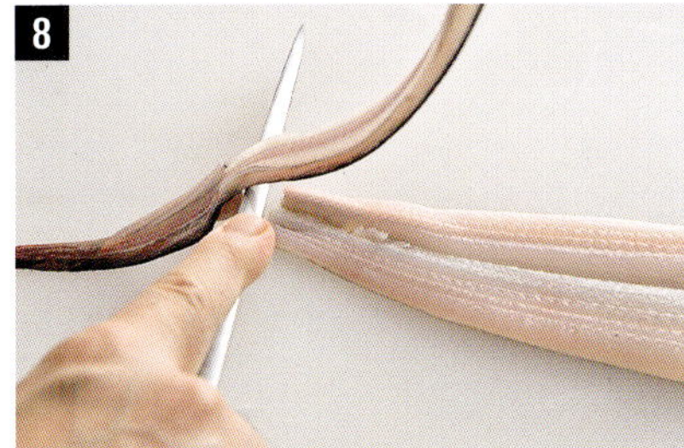

7 Continue cutting toward the tail, separating the spine and central bones from the flesh.

8 At a place about 5 cm (about 2 in.) from the tip of the tail, cut the spine and central bones away from the flesh.

9 The opened *hamo*. The bones may be used for making dashi or grilling sauce.

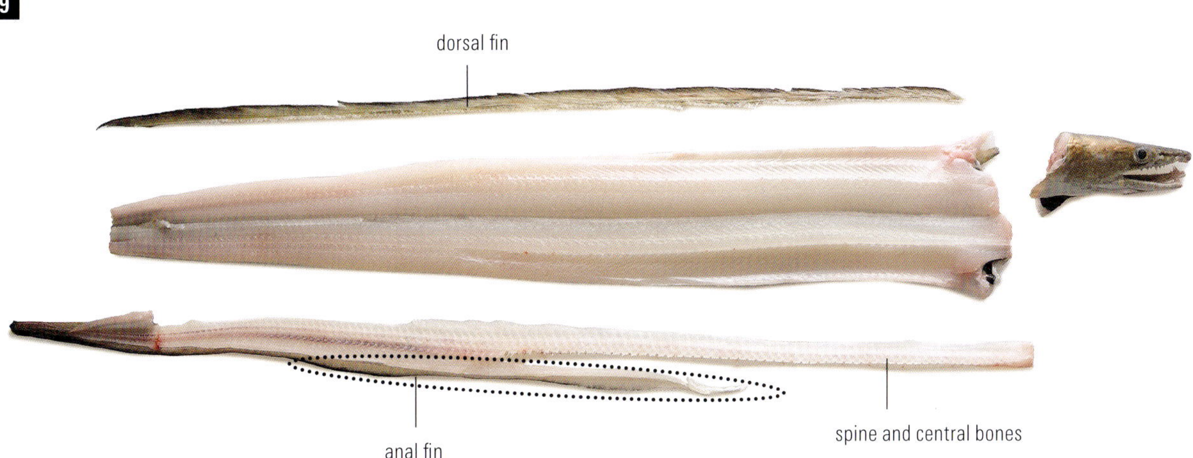

Removing the remnants of the dorsal fin

1 Fold over the flesh at the head end as shown and pull out the remnant of the dorsal fin.

2 Pin down the protruding end of the fin with the knife blade and pull the body with the left hand to detach the fin.

3 Close the body and, with the head end to the right, place with the dorsal side toward you. With the flat of the index finger, feel out the remnants of the dorsal fin and remove with a bone tweezer. The bones of the dorsal fin are hard and cannot be cut with the *honekiri* knife, so they need to be removed carefully with tweezers.

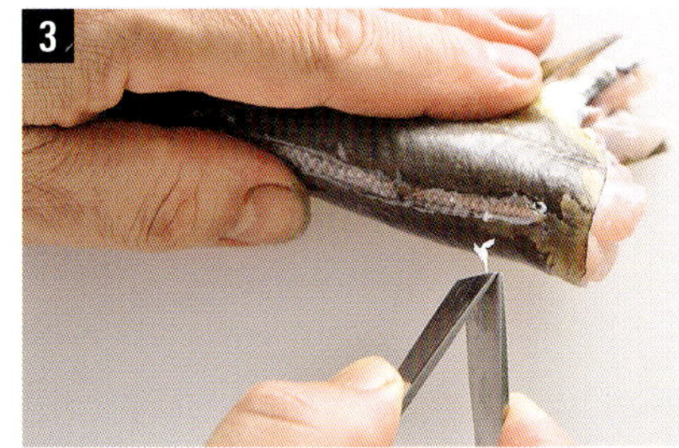

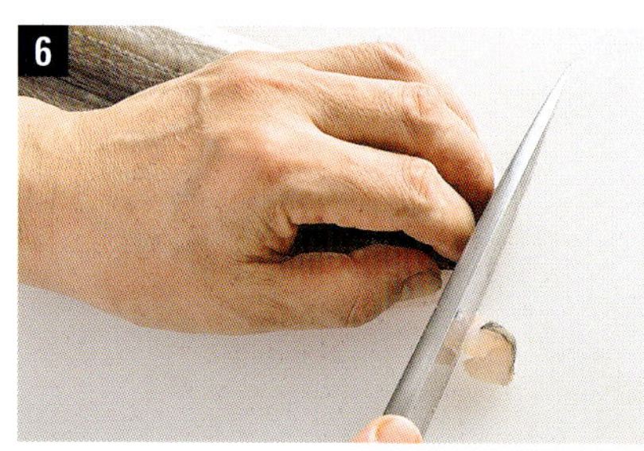

4 Place the body with the skin side up and head end facing you. Place the knife at an angle beneath the collar bone and cut off the pectoral fin together with the collar.

5 Cut off the opposite-side collar bone and pectoral fin.

6 Cut off the frayed part remaining from the base of the head.

7 The body and the collar/pectoral fin parts cut away.

Removing the belly bones

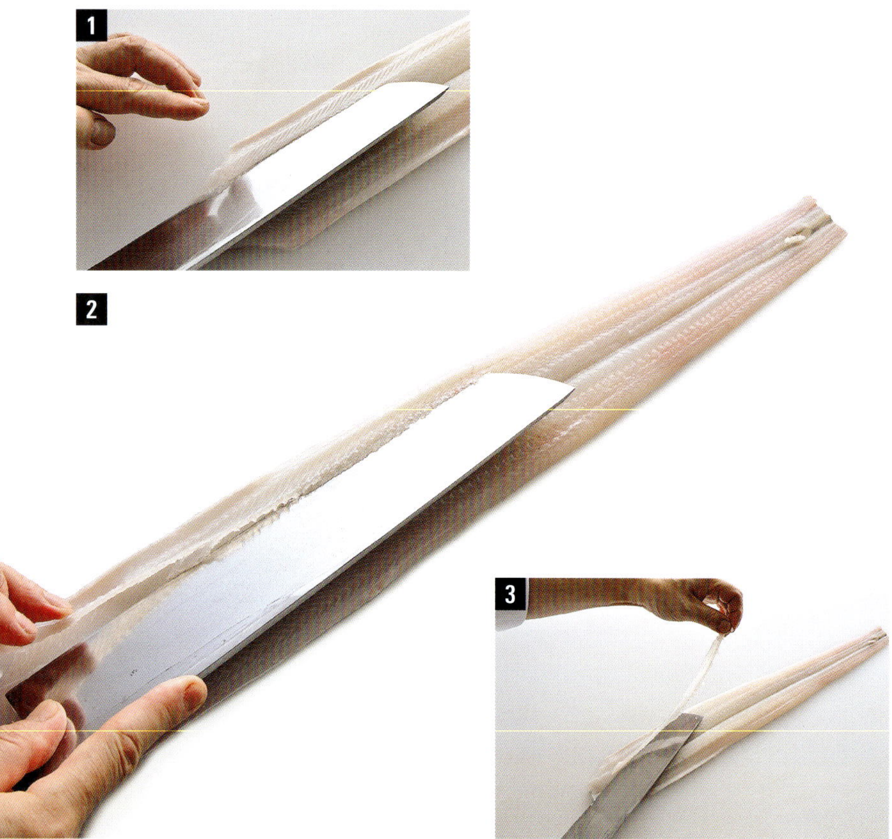

1 Change to the *honekiri* knife (see p. 14). Place the flesh with the skin side down and the head end toward you. Holding the *honekiri* knife horizontally, insert the blade under the base of the belly bones on the farther side, as shown.

2 The belly bones are spread all along the flesh, so insert the knife repeatedly, working from the head end toward the tail, positioning the knife carefully and slicing off the bones.

3 With the left hand, raise the part of the belly bones detached and insert the knife again, slicing off the bones on one side.

4 Place the flesh with the skin side down and the tail end toward you. Holding the *honekiri* knife horizontally, insert the blade under the base of the belly bones on the farther side.

5 Make a shallow cut along the base of the belly bones.

6 Reinsert the knife in the cut made in step **5** and slice off the belly bones.

7 With the left hand, raise the detached part of the belly bones while slipping the *honekiri* knife under the remaining belly bones to remove them.

The belly bones detached from the flesh become ingredients themselves for making dashi, crunchy "bone *senbei*,"* and other uses. The flesh nearest the head is densely filled with bones. The broad section between the collar and anal vent (marked with dotted lines), which is of the highest quality, is used for *hamo otoshi* delicacies and grilled dishes. The flesh in the tail-end section, which is thinner, is often crushed for use in *narutomaki* cured paste rolls.

*The bones are pounded lightly with a wooden pestle, dusted with kuzu starch, and deep fried.

Honekiri slicing technique

Hamo flesh is filled with countless fine bones (intermuscular bones, see p. 73), so is inedible without cutting them finely. The *honekiri* technique makes the flesh palatable.

Place the skin side down and the head end to the right. Lightly dampen the *honekiri* blade with a cloth and tip the blade about 20 degrees to the left while scoring the flesh at 1.2-mm intervals, leaving the skin intact, from head end to tail end (this angle positions the knife perpendicular to the small bones, enabling them to be finely cut).

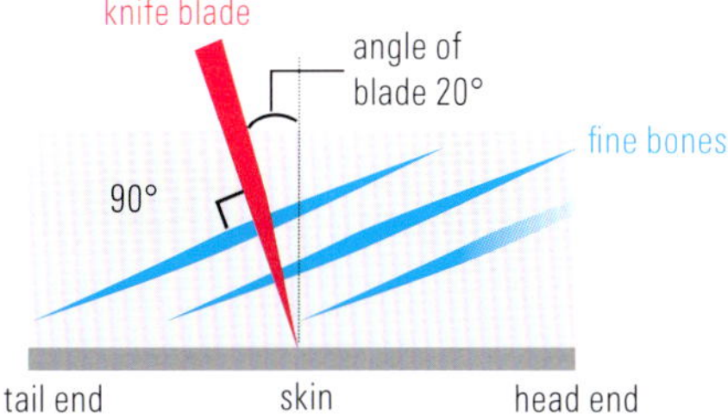

Yakishimo

Lightly grilling fish with the skin on and cooling the skin side on ice is called *yakishimo* (lit., "grilling and frosting") and is used with pike conger, sea bream, and other fish with skin that is rich in umami flavor. The method, for cooling down the grilled side, quickly halting the heating of the flesh, results in a deliciously moist preparation.

1. Place the flesh vertically and secure with a metal skewer at the center of the near end. Handling with the fingers would crush the fluffy texture of the flesh created in the scoring technique, so an extra skewer is used to steady the flesh while inserting a skewer along the length of the piece near the center line, as shown.
2. Insert another skewer along the right edge.
3. Insert a skewer to the left of the center.
4. Insert a fourth skewer on the left edge of the piece as shown: two skewers through the thick flesh at the center and one on each edge where the flesh is thinner.
5. To counteract the tendency of the flesh to curl in grilling and achieve an even tinge from the grilling, slide a bamboo skewer under the outside skewers and over the two inside skewers, as shown, before placing on the grill. Grill at high heat. When the skin side is well browned by the heat, turn over and grill the flesh side for between 30 seconds and one minute (depending on the size of the piece).

6 Finish before the heat has passed completely through the flesh

7 Immediately place skin side down on ice and, taking care to keep the flesh intact, carefully draw out the skewers.

8 Leave on the ice for about one minute; when thoroughly chilled, place on a cloth to absorb excess moisture

9 Cut in two through the center.

10 The bones (*tankikotsu*) at the base of the dorsal fin in the central part are not palatable and should be cut away.

11 Place the pieces lengthwise and slice across in pieces about 2 cm (about 1 in.) wide.

12 Completed *yakishimo* pieces. The flesh is soft and moist and ready to serve.

Otoshi

Otoshi and *yakishimo* are both preparation techniques used to enjoy the flavor of fish or conger skin. Soaking in ice water removes a suitable amount of fat and enhances the flavor. After soaking, the trick is to remove just the right amount of moisture, leaving the flesh soft and moist.

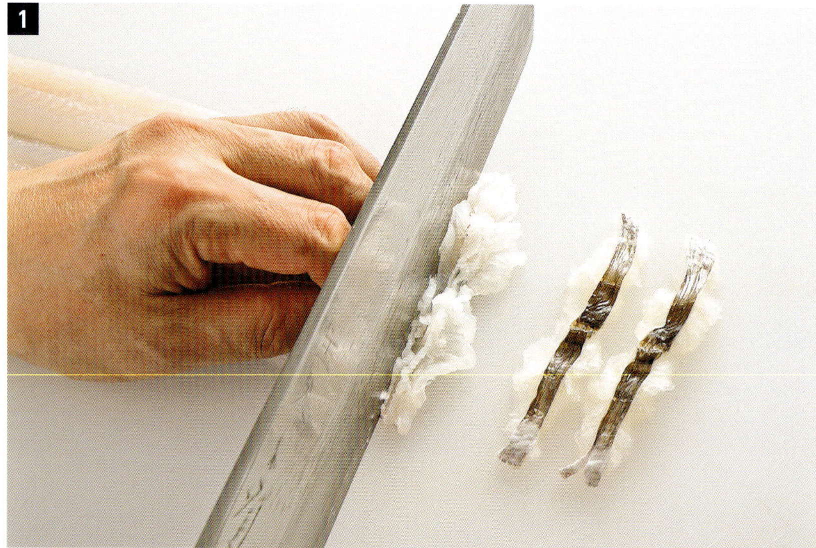

1 Cut off slices of *honekiri*-prepared *hamo* (p. 81) every 5th cut of scoring.

2 Place slices, skin side down, on a mesh ladle and lower into boiling water only as far as the skin for about 10 seconds.

3 Lower completely into the boiling water for a further 5 seconds (the flesh will open out like a flower).

4 Soak in ice water for about 5 seconds.

5 Place on an absorbent cloth.

6 Cover with the cloth and lightly press to soak up excess moisture.

7 Completed *hamo otoshi*. The trick is to remove just the right amount of moisture.

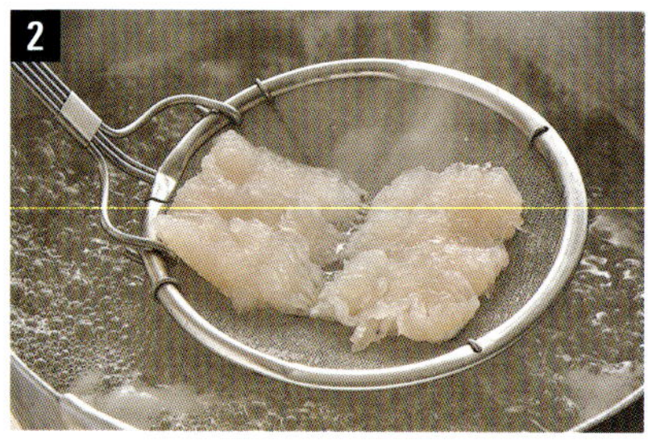

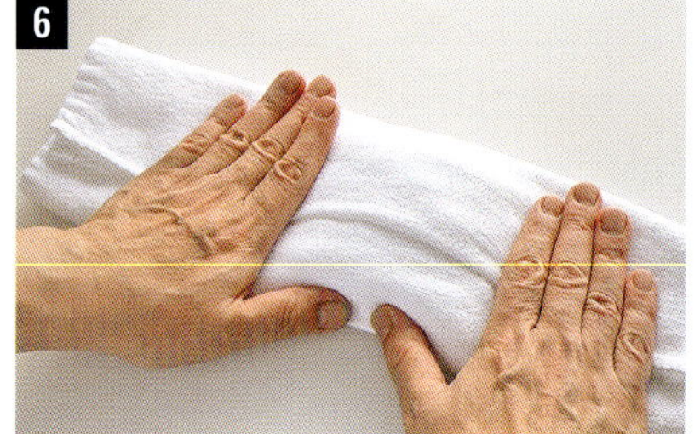

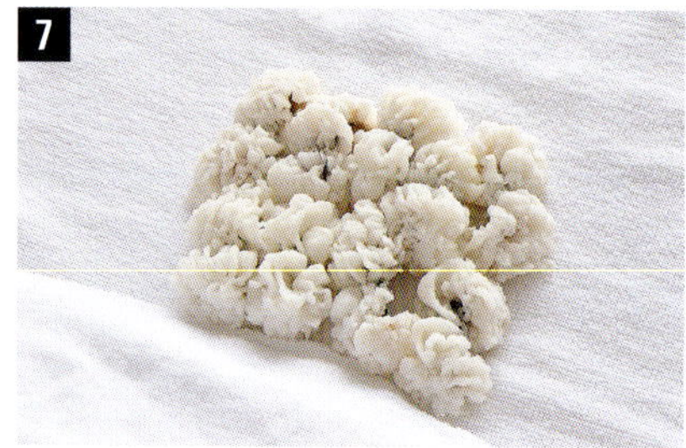

Pike Conger *Yaki-shimo* and *Otoshi*

daikon *ken*
cucumber *ken*
curled cucumber
imo ken
shiso leaves
shiso flowerets
wasabidai
red bud *shiso*
benitade
wasabi

Chapter 2

Carving Shellfish, Octopus, and Squid

Japan's coastal waters, situated advantageously in the path of four major ocean currents, are home to a wealth of ingredients for seafood dishes. In this chapter we present procedures for carving shellfish, octopus, and squid, mainly for sashimi dishes. Even for squid and crustaceans like shrimp, carving techniques differ according to shape and size. When opening shellfish, a *kaiwari* knife is used (see p. 18).

Kuruma-ebi

TIGER PRAWN

Marsupenaeus japonicus

Tiger prawn (*kuruma-ebi*), a large species in the family Penaeidae (order Decapoda), is a favorite in Japanese cuisine, along with the Ise lobster. Preferring temperate waters, tiger prawns live along Japan's coasts from the north (Tohoku) southward as well as along the coasts over a broad area from Southeast Asia to the Indian Ocean. They are nocturnal, concealing themselves on the sandy or muddy sea floor in the daytime.

Tiger prawns have wide, dark-reddish-brown stripes on an almost-transparent, light-brown ground with a bluish tinge, with brown, yellow, and blue stripes on the tail fan. When the shrimp curls up, the stripes on the body form a radial pattern like a cartwheel from which the Japanese name *kuruma-ebi* ("wheel shrimp") derives. *Kuruma-ebi* can grow as long as 25 centimeters. They may be named differently depending on size or weight; for example, large ones, 20 centimeters or longer, are called *o-guruma*, smaller ones *saimaki*, and so on.

Tiger prawns—along with Ise lobsters—have long been widely eaten because they are beautiful in color and have a better flavor than other prawns. They are rich in umami components, and have an especially high content of glutamic and arginine acids. The meat has a dense sweetness and a pleasant texture. When cooked, the shells turn a beautiful red. The wild tiger prawn season is from June to September, but farm-raised tiger prawns are also in plentiful supply. They are served mainly as sashimi, salt-grilled, or deep fried.

PREPARING TIGER PRAWNS

1

Removing the head and shell

1. Grasp the shrimp firmly with the fingers of the left hand, belly upwards, tail to the left, and press down with the left thumb at the base of the head (this grip controls the movement of a still-lively prawn).
2. Placing the right thumb at the boundary between the head and body, remove the head by bending it toward the back.
3. Pull off the head and attached intestine.
4. Change hands, placing the tail to the right with the belly up, and insert the left thumb between the carapace and flesh at the base of the swimmerets.

2

3

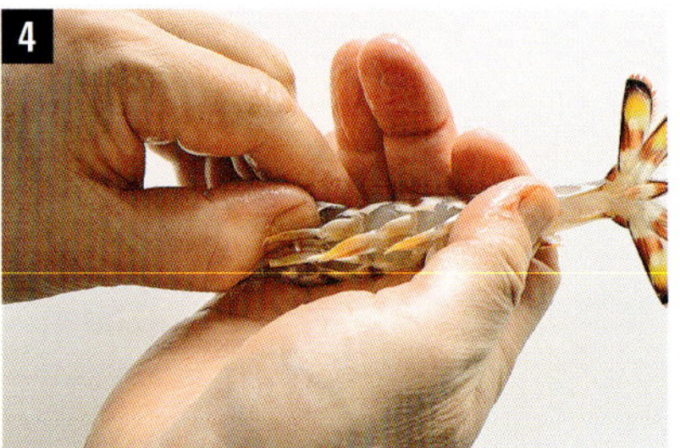
4

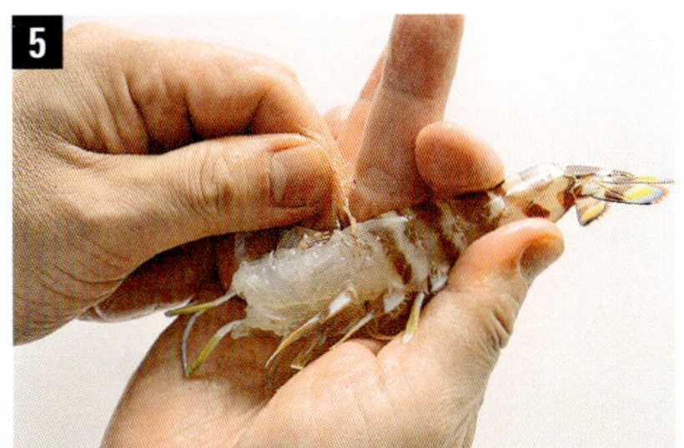

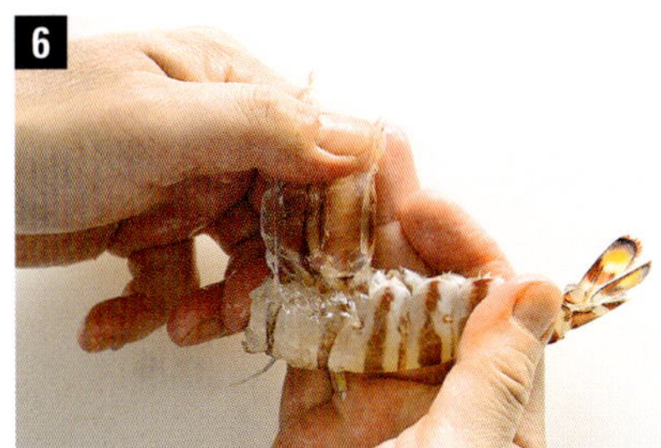

5–6 Holding the body between the index finger and thumb of the right hand, peel off the first two sections of the carapace.

7 Then peel the carapace off from the third section to the tail.

8–9 Remove the carapace from the section at the base of the tail carefully, taking care not to break off the tail.

10 The shell removed (the tail is kept on for further preparations, because it has an appetizing appearance).

Tiger Prawn Sashimi

Kuruma-ebi Tsukuri

Prawn sashimi is served without removing the beautiful tail. The ice bath tightens the flesh and removes unwanted bitterness. If soaked too long, the flesh becomes watery; remove from the ice bath once the tail's sides flare out.

1 Place the shrimp head down to the left, tail up to the right, dorsal side toward you. Make a shallow incision along the center of the back from the base of the tail to the head end.

2 Open the flesh all the way to the head end.

3 Opened shrimp with tail intact.

4 Place in an ice water bath for about 3 minutes. until the flesh opens out "like a flower" (*hana ga saku*). (It will open about one minute earlier if using sake instead of water, but then you will need to rinse it well in running water to remove the sake smell.)

5 Place prawn on a towel, dorsal side up, and lightly press to remove excess moisture.

6 Place with the tail to the left and make a shallow incision at the base of the tail (do not cut through).

7 Bend the tail outward.

8 Cut the flesh in two crosswise, as shown (if quite large, cut in three equal-sized pieces). Cut so that the part without the tail is just slightly larger.

9 Cut the part without the tail in half along the vertical axis.

10 Stack the two pieces cut in step 9 and place the part with the tail attached against it, as shown.

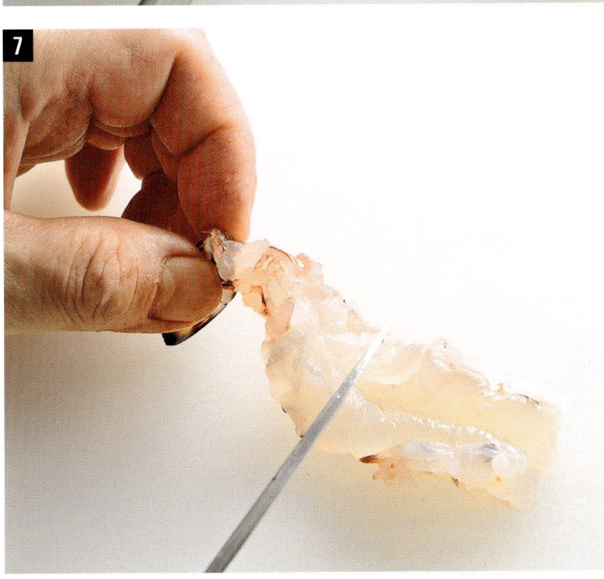

Salt-Grilled Tiger Prawn

Kuruma-ebi Shio-yaki

Simple salt-grilled tiger prawn, whose meat is sweet and soft, is a long-time favorite, generally grilled whole (*sugata-yaki*) and served without removing the head. Skewers are inserted to prevent the body from curling up.

1. Hold the shrimp folded over in the left hand and insert the tip of a bamboo skewer into the transparent membrane at the top of the curve of the carapace in the center of the back.
2. Insert the skewer under the intestine, as shown.
3. Using the skewer carefully, draw out the intestine that passes along the dorsal side.
4. Turn the shrimp over as shown and hold the upper part with the left hand; insert a skewer from the vent under the tail toward the upper part of the body.
5. Insert the skewer just under the surface of the belly along the length of the carapace so as not to damage the meat (skewering in the dorsal side would risk puncture of the *ebi miso* (prawn butter), which would allow the tasty *miso* to spill).
6. Turn the shrimp on its side and push the tip of the skewer out of the body near the head, as shown.
7. The skewered shrimp

The tip of the skewer should be pushed out about 1 cm (½ in.) from the head.

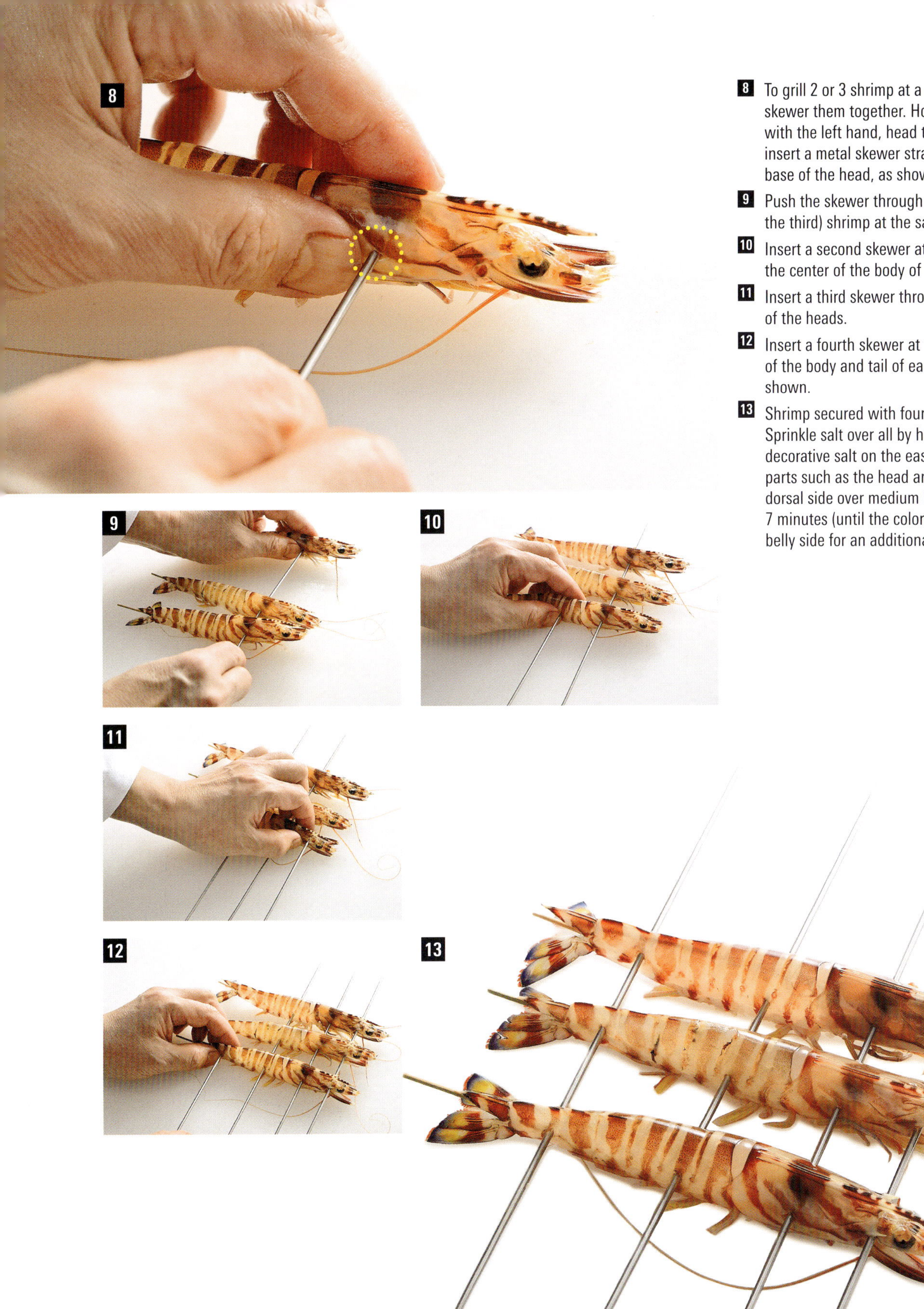

8. To grill 2 or 3 shrimp at a time, metal skewer them together. Holding the body with the left hand, head to the right, insert a metal skewer straight in near the base of the head, as shown.
9. Push the skewer through the second (and the third) shrimp at the same position.
10. Insert a second skewer at a point about the center of the body of each shrimp.
11. Insert a third skewer through the center of the heads.
12. Insert a fourth skewer at the intersection of the body and tail of each shrimp, as shown.
13. Shrimp secured with four skewers. Sprinkle salt over all by hand. Add extra decorative salt on the easily scorched parts such as the head and tail. Grill the dorsal side over medium heat for about 7 minutes (until the color turns) and the belly side for an additional 3 minutes.

Tiger Prawn "Odori" ("Dancing" Shrimp)

uzushio daikon ("whirlpool" daikon)
shiso flowerets
wasabi

Salt-Grilled Tiger Prawns

Ise-ebi

ISE LOBSTER

Panulirus japonicus

Ise lobster refers to several species caught off the coasts of Japan in the family Palinuridae (order Decapoda). It belongs to the Reptantia group of crustaceans that walk on the sea bottom rather than swim. Inhabiting the shallow waters of tropical seas, these are the largest of lobsters fished in Japan and can grow as long as 35 centimeters. They have a pair of long, whip-like antennae, five pairs of legs, and a long abdomen, commonly called the tail. The body is covered with a hard, reddish-brown carapace. With its imposing, finely shaped body and tasty flesh, the Ise lobster has been a symbol of valor and longevity since olden times. As such, it holds special traditional significance as a special ingredient of foods, or as gifts presented on celebratory occasions, and as motifs seen in festive decorations for New Year and other occasions.

The fishing season for Ise lobster is October to April, and they are said to taste best in autumn and winter. The spawning period is May to August, when the flesh is sparer and less tasty, and during this period many areas of Japan prohibit their capture in order to protect the lobster population. Effective Ise lobster-farming methods have not become established, so all those available are caught in the wild; they are sold at the highest prices of all prawns.

Ise lobster meat is sweet and resilient and the yellow, miso-like paste found inside the shell is rich in umami. Ise lobster is often used for dishes that showcase their extravagant appearance, including *sugata-zukuri* (lobster sashimi in the shell), *gusoku-ni* (simmered in the shell), and *onigara-yaki* (split open at the back and grilled in the shell). They are generally carved alive without transpiercing.

CARVING ISE LOBSTER

Removing the head

1 Hold the thick part of the body in the left hand, belly up and tail toward you. With the *deba* knife held horizontally, position the blade tip at the point between the head and tail.

2 Insert the knife tip to sever the meat from the thin shell on the belly side.

3 Moving the knife in and out, cut around just inside the carapace, as shown, in order to detach the meat from the head shell.

4 Insert the blade between the head shell and flesh and begin to remove body from the shell, moving the knife around the body.

5–6 After cutting all around the inside of the head shell, detach the flesh. Then, holding down the end of the tail with the knife (as shown), detach the head from the tail by rotating the head with the left hand.

Removing the thin belly shell

1. Place the tail, from which the head has been removed, belly up with the end of the tail toward you.
2–3. Cut the attachments between the thick outer shell and thin belly shell. Then turn the tail around so that the flippers are to the upper right and cut the attachments between the thick and thin shells.
4. Grip the head-end of the tail with the right hand and lift the belly shell where it is cut away in steps 2–3.
5. Pull away the belly shell in the direction of the tail end, working carefully so that as little flesh as possible adheres to the shell.

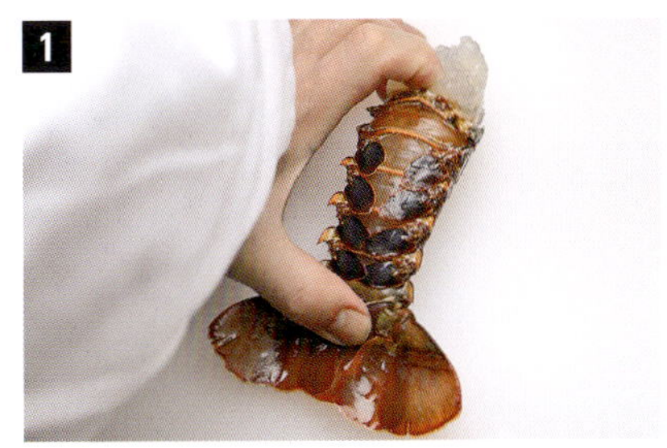

Removing the flesh from the dorsal shell

1. Place the tail—from which the thin belly shell has been removed—with the thick dorsal shell up, head end toward you. With the left hand, lift up the shell somewhat while holding down the tail, as shown. Insert the right thumb to create a space between the flesh and the shell (if the flesh is hard and difficult to dislodge from the shell, insert a spoon to loosen it).
2. Turn the tail over so that the shell is facing down. Insert the thumb in the space between the flesh and shell and shuck the flesh out of the shell.
3. When about half the flesh has been separated from the shell, grasp the flesh with the left hand and pull off up to the tail end while holding down the shell with the right hand.
4. When separated to the end of the tail, cut the attachments to the shell at the base of the flesh and remove.
5. The flesh removed from dorsal shell. When serving "in the shell" (*sugata-zukuri*), set aside the shell for later use.

Sugata-zukuri

Serving fresh shellfish "in the shell" is called *sugata-zukuri* or *ike-zukuri*, with the sashimi served attractively in a fashion that shows off the original form of the lobster. Here, a block of daikon cut on an angle is placed beneath the belly so that the head faces upwards. A chunk lf daikon is also placed under the tail so that it forms a pleasing curve.

1 Place the meat in ice water. This removes sliminess from the surface and tightens the meat.

2 Press lightly with a cloth to remove excess moisture.

3 Place the ice-water-cured meat with the tail end toward you and the belly side facing up.

4 Place the blade of the knife along the center line and draw it toward you to cut the flesh open.

5 If the intestine clings to the meat, pull it out.

6–**7** Between the meat and the shell is a reddish covering membrane. Place the knife in the center of the meat and cut it in two, leaving the membrane on the right side.

8 Turn the right-side flesh (with the membrane attached) over vertically. Shave off the reddish membrane area.

9 Flesh of both sides of the tail and the part with the reddish membrane.

10 Slice the flesh of both sides lengthwise to half the thickness.

11 Cut the slices into four bite-sized pieces at the segments.

12 The flesh cut into four pieces.

13 The flesh with the reddish membrane is thin, so cut into two.

14 Pieces of flesh with the reddish membrane.

Ise Lobster Sashimi in the Shell

uzushio daikon ("whirlpool" daikon)
red and white daikon *ken*
carrot curls

Ko-ika

GOLDEN CUTTLEFISH

Sepia esculenta

The golden cuttlefish (*ko-ika*), in the family Sepiidae (order Sepiida), grows to about 20–30 centimeters, most of its length consisting of the mantle—the oblong main body—which is about 15–16 centimeters long. The mantle contains the calcareous, flat-boat-like endoskeleton—the cuttlebone—on the back side. Flat, undulating fins, called *empera*, are attached on each side of the mantle. The sharp, needle-like spines at the rear end of the mantle gives the golden cuttlefish its alternative name, *hari-ika* (lit., "needle cuttlefish"). Still another name, *sumi-ika* ("ink cuttlefish"), comes from its well-developed ink sac.

Found widely along the coasts from central Japan southward as far as the southern part of Taiwan, golden cuttlefish live in the sandy soil of shallow seas. Nocturnal, they hide in the seabed in the daytime.

The golden cuttlefish belongs to the class Cephalopoda ("headfoot"), a species in which the eyes and the brain are located at the base of the eight short arms and two long tentacles. The tentacles are retractable and capture prey with suction cups on the ends.

The spawning period is spring to early summer, and the golden cuttlefish is thought to taste the best from the winter of the preceding year to early spring. The flesh is thick and has rich umami and sweetness as well as slight stickiness and springiness. Excellent as sashimi, the flesh, which remains soft even when heated, is also deep fried, grilled with salt, and included in simmered dishes. The arms (*geso*) are eaten in stir-fried and other dishes. The large cuttlebone should be removed as the first step in carving.

CARVING GOLDEN CUTTLEFISH

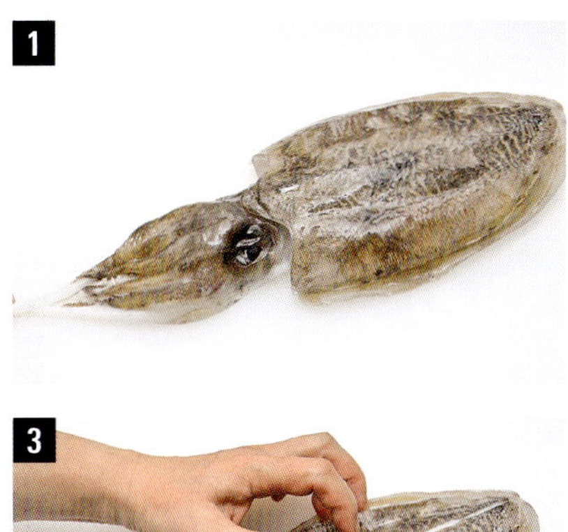

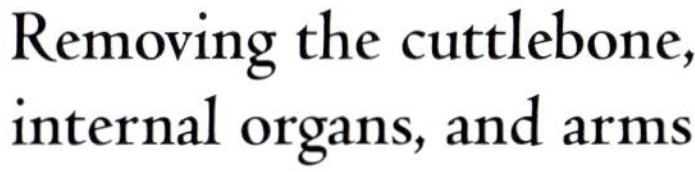

Removing the cuttlebone, internal organs, and arms

1. Place the cuttlefish mantle side up.
2. Steady the body with the left hand and position the tip of the *deba* knife at the far end of the mantle along the center line.
3. Draw the knife toward you, cutting through the skin down to the bone.
4. Pull the skin back on the left and right, revealing the large cuttlebone.
5. With the left hand holding down the arms, lift up the cuttlebone with the right hand.
6. Separate the cuttlebone from the body and remove.
7. Taking care not to damage the internal organs, make an incision in the membrane covering the organs at the center where the body and arms meet (the base of the cuttlebone).
8. Turn the blade of the knife up (*sakasa-bocho*) and make an incision in the membrane at the back end of the body.

9 A membrane covers the internal organs beneath the cuttlebone. Insert the knife, blade facing up as shown, beneath the membrane and slit it open (take care not to damage the organs).

10 Inserting the left thumb into the incision made in step **7**, slide the thumb along and remove the membrane on the left side. Open up the membrane on the right side in like fashion and remove.

11 With the left hand, grasp the arms and the base of the body together.

12–**14** Steadying the body with the right hand, pull up the arms and pull them toward the back of the body. When pulled to the far end of the body, switch hands and continue pulling, separating the arms and internal organs from the body, ink sac and all. If ink is expelled, the flesh will be discolored; take care that the sac is not ruptured.

Removing the skin from the mantle (body)

1. Place the body inside up, skin side down. Starting from the tip of the mantle, insert the thumbs of both hands between the skin and flesh and slide the thumbs toward the base of the mantle, separating about 4–5 cm (about 2 in.) of the flesh from the skin.
2. Gripping the skin firmly with the left hand, roll the flesh away from the skin with the right hand.
3. With about 3 cm (1¼ in.) of skin still attached, hold down on the flesh with the right hand and pull the remaining skin away from the flesh with the left hand.
4. Pull off the skin entirely with the left hand.

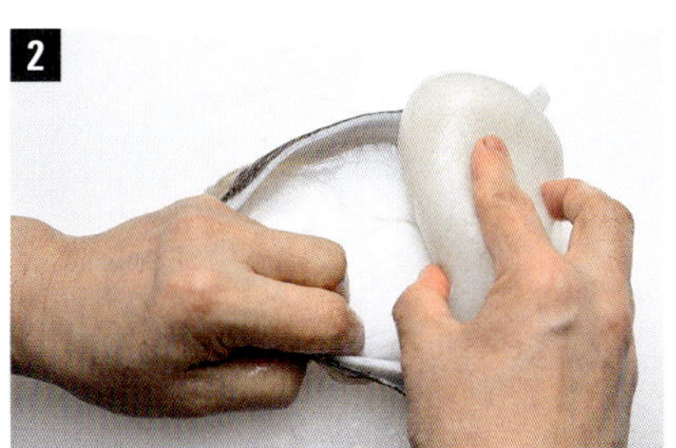

from previous page

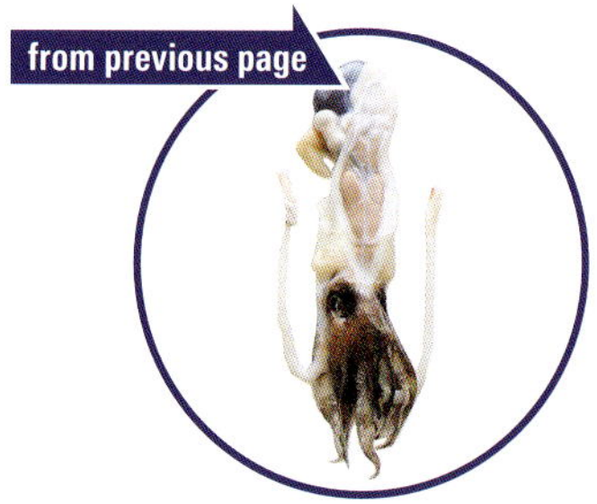

Preparing the arms

1. Place the head end of the cuttlefish with internal organs attached, arms facing left, and cut away the internal organs, leaving the liver (the brown part) attached to the arms.
2. Open out the sac containing the liver with the fingers and remove the organ.
3. The delicate organs can be removed by pushing them out of the membrane and then cutting the tissue attaching them to the body.
4. The arms and liver removed.
5. Cut off the two long tentacles at the base.
6. One at a time, push out the eyes attached to the arms and cut each off with the knife.

1

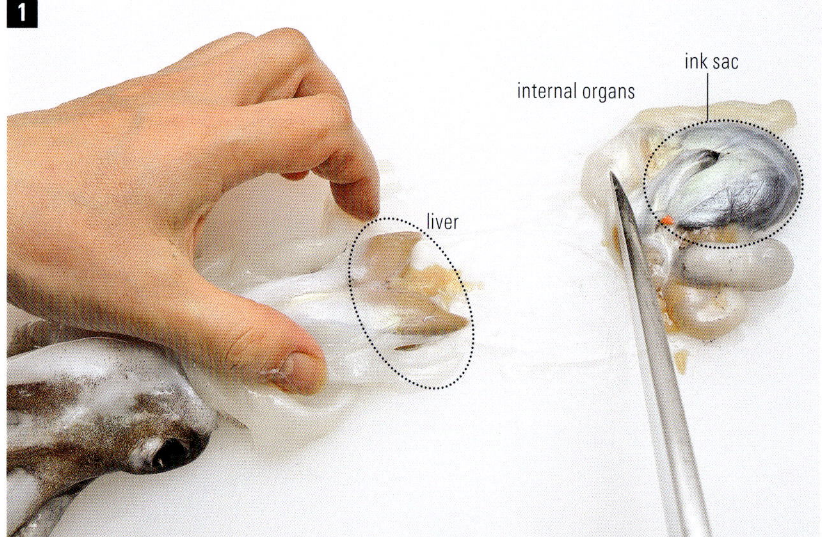

2

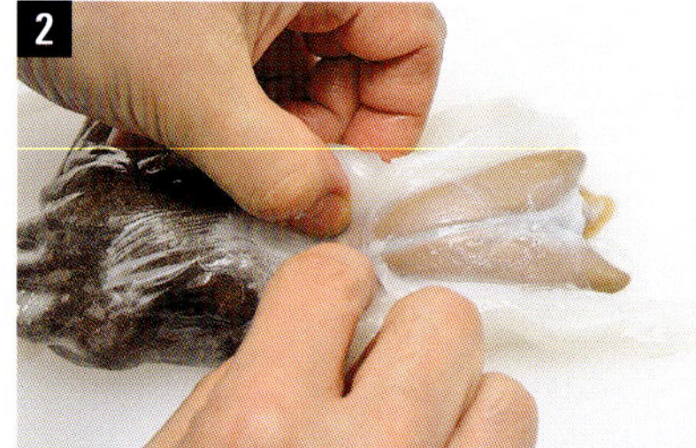

3

4

5

6

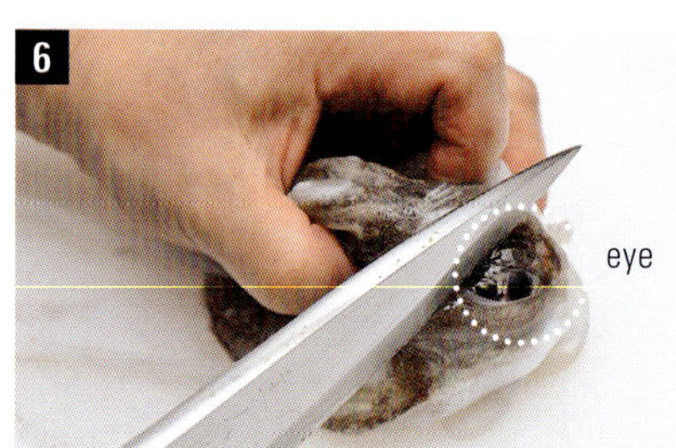

7 At the center of the arms (when spread out radially) is the ball-shaped beak of the squid. With the tip of the knife, push the beak outward and cut it off.

8 Insert the knife into the cavity remaining after cutting off the beak and cut down.

9 Turn the cuttlefish over, make an incision in the center at the base of the arms, and open the circle of arms.

10 Cut off the tough flesh (cartilage) at the base of the arms (below the eyes)

Cleaning the fins

1 The fins of the golden cuttlefish are on the sides of the body, attached to the skin partially removed in step **1** on p. 107. They have a pleasant crunchy texture and can be enjoyed in fine slices served for contrast with the soft flesh of cuttlefish sashimi.

2 Place with the skin side down. From the edge, insert the thumbs between the skin and the fins to separate them (use a cloth for better traction).

3 Hold the fin in the right hand and pull the skin with the left hand, removing it from the fin.

4 Keep pulling the skin until completely removed from the fin.

5 Place with the skin side down. Tough cartilage remains on the parts where the fins were attached; insert the knife vertically along the cartilage and scrape it off with the membrane left on. Remove the fin from the other side of the membrane and scrape off the cartilage with the membrane left on that side as well.

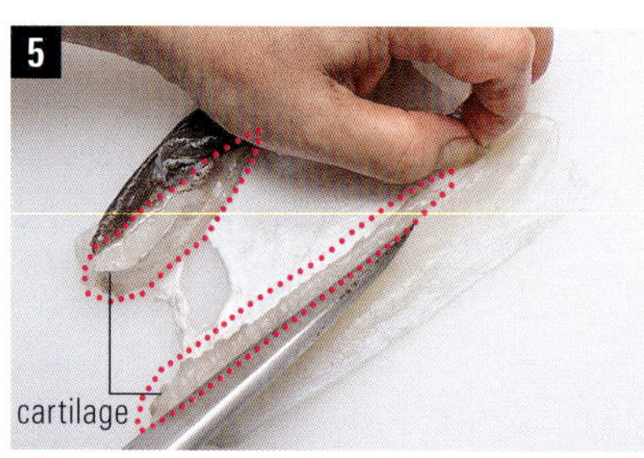

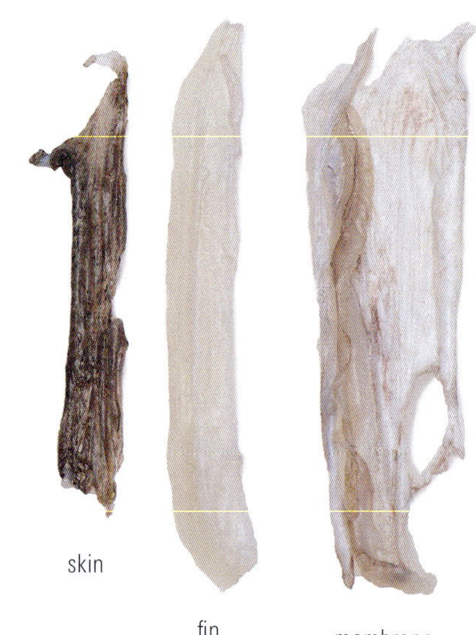

from page 107

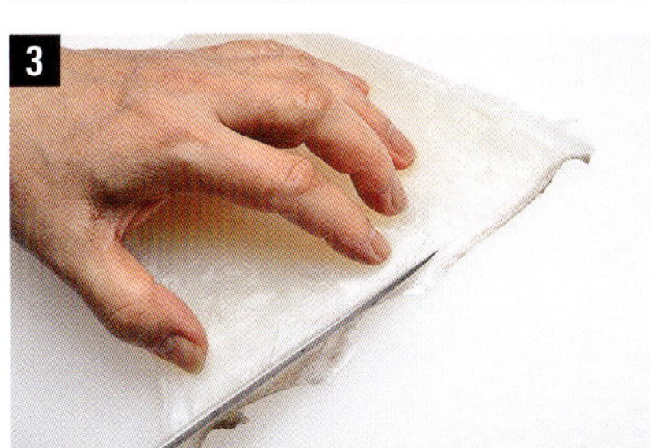

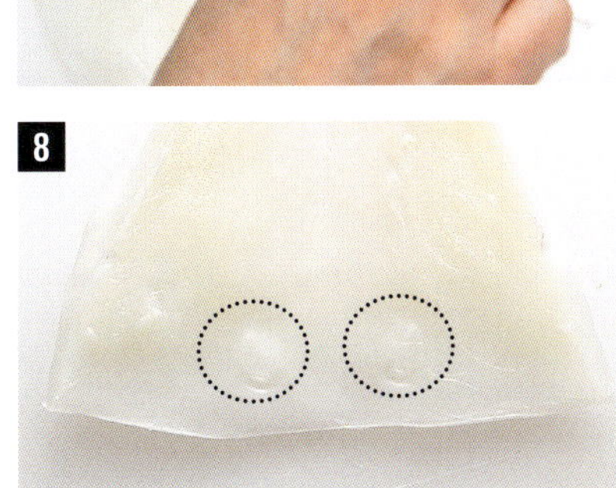

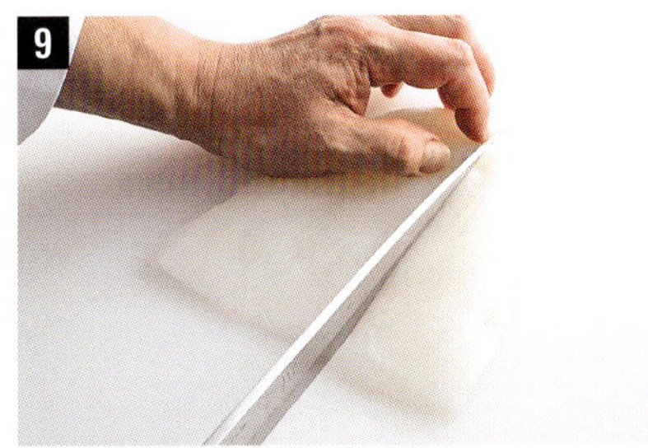

Removing membrane from mantle flesh and creating sashimi *saku* blocks

1 Rinse the flesh in water and remove the surface membrane with a towel or cloth.

2 Place the flesh with the inside surface up. Change to a *yanagiba* knife and place the blade along the head-end edge of the flesh, as shown.

3 In order to make it easier to get a grip on the membrane to peel it off, make a shallow incision about 5 mm (¼ in.) from the edge of the flesh and about 3 mm (⅛ in.) deep (not cutting through the membrane but only through the flesh).

4 Turn the body over. Grasp the edge of the skin at the incision made in step 3 and pull up the skin, pulling it off the flesh.

5 Keep pulling back the skin to the tail end and remove.

6–**7** Using a skewer, carefully separate from the flesh any fragments of skin that may have remained in pulling off the membrane. Pull off any remaining bits of membrane.

8 Remove any lingering fragments of membrane that remain on parts where the flesh is uneven.

9 Cut the cuttlefish flesh from which the membrane has been removed into blocks for making sashimi. Cut the first block from the right side one-third of the flesh, drawing the knife from the tail end toward you. Cut the second block from the left side in the same manner so that the flesh yields three blocks.

to next page

cuttlefish flesh cut into blocks

Kanoko-zukuri

Criss-cross scoring that results in a pattern traditionally called *kanoko*, after the spots on the back of a fawn, is often used for cuttlefish. After scoring, the flesh is scalded and plunged into ice water. The pattern is attractive and also picks up soy sauce for tasty dining.

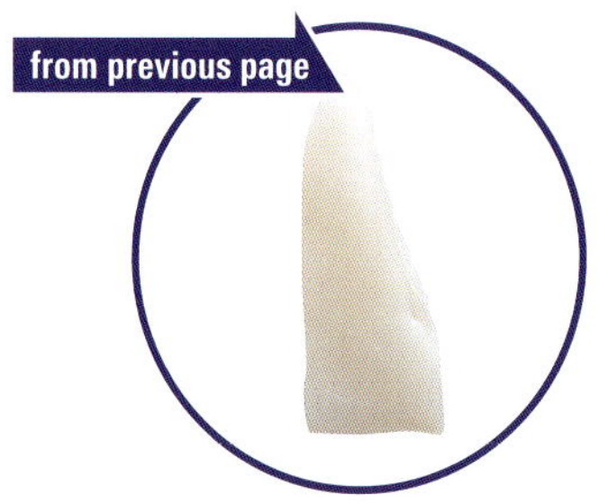
from previous page

1 Place one of the previously prepared blocks of cuttlefish with the tip facing away at an angle of about 45 degrees to the left, with the tip away from you and angled slightly toward the left. Tipping the knife blade slightly to the left, make incisions about 2–3 mm (about ⅛ in.) apart across the width of the entire block, starting at the base, as shown.

2 Turn the tip of the block to the right at an angle of about 45 degrees. From the right side, make diagonal incisions at 2–3 mm (about ⅛ in.) across the incisions made previously.

3 The crosshatching of the incisions forms the "fawn-spot" (*kanoko*) motif. Braise the pieces briefly over a gas burner until the incisions show clearly. Cut the block into 1.5-cm (½-in.)-wide pieces.

Scored Cuttlefish Sashimi

okra
radish *ken*
daikon *ken*
cucumber *ken*
kabocha curls
sansho leaf
grated ginger.

Aori-ika

BIGFIN REEF SQUID

Sepioteuthis lessoniana

Bigfin reef squid, a member of the family Loliginidae (order Teuthidea), has a large mantle, or body, about 45 centimeters in length, with a pair of wide side fins (*mimi*) almost circling it. The Japanese name of this squid comes from the similarity in shape to the *aori*, flaps attached to the saddle on a horse to prevent mud from splashing the rider. The arms are relatively short, and the dorsal side of the squid is dark brown. Males have many short, white horizontal lines, and females have spot-like patterns on the dorsal side. In contrast to the calcareous shell of the golden cuttlefish (p. 104), this squid has a soft, transparent quill inside its mantle.

The bigfin reef squid lives in temperate waters from the Indian Ocean to the West Pacific; in Japan along the coast from part of Hokkaido southward. Its usual habitat is deep waters, but during the spawning season from April to September, it moves to shallower areas near the coast. Those found in shallow waters during this period are prized for their size and taste. The meat is springy and richly sweet, containing ample amounts of amino acid, an umami component. The meat is thick, so it is well suited for sashimi but also for salt grilling and deep frying.

CARVING BIGFIN REEF SQUID

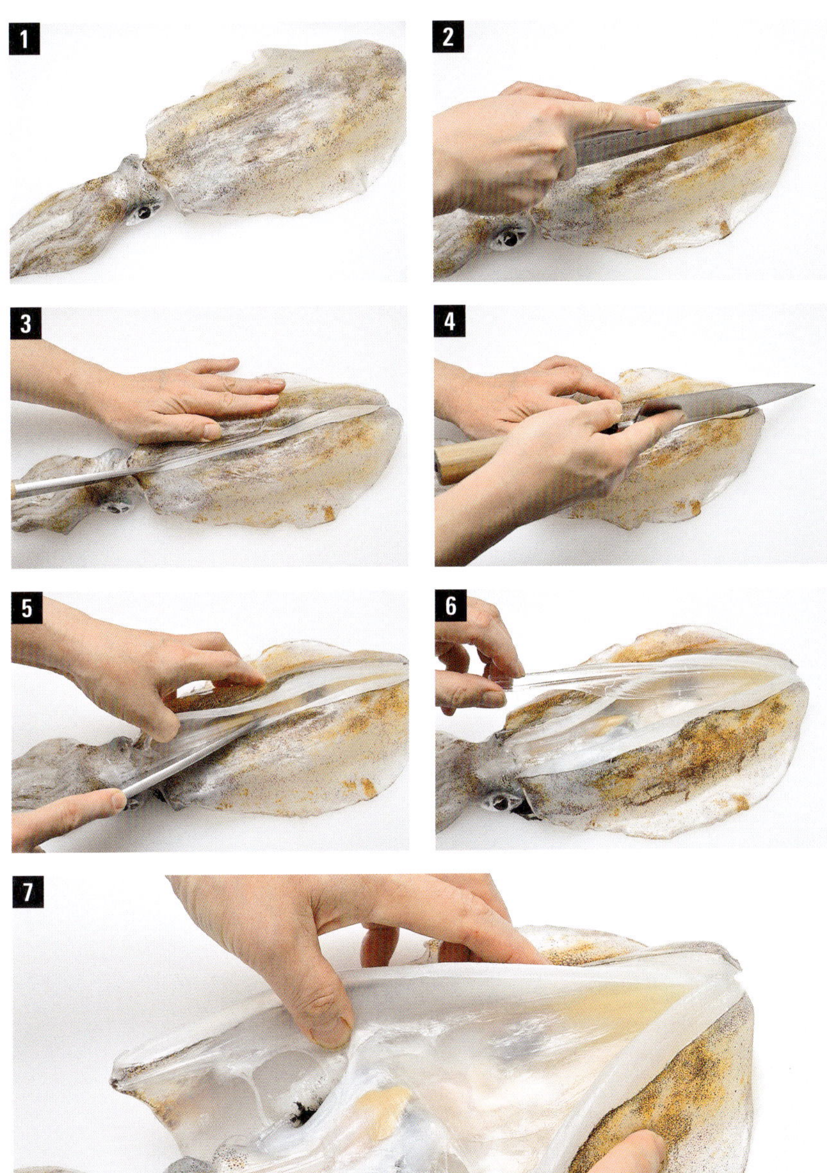

Removing the quill, ink sac, and internal organs

1. Place with dorsal side up, as shown.
2. Steadying the body with the left hand, position the *deba* knife at the center far end of the body.
3. Draw the blade toward you to slit the body at the center down to the quill.
4. Turn the knife over (*sakasabocho*) and insert the knife tip in the slit to complete the cut to the tip of the body.
5. Pull the body open left and right, revealing the quill.
6. Remove the quill, lifting it out with the left hand from the head end.
7. With the thumbs of both hands, open the body left and right.

8 To prevent the ink sac from leaking and discoloring the flesh, remove it first. Pull the arms and internal organs toward the far end of the body and pull out the ink sac.

9 Cut off the ink sac at its base.

10 After cutting off the ink sac wash away any remaining ink in running water.

11 Steadying the body with the right hand, pull off the membrane covering the internal organs.

12 Gripping the body with the right hand, pull the arms with the left hand and separate them (whole) from the body. Wash the body in running water and pat dry with a cloth.

Removing the skin from the flesh

1 Place the flesh side up, skin side down. Starting at the slit made in step **4** on p. 115, insert both thumbs between the skin and the flesh.

2 Sliding the thumbs in and out, remove the skin from the flesh about 3 cm (1¼ in.).

3 Insert the thumb of the left hand into the crease made by separating the skin and flesh and slide it toward the back of the body to separate the skin from the flesh.

4 On the opposite side, insert the thumb of the left hand into the crease and slide it toward the back of the body to separate flesh and skin.

5 Holding down the skin and fins firmly with the right hand, with the left hand, pull the flesh away and up.

6 Pulling with the left hand, separate the flesh from the skin.

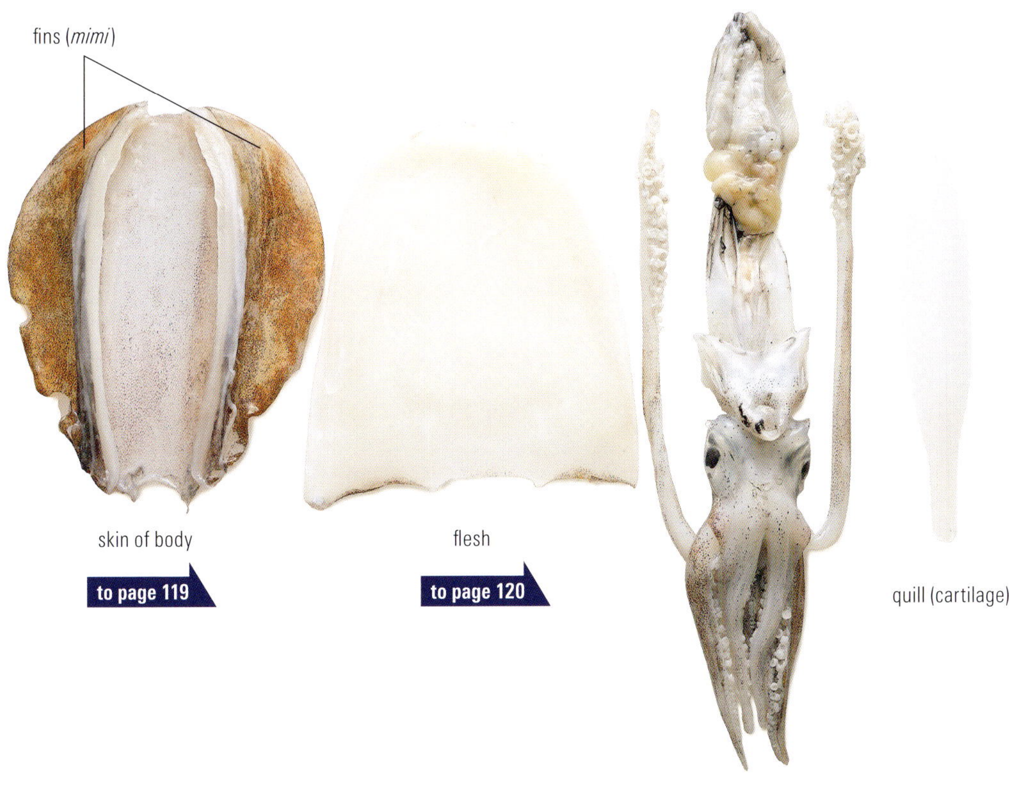

from previous page

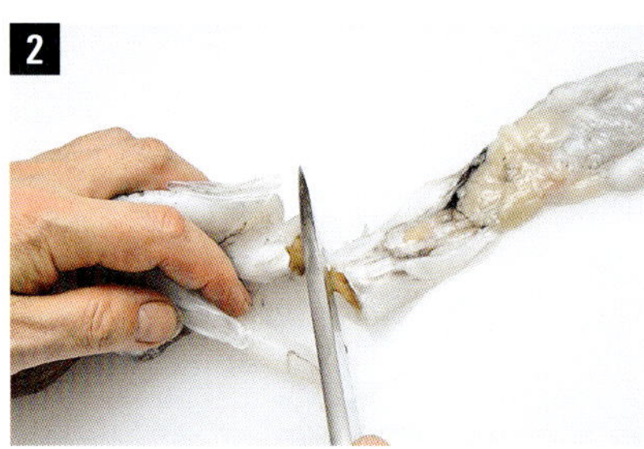

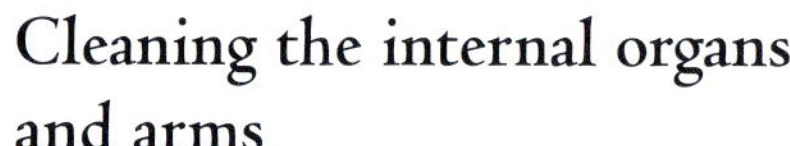

Cleaning the internal organs and arms

1 Place the internal organs away from you and arms toward you, as shown. Make slits along both sides of the liver (dotted line in photo).

2 Leaving the liver on the side with the arms, cut off the membrane-covered internal organs.

3 Holding the arms together with the left hand, pull them back from the cut made in step **2** to push out the eyes.

4 Cut the eyes off from the arms.

5 At the center of the arms is the hard, spherical beak; push the beak away from the arms with the tip of the knife.

6 Holding back the arms with the left hand, cut off the beak.

7 Steadying the arms with the left hand, pull out the two long tentacles and cut them off at the base.

8 Cut the arms off at their base, separating them from the head.

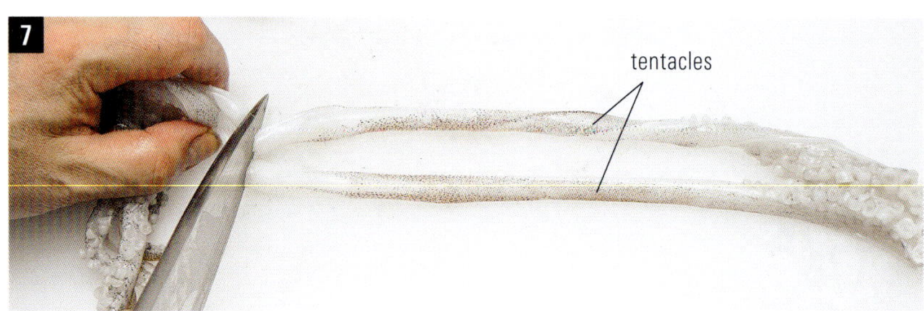

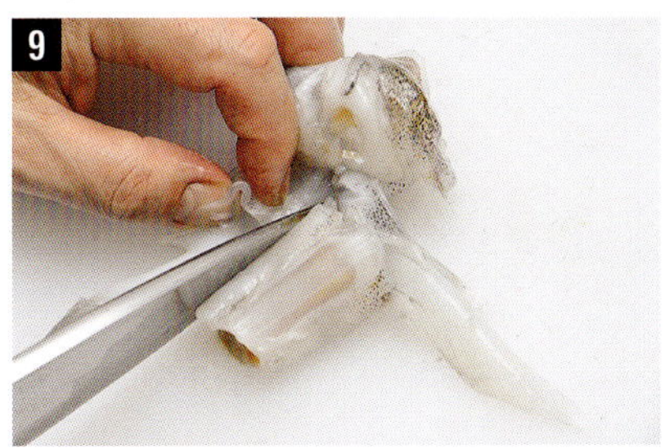

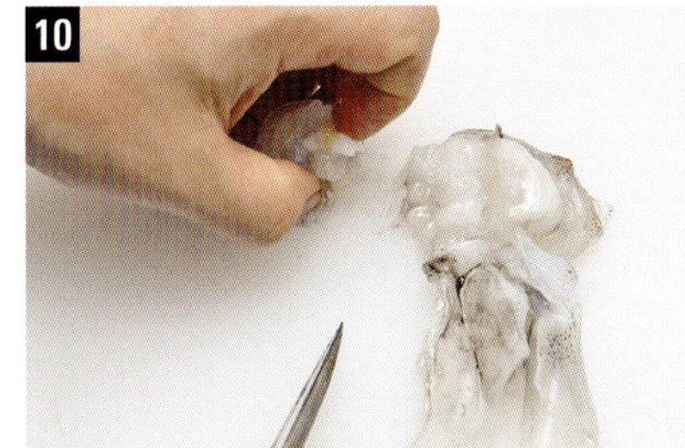

9 Cut the cartilage away from the liver and remove the liver with its membrane intact.

10 Cut off the tough cartilage at the base of the arms (head).

11 Cut off the tough cartilage on the side opposite that cut in step **10**.

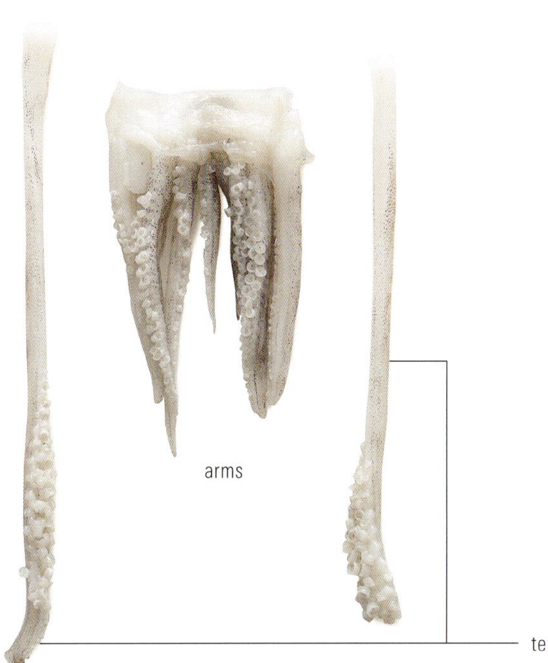

from page 117

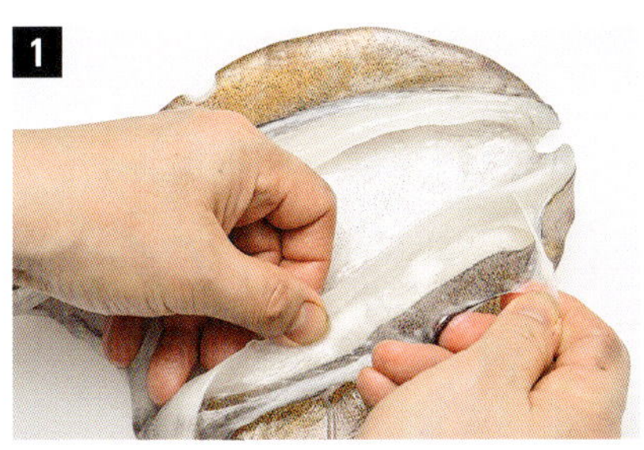

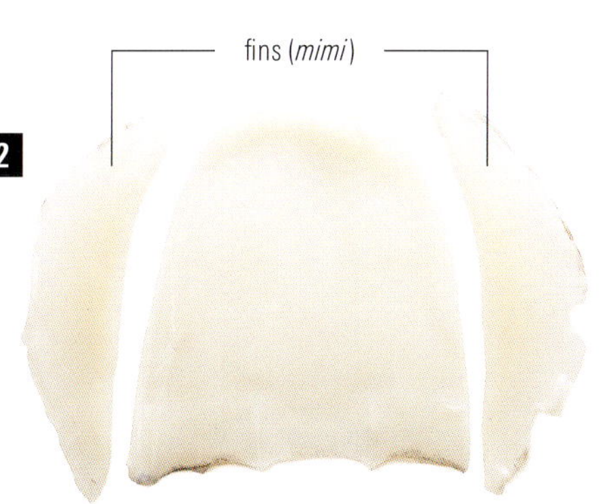

Cleaning the fins

1 To remove the skin from the fins on both sides. Insert fingers between the skin and fins. Holding the skin with the right hand, pull the fin up and away. Remove the skin on the opposite side in a like manner.

2 The fins with skin removed.

from page 117

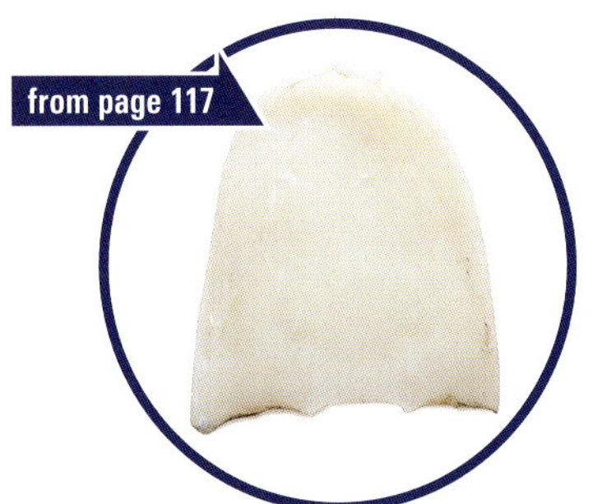

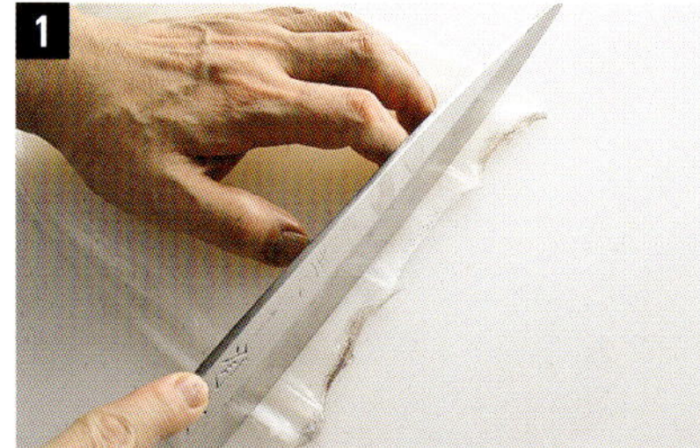

Removing membrane from the mantle flesh

1. Peel off the tough membrane remaining on the side of the body from which the skin was removed. Place the flesh with the inside (abdominal) surface up. Change to a *yanagiba* knife and place the blade about 1 cm (½ in.) from the head-end edge of the flesh (tough part) and make a shallow incision about 3-mm (⅛ in.) deep (not cutting through the membrane but only through the flesh).
2. Grasping the incision along the edge on one side, peel back the membrane from the flesh. Peel back the membrane on the edge of the other side.
3. Trim off the tough cartilage that remains at either side of the flesh, as shown.
4. Turn the flesh over with the tip of the body away from you. Grasp the membrane at the incision made in step 1 and lift it, peeling back toward the tip of the body.
5. When the squid is fresh, the membrane will be stretched tightly over the flesh; pull it toward you firmly.
6. Using the cutting board for leverage, pull back about 1.5 cm (½ in.) of membrane.

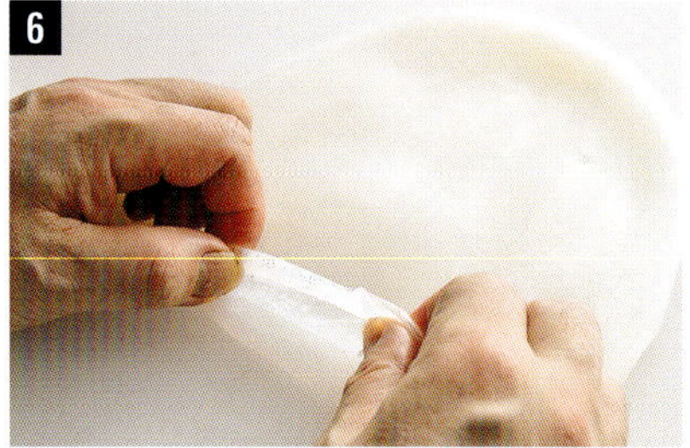

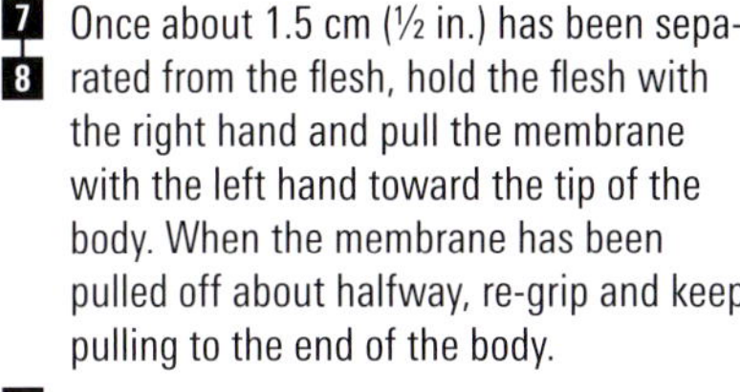

7–8 Once about 1.5 cm (½ in.) has been separated from the flesh, hold the flesh with the right hand and pull the membrane with the left hand toward the tip of the body. When the membrane has been pulled off about halfway, re-grip and keep pulling to the end of the body.

9 Since the membrane is tightly attached all the way to the end of the flesh, grip firmly and pull it off completely. If the membrane is slippery, wrap it in a cloth for better traction. To peel off the membrane on the inside of the flesh, make an incision as in step **1** and peel back the membrane toward the tip of the body. Remove any remaining fragments of membrane on both the inside and outside of the flesh.

flesh after removal of the membranes on the inside and outside surfaces

Cutting *saku* blocks for sashimi

1 Place the flesh from which the membranes have been removed with the outside surface up. Position the knife along its length with the blade tip on the tip of the body.

2 Draw the knife back to the head end, cutting off about one-third to one-quarter of the width (depending on the size of the body) from the right. Cut off a block of similar width from the opposite side.

Hegi-zukuri

This is a variation of *kanoko-zukuri* (see p. 112). Scoring the flesh along the length of the block on the outside and diagonally on the inside makes it easy to create rounded pieces for attractive serving and easy eating. This technique brings out the moistness and umami of bigfin reef squid.

1

2

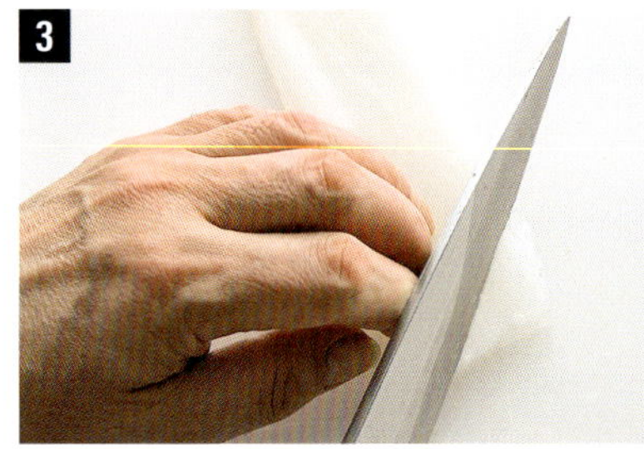

3

4

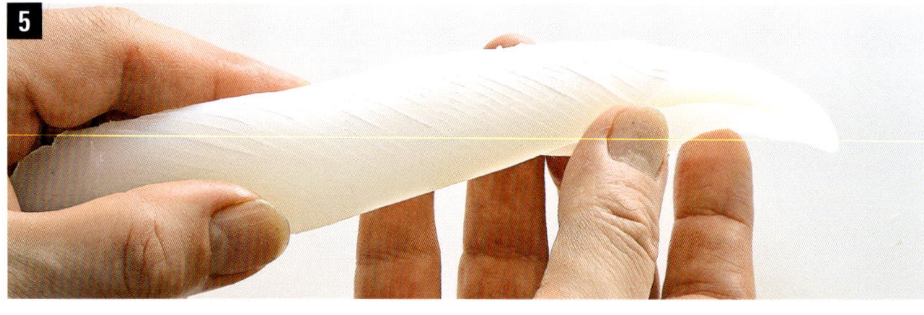

5

6

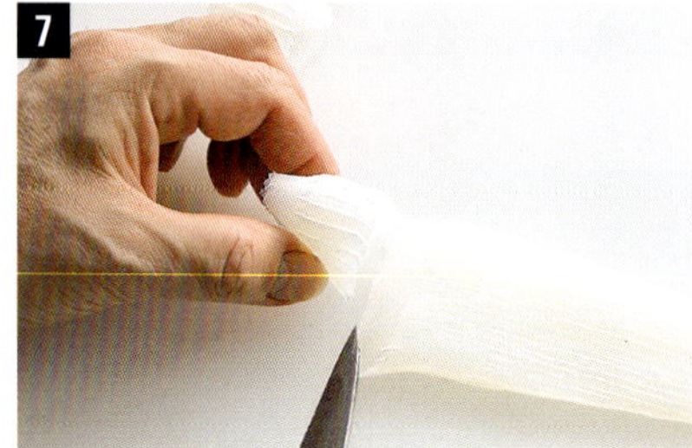

7

8

1 Place the block of squid with the tip at a slight angle to the right, with the outside surface up. Starting on the right edge, score the flesh lenghtwise from tip to base, with incisions about 2 or 3 mm (about ⅛ in.) apart.

2 The block after scoring vertically.

3–**4** Turn the flesh over and place with the tip at an angle to the left. Score the block diagonally with incisions about 2 or 3 mm (about ⅛ in.) apart from the base to the tip. Continue the incisions all the way to the edge of the tip.

5 The block showing the diagonal incisions made on the inside surface.

6 Turn the block over so that the outside surface is up, and place with the tip of the body to the right. Cut the block into 2- or 3-cm (about 1-in.) pieces, cutting into the incisions made in step **1** with the blade angled to the left.

7 With the vertical incisions (the outside) up, bend the pieces into a circle, as shown.

8 Completed sashimi pieces showing off the finely cut incisions.

Bigfin Reef Squid Scored Sashimi

cucumber-skin basket cut with bubble pattern

shiso flowerets

benitade

grated ginger

Kensaki-ika

SWORDTIP SQUID

Loligo edulis

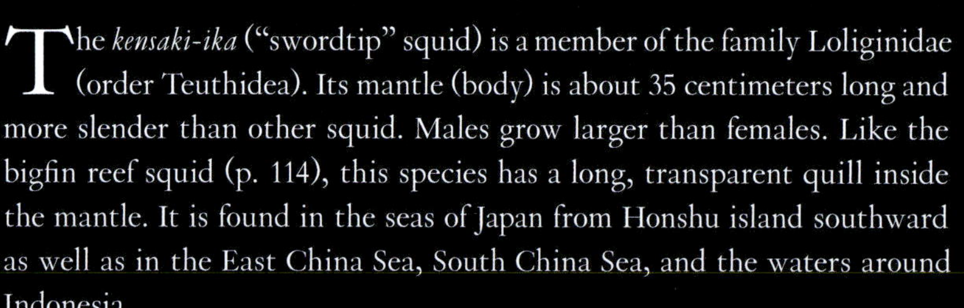

The *kensaki-ika* ("swordtip" squid) is a member of the family Loliginidae (order Teuthidea). Its mantle (body) is about 35 centimeters long and more slender than other squid. Males grow larger than females. Like the bigfin reef squid (p. 114), this species has a long, transparent quill inside the mantle. It is found in the seas of Japan from Honshu island southward as well as in the East China Sea, South China Sea, and the waters around Indonesia.

The squid has other names, such as *aka-ika* ("red squid") and *Goto-ika* (so named because the Goto Islands are a major fishing ground). The swordtip squid varies in form depending on where it is caught. It is almost transparent when very fresh, soon after catch, but grows brownish and then milky white as freshness wears off. For sashimi, choose those with reddish brown skin on the dorsal side and a high degree of transparency.

Swordtip squid generally tastes best in summer, with some variation by area where caught, and the flesh is thinner than that of golden cuttlefish, with a sticky texture and a rich sweetness. It is excellent as sashimi, and the flesh is soft even when grilled. It is also often served deep fried and in simmered dishes. Dried *kensaki-ika* is considered the best for highest-quality *surume* (dried squid).

CARVING SWORDTIP SQUID

Removing the quill, internal organs, and skin

1. Place with the dorsal side up, as shown. Steadying the body with the left hand, position the *deba* knife at the center of the tail tip. Make an incision down to the quill in the center of the skin in the direction of the tip.
2. Turn the knife over, insert the tip of the knife into the incision and cut the center incision all the way to the tip of the body.
3. Remove the transparent quill beneath the skin.
4. With the fingers of both hands, open the body to left and right and, running the fingers under the skin from the tip to the base of the body, detach the membrane covering the internal organs.
5. Holding down the body with the right hand, as shown, pull the internal organs, ink sac and all, out of the body with the left hand.

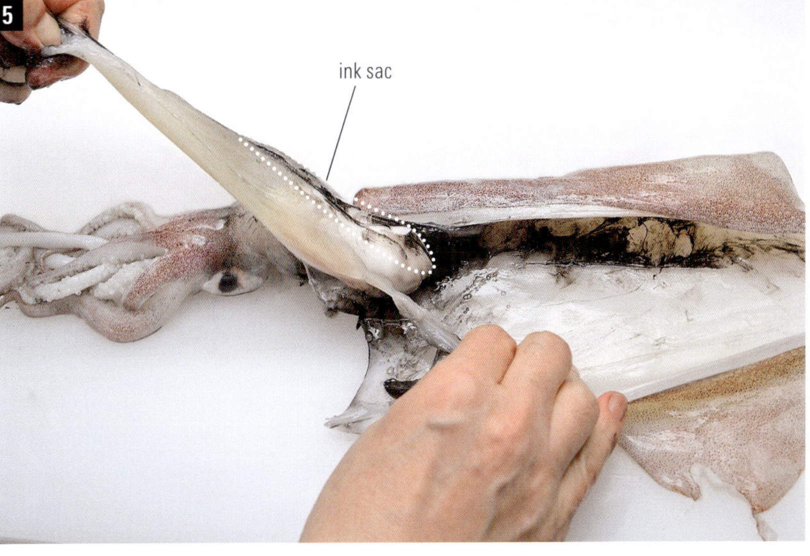

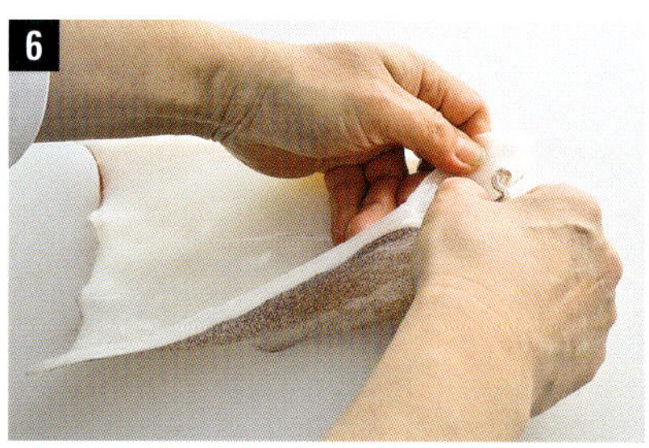

6. If ink spills out of the sac and colors the body, wash the inside of the body. Blot off excess moisture and place the squid with the inside up and skin down. Insert the thumbs between the skin and flesh and remove the skin and fins from the body.

7–8. Pinning down the skin with the right hand, pull the flesh with the left hand and remove it from the skin.

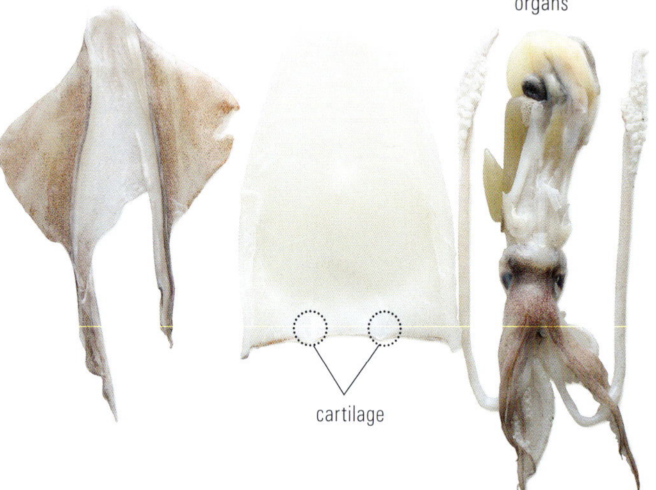

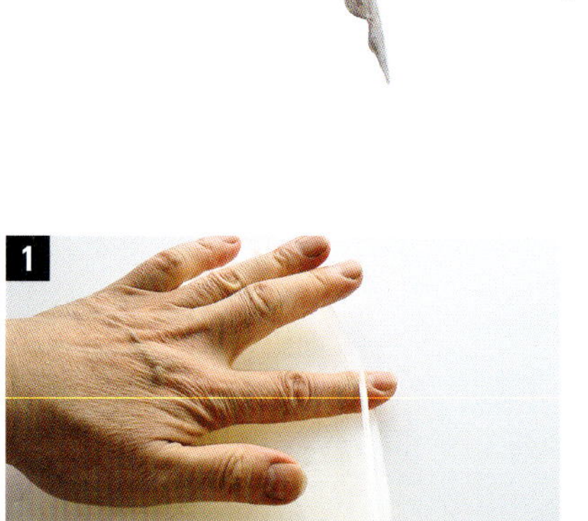

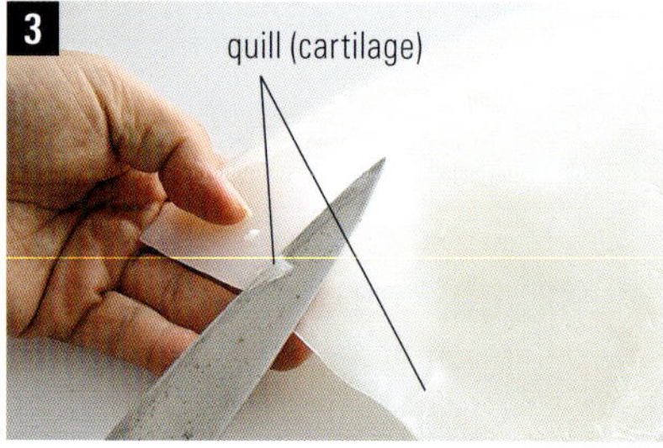

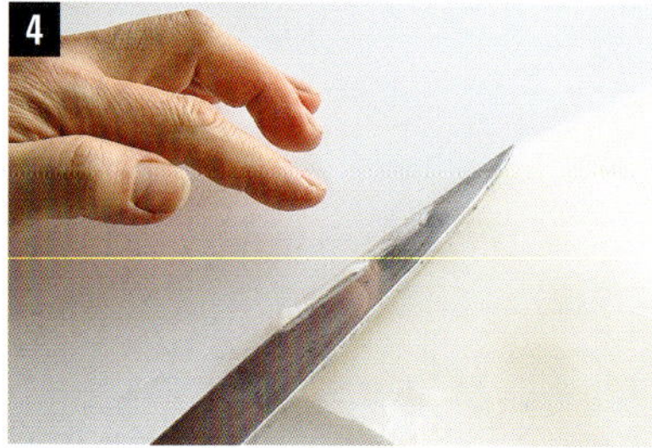

Removing the quill and membrane from the body

1. With the fingers pull off the membranes attached to the inside and outside of the body (they may also be removed by rubbing the surfaces with a cloth).
2. Cut away the tough part at the edge of the base of the body.
3. Slice off the two spots of cartilage beneath the membrane on the inside of the body near the head end.
4. Slice off any fragments of membrane attached to the lumpy parts on the inside surface.

Hoso-zukuri

This cutting procedure is well suited to fish that is slender in proportions, like halfbeak (*sayori*). The knife blade is vertical and the cuts are close together. If the flesh is very thick, it may be sliced into two or three layers before performing the *hoso-zukuri* (fine-cut) technique. Squid has a very springy texture, so scoring the flesh helps to soften it.

Thin-sliced Swordtip Squid Sashimi

cucumber curls
shiso floweret jelly
wasabi

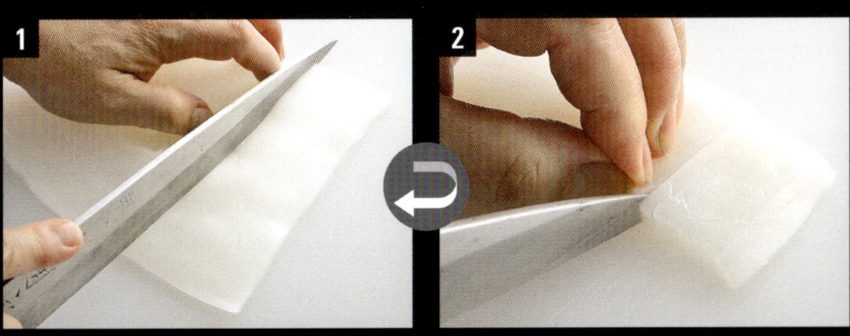

1. Place the *saku* block of squid with the dorsal side up and slanted to the right. From the left side make vertical incisions 2–3 mm (about ⅛ in.) apart.
2. Turn the block to the right and, while holding the block lightly with the left hand, score the flesh at 5-mm (¼-in.) intervals from the right-hand side. Inserting the blade with the tip entering at a high angle will prevent the flesh from sticking to the blade and make it easier to score the flesh evenly.

Zuwaigani

SNOW CRAB

Chionoecetes opilio

The snow crab (*zuwaigani*) is a member of the family Oregoniidae (order Decapoda). They have a rounded and somewhat rotund, "triangular" carapace. Generally, the carapace for males is around 15–18 centimeters wide and that for females is about half that size. While the crab is alive, the carapace is purplish brown with a tinge of grey, but when heated it turns pale red. Different names are used in Japanese for males and females, and their names also vary depending on where they are caught. Among many regional names are *matsuba-gani* ("pine-needle crab") and *Echizen-gani* ("Echizen province crab") for males and *koppe* (apron) and *kobako-gani* ("incense-case crab") for females.

Among more than 10 species of crab marketed in Japan, the snow crab has the highest quality meat and enjoys great popularity. It is one of the most delicious of winter seafoods, especially the leg meat of the male crab has a pleasant texture and a distinctive sweetness. The season from November to February, the cold-weather period following the fishing ban, snow crab is sold at high prices.

PREPARING LIVE SNOW CRAB (MALE)

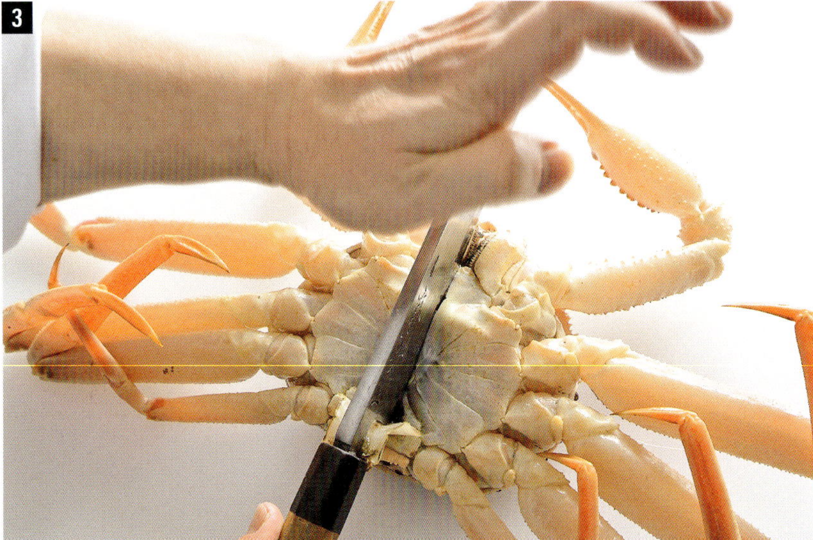

Removing the legs and the *kani miso* (crab butter)

1 Place the head away from you and the ventral side facing up.

2 Place the heel of the *deba* knife at the center top of the abdominal flap and sink it into the shell.

3 Peel back the abdominal flap, place the blade into the incision made in step **2**, and cut the bottom shell in half.

4–5 Bend the legs inward (this bending makes it easier to remove them). Holding the belly side of the body with the right hand, pull and remove the legs on the left side. Remove the legs on the right hand side in the same way.

6–7 Transfer the *miso* in the upper carapace to ice water and immediately rinse and drain (if left in the water, the *miso* will jell and be difficult to remove).

8 Wash the carapace carefully in ice water and blot dry. The *miso* may contain parasites, so it should not be eaten raw but be either grilled or steamed so that it is heated through.

9 Remove the gills (*era*; *gani*) from the left-side legs. Grasp them with a cloth and remove (in many cases parasites are lodged in the joints between the legs and body; sand may remain there as well). Likewise remove the gills from the legs on the right side.

10 To cut off the left-side legs, first place the mouth end away from you. Tip the blade of the knife about 45 degrees to the right and insert at the joint near the base of a leg. Cut off from the ventral side. Cut off all the legs in the same fashion.

11 To cut off the right-side legs, first place the body with the mouth end facing you. As in step **10**, cut off the legs from the ventral side.

12–**13** Place each leg that has been cut off with the base of the leg to the left. Cut off the tip of the leg at the joint, as shown (dotted line in step **12**)

9

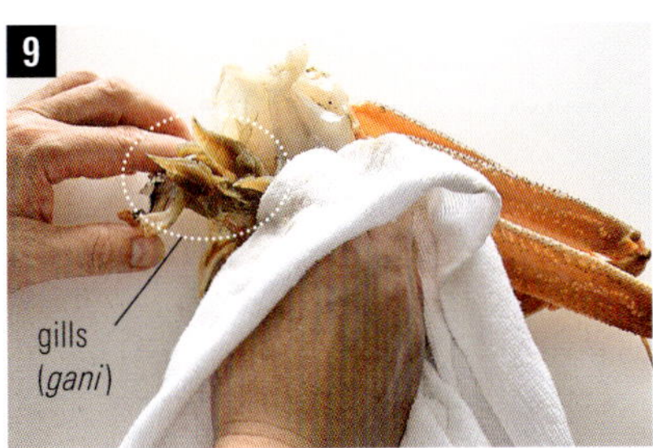

10

11

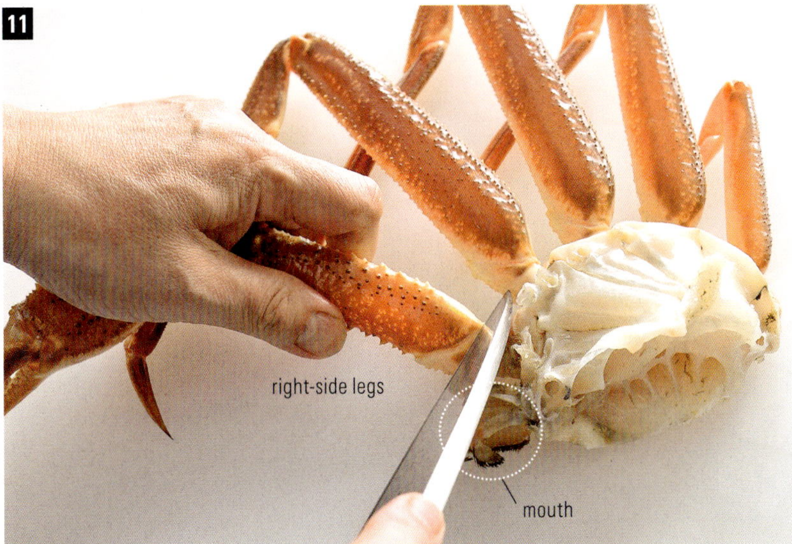

the left-side legs cut off from the body

12

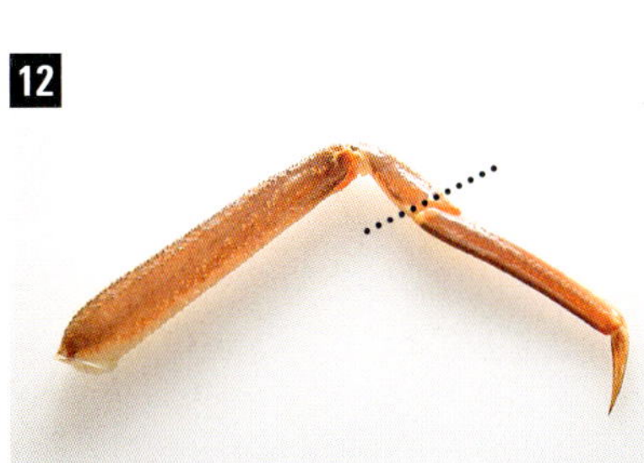

13

from previous page

Curing the leg meat in ice water

1. Bend the joint remaining at the end of the leg (as shown) and stand it on the cutting board (this makes it easier to cut). Insert the blade in the hard part of the surface of the joint.
2. Shave off the hard part of the joint.
3. Place the leg with the base to the right and the "back" of the leg facing up. With the blade facing right (*sakasabocho*), pry up on the horn-like projection and slice through the shell to the right.
4. Continue cutting the shell, in a shaving motion through the center of its hard section all the way to the base of the leg.
5. Cut the connection of the leg shell to the leg base and remove the shell.
6. With the left hand, hold the end shell at the joint (dotted circle), and with the right hand, twist the upper leg (leave the membrane attached to the leg shell, rather than the flesh, to make it easier for the meat to "blossom"; see below).
7. Hold the shell of the leg in the right hand and, with the left hand, pull the end shell outward, separating the flesh from the shell.
8. Place the leg flesh in a bowl of water with sake and ice for about 1 minute until the flesh billows out ("blossoms") as shown.
9. In a separate bowl, wash away the sake to tighten the flesh. Removed to a paper towel to absorb excess moisture.

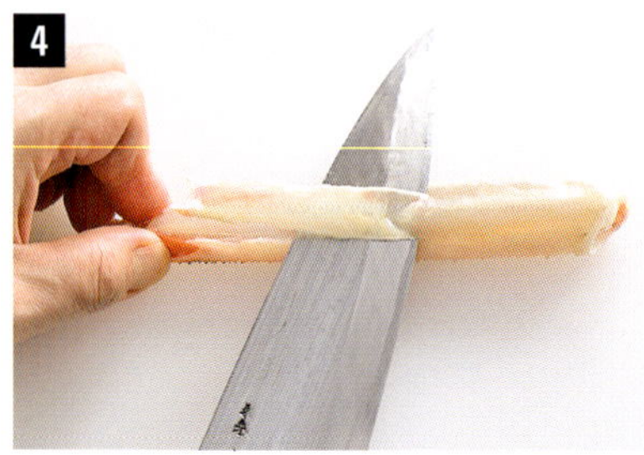

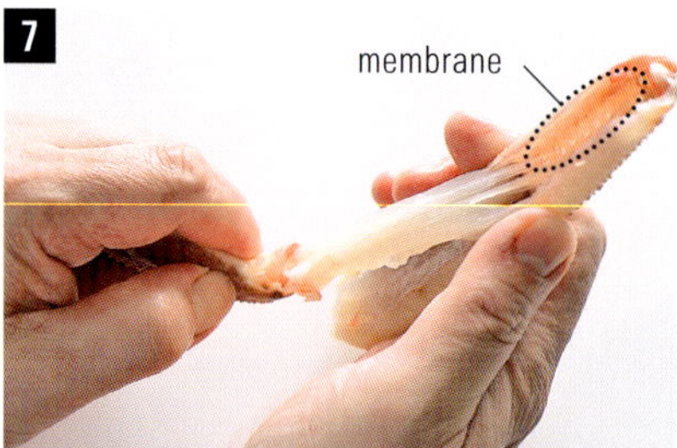

Snow Crab Sashimi in the Shell *Ikezuwaigani-zukuri*

The curing (tightening) of the crab meat in ice water brings out its sweet flavor. It may be served with a basic vinegar flavoring (*kagen-su*; p. 245), with *sudachi* citrus juice, or *warijoyu* (see p. 244) to taste.

Snow Crab Sashimi in the Shell

CARVING BOILED SNOW CRAB (MALE)

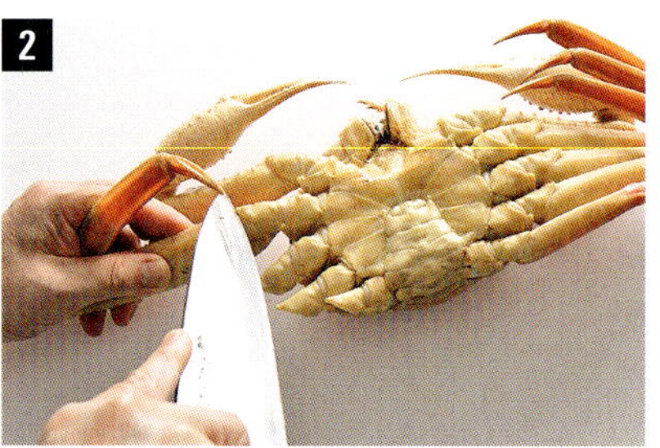

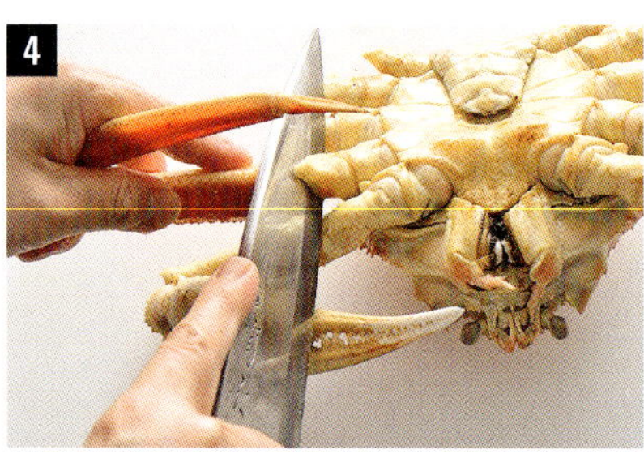

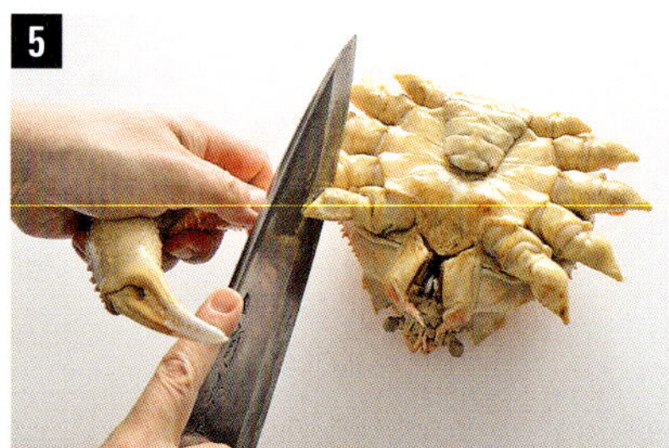

Removing the legs, the *kani miso*, and dividing the ventral flesh

1 Boil the crab in 195°F (90°C) water for about 25 minutes (if placed in boiling water, the crab may struggle, causing its legs to come off).

2–**3** Place the boiled crab ventral side up, head end away from you. Holding the claw with the left hand, turn the knife blade to the right (*sakasabocho*) and insert the knife into the joint closest to the body (adjust the angle of the knife to the contour of the joint for easy insertion). Cut the membrane between the joint and the leg and push the knife in further to the right to cut the leg from the joint. In the same way, cut off all the legs on the left side.

4–**5** Turn the body so that the head faces you. Cut off the legs on the opposite side in the same manner as in steps **2** and **3**, removing all the legs at the joint.

6 With the carapace facing down, grip the body with both hands, and, taking care not to allow the *miso* to spill, pull the abdominal part upward and remove from the carapace.

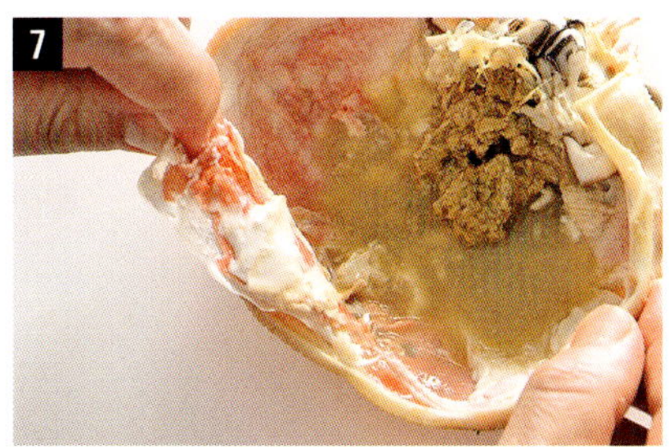

7 Pull off the membrane remaining in the carapace with the fingers.

8 With a cloth, grasp the gills (*gani*) and remove them.

9 Use the knife to remove the carapace membrane remaining on the abdominal part (from when the two were pulled apart).

10 11 Inserting the knife vertically to the side of the central part containing the *miso*, cut off the right third of the body. Cut off the left third of the body likewise.

12 The body, cut into three pieces.

13 Rotate the central part of the body (the part containing the *miso*) 90 degrees and cut it again into thirds, as shown.

14 Cut the two side parts of the body into thirds, as shown.

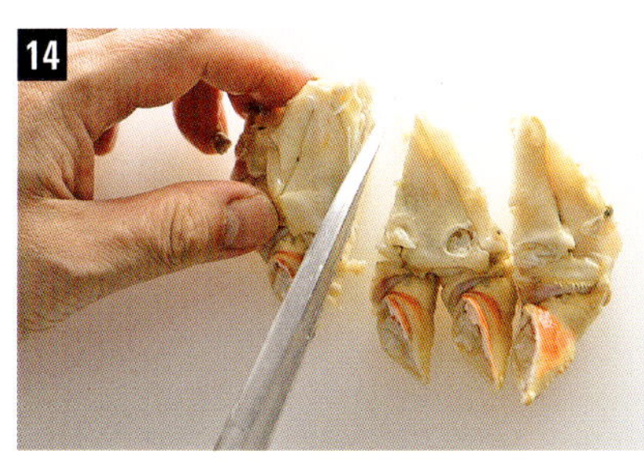

one side of the abdominal part cut into thirds

Removing the flesh from the claw-leg parts

1 Leg with claw (*tsume*).

2 Hold the tip of the claw with the left hand, lifting the end slightly. Place the heel of the blade at the joint closest to the claw (see the dotted line in **1**) and separate the claw from the leg.

3 Hold the leg cut from the claw with the left hand, standing it on the "knuckle," and cut the hard area (whitish part) of the joint from its upper edge.

4 Pushing down hard from above, shave off the hard part of the shell.

5 Stand up the leg part with the joint that had been attached to the claw up. Hold the joint part with the left hand and slice off the central part of the back of the shell.

6 The leg, with the back center part of the leg shell removed.

7–**8** In the same way as described in steps **3** and **4**, grip the claw with the tip up in the left hand, make an incision in the hard shell at the side (whitish part) and shave it off.

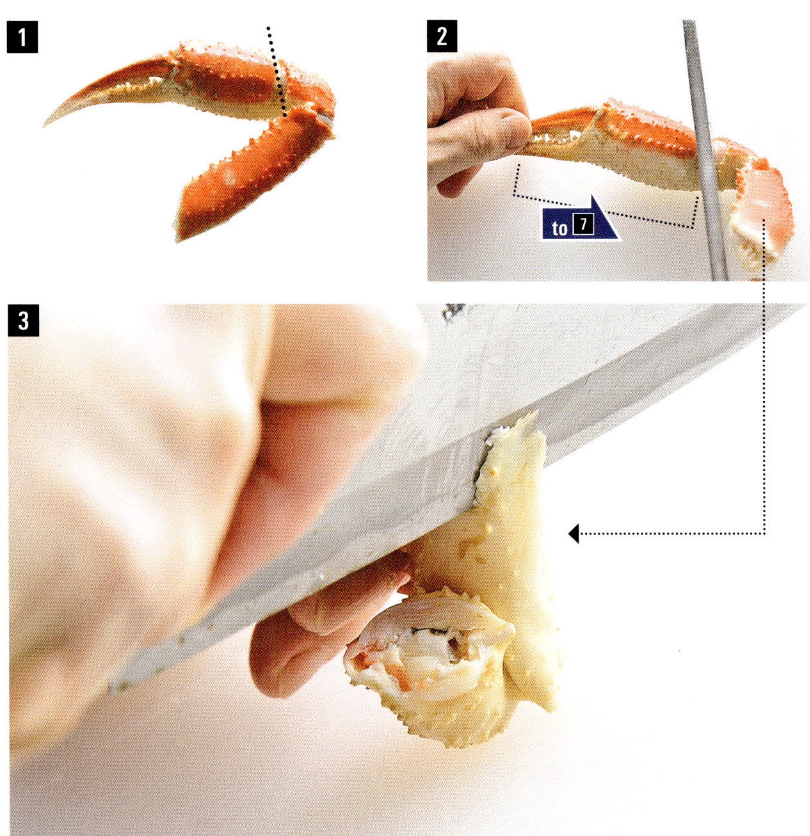

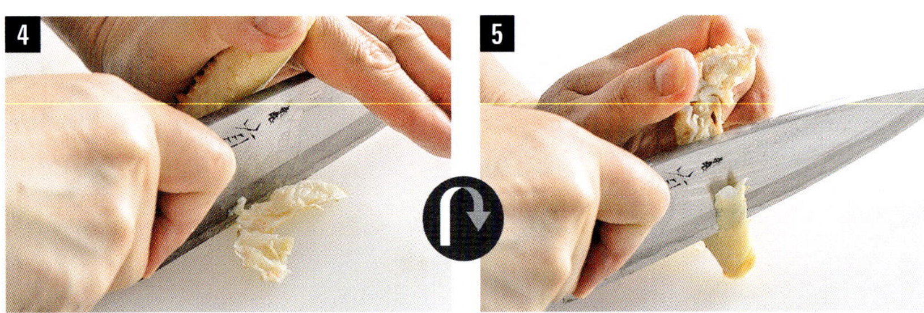

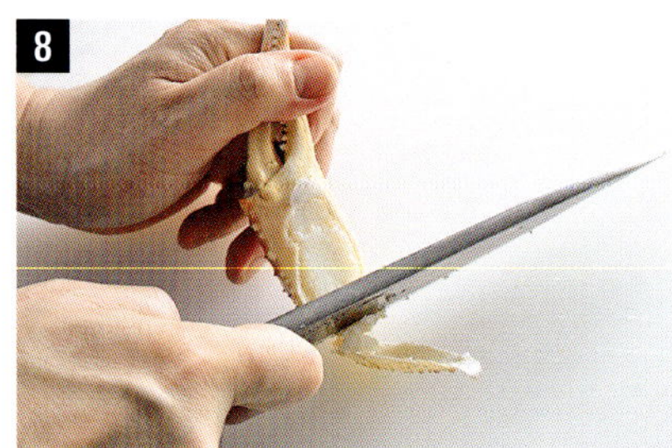

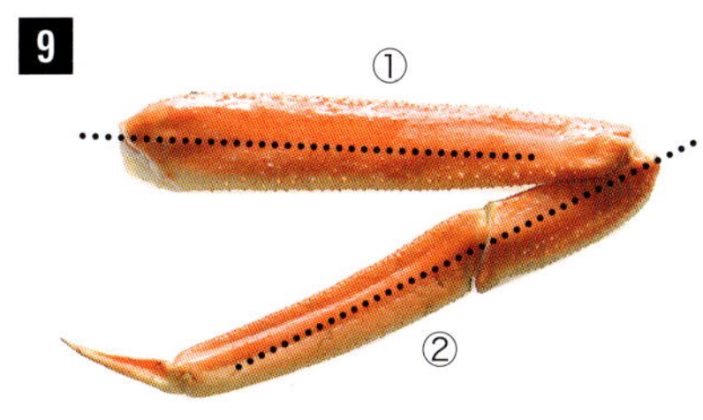

9 Open the shell of the legs without claws in the order ① and then ② (see numbered dotted lines in photo), cut on the back of the leg along the dotted line as shown in steps **10**–**13**.

10 Place the leg with the back side facing up and the base toward you. With the tip of the knife, cut down the center of the shell from the joint to the base.

11 When cut down about half way, stand the leg up and insert the knife; cut down and through the base of the leg.

12 Close the upper leg part near the base and hold together with the left hand; cut the lower part of the leg along the center of the back side of the shell all the way to the joint.

13 Using the knife blade, open the shell to form a "pine-needle" shape.

CARVING BOILED SNOW CRAB (FEMALE)

Removing the legs and mouth

1. Boil the crab in 195°F (90°C) water for about 25 minutes (boil immediately after capture because a stored crab may dehydrate and the flesh will become taut).
2. Insert the knife near each joint at the base of the legs. In order to make it easier to remove the flesh when crushing the shell with the pestle, cut at the wide part (near the joint) of the shell. Cut the legs off close to the joint on both sides of the body.
3. On both sides, cut the claws off at the joint, as shown.
4. With the carapace facing down, grip the body with both hands and, taking care not to allow the *miso* to spill out, pull the abdominal part upward and remove from the carapace.
5. Pull off the membrane remaining in the carapace with the fingers. With a spoon, remove the white froth (when the crab is boiled, water in the body turns to froth) clinging to the carapace.
6. Holding the carapace in the right hand, place the mouth side facing you and bend the mouth toward you to remove at the joint.
7. When removing the mouth, use chopsticks to move the ovaries to the carapace shell.
8. The carapace (left) and mouth (right). Remove any froth left in the carapace. Move parts of ovaries from the mouth part to the cleaned carapace.

1

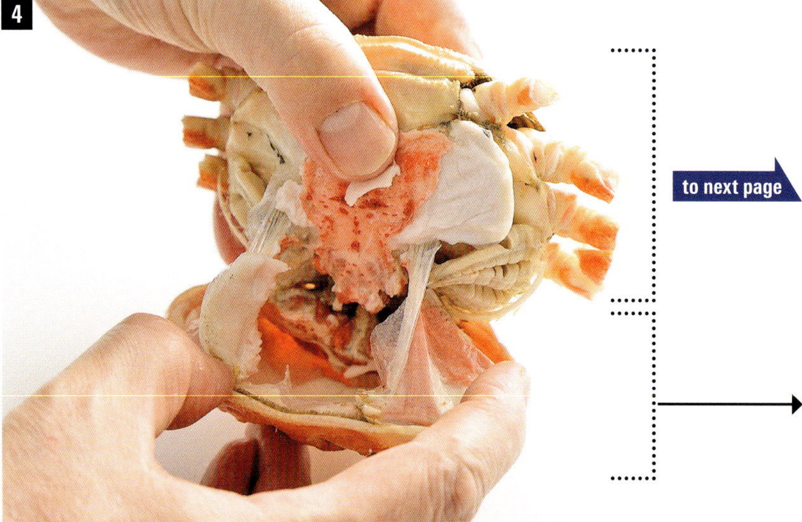

to next page

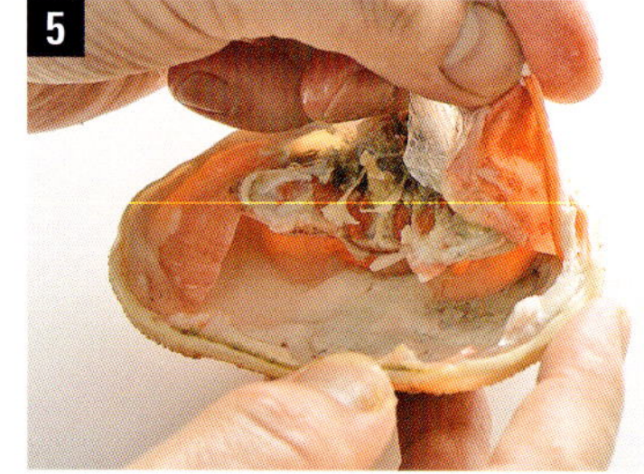

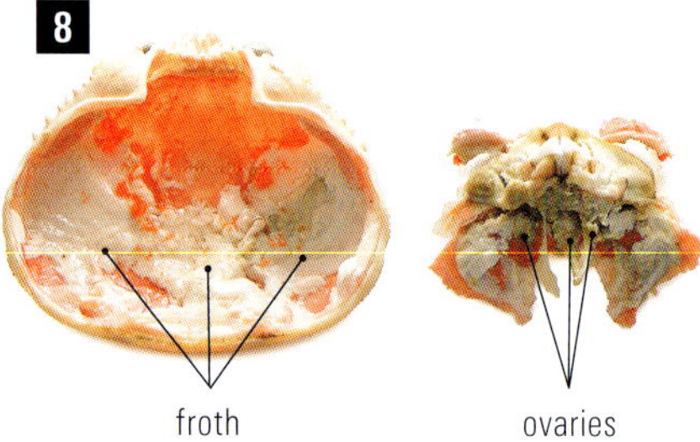

from previous page

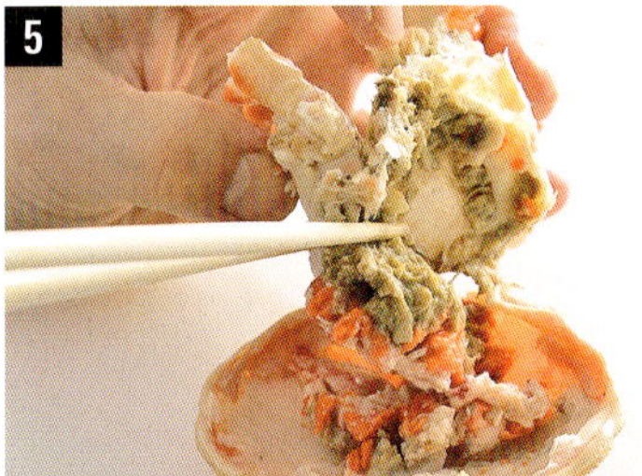

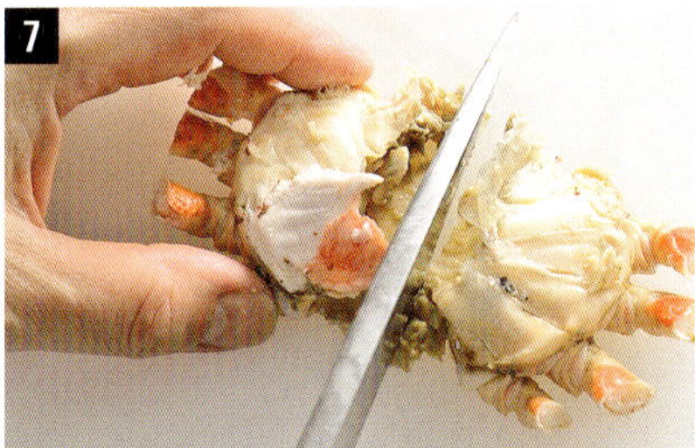

Separating and removing fertilized and unfertilized eggs

1. With the fingers pull off any remaining mouth parts adhering to the body.
2. Remove the fertilized eggs (*sotoko*).
3. The *sotoko* removed. The *sotoko* contains considerable bacteria, so it should be heated through before use.
4. Bend the abdominal part and remove the unfertilized eggs (*uchiko*). The white parts are froth produced in the boiling; remove with a spoon.
5. Scrape out the *uchiko* and *miso* remaining in the abdominal part and arrange in the carapace (step 8 on facing page).
6. The abdominal part with the *uchiko* removed and the carapace containing the *uchiko* ready for serving. The orange-colored *uchiko* eggs can be eaten just as they are.
7. Cut the abdominal part in half in the center.
8. With a spoon, remove the flesh in the openings of the leg shells.
9. Pressing with a wooden roller or pestle (*surikogi*), squeeze out the flesh in the belly part toward the legs, as shown.
10. With the wooden roller or pestle, squeeze the meat of the legs out of the shells.

Boiled Snow Crab in the Shell

Yudezuwaigani Sugata-zukuri

The male crab is much larger than the female and the meat more tasty. Boiling captures the umami of the meat. The carapace may have some black spots on it, and it is said the crab with more of these spots is the more delicious. Serve with *sudachi* and a basic vinegar flavoring (*kagen-su* see p. 245).

Boiled Snow Crab in the Carapace

Yudezuwaigani Koramori

The rich-tasting *uchiko* (unfertilized eggs) of the female snow crab is considered a special winter delicacy. The crab fishing ban is long, and the season is short, from late November to the end of year. *Tosa-zu* jelly brings out the sweetness of the crab meat.

Boiled Snow Crab in the Carapace

tosa-zu jelly (see below)

Boiled Snow Crab in the Shell

hanamaru kyuri
shoyu moromi
sudachi

Tosa-zu jelly

yields about 1.2 kg (2½ lbs.)

3⅓ cups *ichiban* dashi (p. 244)
Scant ½ cup rice vinegar
Scant ½ cup *usukuchi* shoyu
Scant ½ cup mirin
⅓ cup *sudachi* juice
65 g pearl agar

Place all ingredients except the juice in a pot and bring to a boil. When the pearl agar dissolves and froth forms, skim the froth and remove from heat. Cool in the refrigerator.

When liquid jells, press through a sieve (*uragoshi*) and mix in the *sudachi* juice.

Tako

COMMON OCTOPUS

Octopus vulgaris

All edible octopuses are members of the order Octopoda. In Japan alone there are several dozen species, but most sold on the market are *madako* (common octopus), *mizudako* (Pacific octopus), and *iidako* (*Octopus ocellatus*). When people say *tako*, it generally refers to *madako*, a member of the family Octopodidae. The common octopus measures about 60–70 centimeters from the tip of its mantle to the end of its arms, with the arms accounting for three-quarters of the length. It is found in tropical and temperate waters throughout the world, in Japan in temperate waters from the Tohoku region southward. Recognizable for its eight long arms with suckers, the octopus, like squid, belongs to the class Cephatopoda, and the head is located immediately above the "feet" (arms), at the base of which is the mouth. The brain and eyes are immediately above the mouth. What looks like a round head is the mantle, containing the internal organs and gills. Black ink and water are ejected through a funnel on the ventral side. The octopus is a camouflage artist, changing its color and skin pattern to blend in with its surroundings.

Sedentary octopus that inhabits the floor of rocky, coastal waters are in season in summer, while migratory octopus found further offshore are in season in winter. The summer octopus has soft flesh, and the winter octopus has firmer meat, rich in umami. The meat of *tako* has a pleasant texture, satisfying umami, and subtle sweetness. It is enjoyed raw or parboiled for sashimi and in vinegared, simmered, and other dishes.

CARVING OCTOPUS

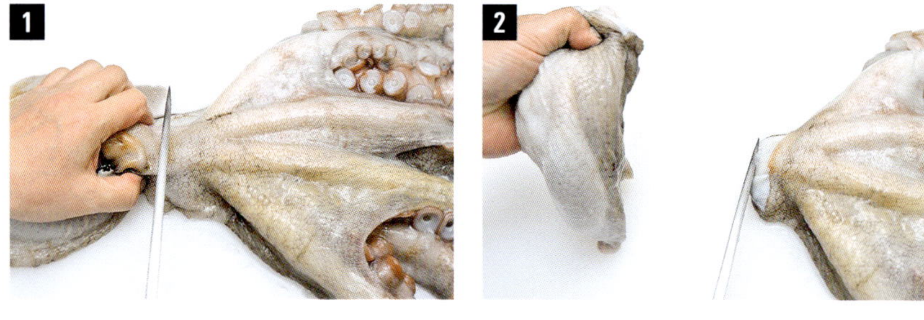

Removing the head and beak

1 Place with the body to the left, arms on the right. Position the *deba* knife at the base of the arms, as shown.

2 Cut apart the body and arms. (When used in cooking, the body is boiled after removing the internal organs.)

3 Lay out the arms with the suction cups facing up as shown. Position the knife just under the beak, located in the center.

4 Cut down through the flesh between the arms, cutting the arms partially apart.

5–**6** Insert the tip of the knife into the cut, pry out the beak, and cut it away from the body.

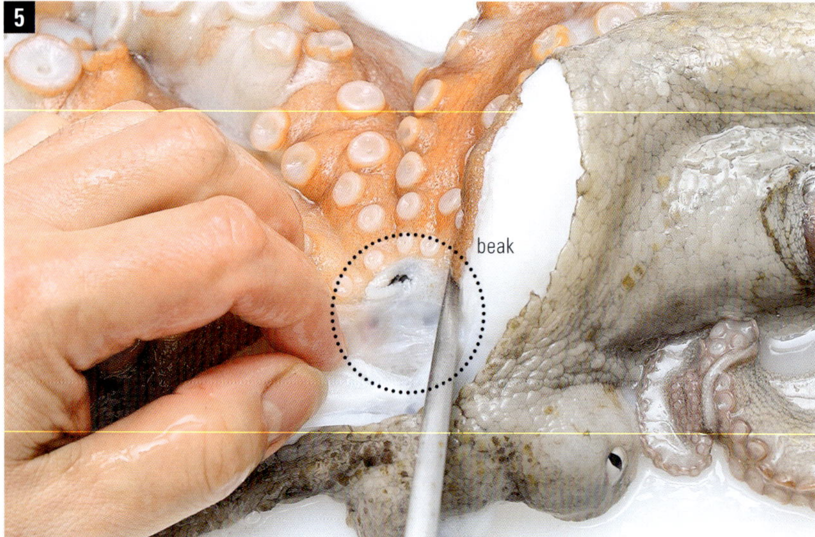

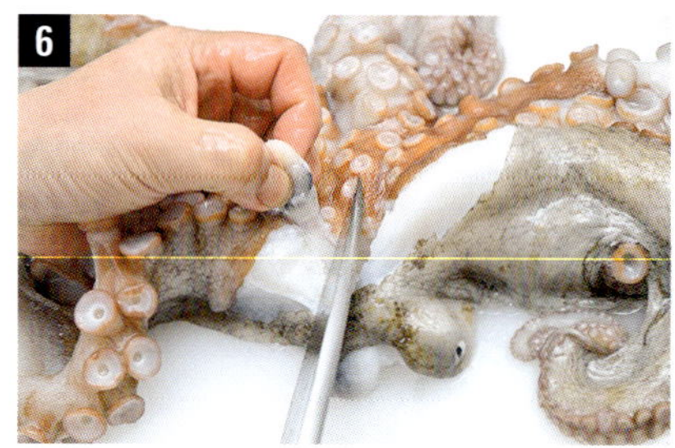

7–8 To remove the mucous from the front surface of the arms, sprinkle a generous amount of rice bran over the surface. (Unrefined salt may be used, but it tends to harden the flesh; rice bran is preferred.)

9 Secure the base of the arms with the left hand and spread the rice bran over the surface of the arms thoroughly.

10 Wash away the rice bran and mucous in running water.

11 Wash out the suction cups of any remaining sand or parasites, cleaning carefully.

12 Wipe away any remaining mucous, debris, and excess moisture with a towel.

13 Turn the arms over and clean in the same fashion.

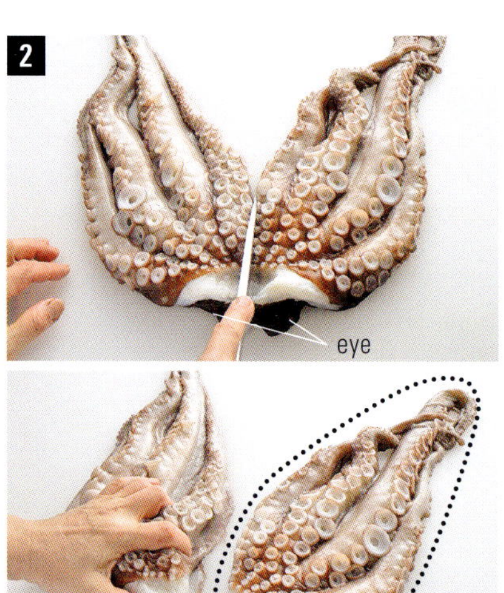

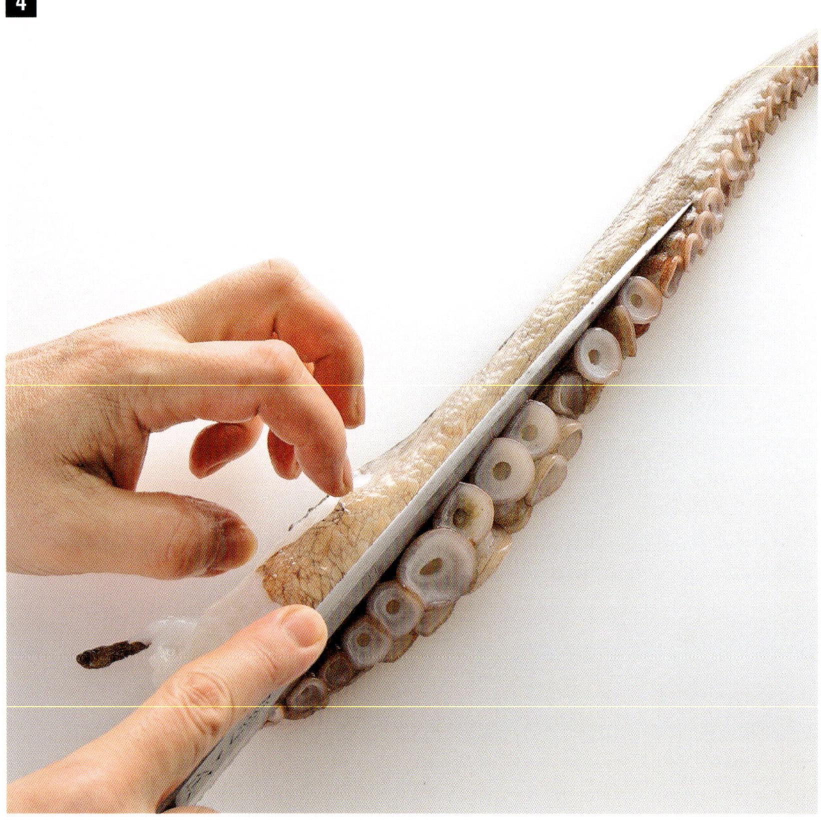

Preparing the arms

1. Place with the suction cups facing up and the base of the arms toward you.
2. Separate the legs with four on each side, as shown, and cut down the center between the eyes (one group for use as sashimi and the other for boiled octopus). Cut the eyes away from the arms.
3. Cut off each of the arms at the base.
4. Place each arm with the suction cups to the right and the base toward you. Change to the *yanagiba* knife and place along the edge of the suction cups.

for boiled octopus, see page 150

5

5 Cut in beneath the suction cups, peeling the skin and suction cups away from the flesh toward the tip of the arm.

6 By rolling the flesh away with the left hand, it will be easier to peel off the skin of an arm with the knife. Remove the skin to the tip of the arm.

7 Remove the skin from all but the narrowest tip of the arm as shown (the tip of the arm is not used).

8 Leaving only the thinnest tip of the arm, cut the skin off from the flesh. (When using the suction cups for a dish, they should be cooked in boiling water.)

Monsen-zukuri

This cutting method is named after its resemblance to a string of old-style Japanese coins, which had a hole in the middle and were grouped on a string. Octopus flesh is very spongy and firm, and this method of partial slicing of the flesh makes this distinctive texture enjoyably palatable.

1. Place one of the octopus arms from which the skin has been removed with the base to the right. Steady the flesh with the left hand and insert the knife straight about 2 mm (⅛ in.) from the edge. (Score the flesh but do not cut through.)
2. Make another partial slice about 2-mm (⅛ in.) wide in the same way,
3. After making four such partial slices, cut through on the fifth one.
4. When the octopus is very fresh, the pieces may jiggle but will quiet down in a little while.

Monsen-zukuri Octopus Sashimi

suction cups scalded in boiling water
umeboshi paste
kabocha curl
shiso floweret jelly
shiso leaves
wasabi

BOILED OCTOPUS

from page 146

Boiling the arms

1. Bring ample amount of water to boil in a large pot.
2. –3. Skewer the arms near the base of each set of four arms with a pair of metal skewers or chopsticks. Lower the arms, tips first, into the boiling water.
4. When the arms are submerged up to their base, remove the skewers/chopsticks so the whole set is beneath the surface.

1

2

3

4

5 Boil for about 2 minutes.

6 When done, skewer again near the base and lift out of the water.

7 Leave for about 5 minutes after removing, allowing lingering heat to pervade the flesh.

Cutting apart the arms

1. Place the set of four arms with the base toward you.
2. With the left hand, grasp three of the arms and cut off the fourth arm on the diagonal, as shown.
3. Place the arm removed with the base toward you and the suction cups to the left. Change to a *yanagiba* knife and insert the knife at the edge where the skin is thick, as shown.
4. Steadying the flesh with the left hand, cut the fold of skin away from the flesh in the direction of the tip of the arm.
5. Place the arm with the base end to the right. Cut off about one centimeter. (The flesh at the base of the arm is quite tough and is not used.)
6. From the edge, cut slices of about 5-mm (¼-in.) thickness.
7. Tenderize each slice by pounding it with the hilt of the knife three or four times.

the fold of skin removed

Vinegared Octopus

Takosu

Thinly sliced octopus doused in flavored vinegar sauce is a standard of summer cuisine. A dab of mellow *kimi-zu* sauce further enhances its enjoyment.

Vinegared Octopus

jabara-cut cucumber
vinegared *myoga* bud
shiso flowerets
kimi-zu (see p. 245)
tosa-zu (see p. 245)
ginger juice

Awabi

ABALONE

Haliotis

Awabi (abalone), in the family Haliotiae (order Vestigastropoda), is a common name for any of a group of medium-sized to large marine snails. They vary in form by species but all share an oval-shaped shell. The aperture of the shell is very wide, the surface is brown, and the iridescent inside surface may be used to make buttons and other accessories. The human use of abalone has a very long history as known from shells found in Jomon period (ca. 15,000–300 B.C.) archaeological sites. *Awabi* has long been closely tied to Japanese food culture. A well-known traditional shrine offering is a strip of dried and stretched abalone called *noshi-awabi*. The *noshi* festoon that is attached or printed on gifts given on auspicious occasions even today is patterned after the *noshi-awabi* offering.

Abalone live along the shallow, 20-meter-deep coastal waters around almost all of Japan. The main four species of *awabi* caught in Japan are: *madaka awabi* (giant abalone), *kuro awabi* (Japanese abalone), and *megai awabi* (Siebold's abalone), as well as *Ezo awabi* found off Hokkaido (formerly called Ezo). The *kuro* and *megai* abalone are the most commonly available on the market. All of these *awabi* species for the table have an oval shell about 15 centimeters (6 in.) along the long axis. Growth to that size takes about four or five years. The number of wild abalone on the market is decreasing, and farm-raised abalone are increasing in supply.

Wild abalone is in season from July to September, and the meat grows thicker prior to the spawning period in autumn. Considered a luxury ingredient, *awabi* is characteristically firm and chewy. It is served as sashimi, grilled, steamed in sake (*sakamushi*), and the like. The liver is prized; it is served with sashimi or used to make *kimojoyu*.

CARVING ABALONE

Removing from the shell

1. Remove dirt and slime from the flesh using a *tawashi* brush (or other short-bristled, firm brush) and wash in running water. Scrub it carefully until it is clean overall. (To enhance the crunchy texture of the flesh, scrub with salt; the flesh will tighten up.)
2. Holding the shell with the left hand, insert the tip of a wooden spatula between the flesh and the shell.
3. Push the spatula in as far as it will go; slide the spatula along the shell while prying the flesh upward to separate it from the shell.
4. When about halfway separated, grasp the flesh with the left hand and pull it off of the shell.
5. The abalone *kimo* (digestive cecum) is located under the curled edge of the shell. Taking care not to damage the liver, insert the thumb at the edge of the shell and separate the liver and attached membranes from the shell.
6. The flesh and the shell after removal.

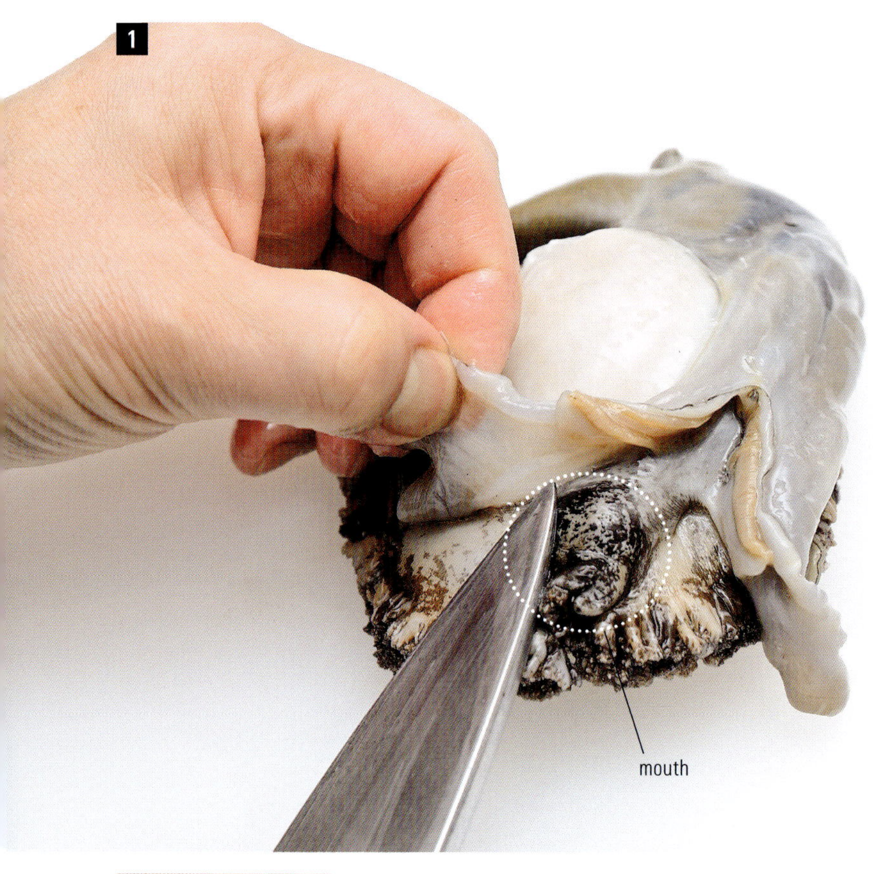

Removing the *kimo*

1. Use the *deba* knife. With the side of the body attached to the shell facing up, place the body with the mouth (see photo, right bottom) facing toward you. Pull up the membrane that is attached to the liver. Position the tip of the knife at the boundary between the membrane and the muscle (*kaibashira*).
2. Make an incision in the membrane and cut it away along the perimeter of the muscle.
3. Pulling the membrane back with the left hand, cut around the edge of the muscle with the tip of the knife.
4. After cutting the full circle, trim away the membrane completely from the muscle.
5. The organs detached from the body. The *kimo* should be scalded and then cooked before serving.

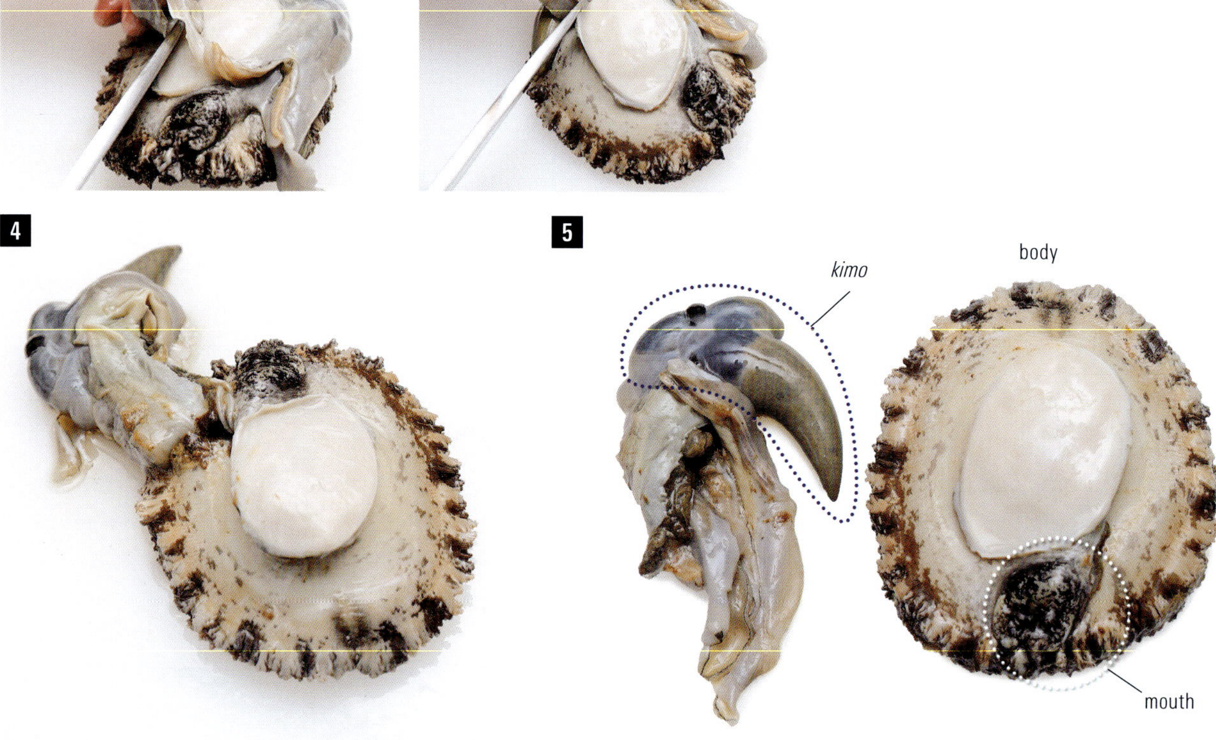

Removing the fringe and mouth

1. Place the body vertically, mouth end down. Insert the knife at the center (opposite the mouth) and cut the fringe (*engawa*) away from the flesh encircling the muscle (not cutting in as far as the muscle).
2. Rotating the body with the left hand, cut off the fringe, severing it at the lower end.
3. Turn the body around and cut off the fringe from the other side, severing it at the lower end.
4. With the mouth end up, cut in from both sides in a v-shape and remove the mouth from the body.
5. The fringe on both sides cut away from the body and the mouth detached. The *engawa* should be thoroughly cooked before using in food preparation.
6. The suction-cup side of the body is often stained from exposure to rocks. Clean carefully.

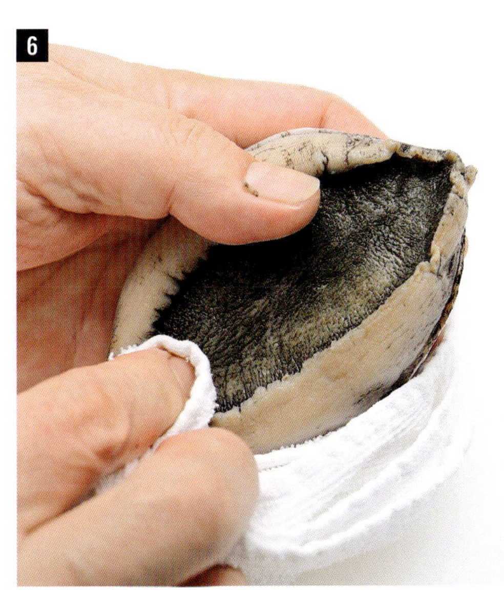

Abalone in the Shell

Awabi Sugatamori

The tough flesh of abalone, octopus, and the like is sliced using the "ripple" (*sazanami*) technique, tipping the blade up and down in a waving motion. The surface of the cut is thus somewhat uneven—like waves on a beach—making it easier to eat and to take up the dipping shoyu. The ripple-sliced flesh is served in the shell, evoking how the abalone looked in its original state, along with morsels of the *kimo* after scalding and cooking.

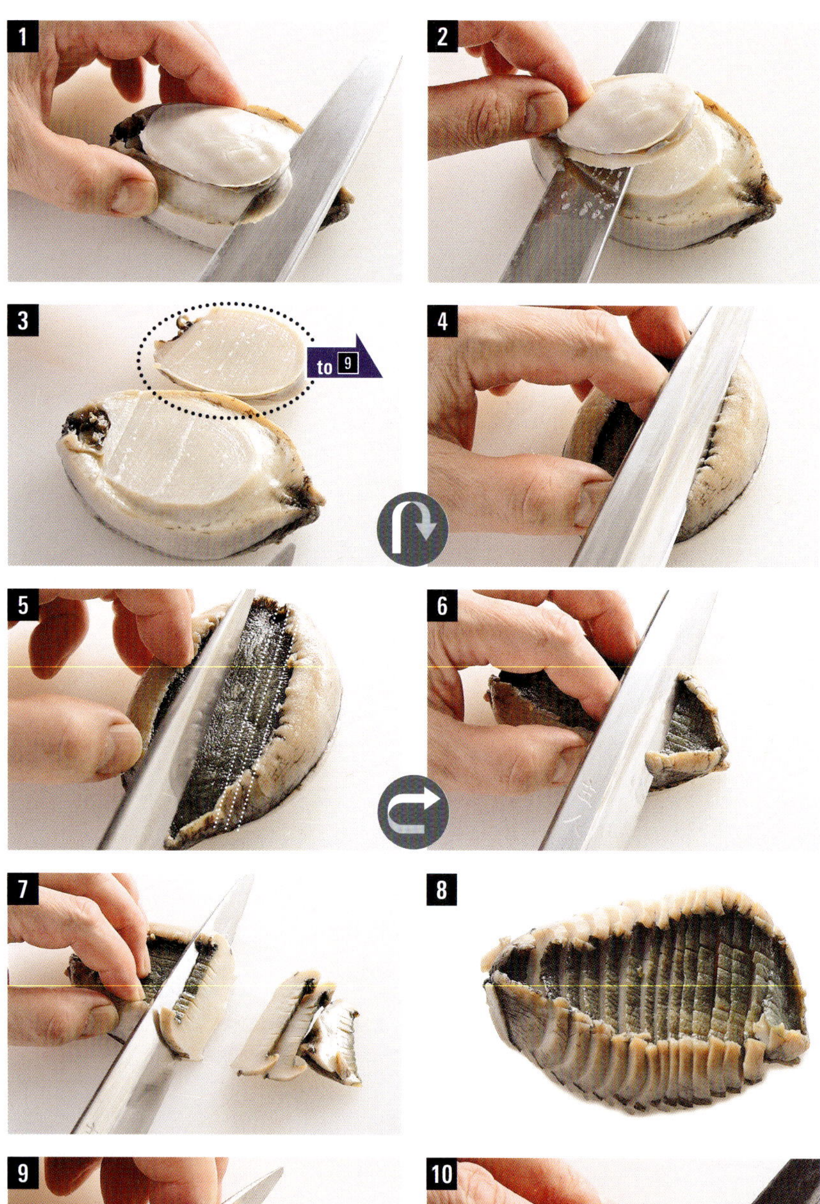

1. Place the prepared flesh with the muscle facing up. Steadying the body with the left hand, insert the *yanagiba* knife blade under the surface of the muscle.
2. Cut off the rounded part of the muscle, making the surface almost flat.
3. The surface with the rounded part of the muscle cut away.

4–5 The flesh is prepared with the *sazanami* technique. With the mouth end away from you, place the body lengthwise. Score the flesh at 2- to 3-mm (about ⅛-in.) intervals from the right side. Continue scoring at 2- to 3-mm intervals across to the left side.

6. Turn the body horizontally to the right. Slightly lifting the left side, insert the tip of the blade at a slight angle (as shown) and cut slices 2 to 3 mm thick.
7. Moving the blade up and down while slicing through, shave off each slice.
8. Reassemble the *sazanami*-cut slices and place them in the shell.
9. Prepare the muscle part of the flesh *sazanami*-style as well. Place the muscle with the previously rounded side up and score the flesh from the right side at 2- to 3-mm intervals. Score across the entire muscle.
10. Turn the muscle to the right and, steadying the end with the left hand, cut a 2- to-3-mm- thick slice with the knife at a diagonal (as shown). Similar to the technique shown in step 7, cut slices about 2 to 3 mm thick.
11. Slices of the muscle cut using the *sazanami* technique.

Abalone in the Shell

abalone *kimo* (scalded)
daikon *ken*
shiso leaves
wasabi

Hamaguri

HARD CLAM

Meretrix lusoria

Hamaguri, in the family Veneridae (order Veneroida), is a bivalve mollusc with a rounded-triangle-shaped shell around 8 centimeters long. The shell comes in various colors, and its exterior surface is flat and glossy, typically with elliptical brown bands. The interior surface is white and ceramic-like.

Found mainly along the coasts of Japan from the southern part of Hokkaido to Kyushu and part of the Korean peninsula, the *hamaguri* inhabits sandy mud bottoms of deep bays fed by freshwater sources. Ise Bay and the Ariake Sea were once famous for clams, but domestically harvested *hamaguri*—known in the fishmarkets as *ji-hama*—are now few in number and sold at high prices. Domestic *hamaguri* has a refined umami and the meat is soft, even if heated.

Like abalone, the *hamaguri* has been part of the traditional Japanese diet since olden times; its shells are found in archaeological sites going back to the Jomon period (ca 15,000–300 B.C.). Each pair of shells of this clam is unique, and shells cannot be matched from other pairs. Because of this, *hamaguri* have long been a symbol of good marriage. On Doll's Day, a clear soup made with *hamaguri* is part of traditional fare with the wish that the girls of a family will find good husbands. The soup is also served at wedding receptions and other auspicious occasions.

Hamaguri is considered tastiest in March and April, prior to the spawning period. Besides clear soup, it is grilled, steamed in sake (*sakamushi*), and included as an ingredient of dressed foods (*aemono*), among others.

CARVING CLAMS

Removing the meat

1. Place the shell with the umbo protuberance facing you and position the tip of the *deba* knife on the hinge ligament at the side.
2. Push down on the hinge ligament to remove it.
3. Insert a clam knife (*kaiwari*; see p. 18) at the spot where the hinge was removed.
4. Hold the clam vertically with hinge up. Cut through the muscles inside and move the knife downward to further open the shell.

Muscles attaching the clam to the shell are located at these four points.

5–6 Scrape the flesh away from the top shell into the lower shell. Pull the top shell back so that it comes off (set aside, since it will be used in serving).

7 Detach the flesh in the bottom shell as in steps 5 and 6.

8 The flesh, detached, arranged in the lower shell.

Grilled *Hamaguri* Clam

Yaki Hamaguri

The flesh, placed in the lower shell, is grilled for 1 or 2 minutes or until it swells up. If the clams are already very salty, the flavor may be adjusted by sprinkling the flesh with dashi. A favorite dish for winter and early spring.

Grilled *Hamaguri* Clam

hana yurine (lily bulb "flower" garnish)

Akagai

BROUGHTON'S RIBBED ARK

Scapharca broughtonii

Akagai ("red clam"; Broughton's ribbed ark) is a bivalve mollusc in the family Arcidae (order Arcoida). In Japan it is found on sandy mud bottoms of deep bays from Hokkaido to Kyushu. Its nearly lozenge-shaped shell grows to around 12 centimeters in length and is characterized by a bulging shape with a dorso-ventral measurement of as much as 9 centimeters. On the shell surface, covered with a dark brown hairy coat, are 40–42 radial ribs that flare out from the hinge. Like mammals, the clam has hemoglobin, so its blood is red, which makes the meat reddish, hence the clam's Japanese name. The shells have tiny teeth along the straight hinge line, and the shells fit together very tightly.

The taste of the clam declines during and around the May–October spawning season, and the meat grows thicker and tastier winter to spring. Featuring flesh of a bright red color with a slight astringent taste, *akagai* is served mainly as sashimi and in dressed foods (*aemono*). Boiled, the mantle (*himo*) around the main body is also considered a delicacy.

CARVING ARK SHELL

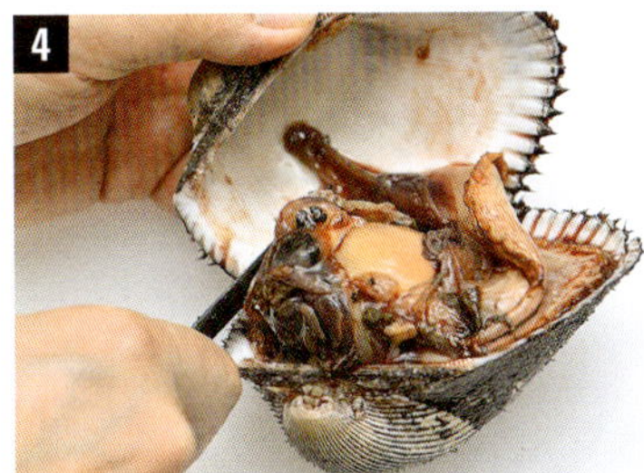

Removing the meat

1. Wash the shells well in water and place with the hinge to the right, gripping the shell with the left hand. Keeping the shell steady, position a clam knife (*kaiwari*) at the center of the hinge.
2. Push the knife into the crevice at the hinge and twist to leverage the shells apart.
3. Insert the knife into the shell, cut the muscle attachments to separate the body from the shells.
4. Scrape the body from the top shell into the lower shell.
5. Insert the knife into the shell and cut the muscle attachments and body from the lower shell in the same way as in step 3 and remove the *akagai* body. Wash off the blood in running water.

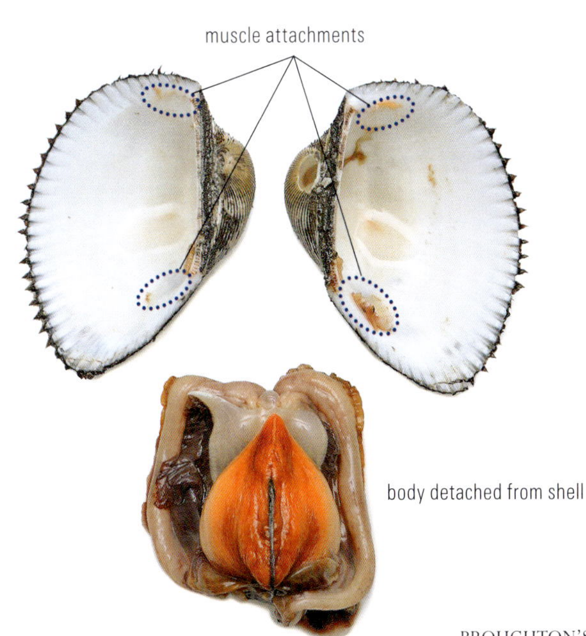

Preparing the mantle: Separate the mantle and body

1. Place the body with the thick part of the mantle (*himo*) to the right. Hold the body with the left hand (as shown) and position the *deba* knife where the body connects to the mantle.
2. –3. Cut in while lifting the body with the left hand, and detach the body from the mantle.
4. Place the mantle with the thick part away from you. With the tip of the blade, cut away the membranes attached to the mantle.
5. Turn the mantle over and cut away the membranes on the back.
6. Cut away the internal organs (dark parts) attached to the membrane.
7. Cut away the internal organs attached to the end of the muscle.

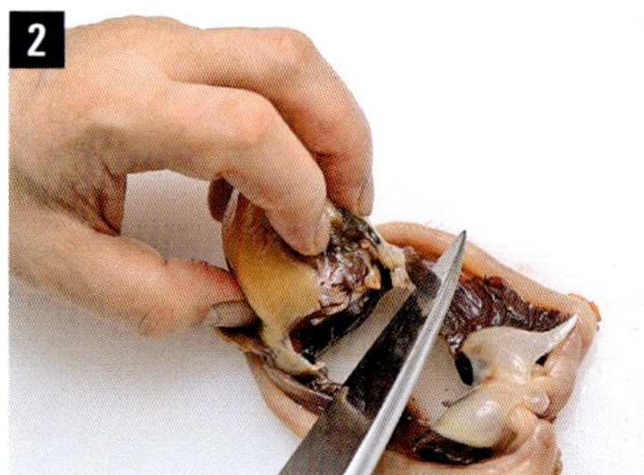

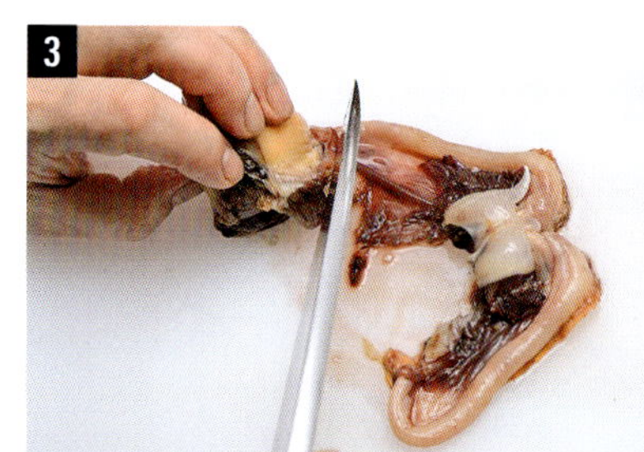

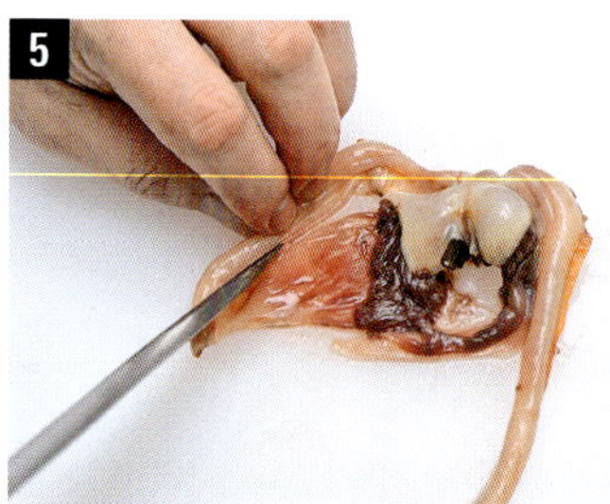

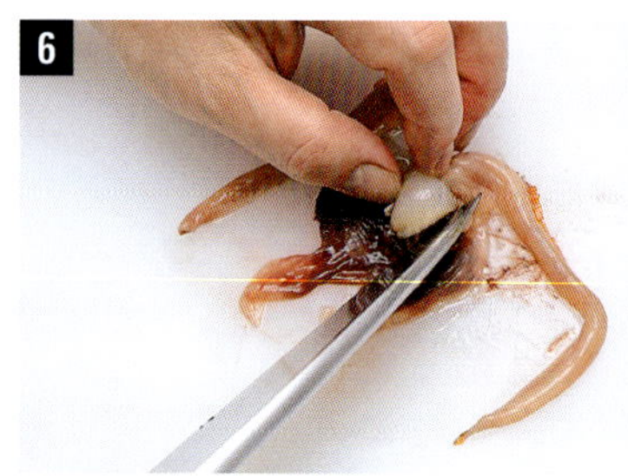

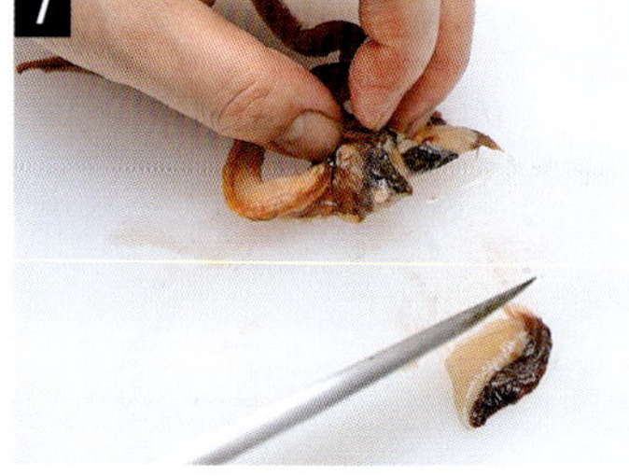

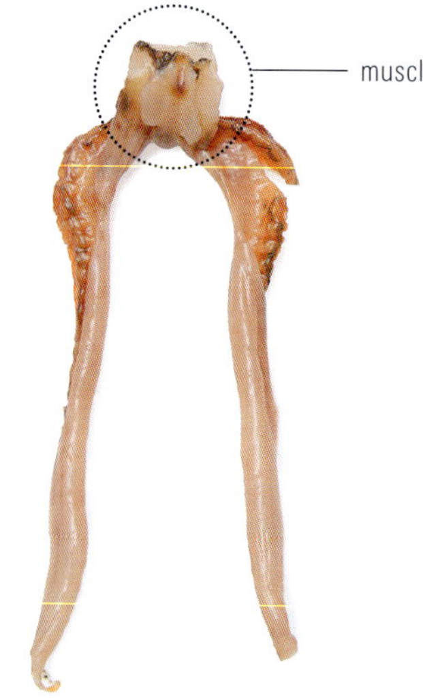

the prepared mantle (*himo*)

the body, separated from the mantle

Removing the internal organs from the body

1 Lay the body down with the internal organs facing you and position the knife at the center of the organs.

2 Open out the body to left and right without cutting it entirely in two.

3 The body opened butterfly style. The internal organs on either side are to be discarded.

4–**5** Position the knife at the base of the organs and cut the organs away from one side of the body in a scooping motion.

6 Cut the organs away from the other side. In certain seasons, the organs are edible but should be cooked.

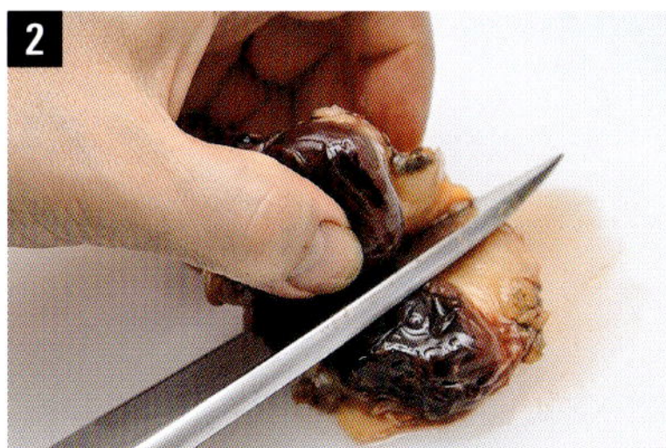

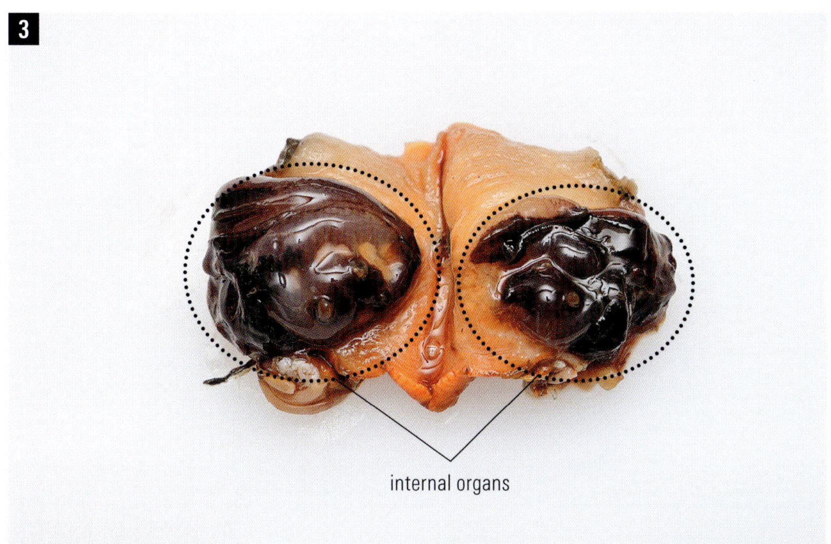

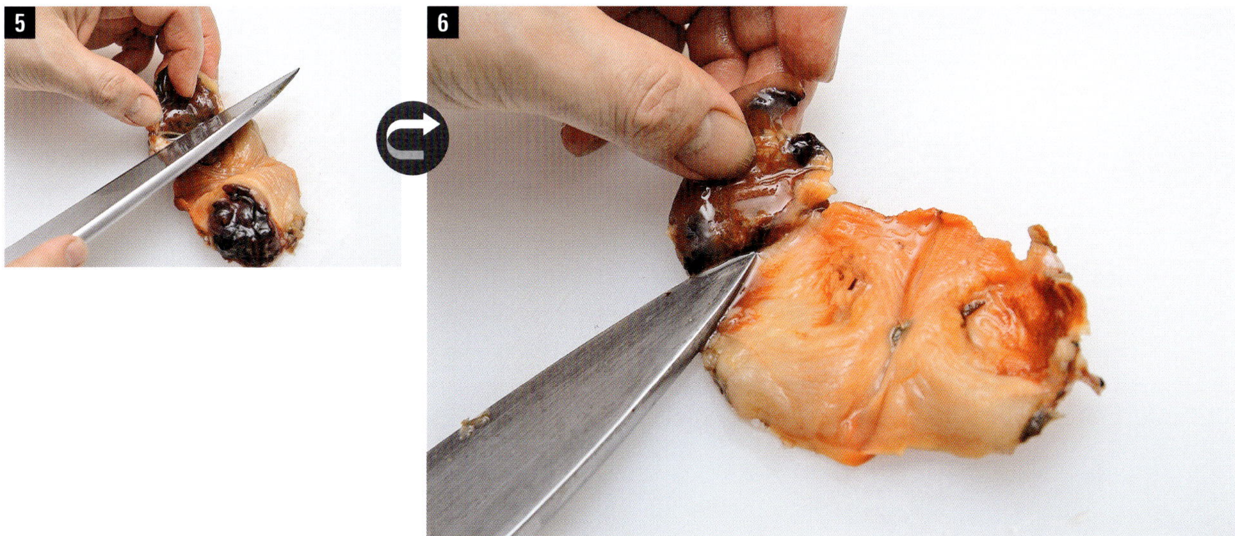

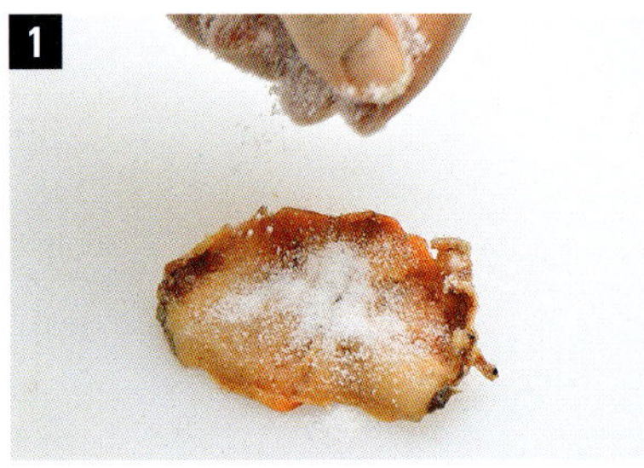

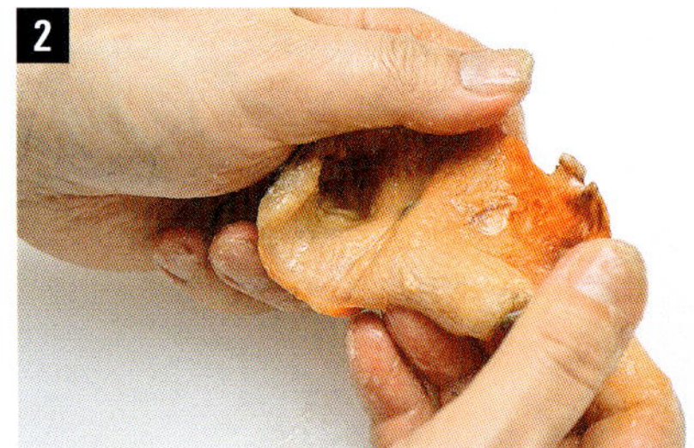

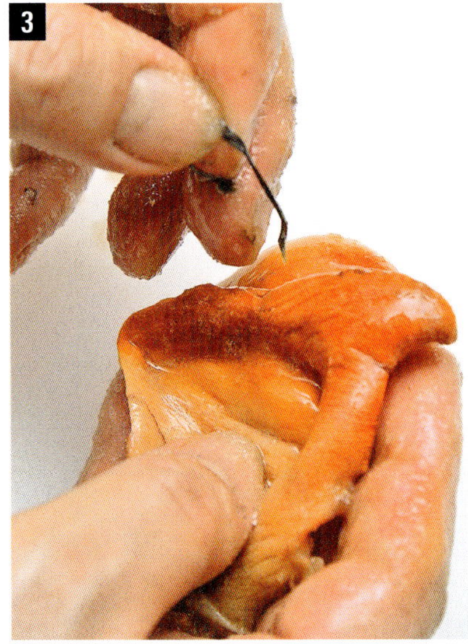

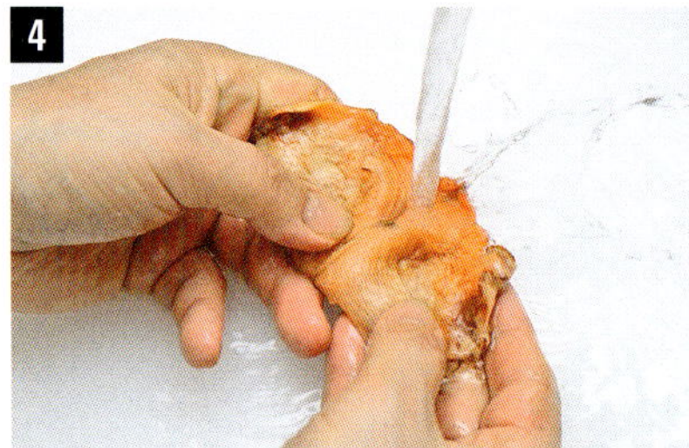

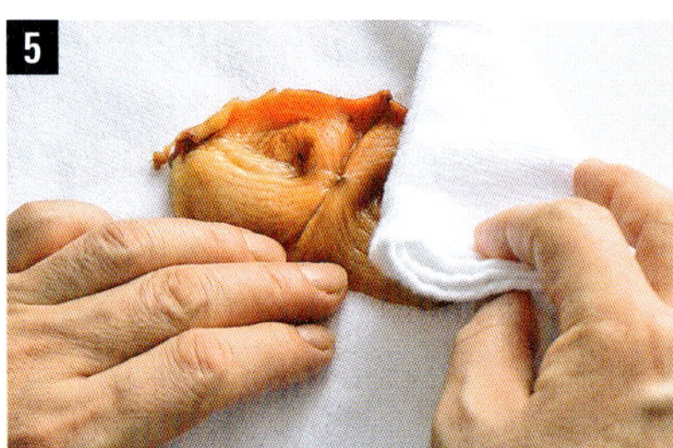

Remove the sliminess from the flesh and mantle

1. Sprinkle about a teaspoon and a half of salt over the flesh.
2. Work the salt in over the entire flesh to pervade the slime and debris.
3. Remove any seaweed or other debris adhering to the flesh.
4. Wash thoroughly in running water to remove salt along with the slime and debris.
5. Blot the flesh dry with a cloth.
6. Sprinkle the mantle with salt as in step 1.
7. Work the salt into the muscle and mantle to pervade the slime and debris.
8. Wash thoroughly in running water to remove salt along with the slime and debris.
9. Blot dry with a cloth.

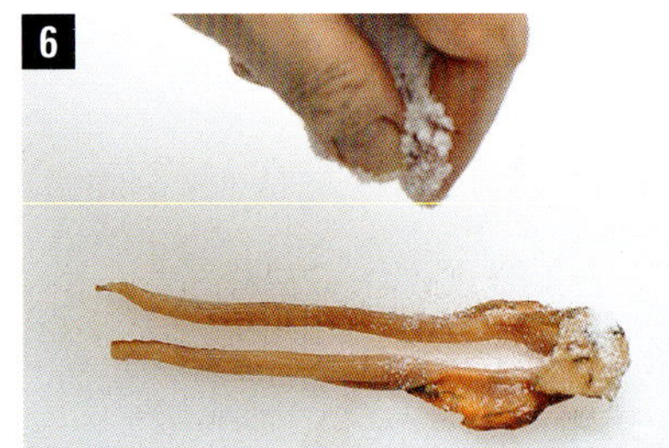

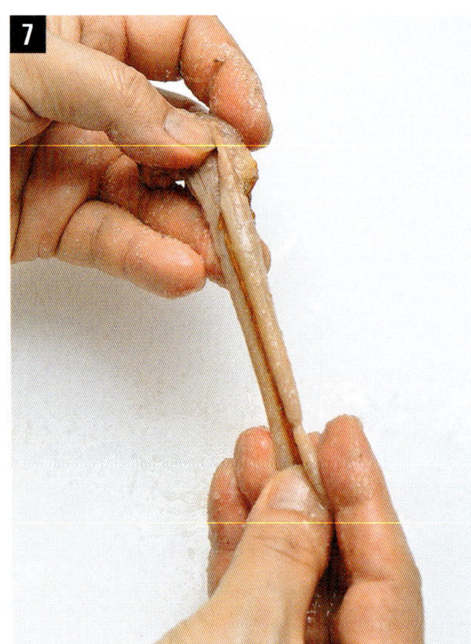

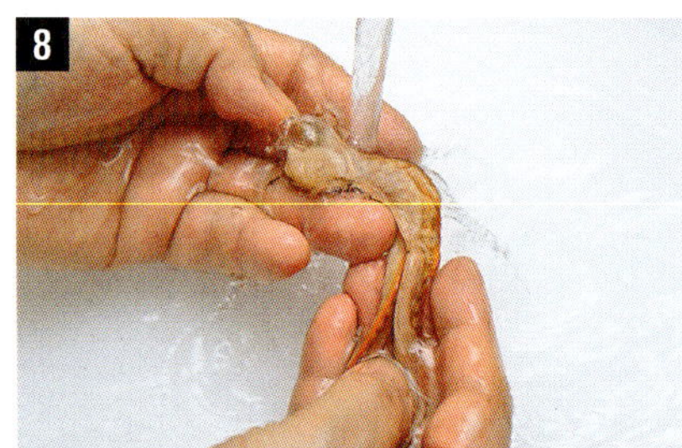

Prepare the flesh and mantle

1. Place the flesh with the side where the internal organs were attached facing down. Cut off any remnants (blackish parts) of the internal organs remaining around the edges.
2. Turn over and trim off any remnants of the internal organs on the "back."
3. Place the mantle part on the board with the muscle (*kaibashira*) end toward you. Cut in two through the center of the muscle.
4. Cut off the remnant of organs attached to the muscle.

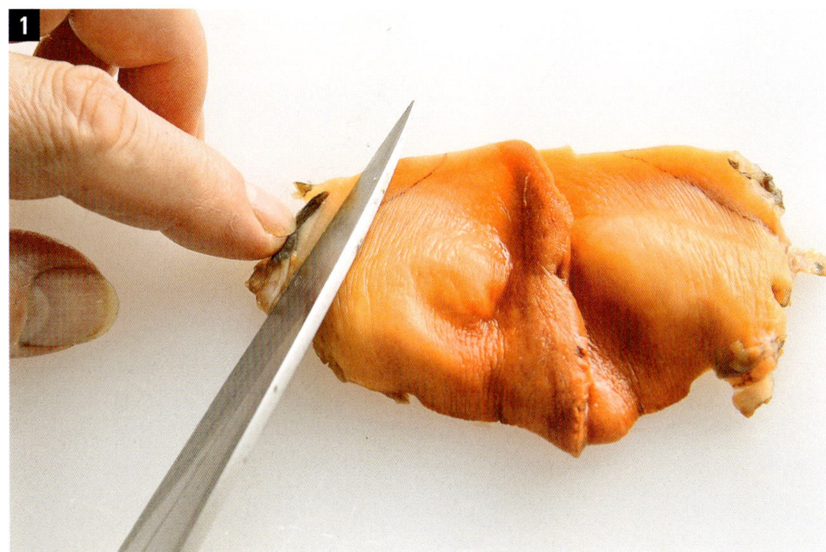

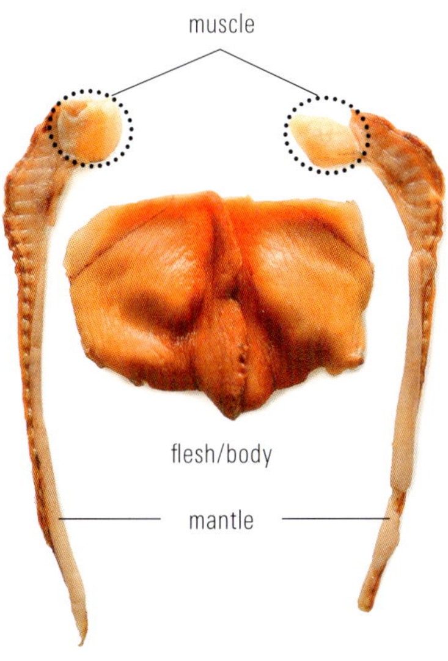

Kanoko-zukuri

After scoring the flesh of ark shell in the *kanoko* (fawn-spot) pattern and pounding the surface on a board, the meat tightens and the ridges bulge, an effect that is called *ichigo-zukuri* (strawberry cut) or *ichigo-akagai* (strawberry ark shell).

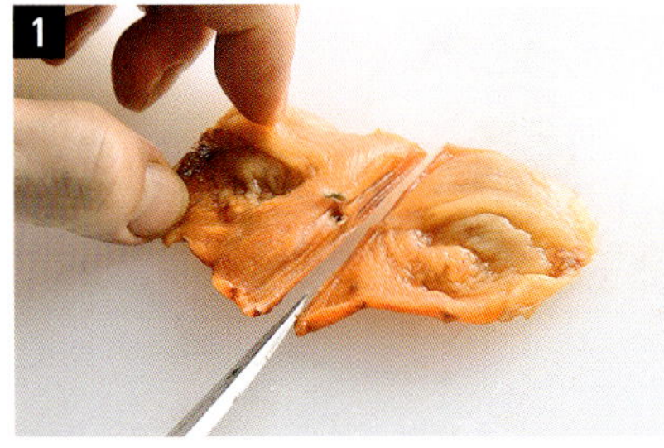

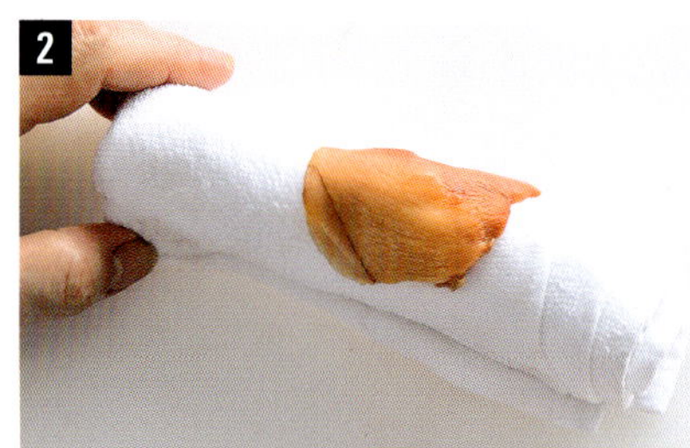

1. To cut the prepared body flesh in two, place with the inside (to which the internal organs were attached) up. With the knife tilted slightly to the right, cut in two through the center.
2. Roll up a damp towel (as shown) and place a half piece of flesh over the towel, with the outside up.
3. Score the flesh on the diagonal at 2- to 3-mm (about ⅛-in.) intervals, leaving about 5 mm (¼ in.) on either side.
4. Score the flesh on the opposite diagonal, likewise at 2-to 3-mm intervals (also leaving about 5 mm on either side).
5. The ark shell meat scored in the *kanoko* (fawn-spot) pattern. Placing over a rolled towel makes it easier to score the flesh.
6. With the scored side up, throw the flesh hard against the cutting board (once only).

Serve after the meat tightens, causing the "spots" to bulge.

Kiku-zukuri

The *kiku-zukuri* (chrysanthemum-cut) technique consists of straight-line scoring of the flesh. Placing two rounded pieces of flesh together makes an arrangement that looks like a just-opening chrysanthemum flower.

1 Place the remaining piece of the flesh with the inside (the side to which the internal organs were attached) down over a rolled-up towel. Score the flesh on the diagonal at 2- to 3-mm (about ⅛-in.) intervals (leaving about 5-mm or ¼ in. unscored on either side).

With the scored side facing up, throw the flesh hard against the cutting board (once only), a process that makes the flesh rounded in shape. Arrange on a plate in a curved shape.

Karakusa-zukuri

The *karakusa-zukuri* (arabesque-cut) technique is used for seafood sashimi with a springy texture. Fine incisions are made but without cutting all the way through.

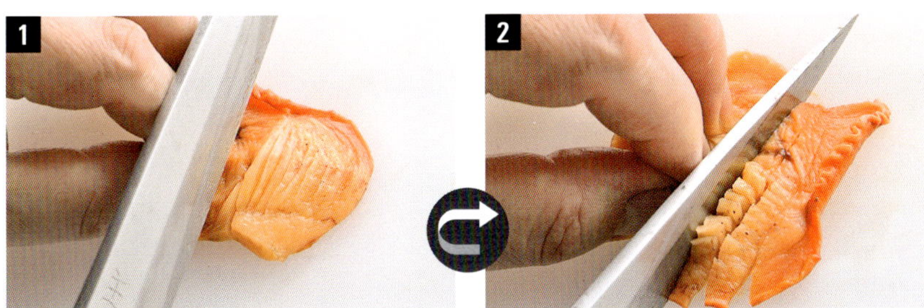

1 Place the halved piece of flesh with the inside (the side to which the internal organs were attached) facing up. Score the flesh from the right side at 2- to 3-mm intervals.

2 Turn the piece 90 degrees and score at 2- to 3-mm intervals from the right side, leaving 1 cm (½ in.) at the top uncut.

3 Cut into 1.5-cm (½-in.)-wide pieces.

Serve after throwing the flesh hard against the cutting board (one time).

Yatsude-zukuri

The flesh is cut in a fan shape like the leaves of the Japanese aralia shrub. An arrangement of ark shell sashimi in the *kanoko-zukuri*, *karakusa-zukuri*, and *yatsude-zukuri* (Aralia-leaf cut) shapes offers a variety of textures and visual patterns to delight the eye and palate.

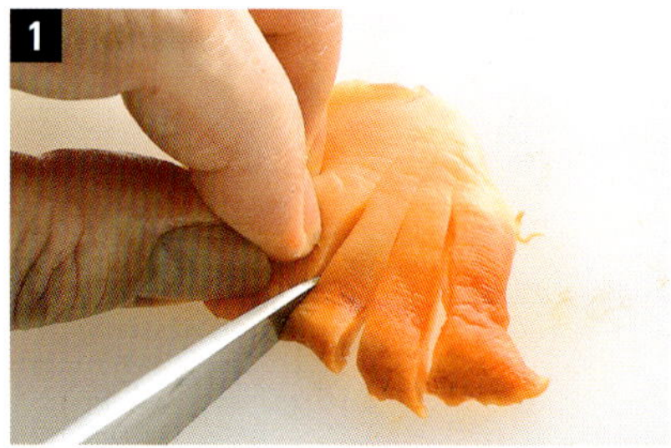

1 Place the half piece of ark shell flesh with the upper side up and the redder end toward you. From the right side, cut in at 5-mm (¼-in.) intervals toward the hinge as shown (leaving about 1 cm (½ in.) at the top uncut).

2 Make a total of about 5 or 6 incisions, as shown.

Strike the flesh forcefully against the cutting board and serve when the flesh swells out.

Preparing the Ark Shell Mantle

Ark shell mantle (*himo*) is served not only as an ingredient of sushi and sashimi but also dressed foods (*aemono*) and other dishes. It is prepared after first rubbing it well with salt and removing any debris or sliminess.

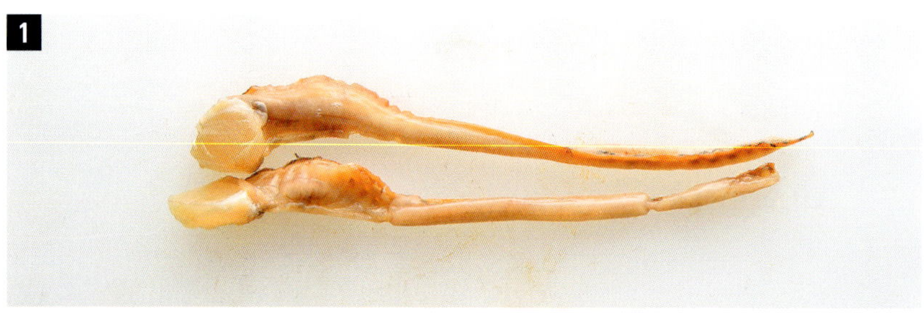

1 Place with the muscle facing left.

2 Lay the two pieces of the mantle together and cut into three pieces of equal length (should be of a length that is easy to eat).

mantle cut into pieces

Ark Shell Sashimi

daikon *ken*
matsuba-udo stalk
hamabofu
shiso leaves
uzushio daikon ("whirlpool" daikon)
benitade
wasabi

Sazae

HORNED TURBAN

Batillus cornutus

Sazae, horned turban, is a species of sea snail in the family Turbinidae (order Vetigastropoda). It mainly lives in the rocky coastal waters (up to 30 meters deep) around Japan from the southern part of Hokkaido to Kyushu. Prized as a delicacy since olden times, *sazae* is one of the species of marine snail harvested in largest quantity in Japan.

Found along both the Japan Sea and Pacific coasts, horned turban of the Japan Sea side (the Tsushima Warm Current) are mostly small in size, about 10 centimeters in shell length, whereas those of the Pacific side (the Kuroshio Current) tend to be larger, sometimes growing up to more than 20 centimeters. Generally, the horned turbans inhabiting rougher seas are likely to have horny protuberances while those of quiet inland sea waters less so. Both have a hard, rocky lid (the operculum) to which the spiral snail body is firmly attached. Taste differs little according to size, habitat, or presence of horns.

CARVING HORNED TURBAN

Insert the clam knife (p. 18) in the crevice at the side.

1

2

3

4

Remove the snail from the shell and remove sliminess

1. Hold the shell with the lid facing toward you and insert the clam knife (*kaiwari*) into the crevice around the operculum.
2. Move the knife around the circle of the shell opening, prying the body outwards.
3. Once the operculum is free (still attached to the body), insert the fingers of the right hand and pull out the *kimo* (digestive cecum) entwined in the whorl behind it, taking care not to break up the organ.
4. The snail body with operculum attached and the shell from which it was removed.

5

6

7

8

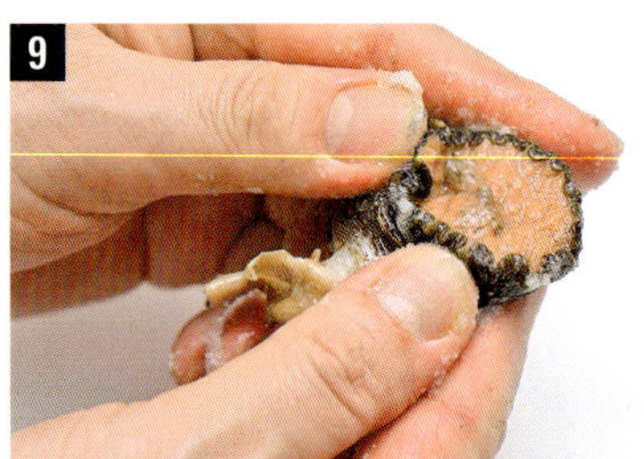

9

10

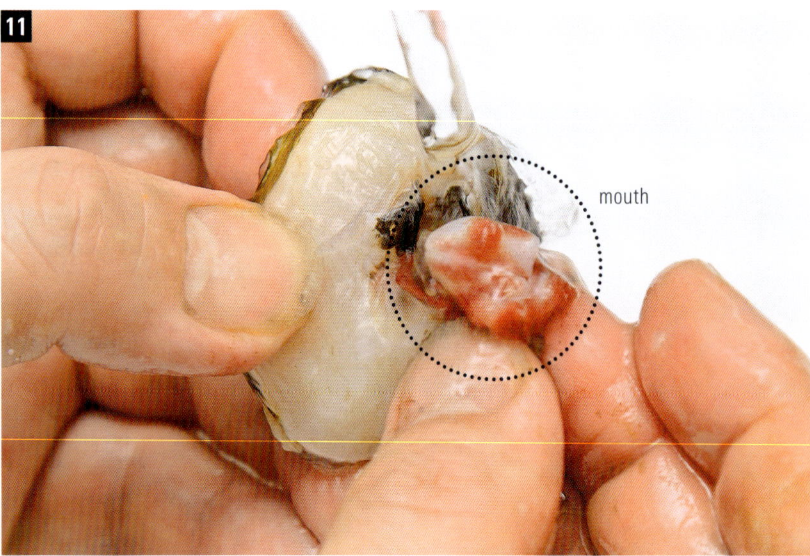

11

5 Place the operculum to the right and cut off the internal organs from the body with a *deba* knife, as shown.

6–7 Insert the clam knife in the crevice between the operculum and body. Push the knife down and cut the lid off.

8 Rub salt into the body to remove debris and sliminess.

9 Rub salt into the suction foot and work in well to cleanse the flesh.

10 Wash away any sliminess and debris along with the salt.

11 While washing, pinch away the red mouth attached on the lid side of the body. Blot away excess moisture.

Cleaning the internal organs

1. Cut the *kimo* away at its base.
2. –3. Cut the muscle away from the internal organs that had been attached to the *kimo*. Cut the other muscle off from the fringe and organs (which are not edible).
4. Sprinkle salt on the muscles.
5. –6. Work in the salt thoroughly. Clean thoroughly. Wash well in running water.
7. Blot away excess moisture. The darker parts especially tend to retain dirt, so wipe well.
8. The body, muscles, and liver, separated. The *kimo* may be served after first boiling in salt water.

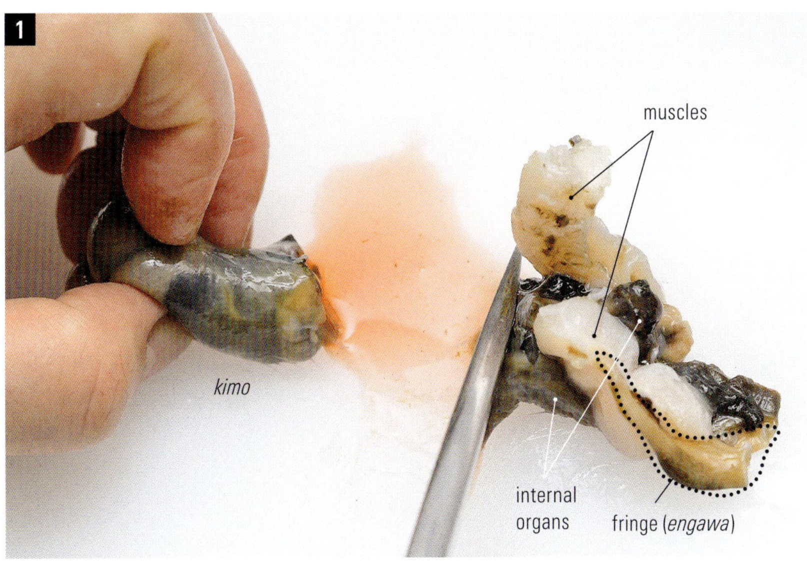

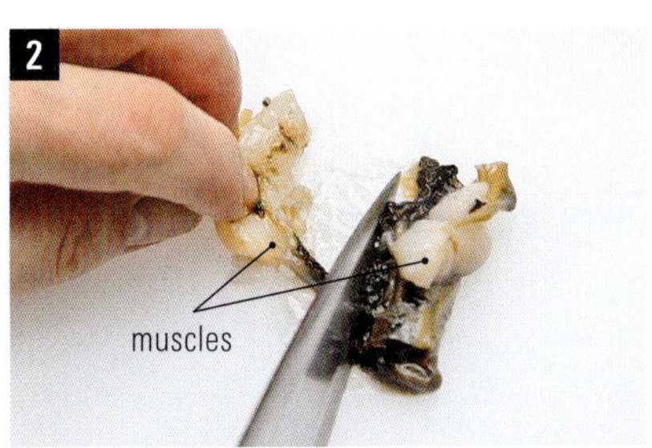

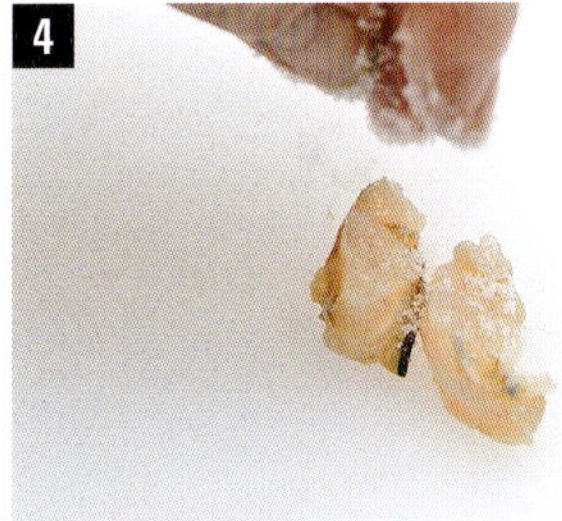

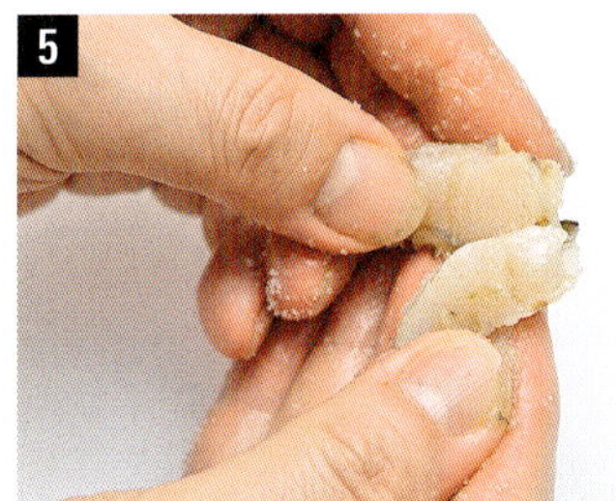

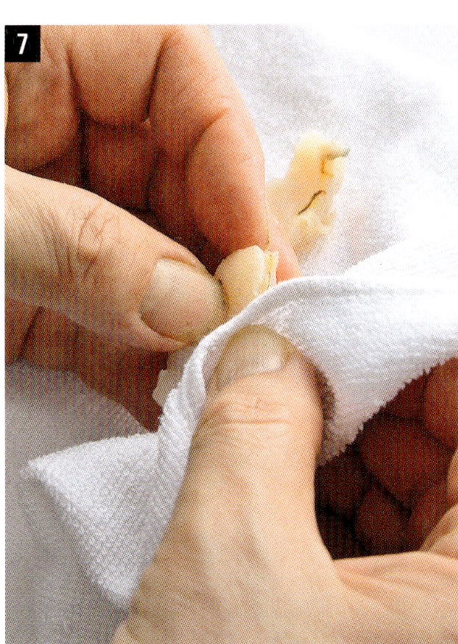

8

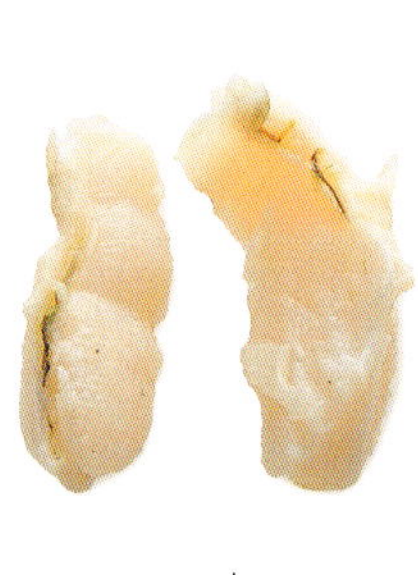
muscles

remnants of fringe (*engawa*)

kimo

Horned Turban *Sazanami-zukuri* *Sazae Sazanami-zukuri*

When serving sashimi (*tsukuri*) style, the suction foot is cut into thin strips *sazanami* style (see p. 158). The suction area is sliced off thin to make a flat surface on the remaining portion. The *kimo* is boiled and served together with the muscles.

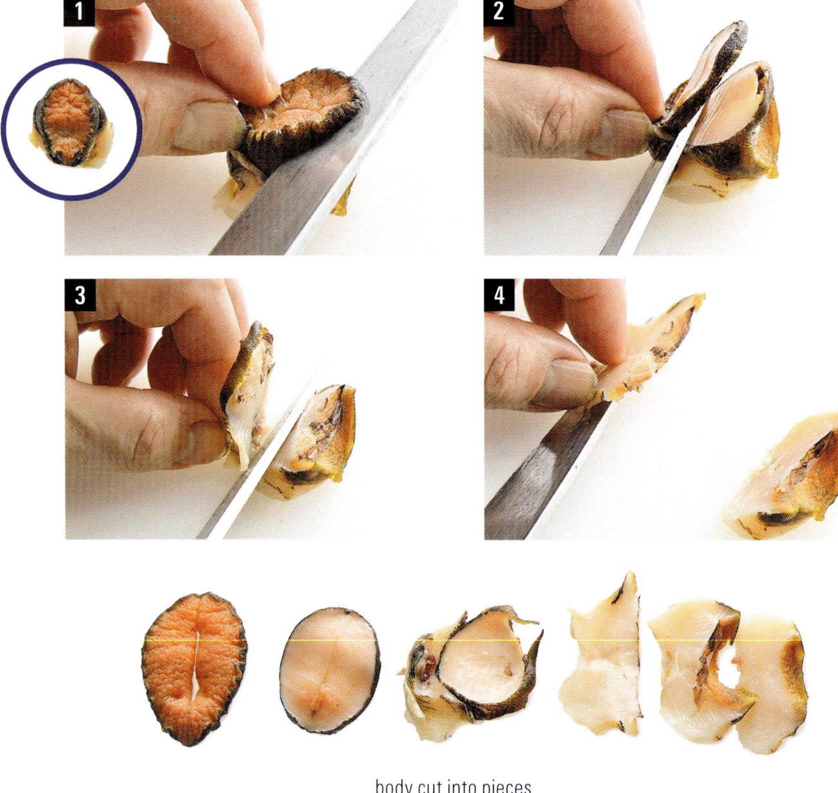

body cut into pieces

1–**2** Place the body with the suction foot facing upward, as shown. Steadying the body with the fingers of the left hand, use the *yanagiba* knife, held at a low angle, and shave off a 2-mm (⅛-in.) slice at the top (the flesh is tough, so cut thin).

3 Place the remaining flesh vertically. With the blade at a low angle, cut off the hard part at a point about one-third from the right. Cut the hard part further into three thin pieces.

4 With the knife horizontal, cut the remaining flesh into 2-mm slices, following the *sazanami-zukuri* style (see p. 158).

5–**6** Cut off any residue of the lid remaining on the muscles.

7 Cut off any remnants of the mantle remaining on the muscles.

8 Boil the *kimo* for 2 to 3 minutes in 2 percent salt water by weight to remove unpleasant odors.

9 Cut the *kimo* in two at the center.

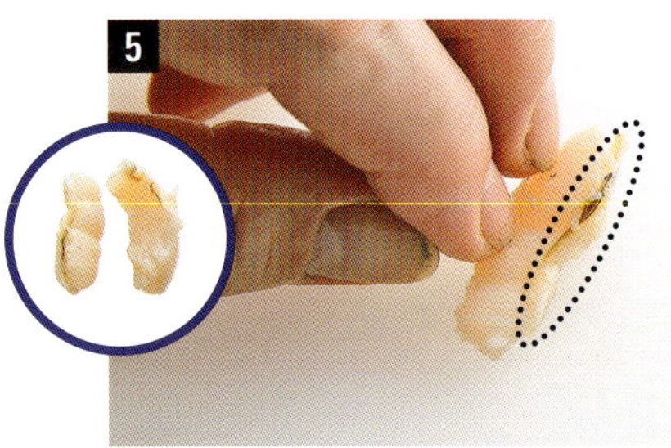

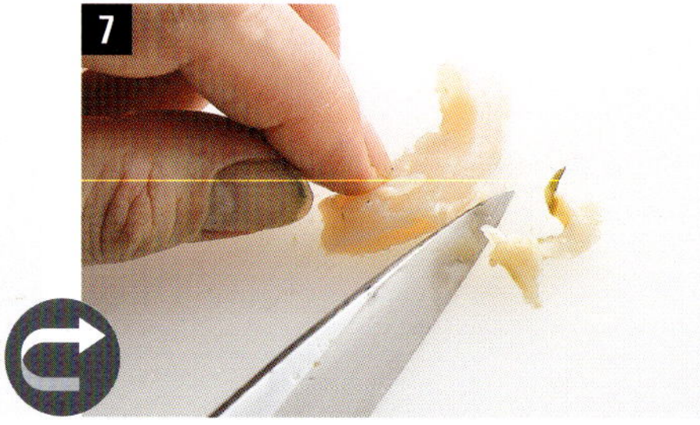

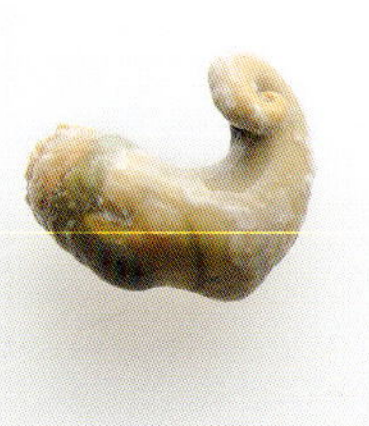

Horned Turban *Sazanami-zukuri*

daikon *ken*
cucumber *ken*
hamabofu
sakura-so (primula) petals
wasabi

Horned Turban Grilled in the Shell *Sazae Tsubo-yaki*

Along with sashimi, *tsubo-yaki* (grilled in the shell) is one of the two leading ways for enjoying the horned turban, an ingredient featuring the fragrance and taste of the sea. The flesh and *kimo* are cooked together and then placed in the shell, adding dashi before grilling.

1. Prepare lily bulb and *mitsuba* for adding to the *tsubo-yaki*. Clean the "petals" of the lily corm and steam them for 10 minutes at 195°F (90°C); sprinkle with salt (0.8–1.0 percent by weight). Cut the *mitsuba* in 2-cm (about 1-in.) lengths.
2. Bring seasoned dashi (4 T *ichiban* dashi [p. 244]; 2 T de-alcoholized sake; 1 T each mirin and shoyu) to a boil, add prepared flesh, muscle, and liver (preparation and cutting same as for *sazanami-zukuri*) along with a slice of ginger (cleaned, skinned, and cut about 3-cm or 1¼-in. thick), and cook about a minute and a half over medium heat.
3. Remove the ginger from the liquid and insert into the shell, trimming the size (according to the size of the shell and the amount of ingredients) to serve as a base upon which to arrange the ingredients.
4. –5. Arrange in layers, liver, flesh, lily bulb, flesh, lily bulb, flesh, in that order.
6. Place stems and leaves of *mitsuba* on top.
7. Pour in the dashi from the pot until it fills the bowl of the shell. Place the shells on a grill and grill slowly over medium heat. (Remove from heat after the dashi boils.) If the dashi boils over, add more to fill the shell.

1

2

3

4

5

6

7

Horned Turban Grilled in the Shell

mitsuba
hajikami (pickled ginger)

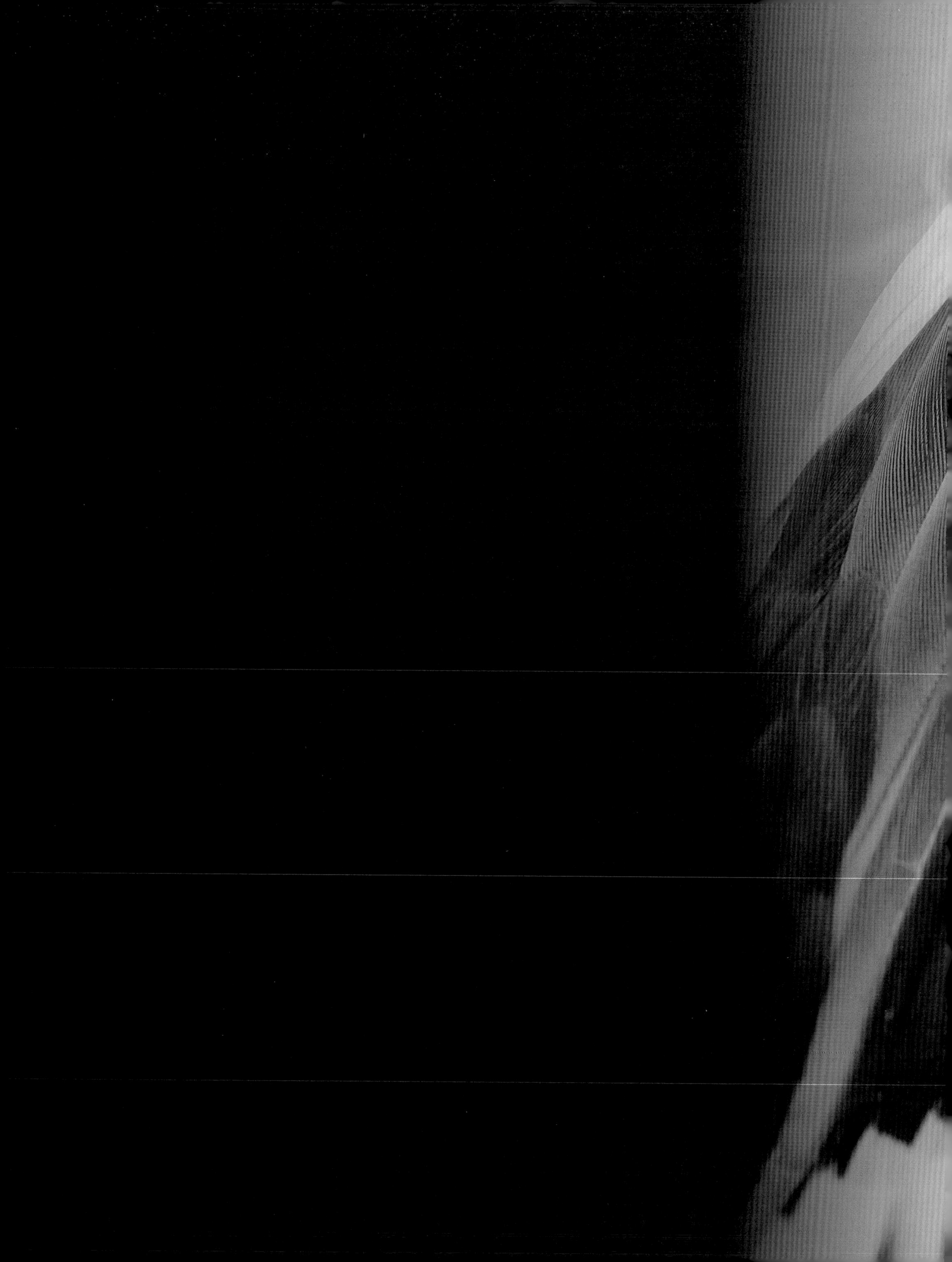

Chapter 3

Carving Poultry

For many centuries of Japan's history the tenets of Buddhism, which prohibit the consumption of the flesh of four-legged animals, prevailed widely throughout society, and for this reason poultry and wild fowl were frequently used in cooking. Here we introduce the procedures for carving chicken, duck, and quail. Chicken and duck are divided into parts easily used for cooking, but for quail, here we give instructions for butterflying this small and fine-boned bird.

Niwatori

CHICKEN

Gallus gallus domesticus

Belonging to the family Phasianidae (order Galliformes), chicken is the leading type of poultry farmed throughout the world. Chicken for meat is marketed in Japan as mass-market broilers, heritage-bred chicken (*jidori*), and "brand chicken" (*meigaradori*). Broilers, also called *wakadori* ("young chicken"), refers to the fast-growing breeds raised specifically for meat. They reach slaughter weight in a short period, at approximately 50 days of age. Heritage breeds include *Hinai-jidori* (Akita prefecture), *Satsuma-jidori* (Kagoshima prefecture), and *Okukuji-shamo* (Ibaraki prefecture), originating in indigenous chickens. Growing more slowly than broilers, they reach the slaughter weight at 80 or more days of age. Strict criteria define the *jidori* category, including at least 50 percent genes of indigenous chicken and evidence of pedigree. The meat quality of *jidori* varies depending on the breed, but generally is firm and springy in texture and rich in taste. "Brand chickens" are raised in Japan and have been more successful in breeding than *jidori*, and producers have developed various innovations in the way the birds are fed and how the meat is delivered.

In cooking, purchase of whole chicken is preferred, and generally the internal organs have already been removed. The chicken's head, and especially the feet, which touch the ground, harbor bacteria. Carving is made easier, therefore, by removing the head and feet first. You may cook a chicken whole, as with roast chicken, but often the bird is butterflied or carved into separate parts for various dishes. For Japanese cuisine, chicken breast, thigh, and tenderloin (*sasami*) are mainly used, and the *tori-dashi*, or broth made from the bones (*gara*), serves as a base for chicken dishes.

CARVING CHICKEN

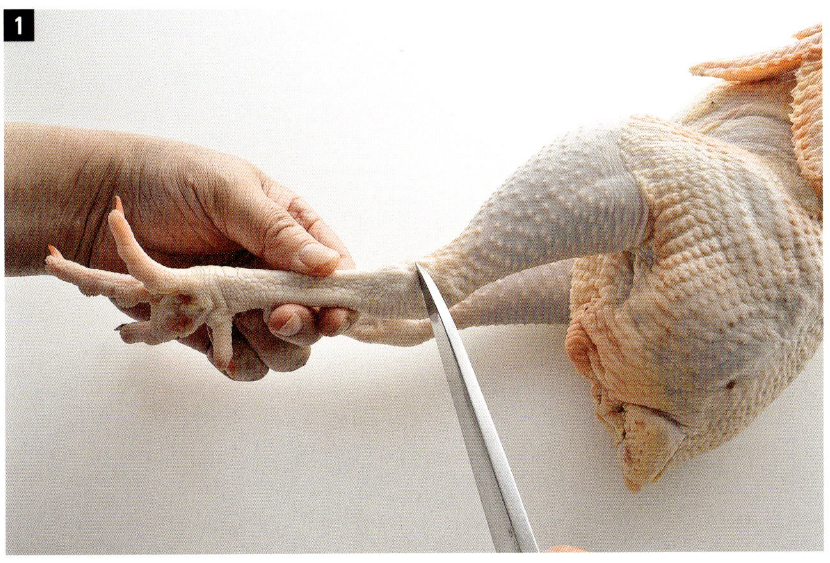

Removing lower legs

1 Place the chicken with legs to the left, breast-side away from you. Grip the left leg as shown and position the tip of the *deba* knife at the leg joint.

2–**3** Cut through the skin around both leg joints.

4 Grip the left leg above and below the joint, as shown.

5 Twisting both hands in a wringing motion, separate the bones at the joint.

6 When the joint has come apart, pull the lower leg away, pulling out the tendons with it. Remove the right lower leg in the same way.

7 The lower legs with their tendons after removal.

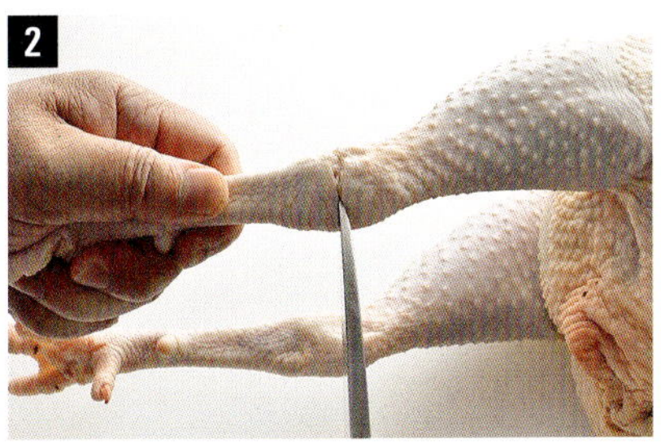

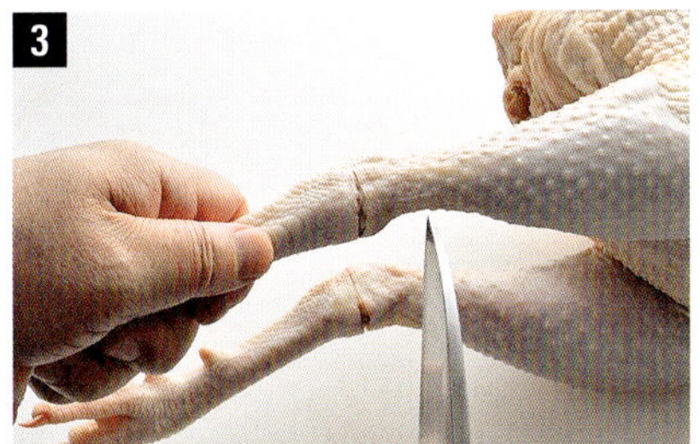

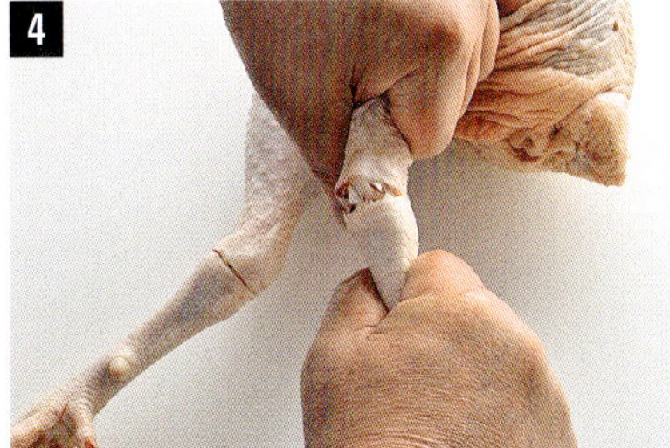

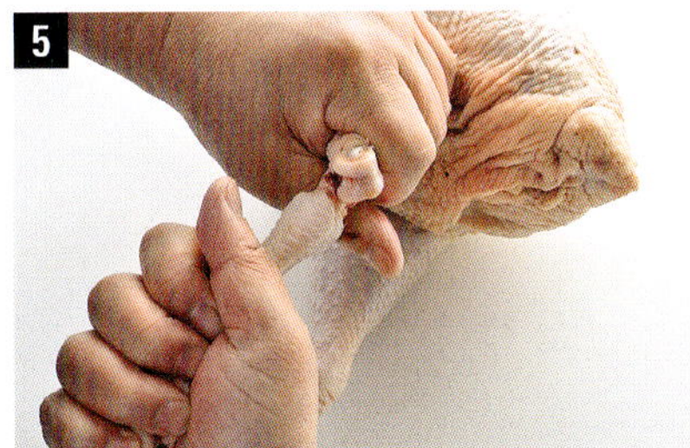

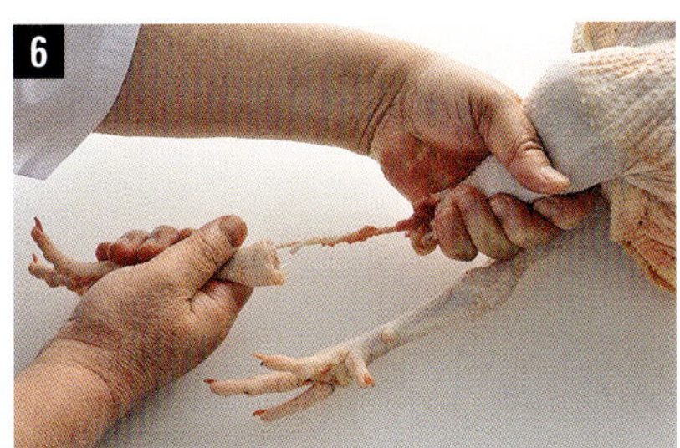

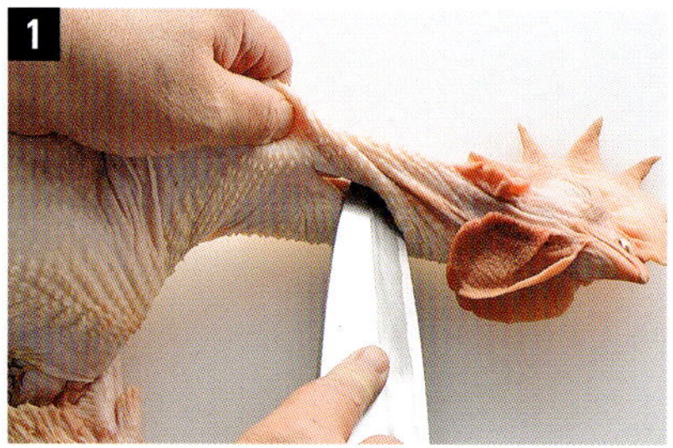
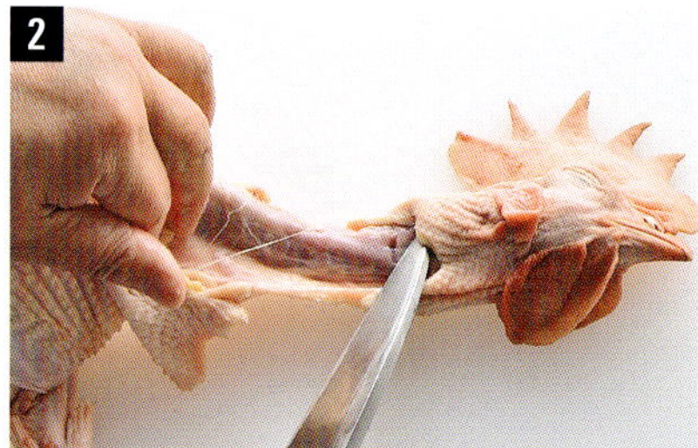
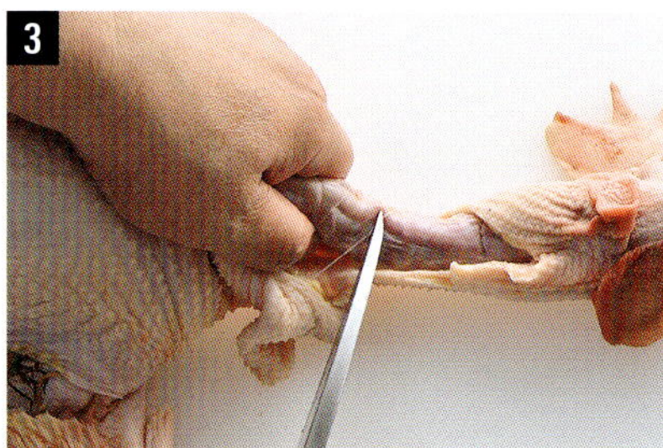
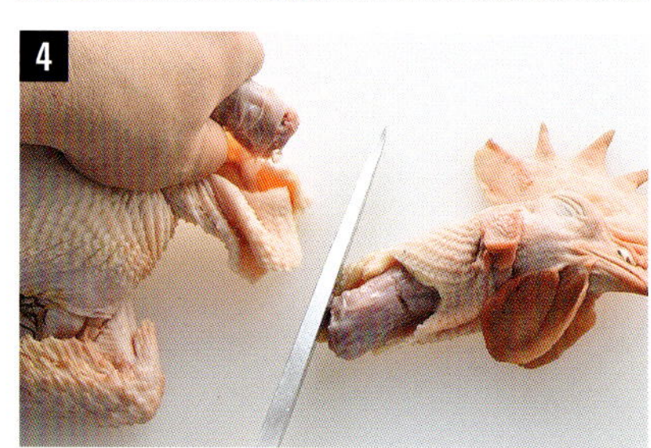

Removing the head

1. Place with the head to the right, breast side facing toward you. While pulling back the skin at the neck with your left hand, as shown, turn the blade of the knife to the right and make an incision in the skin at the base of the head.
2. With the tip of the blade, cut the skin where the incision was made in step 1 and peel the skin off toward you.
3. Make an incision in the flesh around the joint of the neck with the tip of the knife.
4. Place the tip of the knife in the incision made in step 3 and strike the back of the blade, cutting down hard through the neck to remove the head.

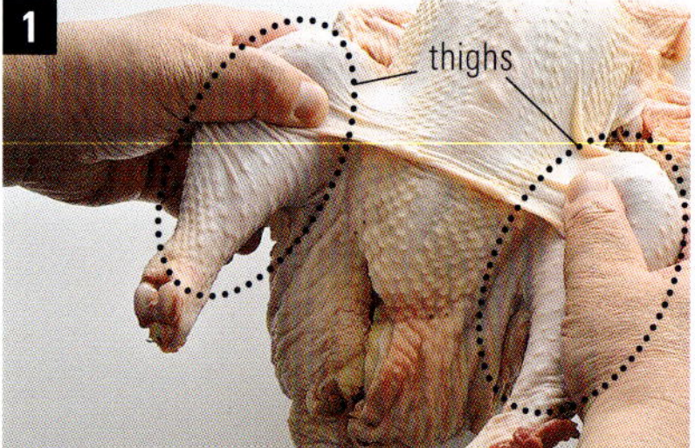

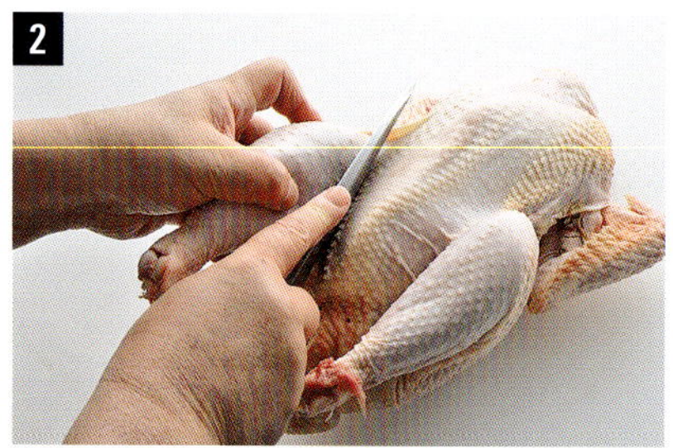

Removing the thighs

1. Breast side up, legs toward you, grip the thighs at the base on both sides. Manipulate the joints until they loosen, making it easier to insert the knife.
2. Place the knife at the base of the bird's right leg.
3. Draw the knife toward you and from the base of the thigh toward the rump (dotted lines in the photo), cutting through the skin. Make a similar cut from the base of the bird's left thigh.

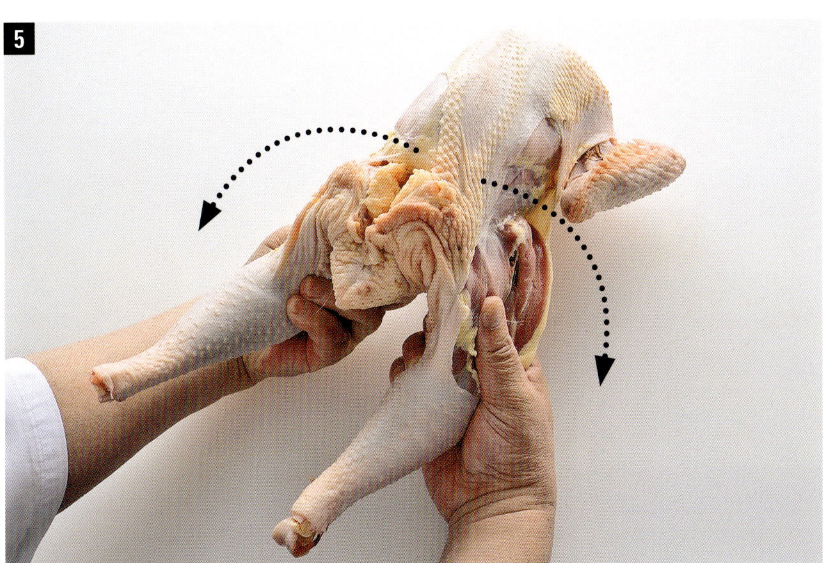

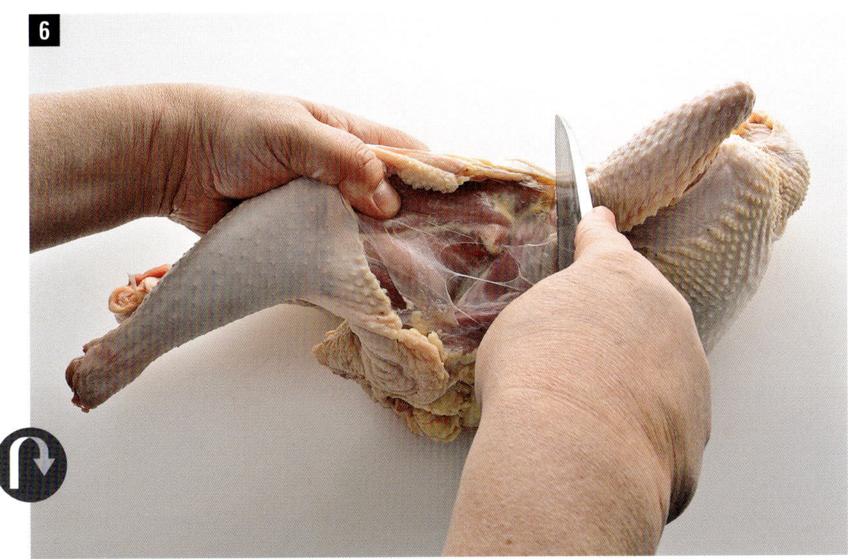

4 Grip both thighs at the base, as shown. Insert the thumbs in the incisions made in step **3** and open out the thighs.

5 Fold the thighs back toward the spine (as shown) to separate the bones at the joints.

6 With both thighs folded over the back, place the body with the breast to the right. Grip the right thigh with the left hand and make an incision at the base of the thigh.

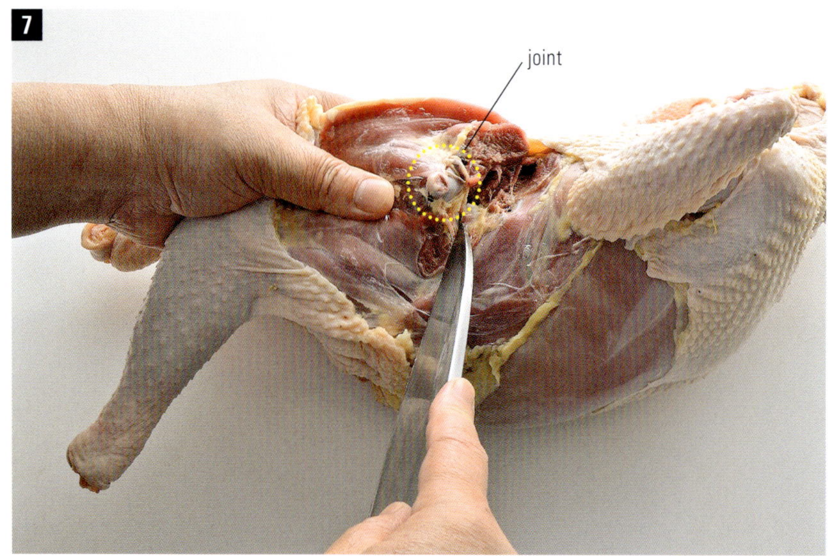

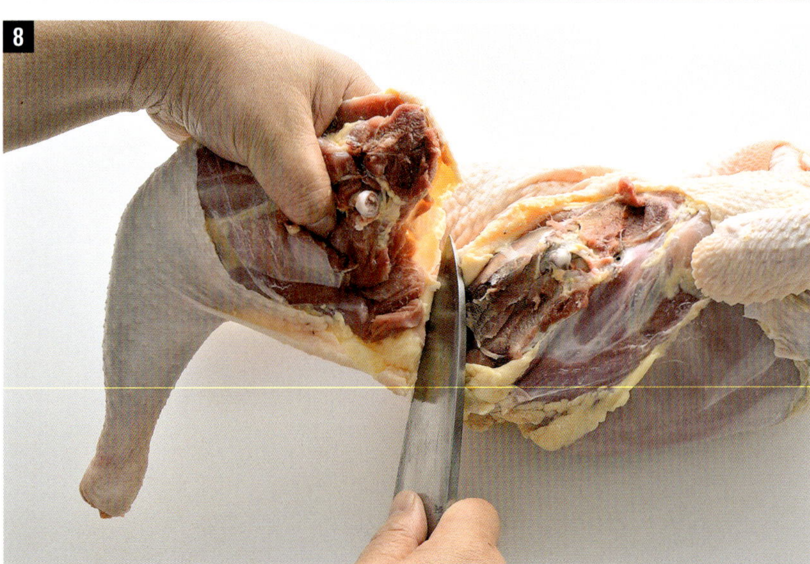

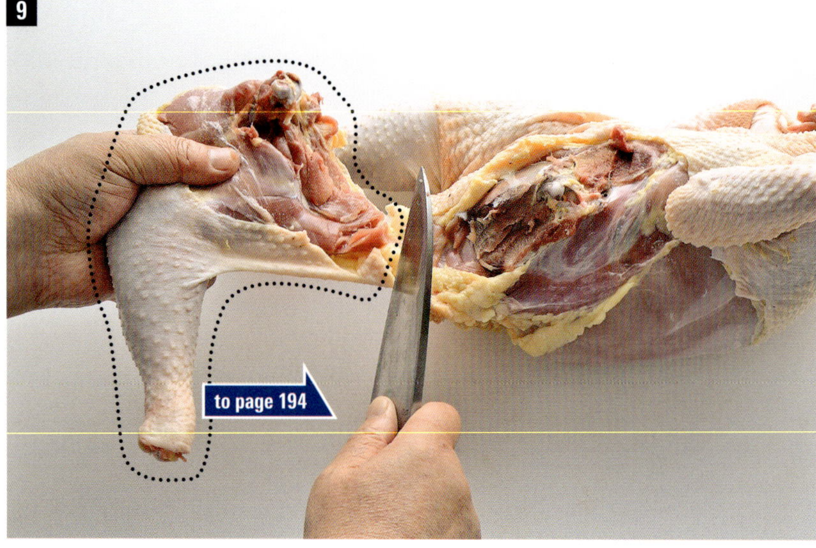

7 With the left hand, grip the incision made in step 6 firmly and push out the base of the joint, as shown. Position the knife at the joint and cut through the muscles around the joint, separating the joint. Cut in further along the thigh bone, slicing through the rest of the flesh, leaving the skin intact.

8 Using the knife to firmly pin down the skin connecting to the breast, grip the thigh at the base and pull it outward, removing the thigh as if to tear it away, skin and all.

9 Cut through the skin on the breast side and remove the right thigh.

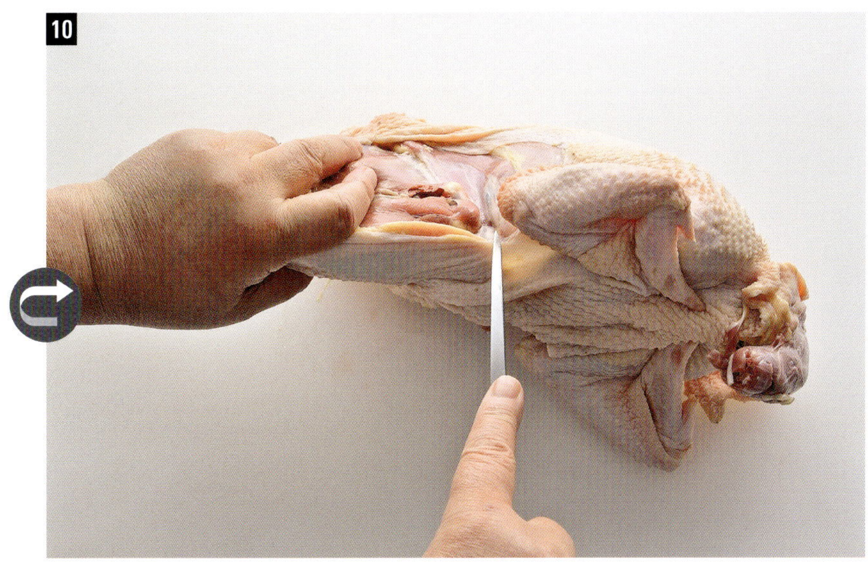

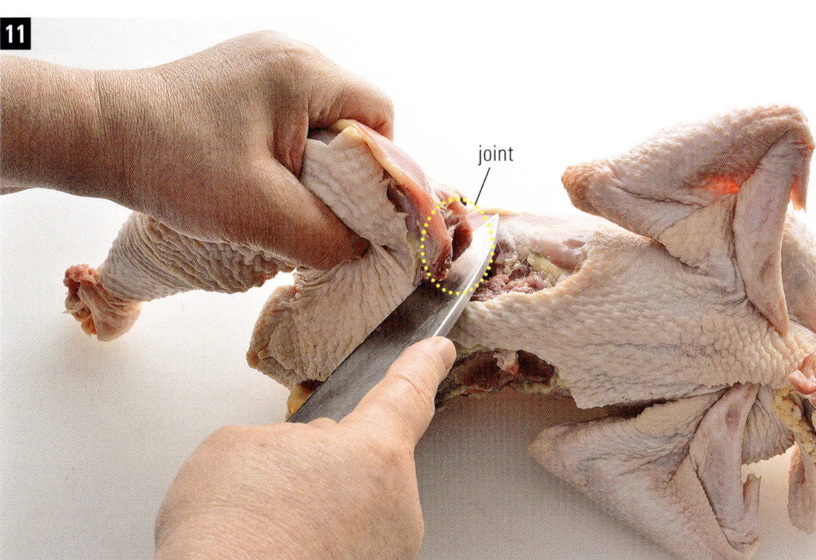

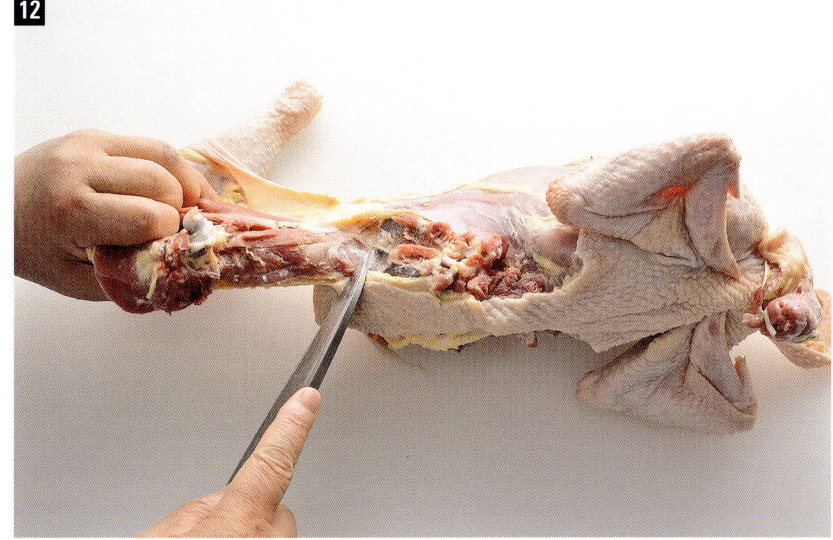

10 Place the bird with the left thigh up, spine side toward you. Lifting the thigh with your left hand, position the blade at the base of the thigh, then cut along the base of the thigh in the direction of the spine.

11 Lifting the thigh with the left hand, slice in with the knife at a low angle (as shown) and start cutting through the base of the thigh. As in step **7**, push the bone so that the joint rises up and cut the muscles around it.

12 Following the same procedures as in steps **8** and **9**, remove the left thigh.

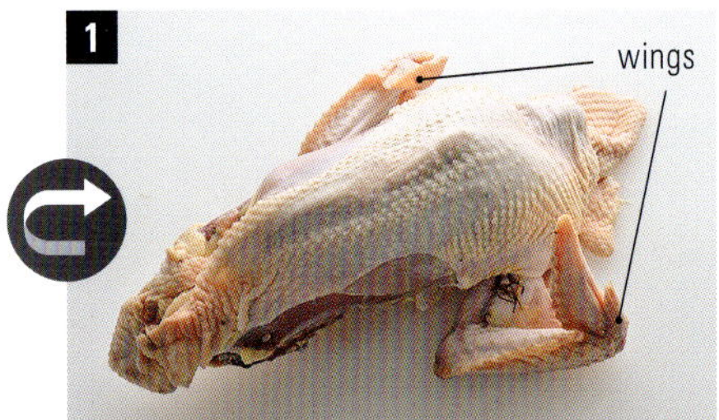

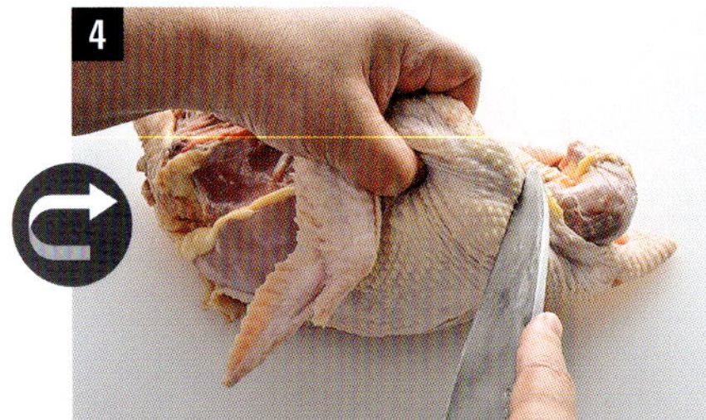

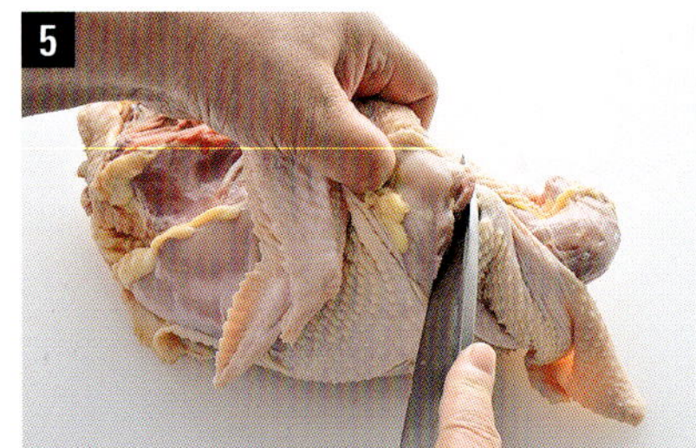

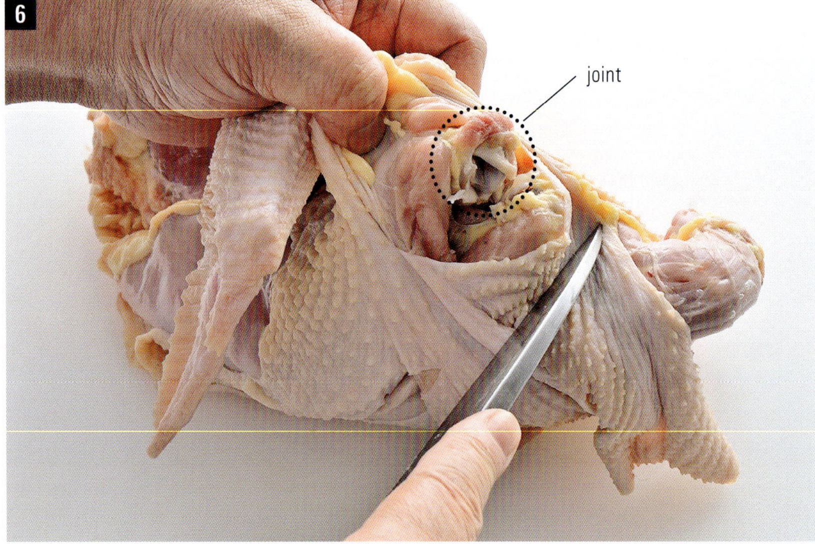

Removing the wings and breast meat

1. Place the bird breast side up, neck end away from you.
2. Insert the knife along the left side of the breastbone at the neck end (see dotted line in photo).
3. Cut toward the tail end (as shown), along the left side of the breastbone.
4. Place with the head end to the right, breast side facing you. Position the knife just above the joint at the base of the right wing.
5. Cut through the skin and keep on cutting down to the joint.
6. With the fingers of the left hand, push out the joint at the base of the wing.

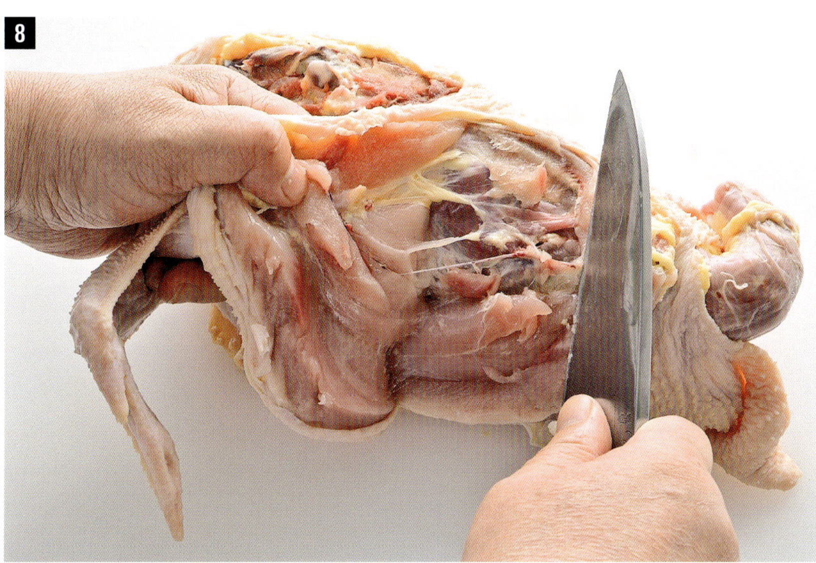

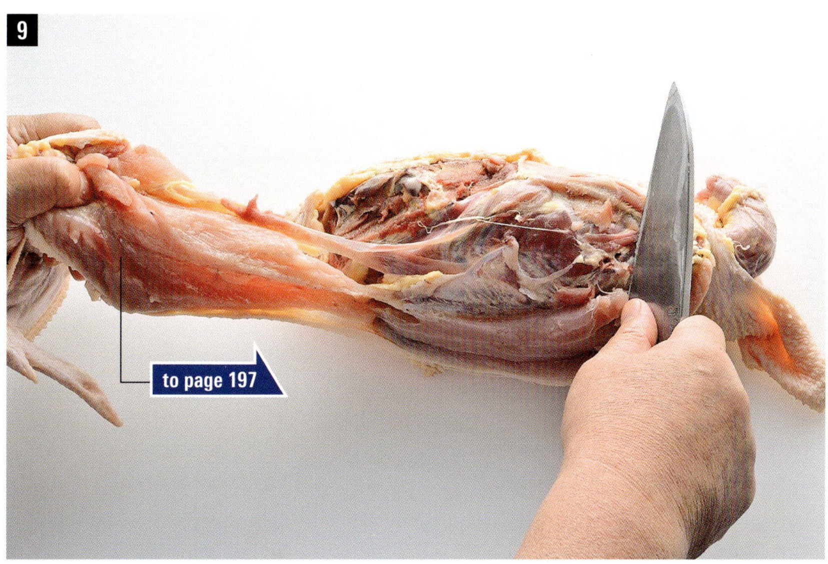

7 Placing the blade at the joint and steadying the body with the knife, pull out the wing, muscles and all. Cut through the muscles to detach the wing.

8–**9** Steadying the body at the shoulder area with the knife, grip the wing at the base with your left hand and pull (as shown). Keep pulling until the wing and breast separate from the breastbone.

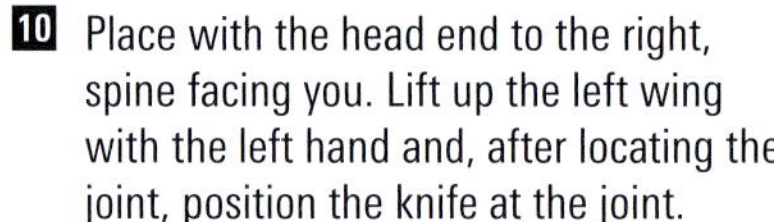

10 Place with the head end to the right, spine facing you. Lift up the left wing with the left hand and, after locating the joint, position the knife at the joint.

11 Hold the wing with the left hand and cut through the skin at the joint located in step 10. Then cut through the joint completely.

12 Cut in further, cutting the muscles around the joint.

13 With the blade facing right (*sakasa-bocho*), insert the knife into the incision made in step 11 and push the tip of the knife all the way through.

14 Continue cutting through to the neck end, cutting down to the base of the wing.

15 Holding down the body at the shoulder with the knife, grip the wing with the left hand and pull it off.

16 Keep pulling, detaching the left wing and breast meat from the body.

17 The body with the breast meat and wings removed

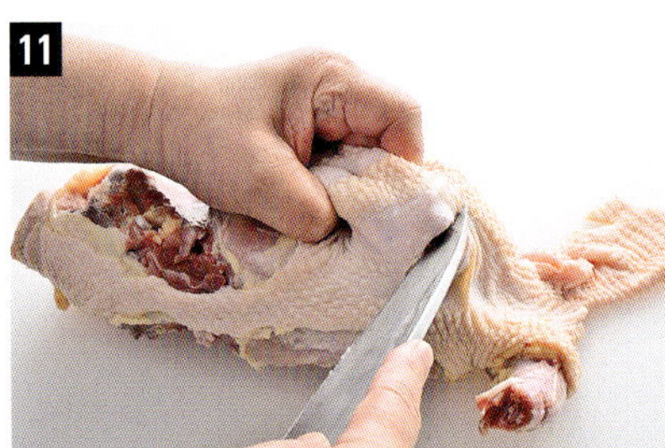

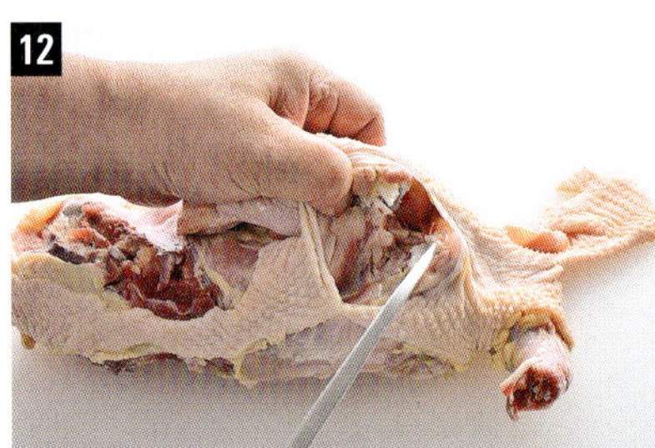

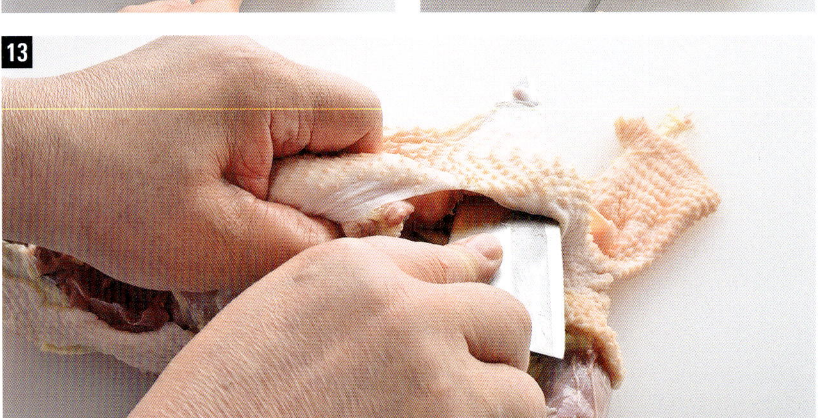

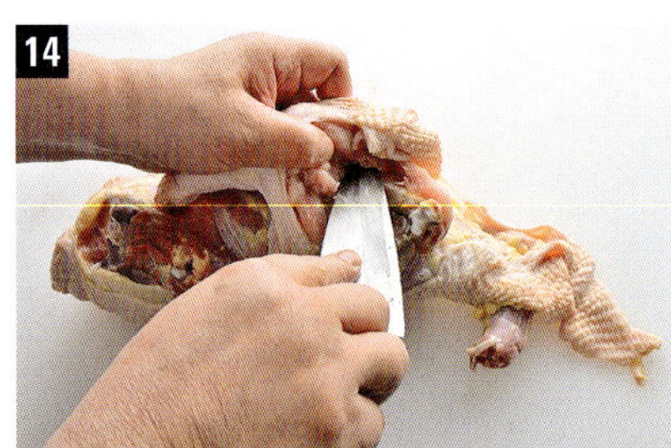

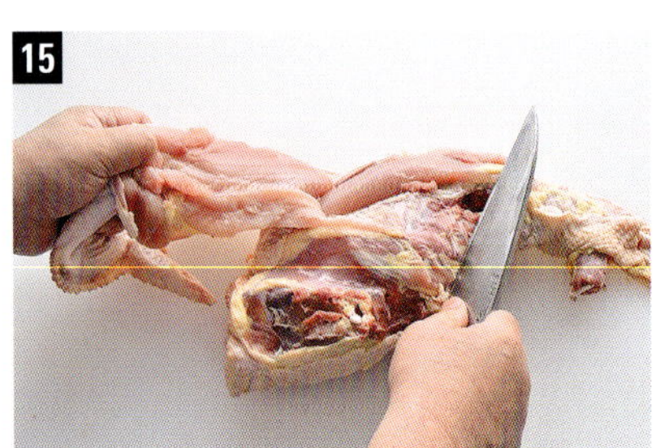

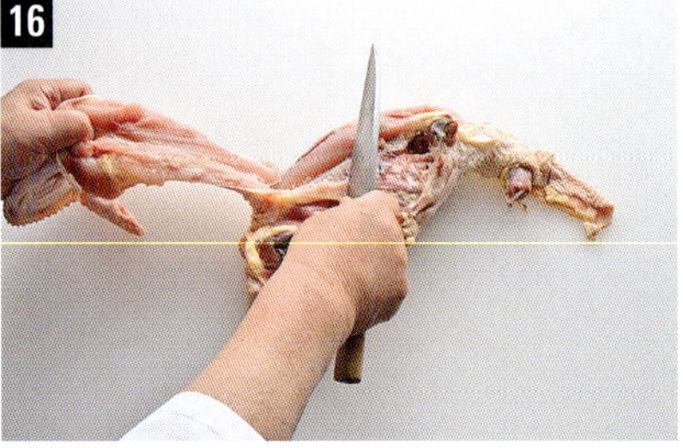

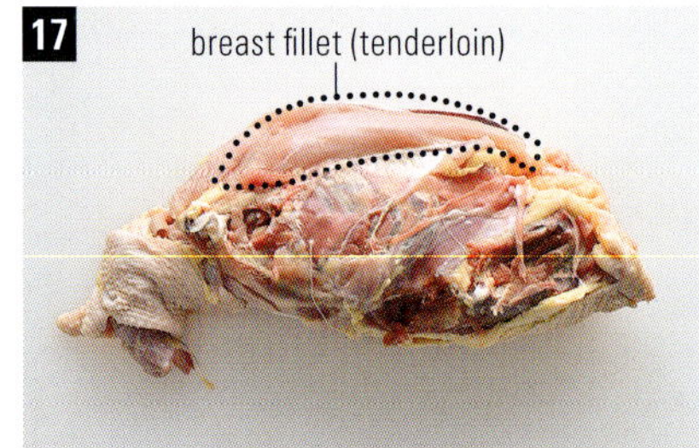

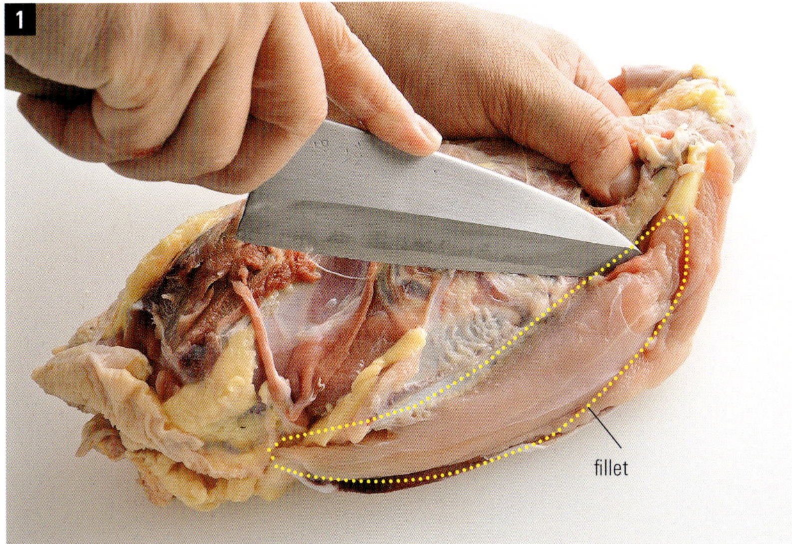

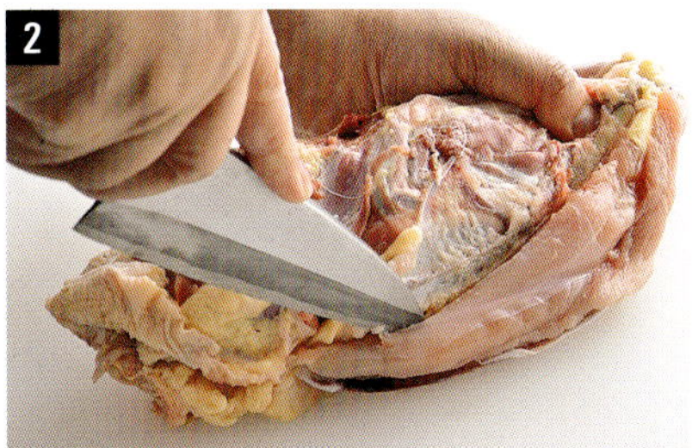

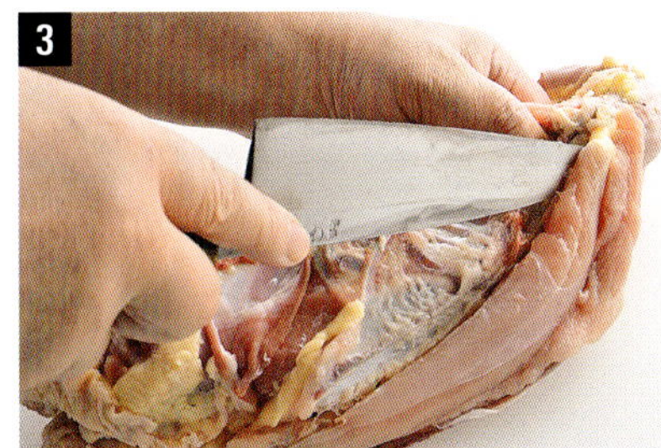

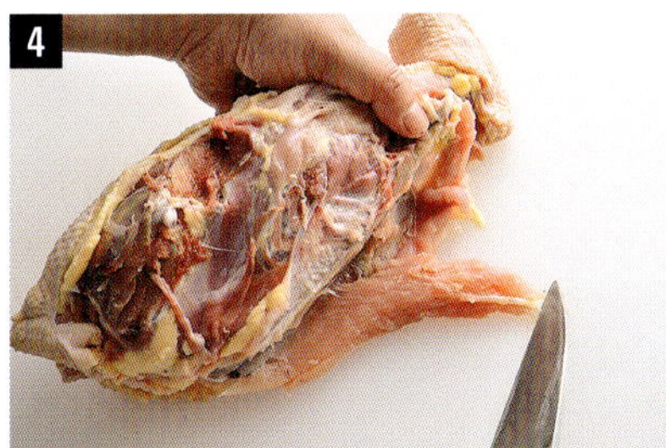

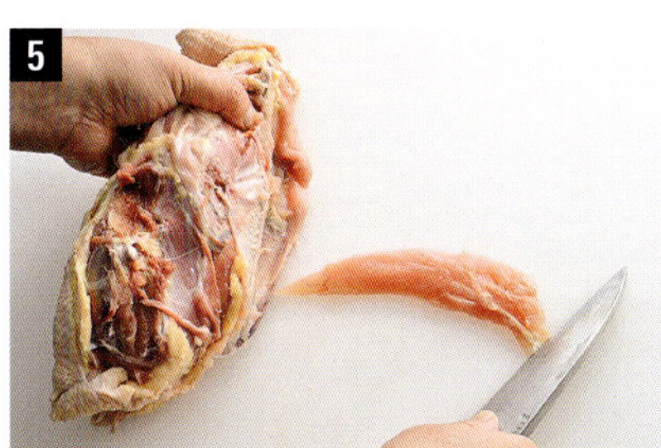

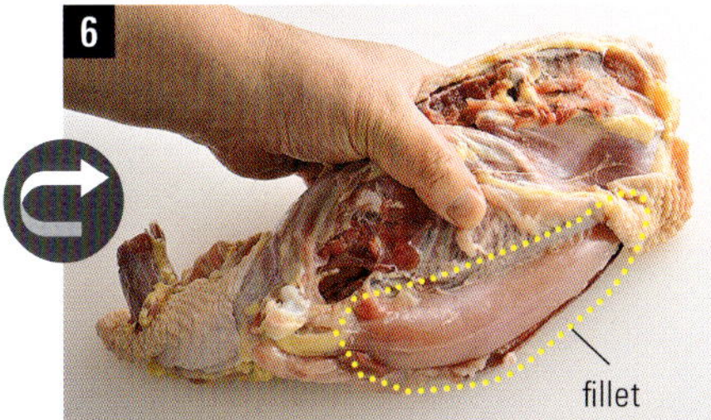

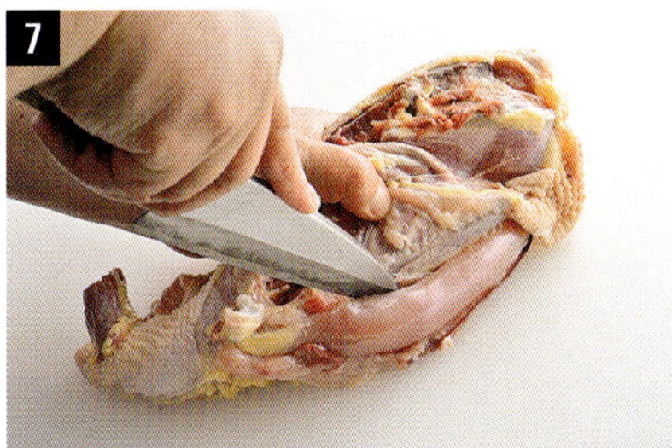

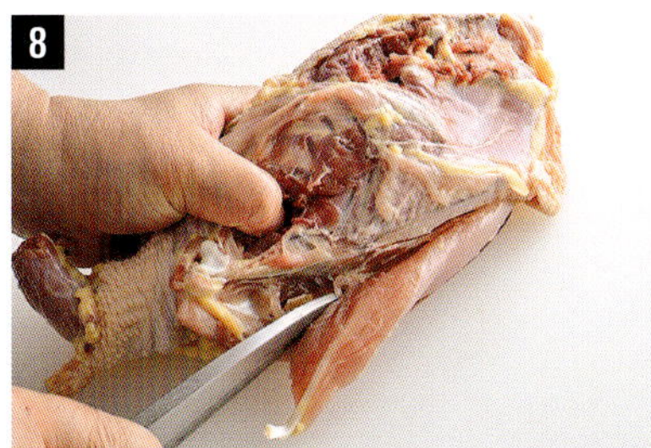

to page 198

Detaching the breast fillets

1. To detach the two breast fillets (*sasami*) attached to the rib cage, place the body (from which the breast meat and wings have been removed) with the neck end away from you, breast side facing you. Position the tip of the knife where the breast fillet joins the body at the head end.
2. Draw the knife tip toward the tail end along the edge of the fillet, detaching it from the rib cage.
3. Reverse the direction of the blade (as shown) and cut off the tendon at the base of the fillet on the head end.
4. Pinning down the tip of the tendon (detached in step 3) on the cutting board with the tip of the knife (as shown), grip the body at the shoulder and pull.
5. Keep on pulling until the fillet is detached.
6. Turn the body around so that the head end is facing you.

7–8. Position the tip of the knife where the breast fillet joins the body and cut under the edge toward the head end. Keep on cutting it away and cut the tendon at the base of the fillet on the head end.

9. Pin the tip of the tendon (cut in step 8) to the cutting board with the knife and detach the fillet as described in step 4.

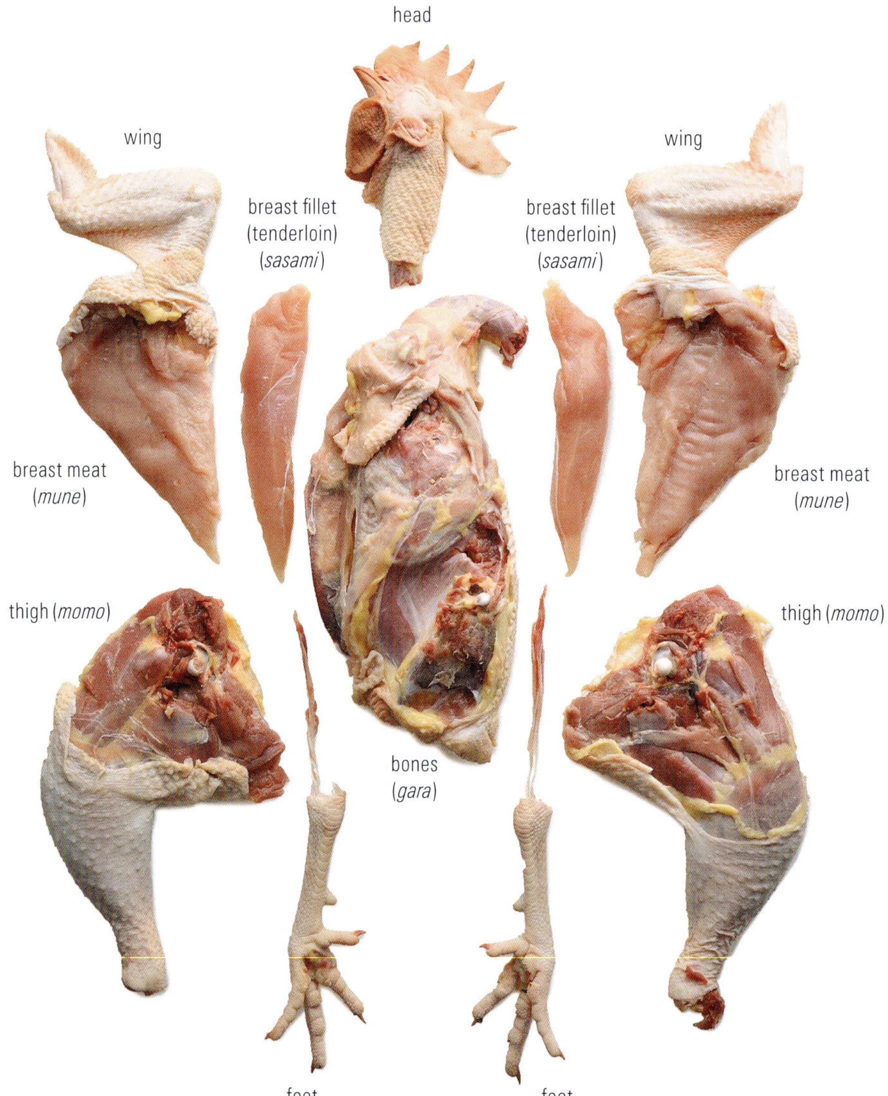

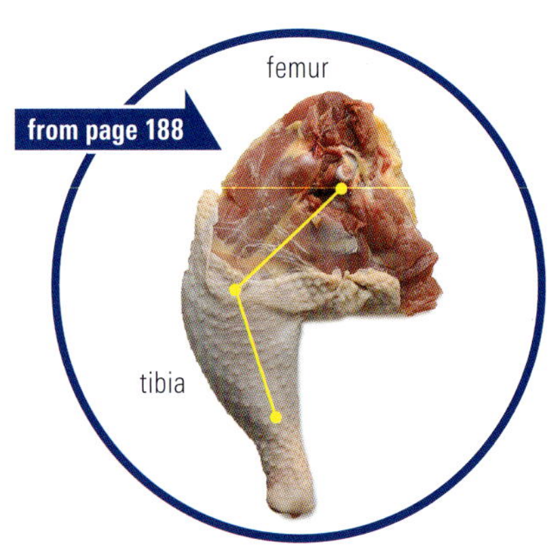

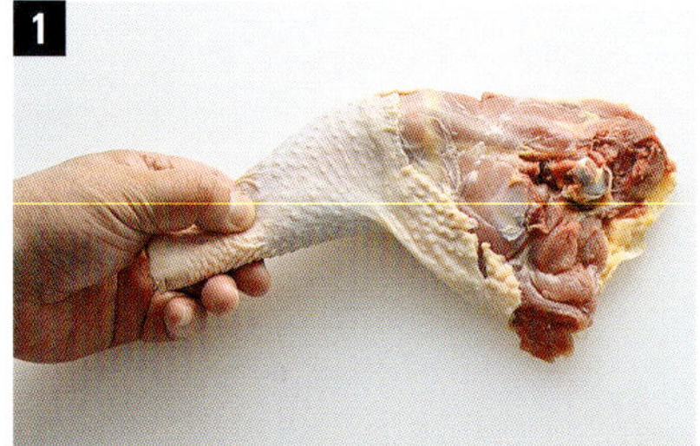

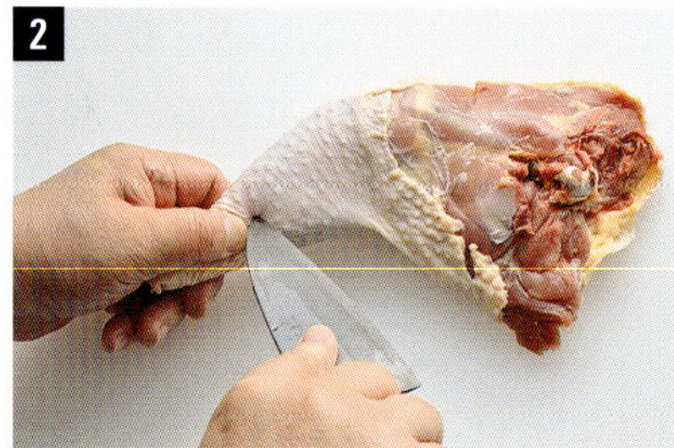

Removing the bones from the thigh

1. The leg has two main bones (the femur and the tibia, see p. 29) connected at a joint. Grasp the end of the right thigh with the left hand, checking the position of the tibia bone with your thumb.
2. With the blade of the knife facing right (*sakasabocho*), pierce the skin over the tibia bone just to the right of your thumb.

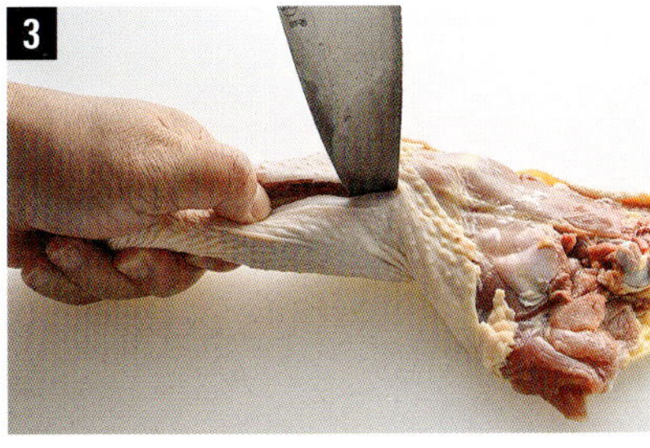

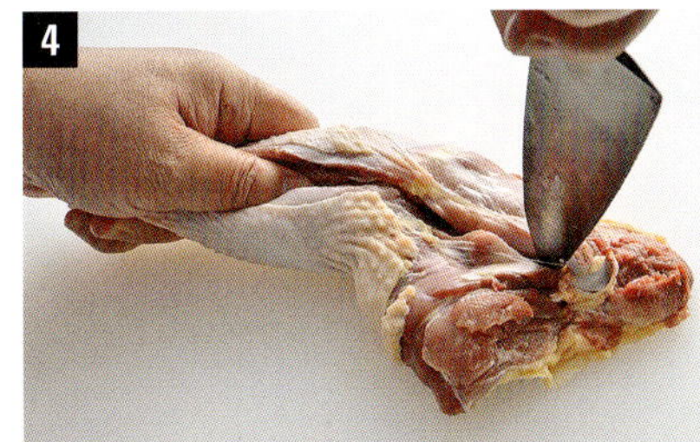

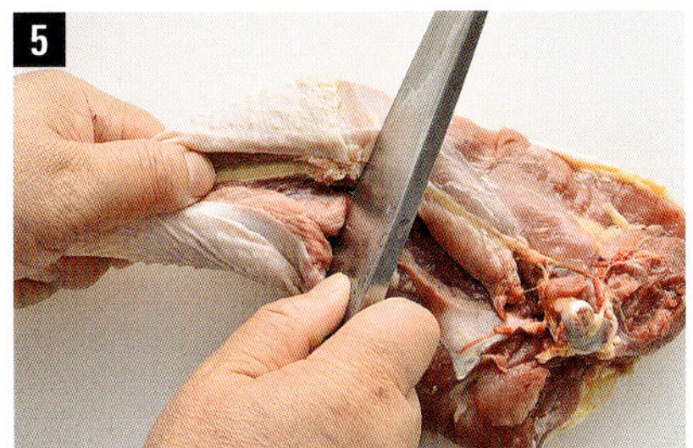

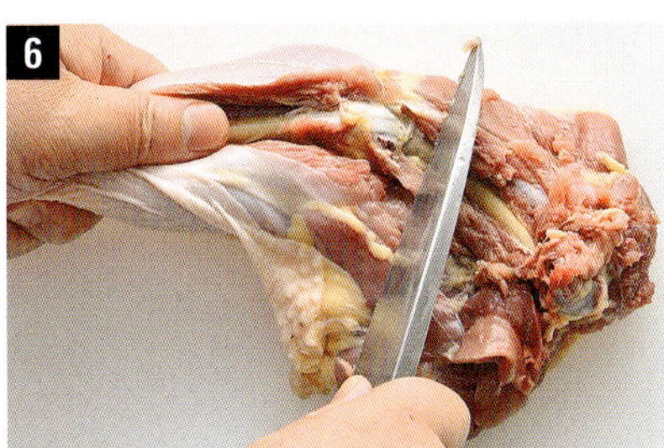

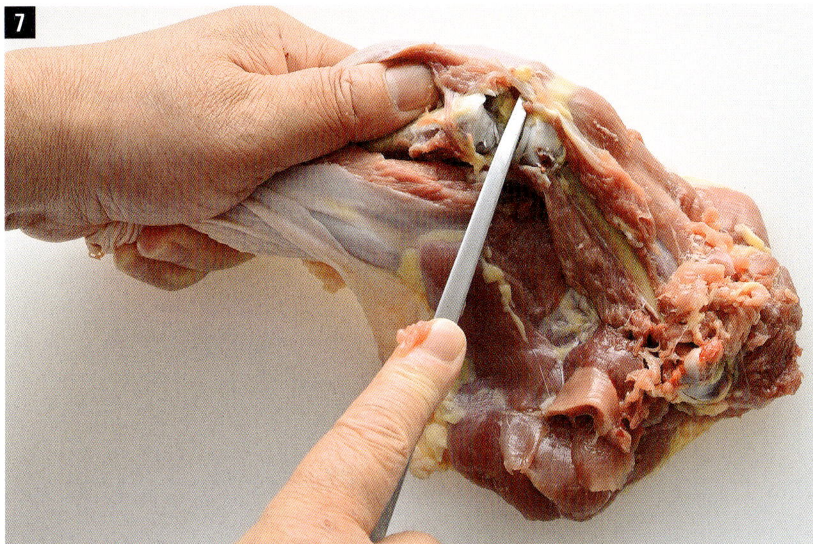

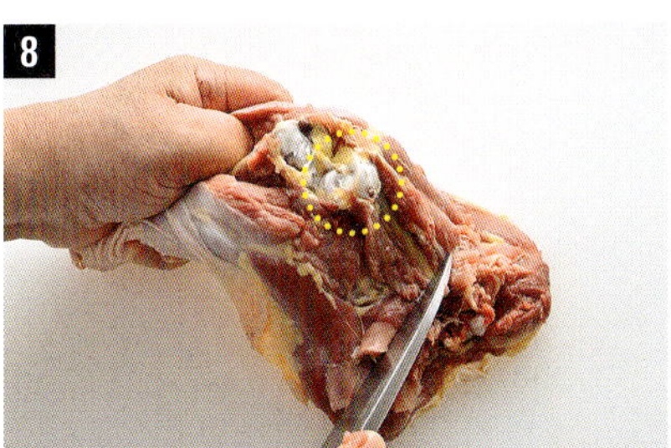

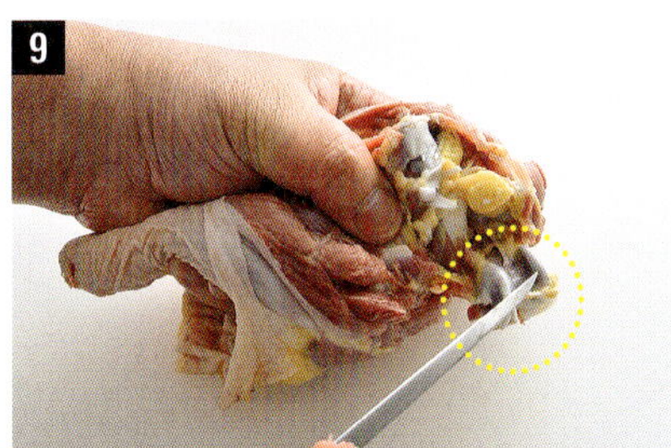

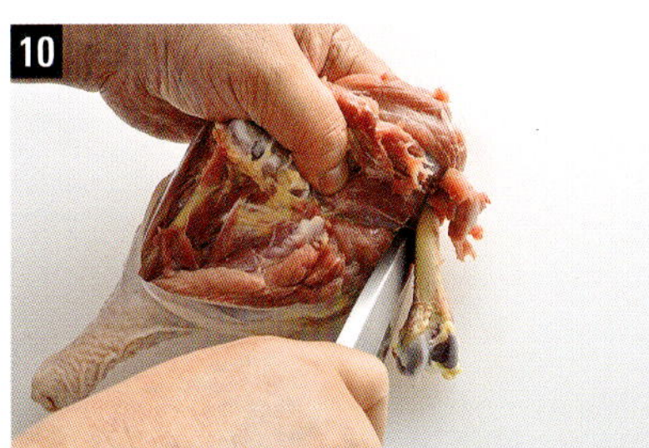

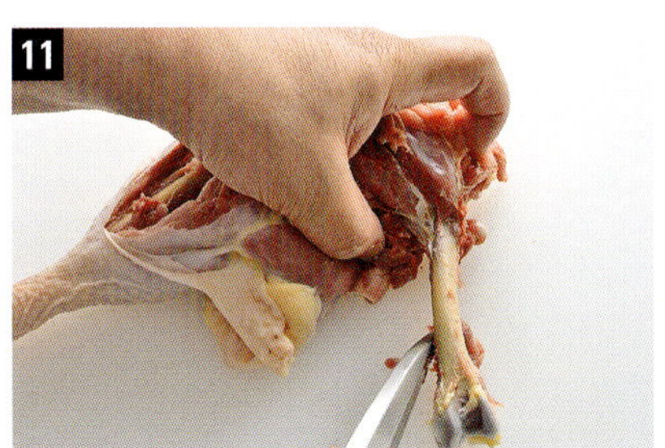

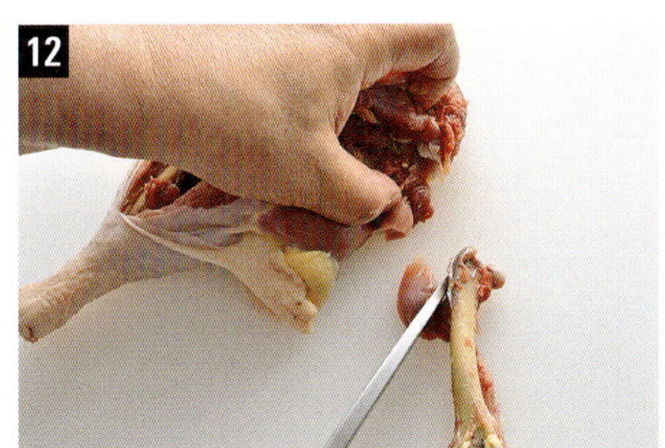

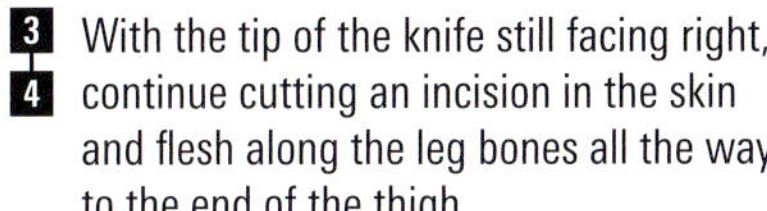

3–**4** With the tip of the knife still facing right, continue cutting an incision in the skin and flesh along the leg bones all the way to the end of the thigh.

5 With your thumb in the incision started in step **2**, scrape the flesh off toward the foot end to reveal the bone.

6 Scrape off the flesh around the femur near its base, detaching the flesh from the bones. Pinning down the flesh with the knife as shown, grip the lower part of the tibia and lift it slightly (as shown).

7 Cut the tendons around the joint and separate the bones at the joint.

8 The two bones separated.

9 Keeping the thumb in the incision made in steps **2** and **3** (as shown), fold back the femur, cut the tendons around the bone, and pry out the end of the bone with the knife tip.

10 Cutting the flesh away from the femur, detach it from the thigh meat.

11 Severing the attachments to the meat, remove the bone.

12 The femur detached from the leg meat.

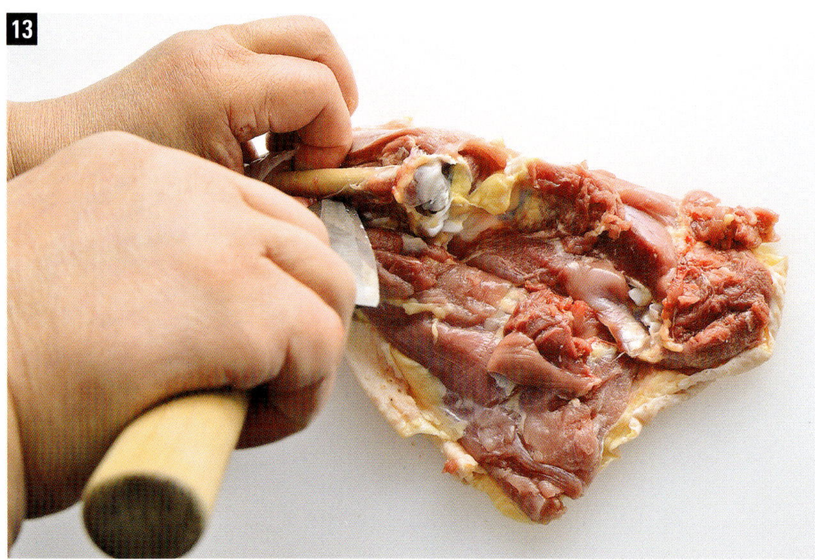

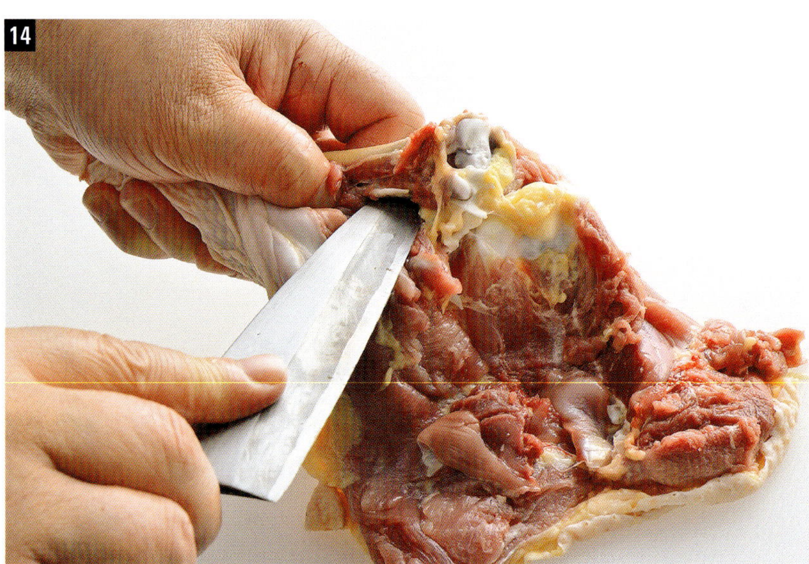

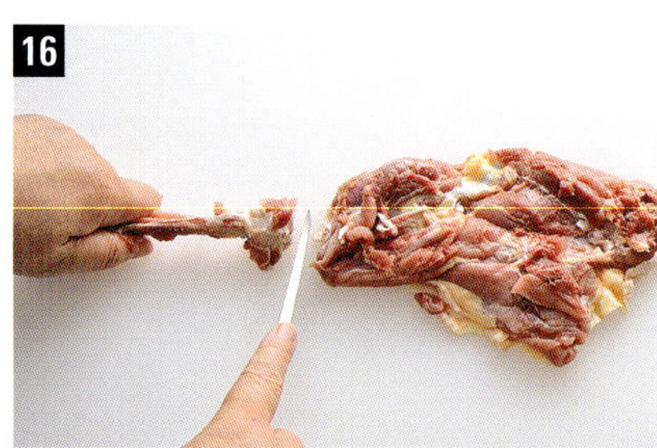

13 With the knife facing right (*sakasabocho*), insert the blade under the tibia toward the foot end.

14 Holding the tibia bone with the left hand, start cutting the flesh away from the bone.

15 Pinning down the flesh with the flat of the knife, as shown, pull up on the tibia bone with the left hand. Insert the knife at the connection between flesh and bone and keep cutting them apart.

16 Turn the tibia over to the left and cut off at the connection between bone and flesh. Detach the femur and tibia bones from the other leg in the same fashion.

17 Leg meat after detaching the bones.

from page 191

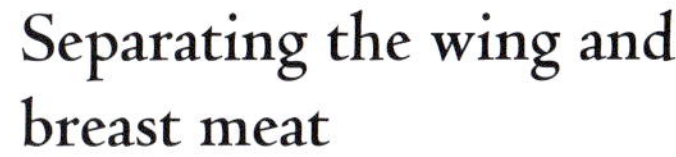

Separating the wing and breast meat

1 Place the right-side wing (and breast meat) with the wing to the left, the underside facing up.

2 With the joint pointing upward, grip the wing tip in the left hand and with the thumb locate the position of the bones. With the blade facing right, insert the knife tip through the skin and under the bone.

3 Pulling with both hands, widen the incision made in step **2**.

4 Insert the tip of the knife into the opening and pry out the bone, stripping the flesh away from it.

5 Holding the bone pried out in step **4** with the left hand, cut apart the flesh and bone.

6 Insert the fingers under the bone and make an opening by inserting the tip of the right-facing knife between the bone and flesh.

7 Fold the wing over the breast meat and hold them together; insert the blade in the opening formed in step **6**.

8 Cut the joint and separate the breast meat from the bone.

9 Place the breast meat with the wing to the left, lift the bone, insert the blade at its base, and cut in. Keep on cutting and detach the wing from the breast meat. Separate the left-side wing and breast meat in the same way.

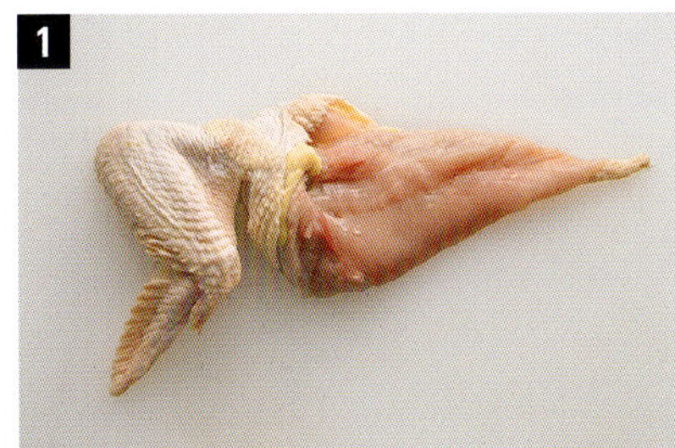

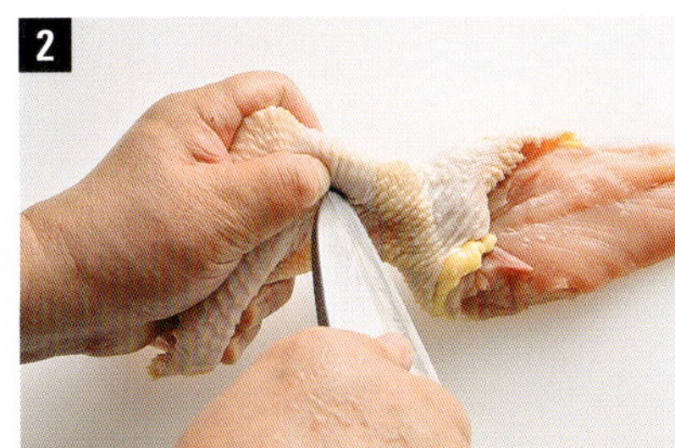

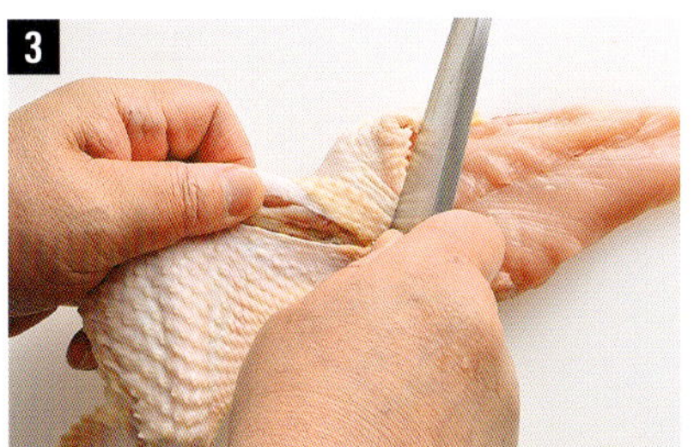

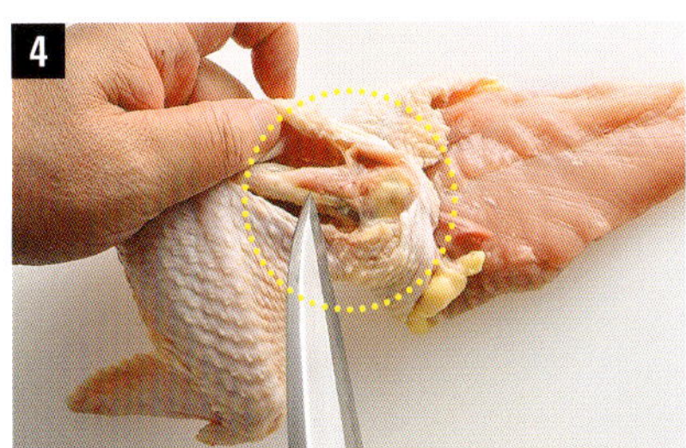

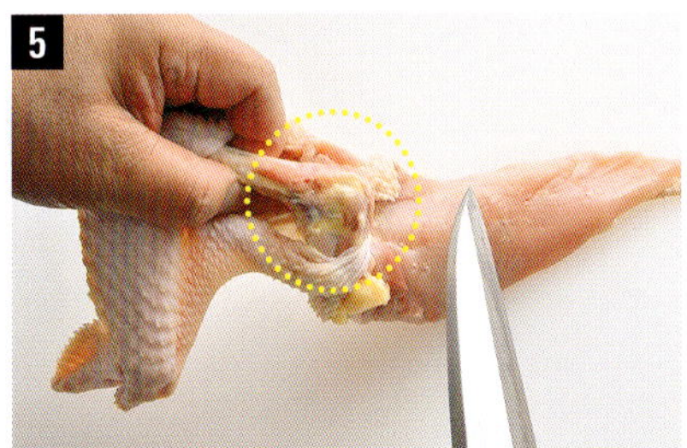

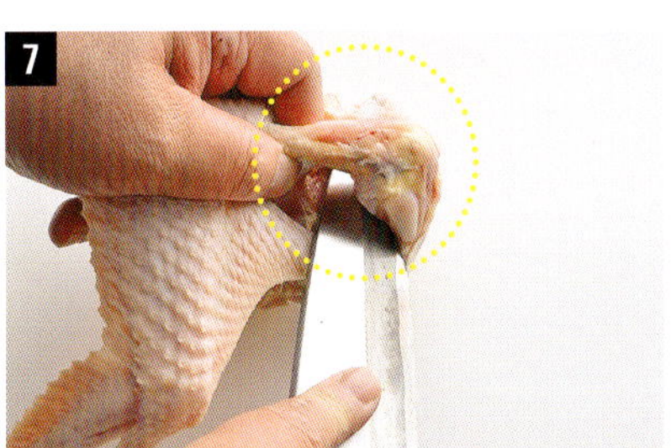

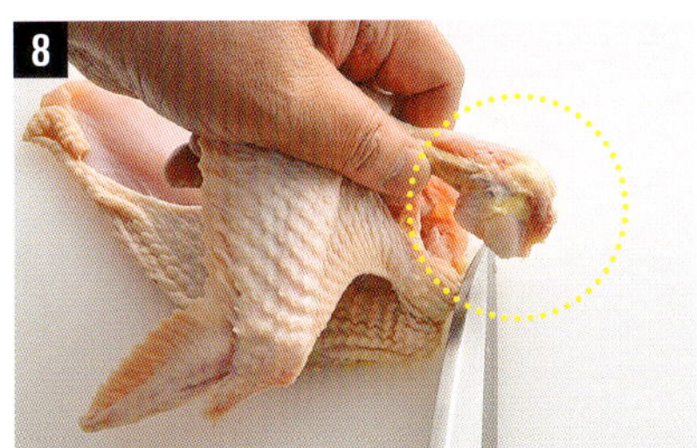

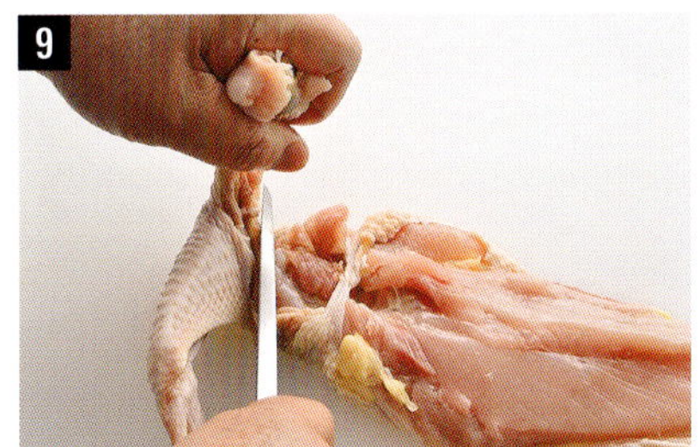

the right wing detached from the breast meat

from page 193

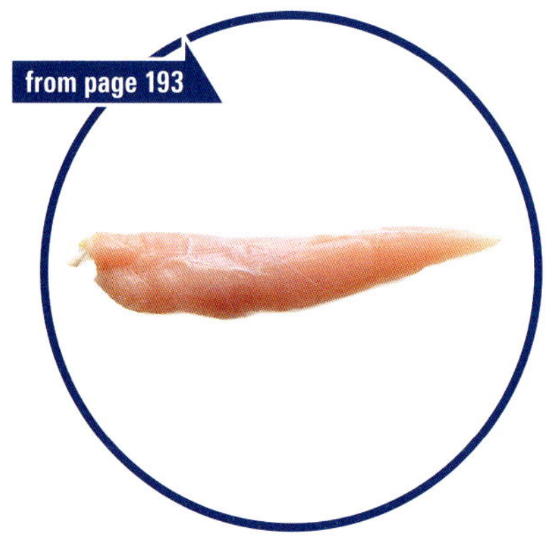

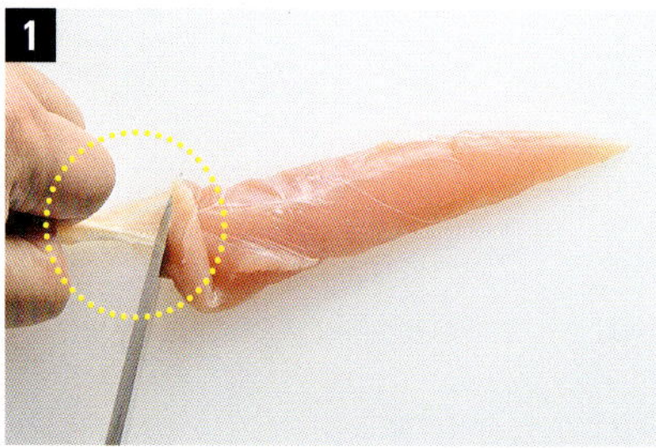

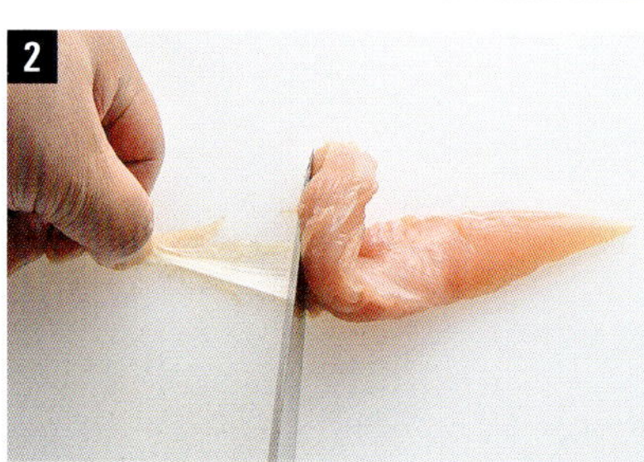

Removing the tendons from the breast fillet

1–2 The tendons attached to the fillet (*sasami*) are very tough, so should be removed. Insert the knife blade between the tendon and the flesh and, with the knife blade, fold the flesh over toward the tip end. While pulling on the tendon with the left hand, detach from the flesh.

the fillet with the removed tendon tissue

Kuwayaki-Style Glazed Chicken

Tori Kuwayaki

Chicken and duck are often used in making *kuwayaki*, a dish consisting of pan-fried meat or vegetables covered with a thin, sweet glaze. Its origins are thought to go back to farmers who would feed themselves in the fields by capturing wild birds and cooking the meat using a hoe (*kuwa*) as a frying pan. The meat is not marinated in this recipe but glazed while cooking.

Serves 4

- 400 g (13⅓ oz.) chicken leg meat
- *Kuwayaki* sauce
  - 60 ml (¼ cup) sake
  - 1 Tbsp. plus 2 tsp. mirin
  - 1 Tbsp. plus 2 tsp. shoyu
  - ½ Tbsp. sugar
- ¼ tsp. powdered *sansho*
- 4 chestnuts
- 2 gardenia (*kuchinashi*) pods, cut in half
- 500ml (about 2 cups)+200 ml (about ¾ cup) water
- 6⅔ Tbsp. sugar
- 4 chrysanthemum leaves

1 Peel the chestnuts and the cut away the bitter skins with attractive cuts. Soak in water for a few hours to remove bitterness before simmering. Place the cut gardenia pods in a saucepan of about 500 ml water over high heat. When water turns bright yellow, add the chestnuts; after water comes to a boil again, cook for 7–8 minutes until the chestnuts turn yellow. Place 200 ml water in a saucepan and add the sugar; place on low heat and, after sugar dissolves, add chestnuts; cook over low heat for 15–20 minutes, covering with a paper towel drop-lid to prevent water from evaporating. Remove from heat and cool in the pan.

2 Mix the sauce ingredients well until the sugar dissolves. Score the surface of only the thickest parts of the leg meat and dust with flour (extra). Heat oil (extra) in a pan and fry meat with the skin side down over medium heat. When well browned, turn over and continue cooking 4 or 5 minutes more. Pour in part of the sauce and spread it over the meat; turning the meat in 2–3 minutes, until well glazed.

3 Slice the cooked chicken into 2-cm (about 1-in.) pieces and serve in a dish, dousing with the remaining sauce. Garnish with a sprinkling of *sansho* powder, a chestnut, and a chrysanthemum leaf.

Kuwayaki-Style Glazed Chicken

sweet simmered chestnut
chrysanthemum leaf
powdered *sansho*

Magamo

MALLARD

Anas platyrhynchos

A member of the family Anatidae (order Anseriformes), the mallard duck (Jp. *magamo*) is the largest of all the wild ducks and has a plentiful amount of meat. With their glossy green heads and white ring around the neck, male birds are called colvert duck (from the French *col-vert*). Their meat has a chewier texture and richer flavor than that of female birds. The latter features thicker fat under the skin as well as softer meat. The meat of both males and females has a strong tinge of red and a distinctive taste. Birds that walk on the ground like chickens have well-developed thighs, but, with birds that fly in the air like ducks, the area from the wing to breast is well developed. The game shooting season is November to February, and mallards migrate to all parts of Japan as winter birds, so their meat is considered best in winter. Most duck on the food market in Japan is farmed *aigamo*, a cross between mallard and domestic duck. In cooking, mainly male hybrid duck is used. Many different breeds have been developed, but the French barbary (Muscovy) duck is most widely marketed.

Duck available in poultry markets is invariably dressed, so there is no need to handle the internal organs. As the head will hinder carving and its feathers harbor bacteria, it should be removed first.

The custom of eating wild birds is very old in Japan, and in the Edo period (1603–1867) mallard duck was a favorite delicacy. In fine Japanese cuisine, the breast meat is mainly used and the leg meat is minced and made into meatballs. Duck becomes dry and tasteless if heated for a long time, so care must be taken to use preparation methods that expose it to heat for the shortest possible time to retain its rich umami flavor.

CARVING MALLARD

Removing the wings and head

1. Place with the legs toward you and the breast side up. With the left hand pull out the right wing and spread out.
2. Insert the *deba* knife at the joint between the upper part (*teba-moto*) of the wing and the outer part (*teba-saki*), or outer part.
3. Cut down and detach the wing at the joint. The wings harbor bacteria, so are not used in cooking.
4. Place with the head toward you, breast-side up, and cut off the left wing in the same manner.
5. With the head facing to the right, cut off the head at its base, as shown.

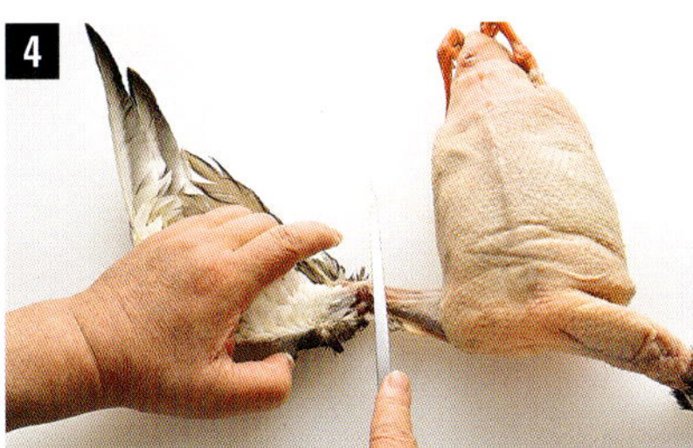

duck with head and wings removed

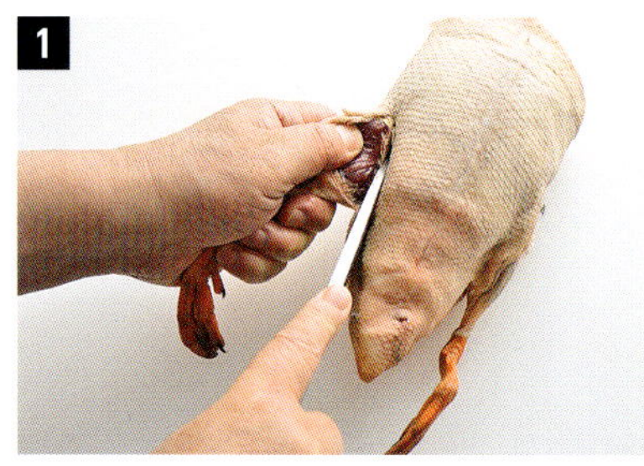

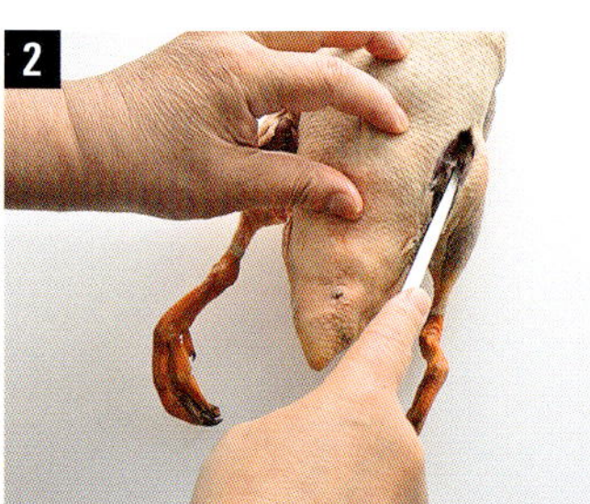

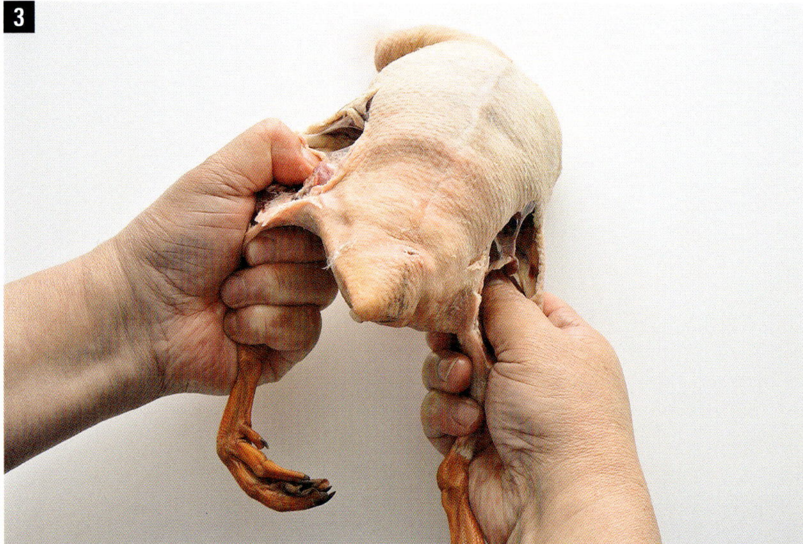

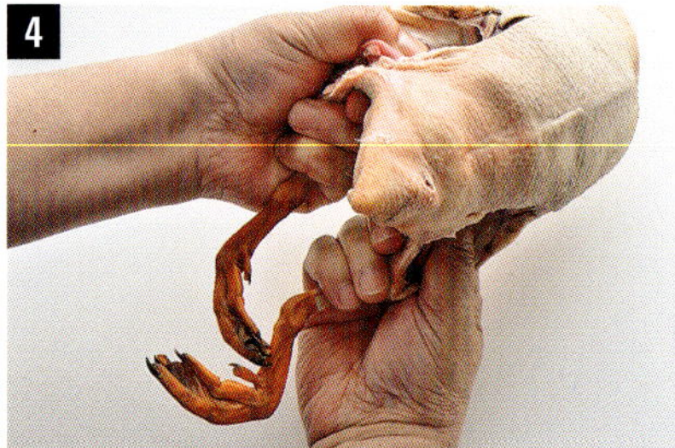

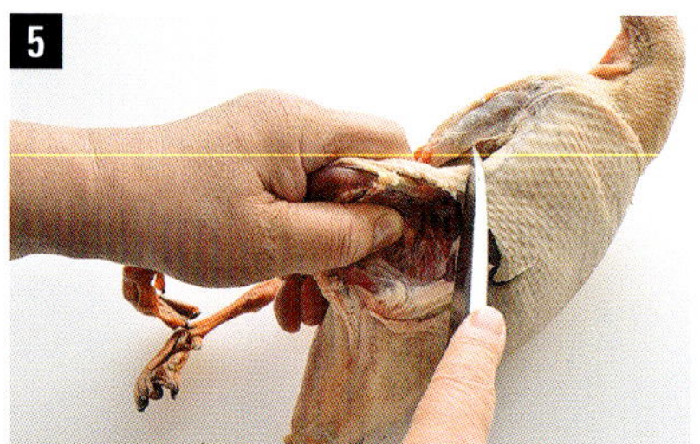

Removing the legs

1 Place the bird with the breast side up, legs toward you. Position the knife at the base of the bird's right leg and draw the blade toward you, cutting through the skin at the base of the thigh.

2 Likewise, cut through the skin of the left thigh.

3 Using both hands, grip the thighs, insert the thumbs into the incisions made in steps 1 and 2, and locate the joints.

4 Fold the thighs back over the spine, forcing the thigh bone out of the joint on each side.

5 Placing the breast side to the right, insert left thumb into the incision made in step 1, grasp the base of the right thigh, and make an incision in the skin, as shown.

6–7 Pulling out the thigh with the left hand, cut through the joint and surrounding skin and muscles. Pulling the leg away, cut through the skin, and separate the right leg from the breast meat.

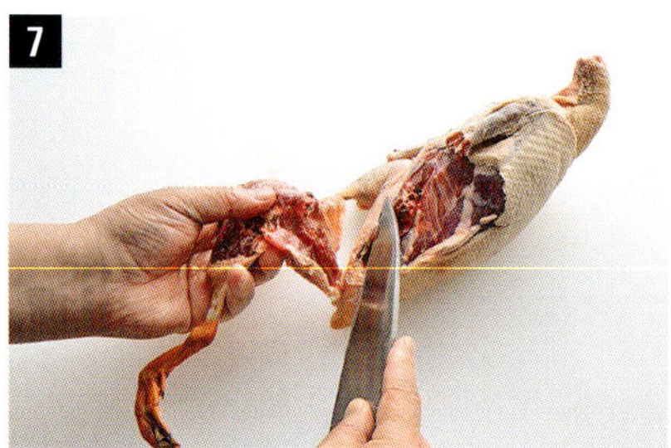

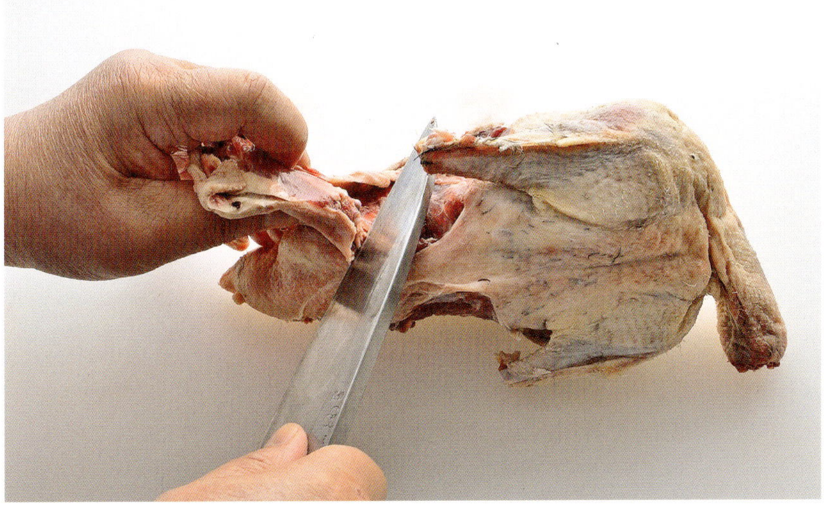

8 Place the head end to the right and the spine toward you. Lift up the left thigh with the left hand.

9 Make an incision in the skin at the base of the thigh.

10 Cut through the joint and surrounding skin and muscle in the same way as described in steps **6** and **7**, and detach the left thigh.

Detach the base of the wing and the breast meat

1–**2** To remove the breast meat from the body with the upper wing attached, place the head end away from you, breast side facing you. Make an incision from the base of the neck down the center of the breast, cutting along the left side of the breastbone. Cut the incision all the way to the base of the tail.

3 With the head end to the right and breast side facing you, place the knife over the joint at the end of the right wing bone.

4 Cut in around the joint.

5 Insert the left thumb into the incision made in step **4** and open it out as shown. Cut the joint and surrounding skin and muscles, and detach the joint.

6 Cut the skin from the base of the wing joint to the spine, connecting with the cut made in step **1**.

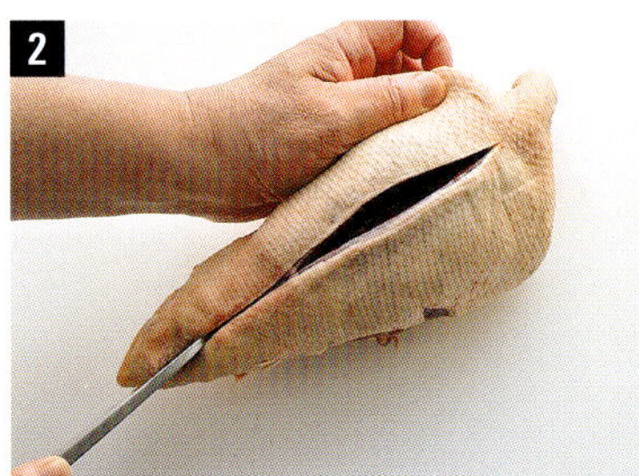

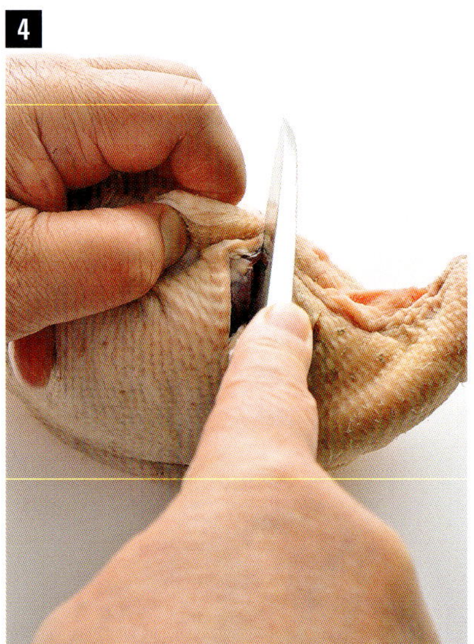

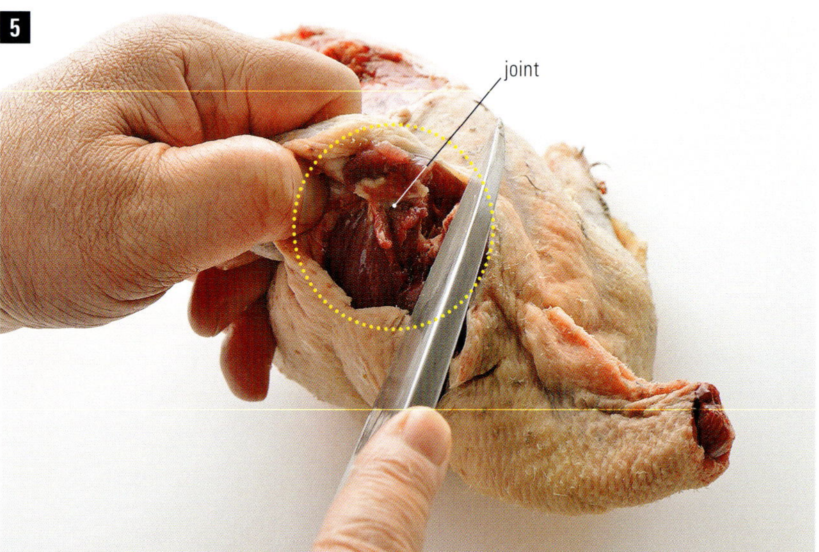

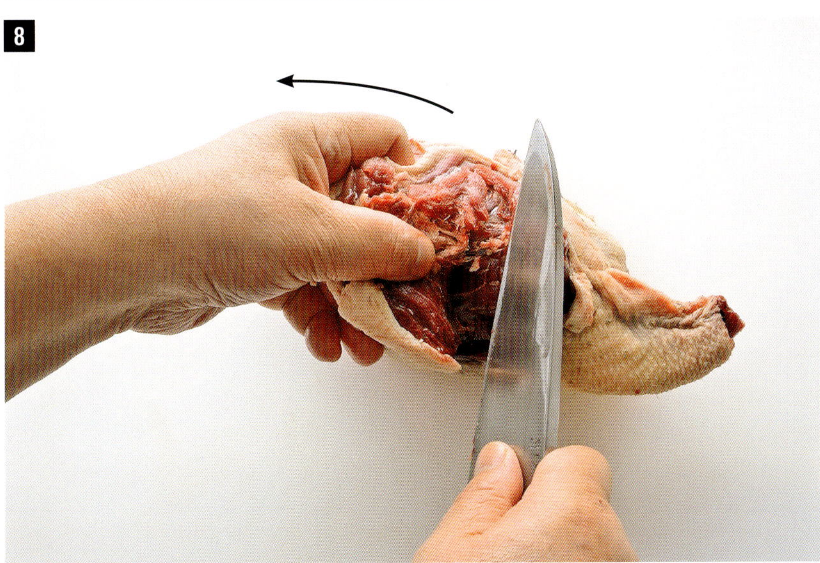

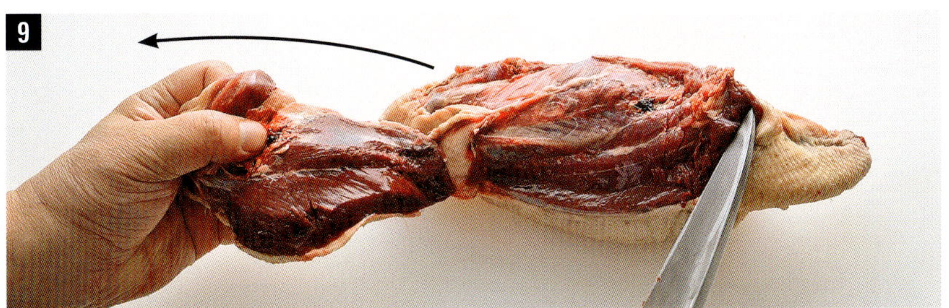

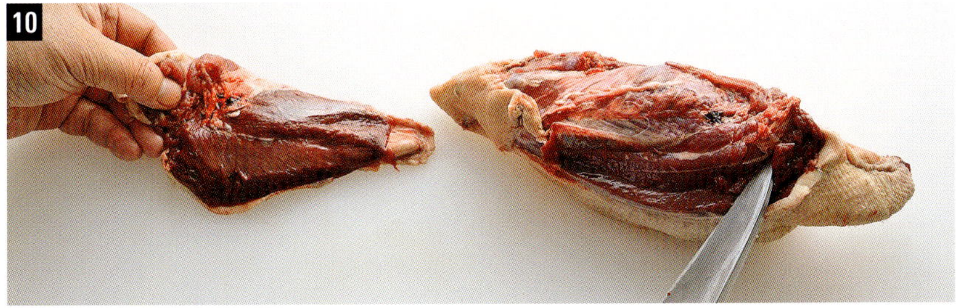

7 With the blade turned to the right, make an incision in the skin on the spine side at the base of the wing.

8 Steadying the shoulder of the bird with the knife blade, grip the upper wing with the left hand and pull, as indicated by the arrow.

9 Keep pulling, detaching the breast meat along with the upper wing from the body.

10 The breast meat with the wing base attached, separated from the body.

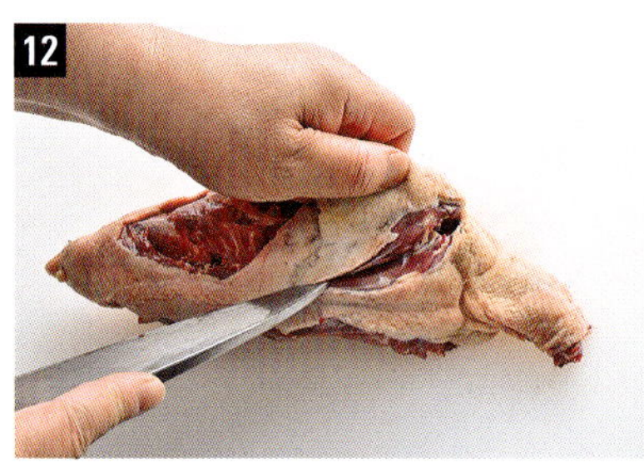

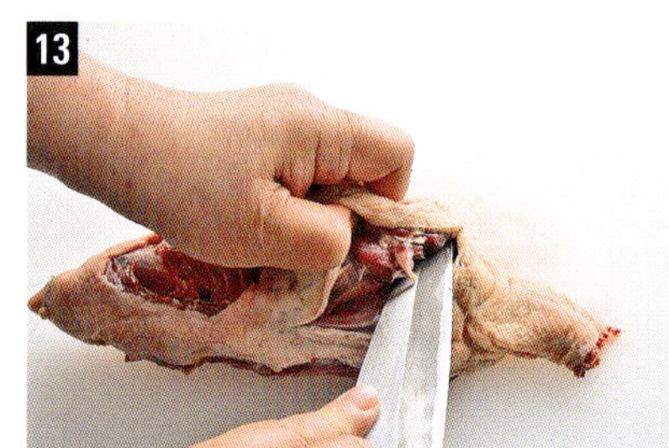

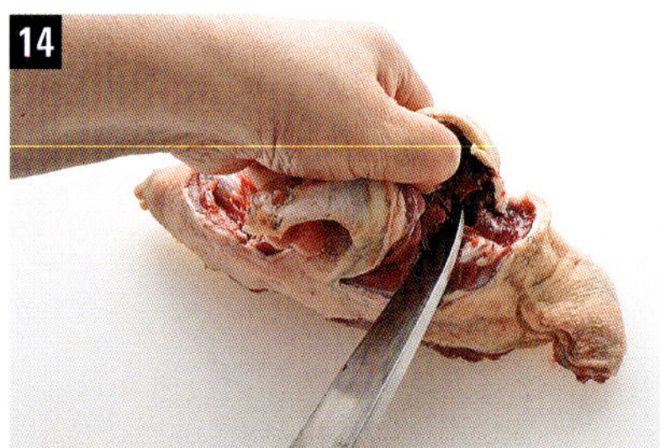

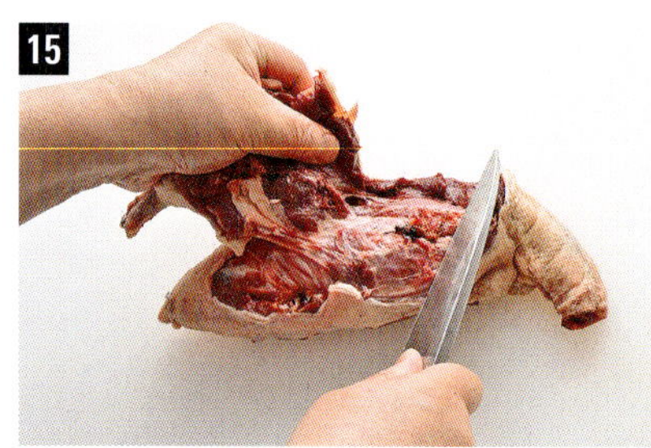

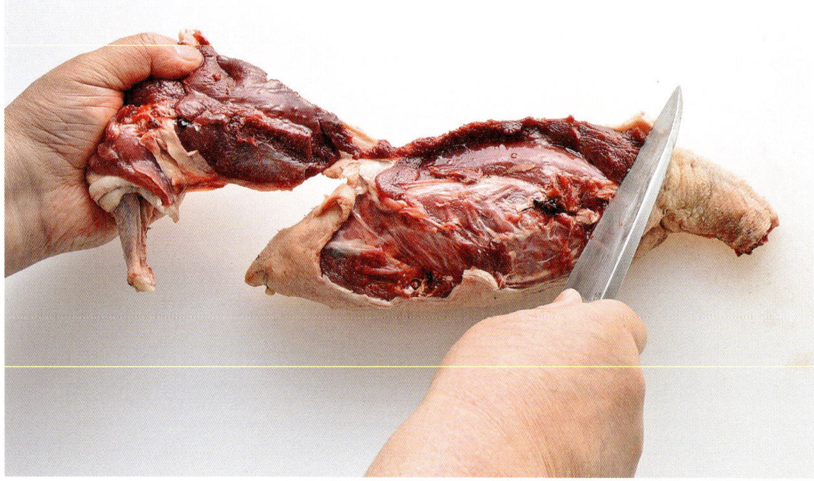

11 To detach the base of the left wing and breast meat, place the bird with the head end to the right and the spine facing you. Lift up the wing, locate the joint, and position the knife over the joint.

12 Cut under the scapula (*kenkokotsu*; see p. 29), and cut an incision down toward the tail, up to the middle of the body.

13 Turning the blade to the right, make an incision at the upper wing on the breast side.

14 With the left hand, lift up the wing as shown, and cut the skin and muscles around the joint to detach the joint. Reinsert the knife at the base of the wing and start cutting away the breast meat and wing base from the body.

15–**16** Steadying the shoulder of the bird with the knife blade, grasp the upper wing with the left hand and pull. Keep pulling and detach the upper wing and breast meat from the body.

Detaching the breast fillets

1. To detach the pair of breast fillets located on the breastbone, place the head end away from you, breast side down. Position the tip of the knife at the connection between the base of the fillet at the neck end and the ribs.
2. Turn the knife so the blade faces up and cut the tendon attaching the fillet to the body at the head end.
3. Insert the knife at the end where the fillet has been detached in step 2 and cut along the ribs all the way to the tail.
4. Pin the end of the tendon cut in step 3 to the cutting board with the tip of the knife (as shown) and, gripping the bird at the shoulder, pull from the fillet.
5. Pull until the fillet is completely detached.

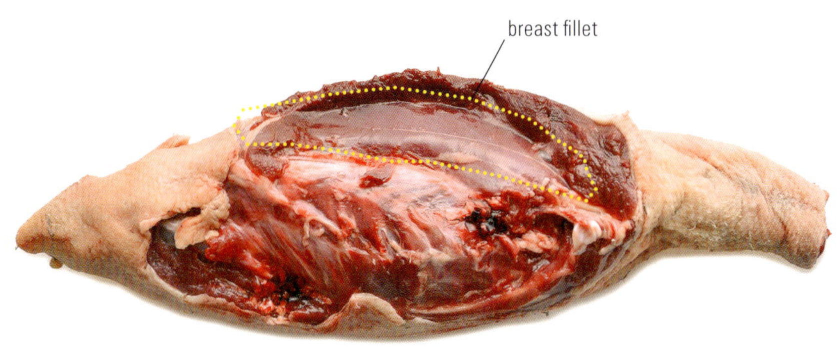

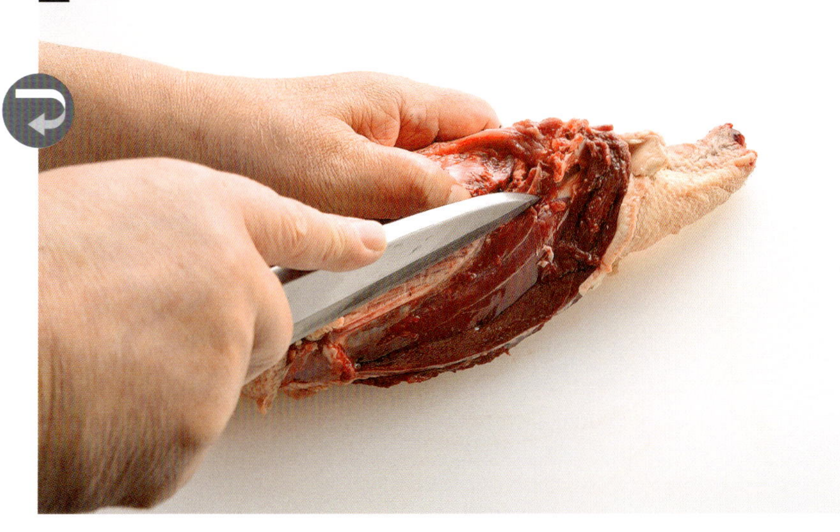

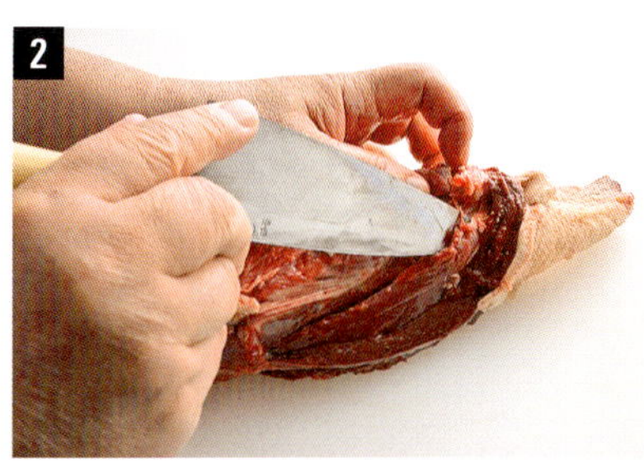

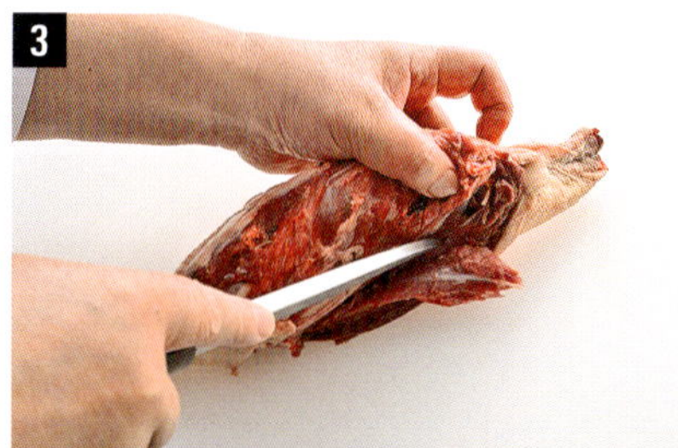

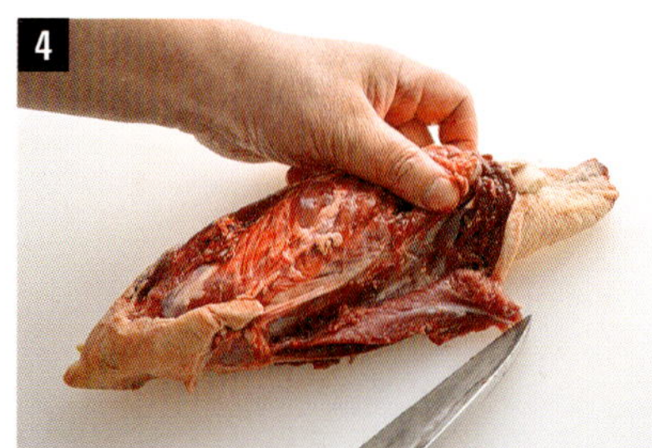

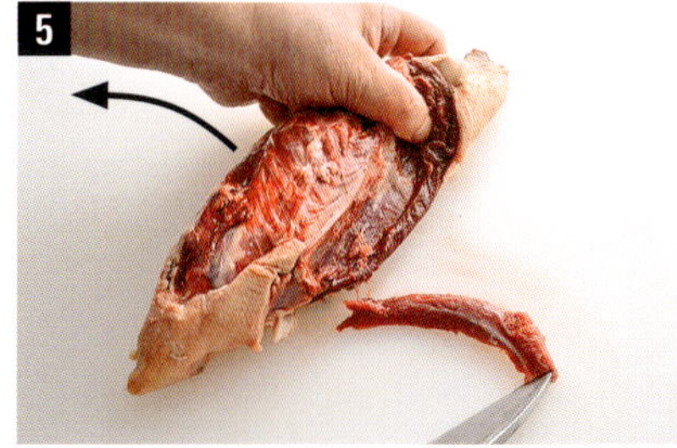

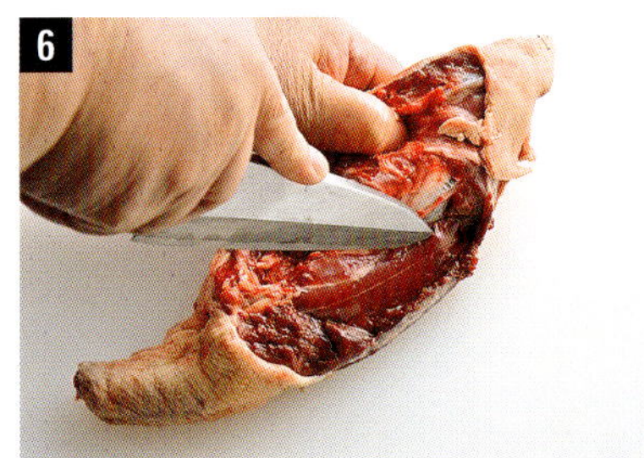

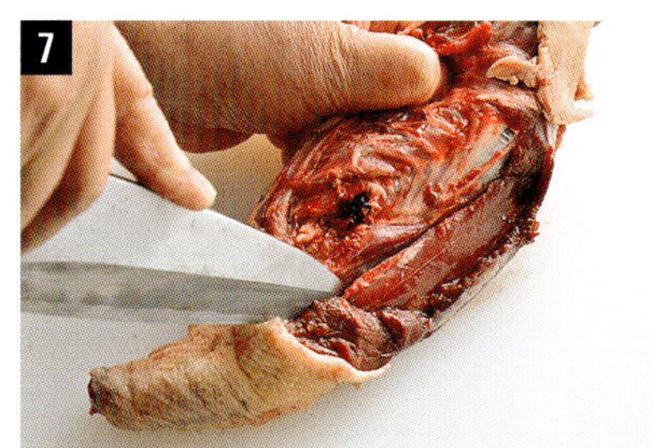

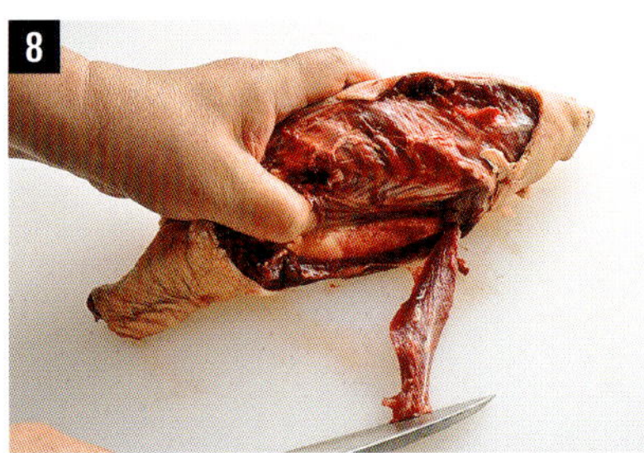

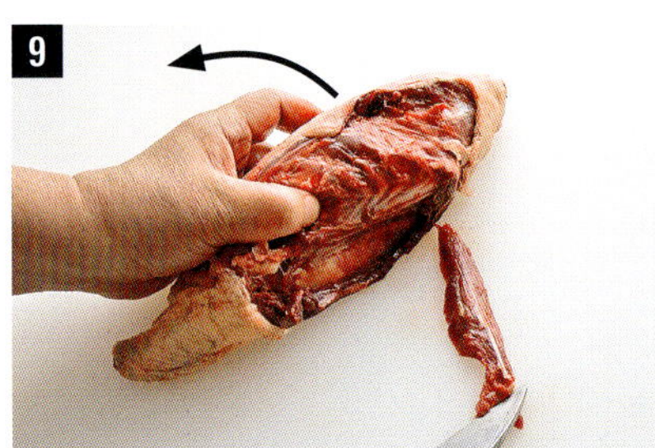

6 To remove the fillet on the opposite side. turn the body, positioning the head toward you. With the tip of the knife, cut through the connection between the fillet and the ribs.

7 Insert the knife where the connection is cut off in step **6** and start cutting the fillet away from the ribs in the direction of the head.

8 Cut the tendon attaching the fillet to its base at the neck and hold down the end of the tendon with the tip of the knife (as shown).

9 Pull the body away from the fillet and separate the two completely.

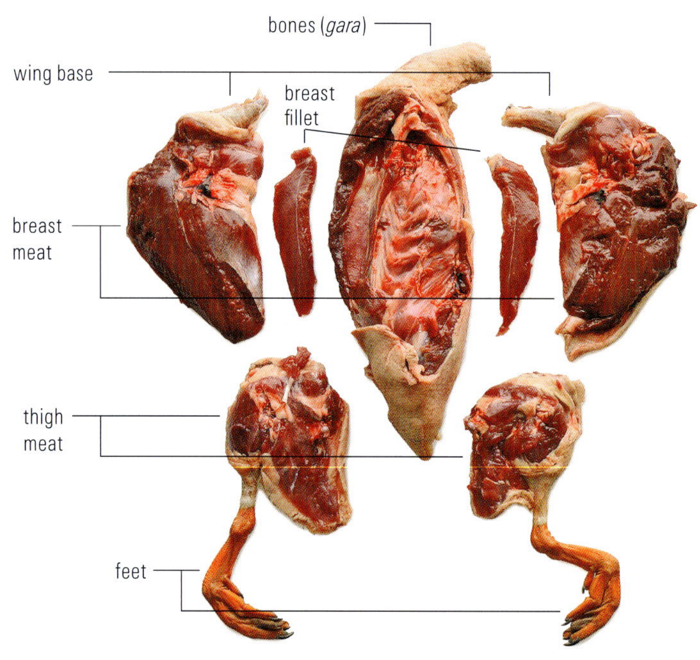

Steamed Duck Breast *Kamo Rosu*

Duck breast has very firm and substantial as well as soft meat and with a moderate amount of fat and a strong, savory flavor. The skin side is pan fried to bring out the aroma of the meat and remove excess fat. Here we smother the meat in a sweet-salty broth. The flavors permeate the meat, so all that is needed is a dab of mustard as a condiment.

Serves 5-6

2 duck breasts (500–600 g or about 1½ lbs.)

Steaming broth

- 360 ml (1½ cups) sake
- 3 Tbsp. *koikuchi* shoyu
- About 1 Tbsp. *usukuchi* shoyu
- 1⅔ Tbsp. sugar
- 2⅔ Tbsp. *karashi* mustard

1 Remove the tendons and excess fat and score the skin (not cutting as far as the flesh) with 1-cm (½-in.) cross-hatching.

2 Heat the frying pan over low heat and place the breasts in the pan, skin down. Fry over low heat to release excess fat until the surface is crispy and aromatic. Soak up excess fat in the pan frequently with a paper towel. Fry only the skin, taking care not to heat the meat,

3 Combine the broth ingredients and place over high heat to release the alcohol. Then cool.

4 In a zip-lock vacuum bag, place one duck breast each along with 150 ml (scant ⅔ cup) of the steaming broth, and steam for one hour at 136°F (58°C). Then cool.

5 Slice into 7–8 mm (about ⅓-in.) pieces and serve with *karashi* mustard.

Steamed Duck Breast

karashi mustard

Uzura
QUAIL
Coturnix japonica

A member of the family Phasianidae (order Galliformes), the quail (*uzura*) is small, about 20 centimeters in length. Its wings are light brown and turn even paler in winter. The species of quail that is a traditional game bird familiar to Japanese since olden times is listed as a vulnerable species that faces a high risk of extinction in the wild. Since its hunting is prohibited, almost all quail sold for food are farmed. The farming of quail in Japan is largely for the purpose of egg production, and most of the quail raised for meat is imported from Europe. Male quail reach 160 to 200 grams (internal organs removed) in about 70 days, and females 200 to 250 grams. The females begin to lay eggs 80 to 90 days after they hatch, and their meat immediately before that is said to be tender and best suited for eating.

The quail's body is small, so it is usually butterflied instead of carved into its different parts. Before splitting, sear the flesh lightly to burn off the remaining pin feathers. Whole quail on the market are sold defeathered and gutted, but the esophagus remains. So, when the head is cut off, the aesophagus should also be removed. Compared with chicken, quail meat is firmer—all the firmer because of its small size—and is rich in flavor and pleasant to the palate. The butterflied bird is served broiled and the like, and the bones, which may be thin and soft, are pounded together with the meat to make meatballs (*dango*; *gan*).

CARVING QUAIL

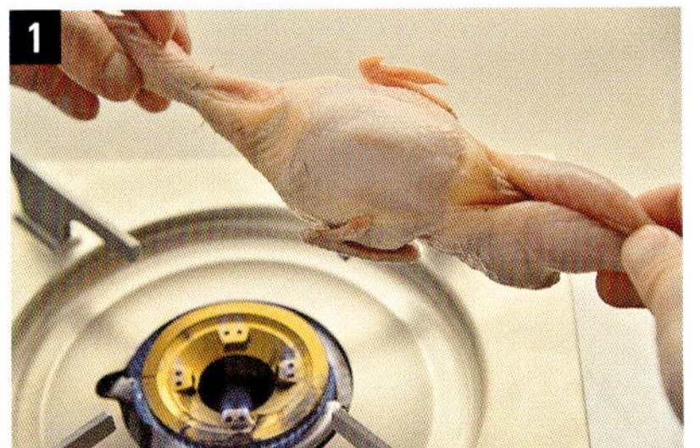

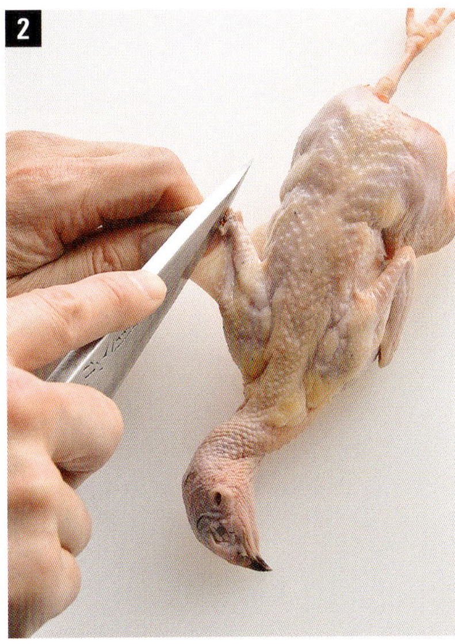

Sear off the pin feathers and remove the wings

1. Holding the bird by the legs and head, burn off the remaining feathers.
2. Place with the head toward you, spine side up. Pull out the right wing and insert the knife at the joint between the wing and the wing base.
3. Cut right through the joint, detaching the wing.
4. Place with the head toward you, breast side up and cut off the left wing.

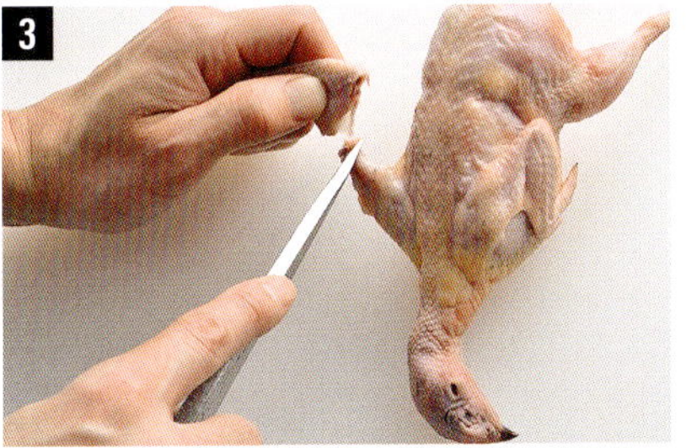

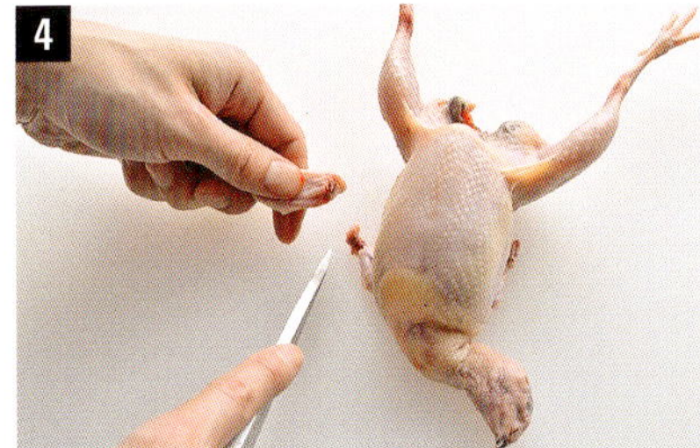

Remove the head and esophagus

1. Place the head to the right, spine toward you. Hold the base of the neck with the left hand and make an incision just behind the eyes.
2. Cut down through neck and locate the esophagus.
3. With the left hand holding the neck, pin the head with the knife blade and pull the neck, separating the head from the neck (as shown).
4. The head and esophagus separated from the neck.

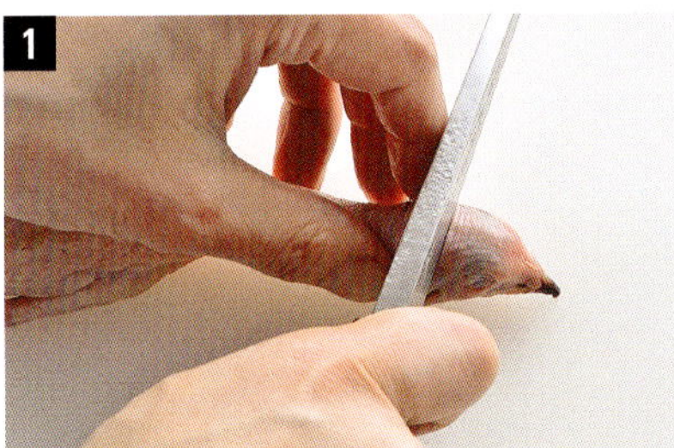

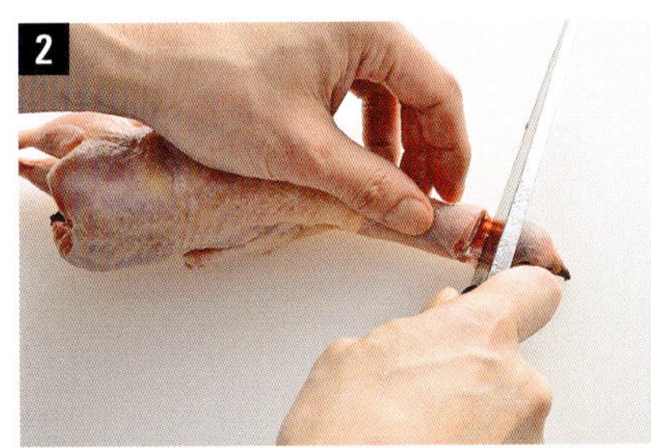

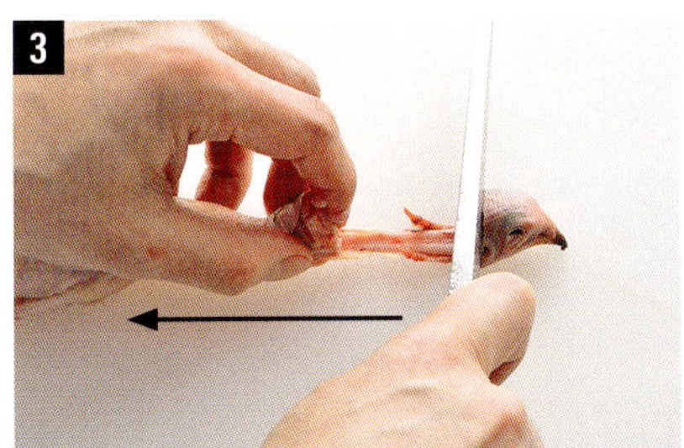

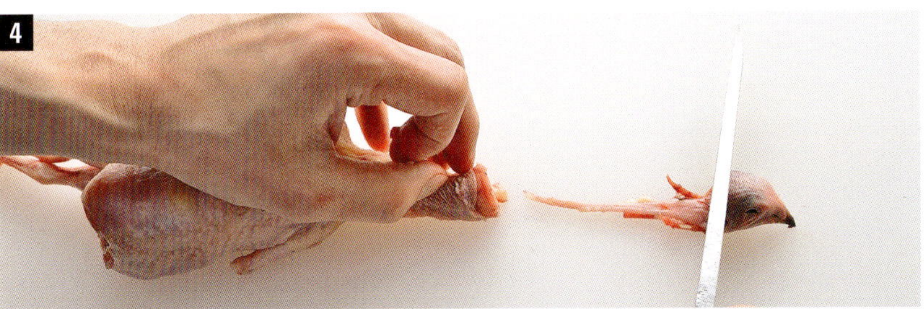

Butterflying quail

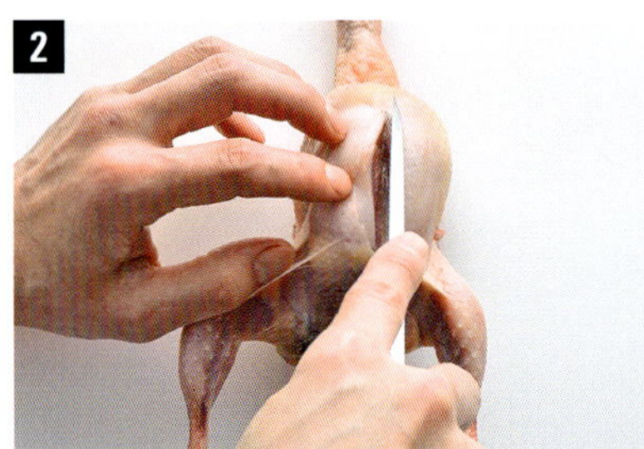

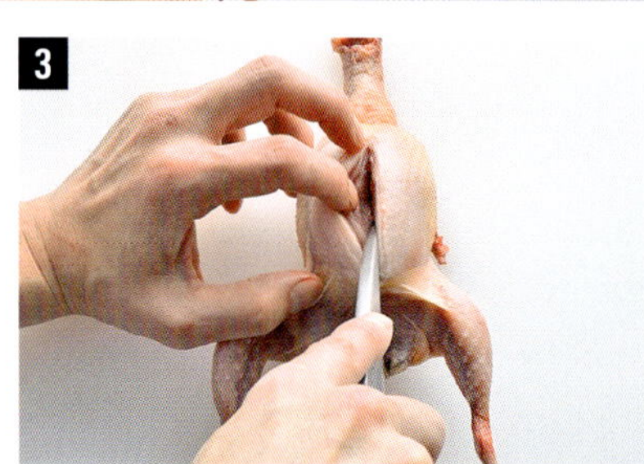

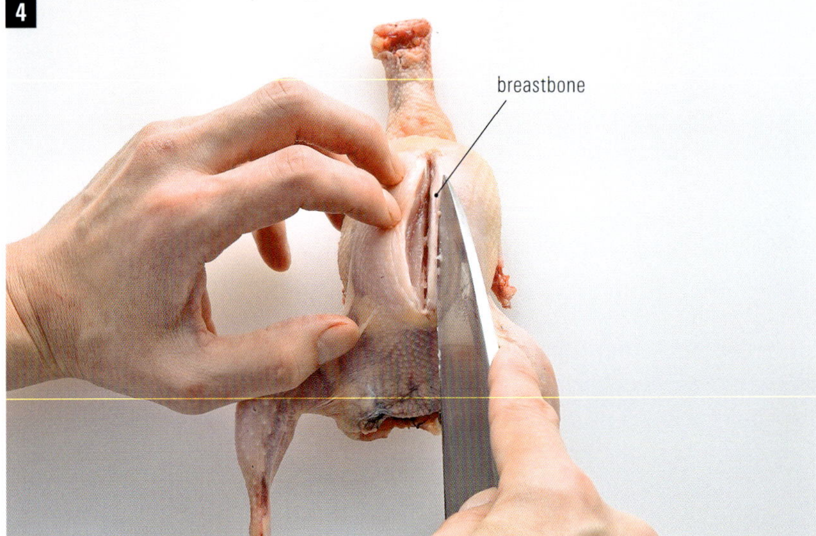

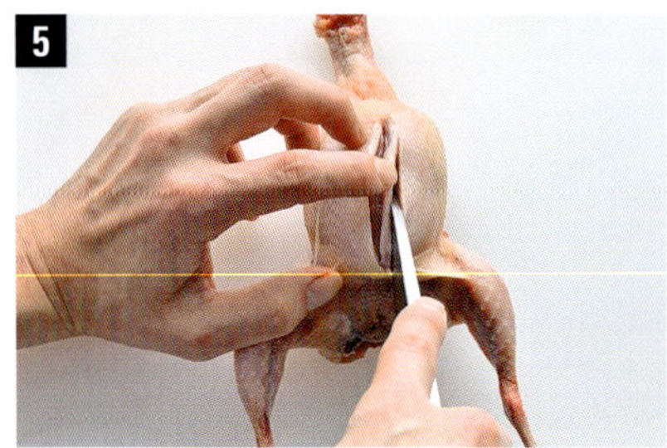

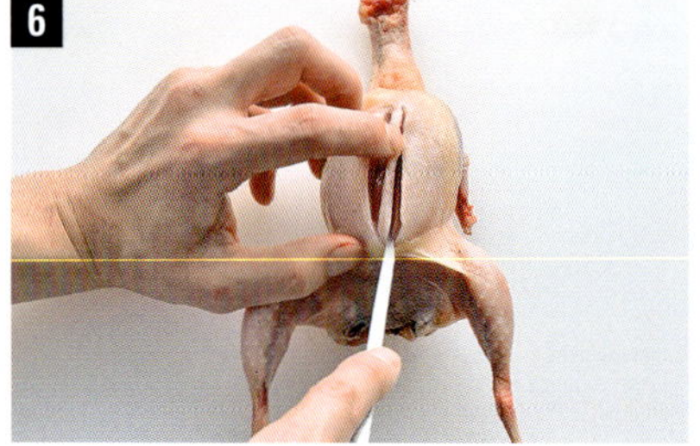

1 Place the bird with the legs toward you, breast side up. Position the *deba* blade along the center line at the base of the neck, just to the left of the breastbone.

2 Draw the knife toward you, making an incision along the breastbone.

3 Pull back the opening with the fingers of the left hand to get a clear view, reinsert the blade in the incision made in step **2**, and deepen the cut from the breastbone down to the rib bones.

4 Place the knife along the right side of the breastbone.

5 Draw the blade toward you, making an incision along the right side of the breastbone, as in step **2**.

6 Reinsert the tip of the knife in the incision made in step **5** and deepen the cut from the breastbone down to the rib bones.

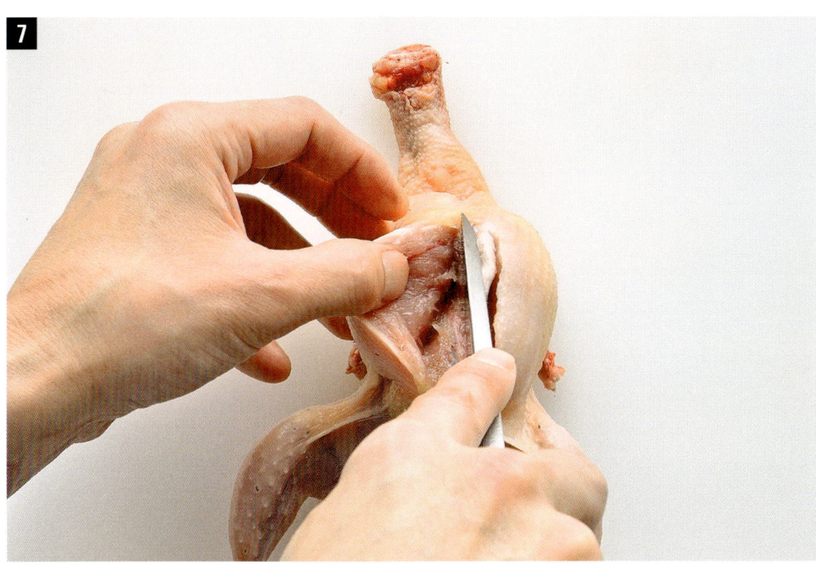

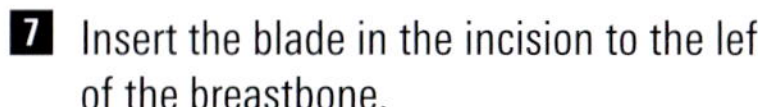

7 Insert the blade in the incision to the left of the breastbone.

8 Cut in over the rib bones visible beneath the breastbone.

9 Reinsert the knife in the incision made in step 8 and draw it gently toward you to cut the meat away from the rib bones.

10 Cut down to the base of the joint of the bird's right leg.

11 Insert the blade at the joint at the end of the right wing bone and separate the bones at the joint.

12 Cut the muscles around the joint.

13 As in steps 11 and 12, separate the bones of the joint of the right leg and cut the muscles around the joint.

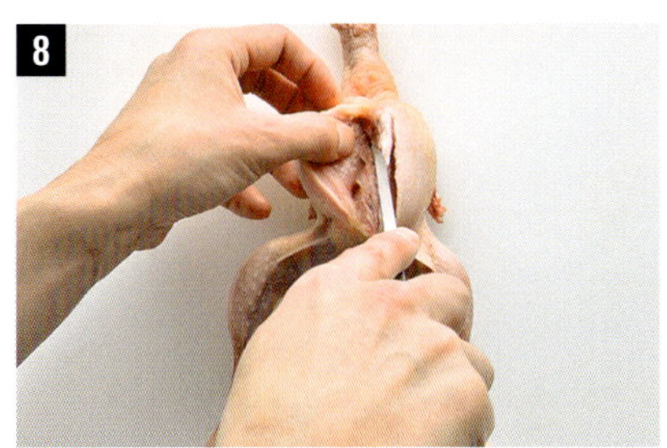

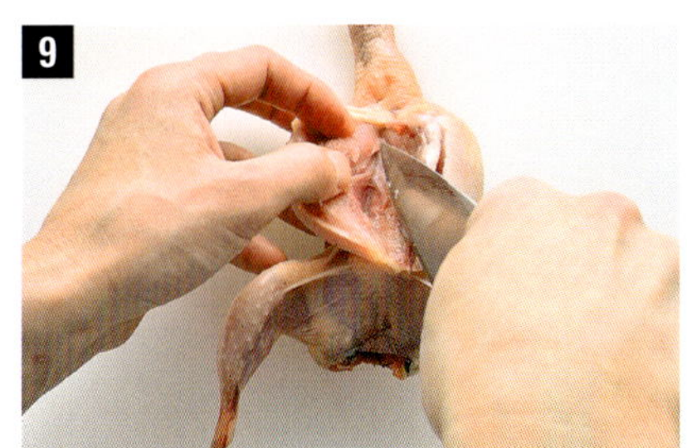

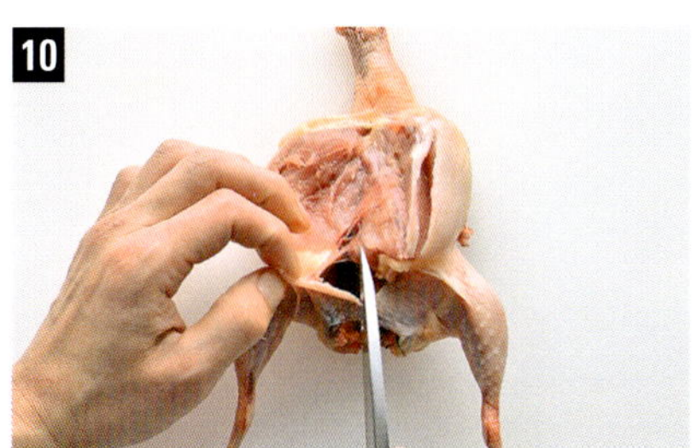

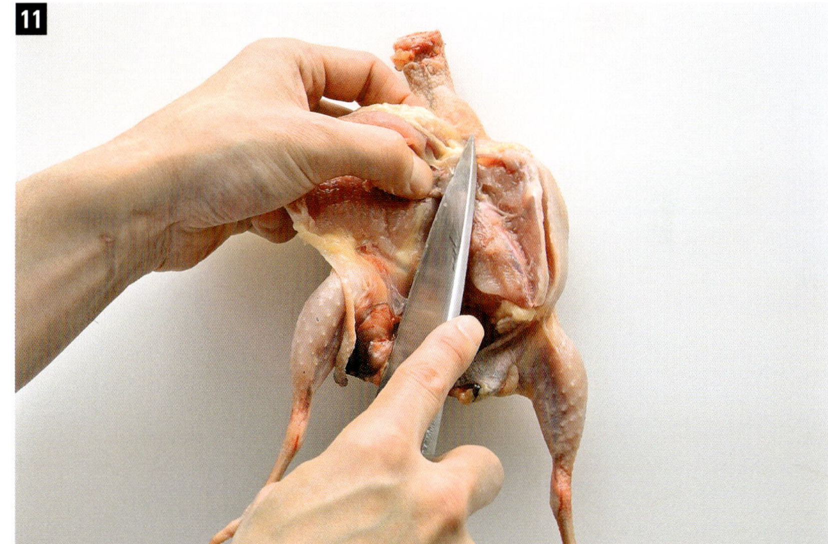

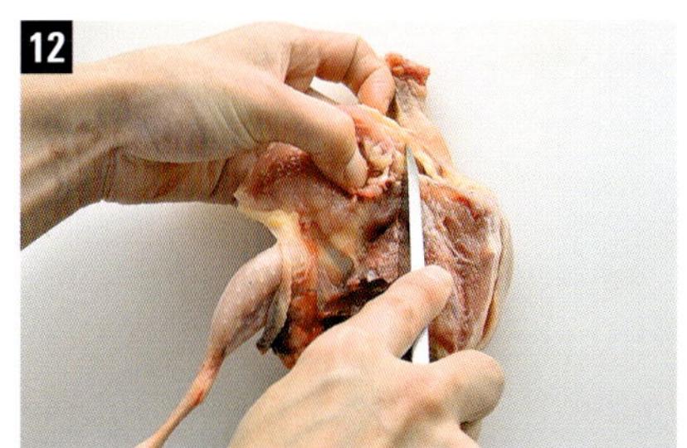

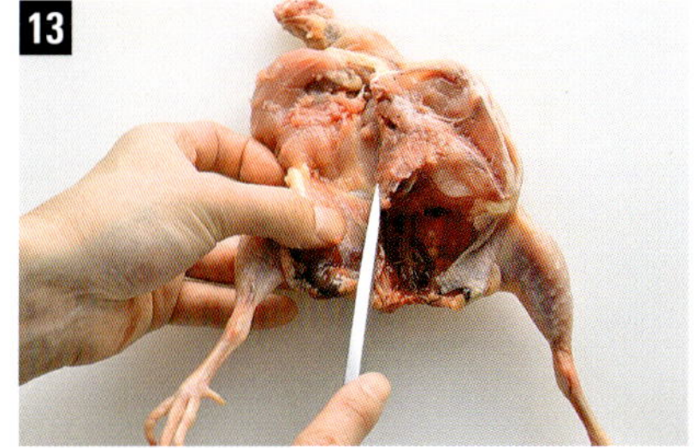

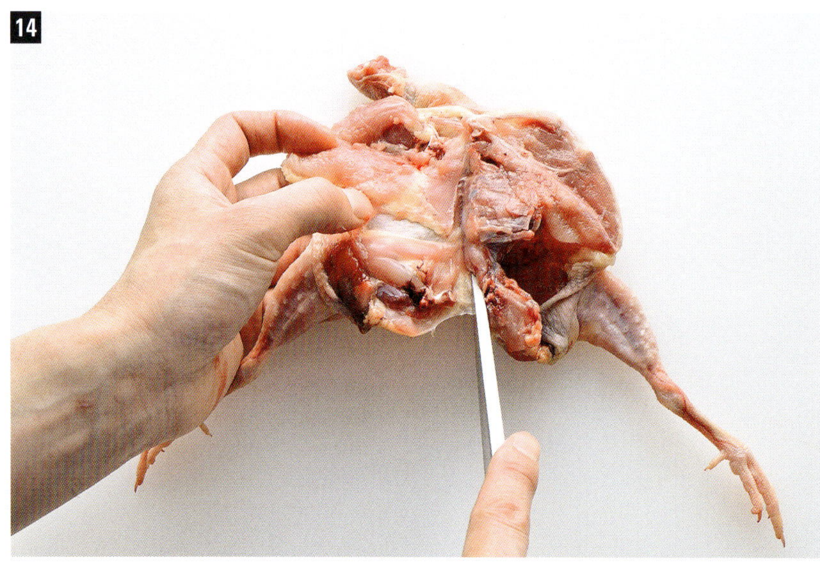

14

14 Make an incision from the base of the leg along the rib cage, making several passes with the knife until the meat on the spine side is separated from the rib bones.

15 Turn the bird so that the head end is facing you.

16 Insert the knife in the incision made in step **5**.

17 Cut toward the head end along the ribs beneath the breastbone.

18 Reinsert the blade in the incision made in step **17** and draw it gently toward you to cut the meat away from the rib bones.

19 Insert the blade at the joint at the base of the bird's left wing bone and separate the bones of the joint.

20 Cut the muscles around the joint.

21 Insert the tip of the blade in the joint at the base of the the bird's left leg and cut to separate the bones of the joint.

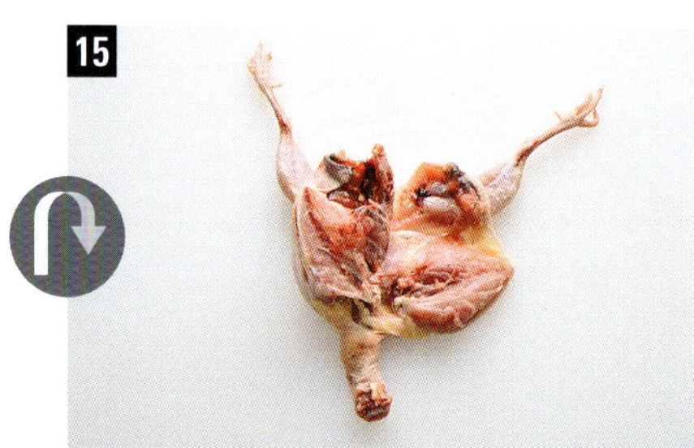

15

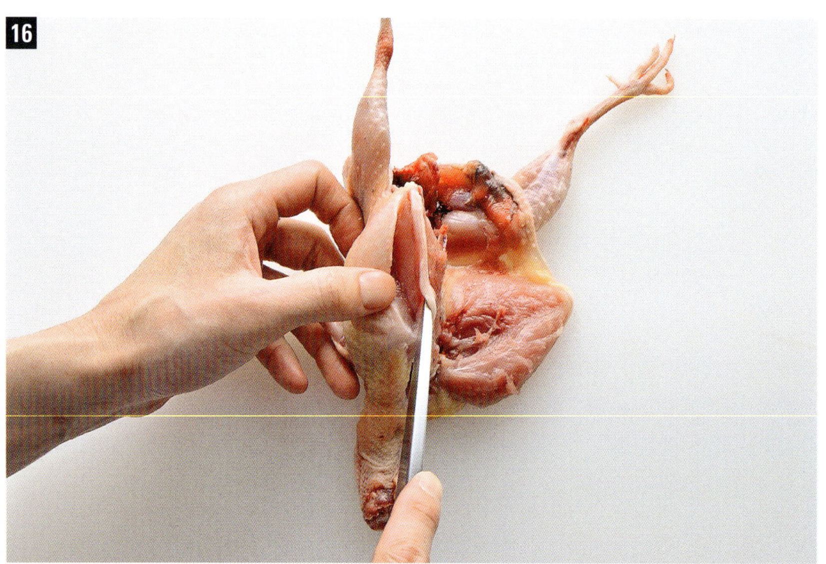

16

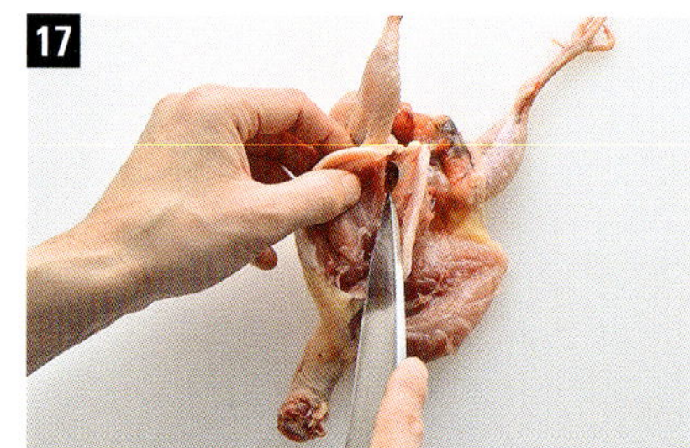

17

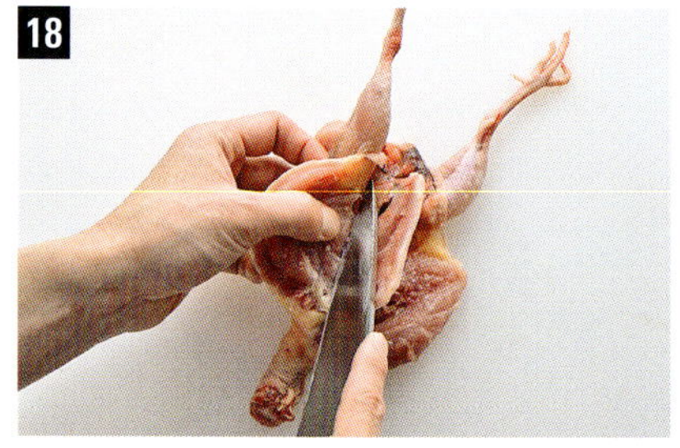

18

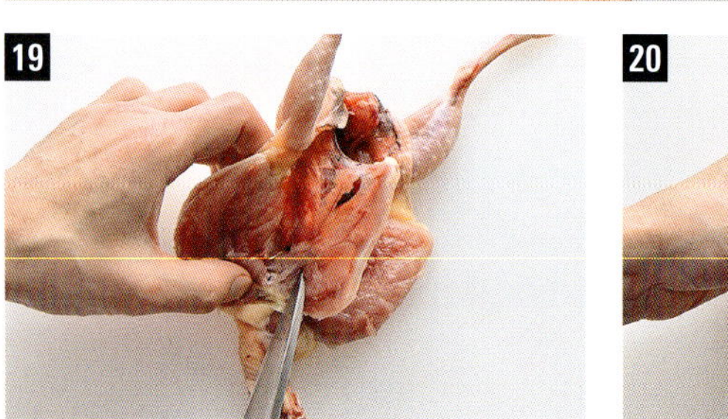

19

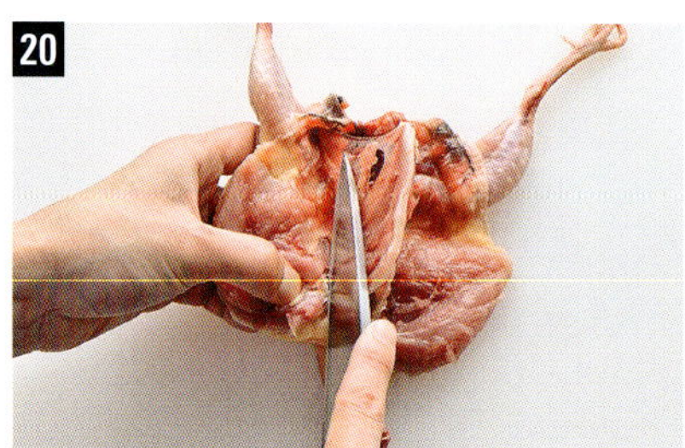

20

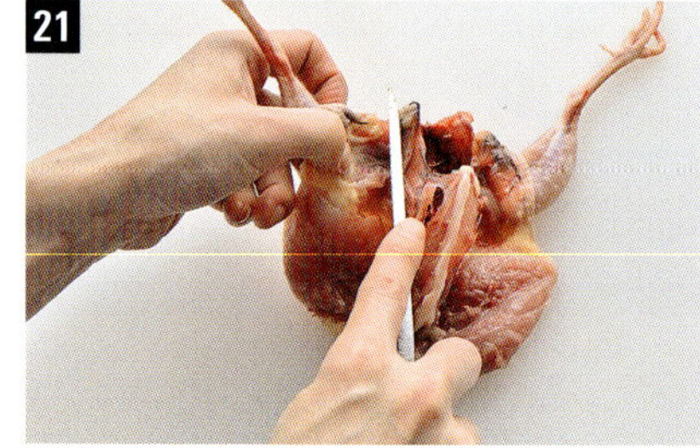

21

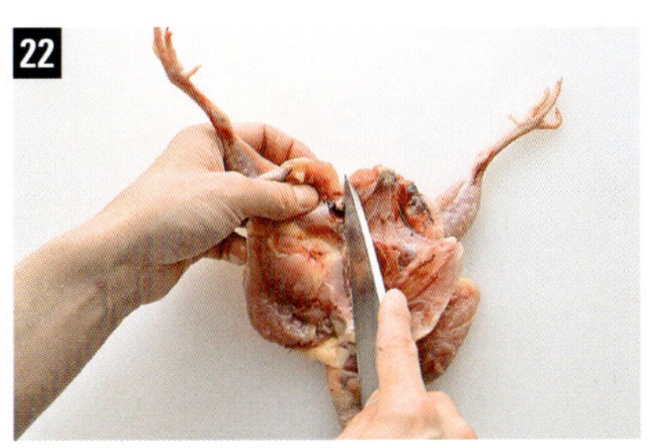

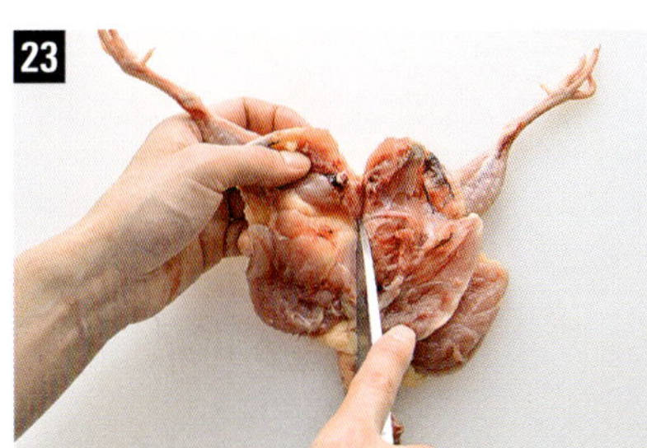

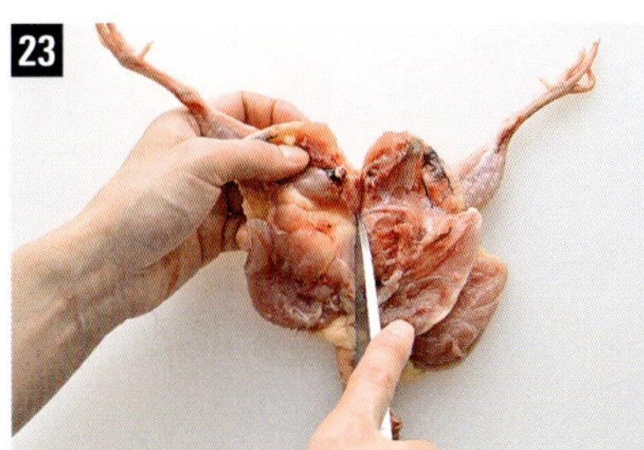

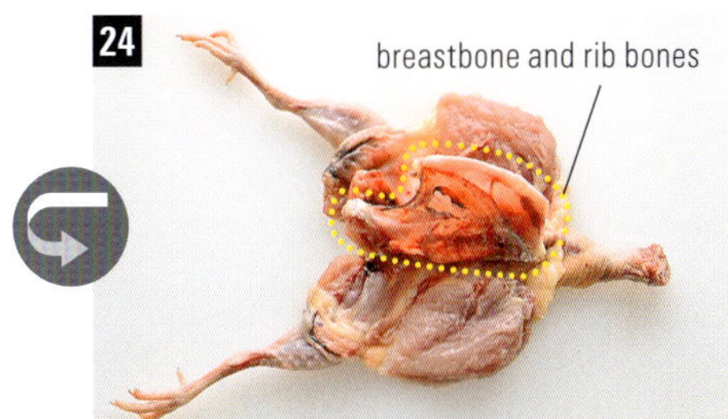

25

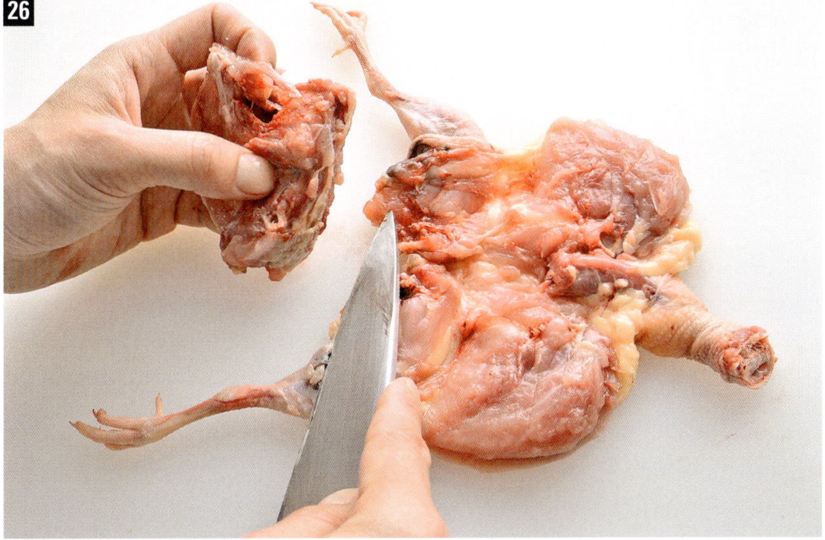

22 Cut the muscles around the joint.

23 Insert the knife from the base of the leg meat to the base of the rib bones. Drawing the knife toward the head end in several passes, cut in to separate the meat at the neck end from the rib bones.

24 Place the head end to the right, breast side up.

25 Gripping the rib bones with the left hand and lifting them, position the knife at the base of the rib bones at a low angle. Cut under the rib bones, separating them from the breast meat.

26 The rib bones and breastbone removed together, and the butterflied bird.

Removing the bones from the thigh meat

1. Place the butterflied bird with the cut surface up and the legs to the left, as shown.
2. Steady the bird's left leg and insert the tip of the knife on the inside of the bone at the joint between the leg and the foot, as shown
3. Continue the cut along the inside of the bone to the end near the base of the thigh.
4. Cut as in step 3 also along the outside of the bone, to expose the bone.
5. Separate the joint between the two leg bones (femur and tibia)

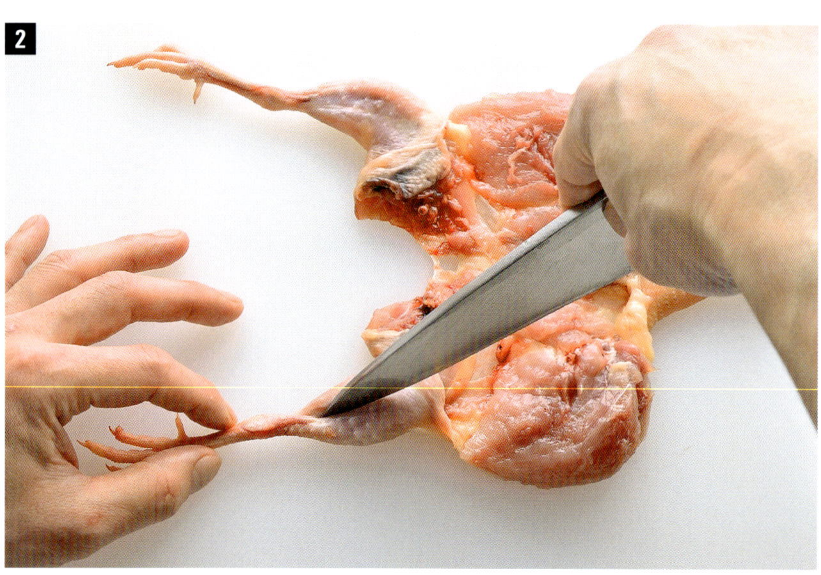

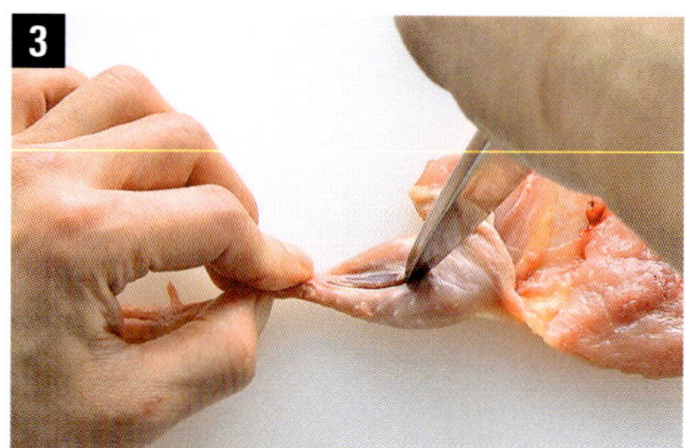

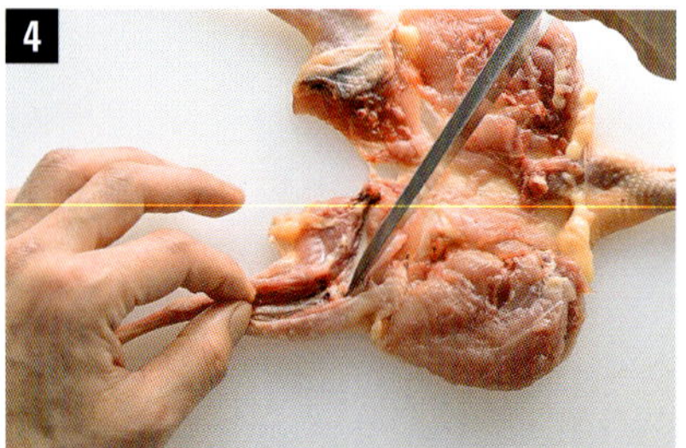

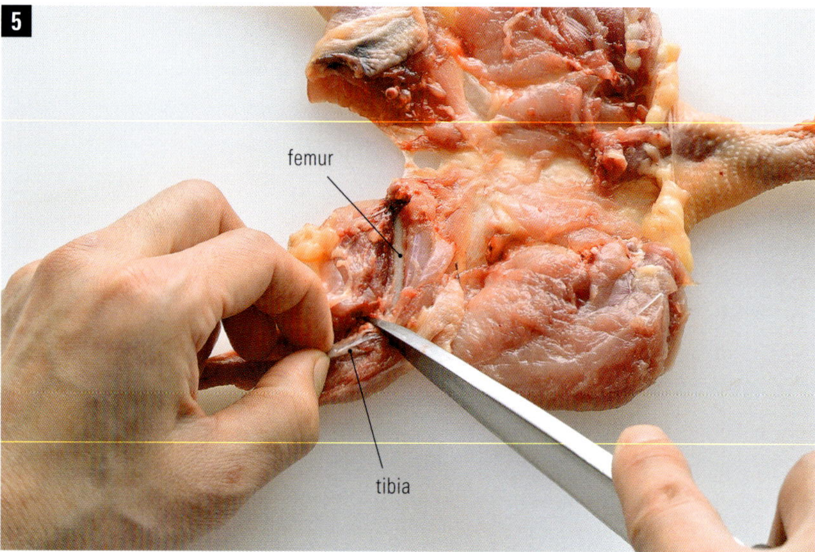

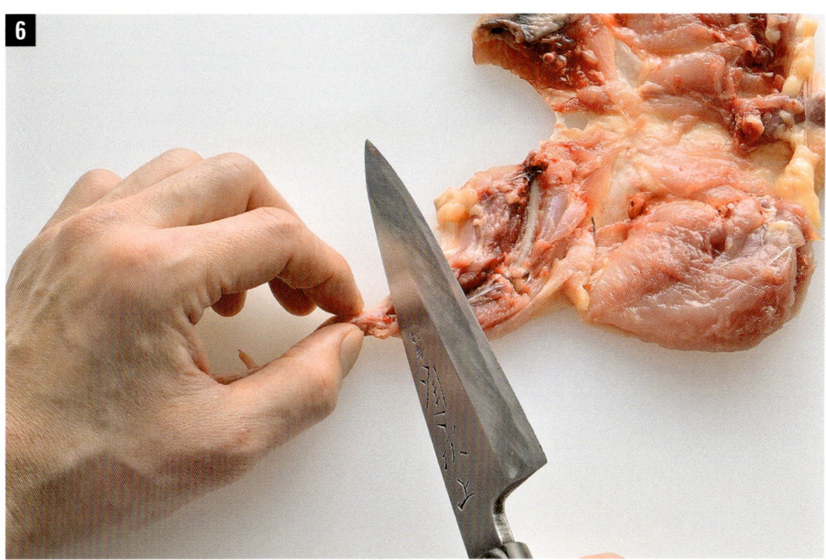
6

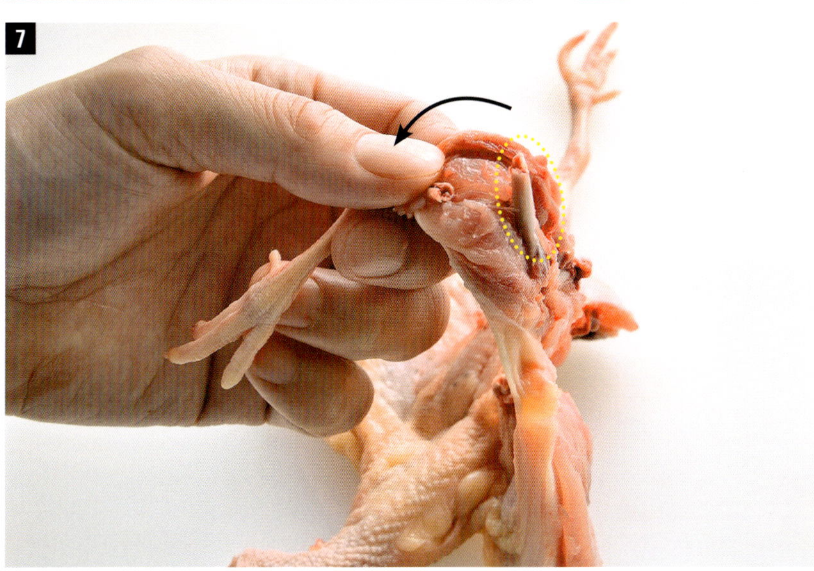
7

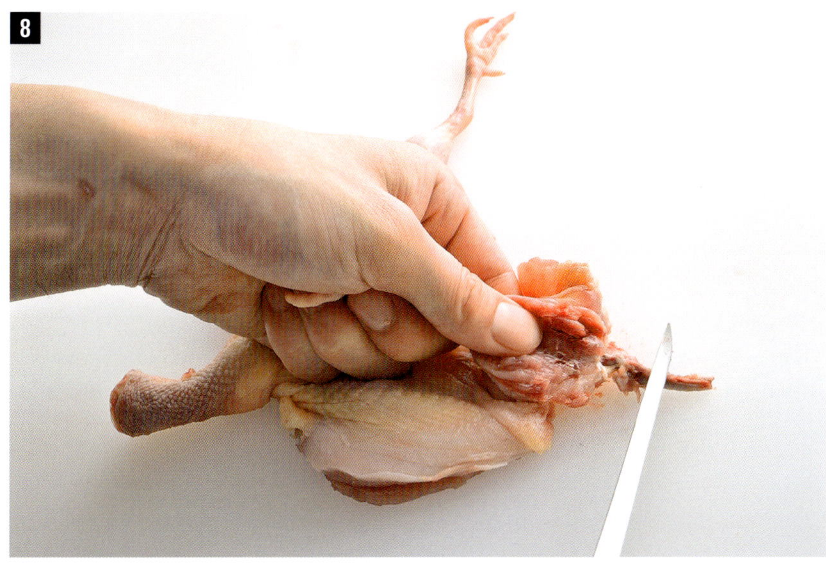
8

6 Strike the joint between leg and foot with the spine of the knife to break the bone.

7 Bend back the foot to expose the tibia.

8 Bend the meat so that the bone exposed in step 7 sticks out. Pin the bone to the cutting board with the blade (as shown) and push it out of the meat.

9 Place the blade at the joint and cut the bone away.

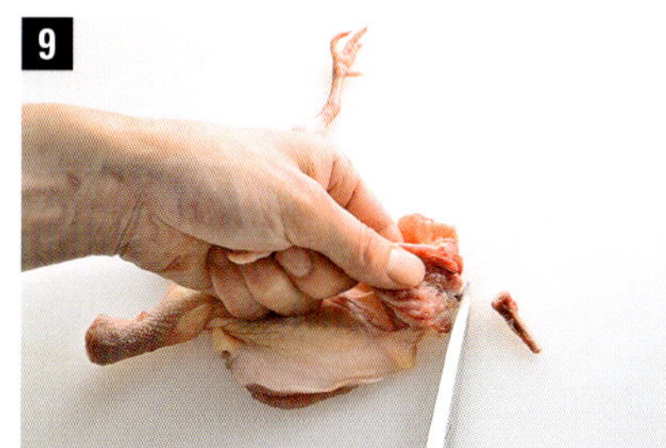
9

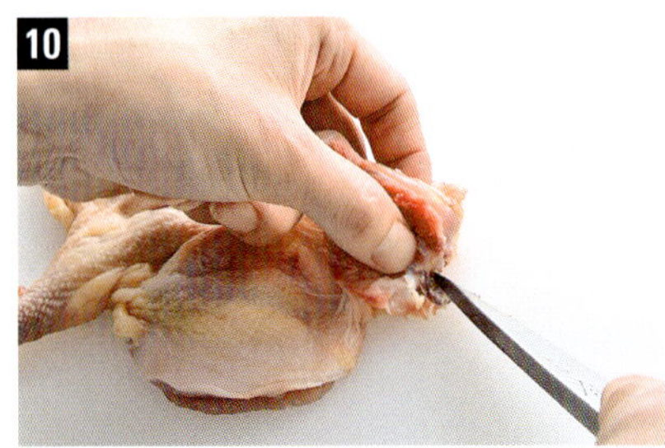

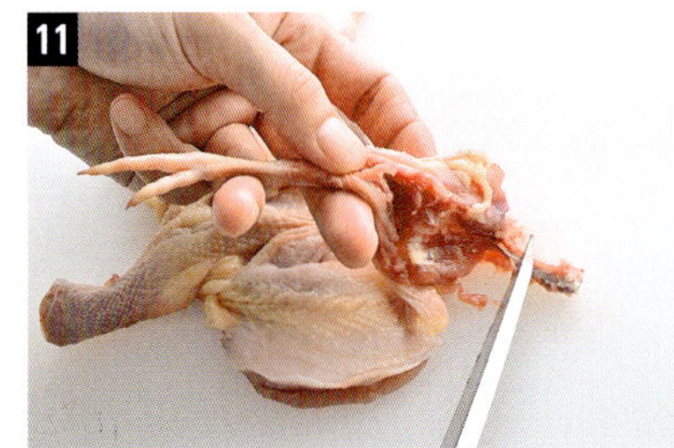

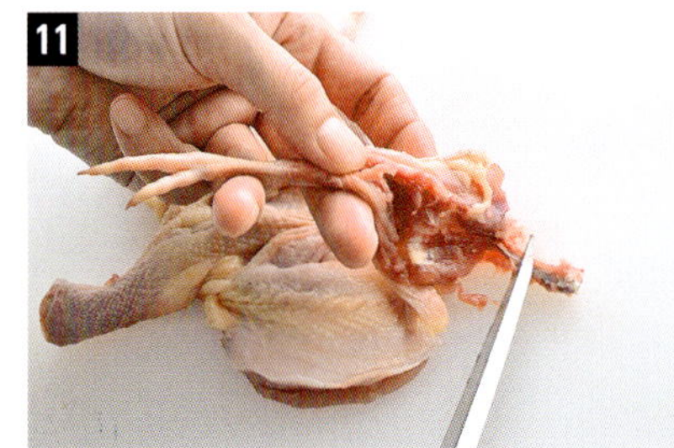

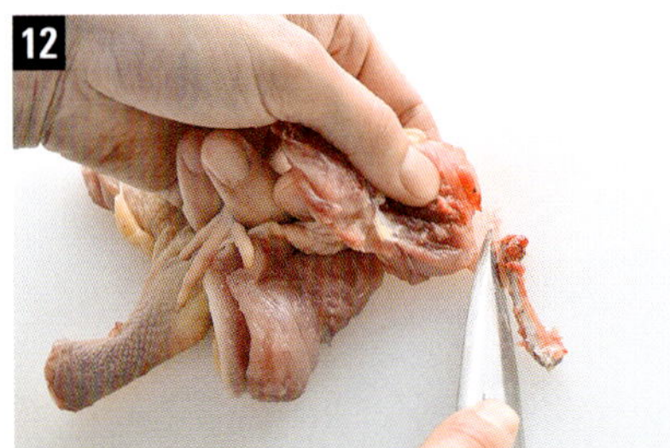

10 Cut the tendon at the end of the femur at the base of the thigh.

11 Pull the end of the bone out of the meat with the tip of the blade and pin it to the cutting board.

12 Keeping the edge of the bone pinned to the board, pull the leg with your left hand to expose the bone before you cut it away. Follow the same procedure for the right leg, removing the bone near the base of the thigh.

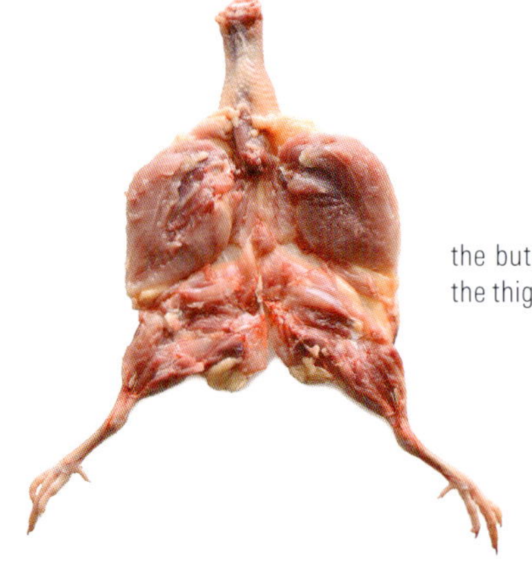

the butterflied bird with the thigh bones removed

Marinated and Grilled Quail

Uzura Tsuke-yaki

The butterflied bird is marinated beforehand to season it well and also dipped in sauce while grilling. A sweet marinade is well suited to quail, which has a stronger taste of wild meat than chicken. It scorches very easily, so the charcoal fire should be very carefully adjusted.

Serves 4

2 quail

Marinade (easy-to-use-quantity)

- 500 ml (generous 2 cups) sake
- 300 ml (1¼ cups) mirin
- 200 ml (scant 1 cup) *koikuchi* shoyu
- 50 ml (scant ¼ cup) *tamari* shoyu

2½ Tbsp. glucose syrup (*mizuame*)

About ¼ tsp. powdered *sansho*

4 pieces sweet potato, each 10 g (⅓ oz.)

500 ml (about 2 cups)+200 ml (about ¾ cup) water

6⅔ Tbsp. sugar

2 gardenia (*kuchinashi*) pods, cut in half

¼ tsp. black sesame

1 Butterfly the quails and remove the thigh bones. Make the marinade. Place all the ingredients in a pot and place over high heat. When the sauce boils, reduce to medium heat and simmer until alcohol is burned off and liquid reduced to about two thirds of original amount. Remove from heat and cool to room temperature.

2 Cut 10-g (⅓-oz.) pieces of sweet potato with one surface on the diagonal. Place about 500 ml (2 cups) water with the gardenia pods, each cut in half, in a pot over high heat. When the water begins to turn yellow, add the sweet potato pieces. After the liquid returns to a boil, reduce heat to low and simmer sweet potato for about 5 minutes until it turns yellow and is cooked through. Remove from water, place in a sieve, steam for about 5 minutes, and let stand to cool and allow excess moisture to evaporate. Place 200 ml water and sugar in a saucepan over high heat. When the water comes to a boil, lower heat, add the sweet potato, and simmer for about 10 minutes. Allow to cool in the pot.

3 Marinate the butterflied quail for about 5 minutes (for small birds, it may be enough to simply dip them in the marinade). Place meat side down on a pre-heated grill and grill until the liquid dries, then turn over. Grill the skin side likewise until the liquid dries, then dip the butterflied bird in the sauce and continue grilling. Grill both sides until they are well browned and lustrous with sauce.

4 Cut the butterflied bird to separate the breast and thigh meat, dust with *sansho* powder and arrange on in a serving vessel. Add sweet potato pieces garnished with black sesame seeds.

Marinated and Grilled Quail

sweet-simmered sweet potato
powdered *sansho*

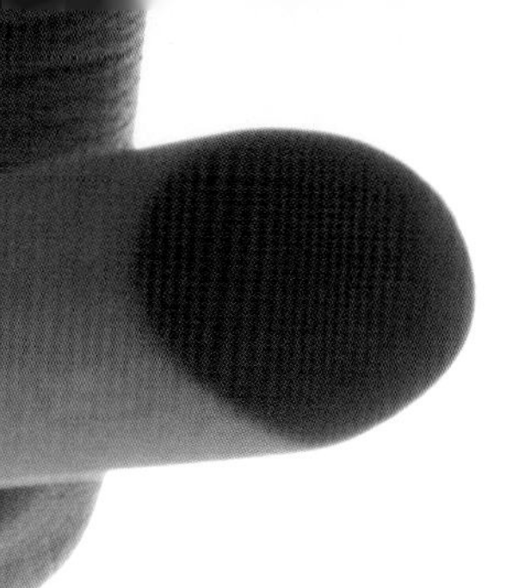

Chapter 4

Vegetable Cutting Techniques

Cutting of vegetables in Japanese cuisine includes a variety of techniques used for basic preparation and cooking as well as for decorative peeling and procedures to create garnishes for color and a sense of the seasons. This chapter presents the necessary, basic procedures as well as some of the widely used decorative cutting methods.

Basic Vegetable Cutting Techniques

Cutting of ingredients to uniform shape and size not only makes dishes easier to prepare and more attractive when served but promotes the even penetration of seasonings. The cutting techniques explained here are the most basic in Japanese cuisine. They are performed using mainly the *usuba* knife.

Sengiri "Fine strip" cutting (shredding or julienning)

The *sengiri* technique is used for cutting strands from thin slices or peels made by the *katsuramuki* rotary technique; the width of the strands varies depending on the dish. This is also the method used for the shredded-daikon garnishes (*ken*) for sashimi.

1 Cut the vegetable lengthwise into 5- to 6-cm (2¼-in.) cylindical pieces. Peel off the outer layer of each cylinder; quarter the cylinder, cutting into blocks through the vertical axis. Lay one of the quarters lengthwise with the rounded surface facing you.

2 With the fingers of the left hand straddled over the block and the thumb steadying it at the top, position the knife parallel to the cutting board with the tip slightly raised, keeping the heel of the blade close to the board, as shown. Cut into the top right front edge of the block and slice off about 1 mm. Keeping the heel of the blade close to the board, cut the next slice from the block beneath the cut slice.

Move the knife in an elliptical motion circling toward you, completing the cut at the knife's tip. Steady the cut slices with the left thumb, sliding the cut slices slightly back from the edge and leaving the staggered slices in place, as shown. With the left thumb, press the stack away from you to form a staggered pile.

3 Line up the slices across the cutting board so that they are slightly overlapping.

4 Curling the fingers of the left hand with the knuckles lightly touching the back of the knife, slice the staggered pieces vertically into fine, even strands about 1 mm wide.

1

2

3

4

Five-color *Kimpira*

Goshiki Kimpira

This colorful salad features green, white, yellow, and other vegetables all cut to the same dimensions using the "clapper" cut (*hyoshigi-giri*) technique explained on p. 227. The ingredients may vary from one season to another, and the satisfaction of the dish can be assured by using celery, green beans, and other crunchy vegetables.

Serves 4

50 g (1⅔ oz.) *kabocha* squash

50 g (1⅔ oz.) carrot

50 g (1⅔ oz.) celery

50 g (1⅔ oz.) green beans

50 g (1⅔ oz.) shiitake mushroom

1 Tbsp. + ½ tsp. roasted sesame

0.3 g *ichimi togarashi* chili pepper

1⅓ Tbsp. sesame oil

1 Tbsp. sugar

Generous 1 Tbsp. shoyu

1. Peel the squash and carrots and cut into 4-cm (about 2-in.) long, 5-mm (¼-in.)-square *hyoshigi-giri* strips. Remove the strings from celery and cut in strips of the same length and thickness. Cut green beans in half vertically and then into 4-cm (about 2-in.) lengths. Remove stems from the shiitake mushrooms, slice each cap into half its thickness and then into 5-mm (¼-in.)-thick strips.
2. Heat sesame oil in a frying pan and sauté vegetables over high heat for about 2 minutes. Add sugar and shoyu and continue frying over high heat while mixing well.
3. When the seasonings have been well absorbed and the excess moisture mostly evaporated, sprinkle over the red pepper flakes and roasted sesame seeds (1 Tbsp.) and remove from heat. Arrange in a dish and top with the remaining (½ tsp.) roasted sesame seeds.

Five-color Kimpira

roasted sesame

ichimi togarashi chili pepper

Araregiri "Hailstone" cut (dicing)

Cubes cut between 2 and 2.5 mm—likened to the size of hailstones (*arare*)—are used for ingredients of dressed foods (*aemono*) and toppings for clear soup dishes (*wanmono*). See *sainomegiri* (p. 228) for slightly larger cubes.

1. Cut the vegetable lengthwise into 5- to 6-cm (2¼-in.) cylindrical pieces, as in *sengiri* step 1. Quarter the cylinders. Lay one of the quarters lengthwise with the rounded surface facing you. From the right edge, cut into slices about 2 mm thick.
2. Align the slices so they are slightly overlapping and slice them vertically from the right into 2-mm-wide strips.
3. Align the strip ends and lengths and turn 90 degrees to the right. Cut into uniform 2-mm cubes from the right end.

1

2

3

Mijingiri Mincing

Diced cubes, even finer than for *araregiri*, should be about 1.5 mm square. *Mijingiri* is used for dressings, ingredients of clear soup dishes and steamed dishes, and for garnishes (*yakumi*).

1. Cut the vegetable, as in *sengiri* step 1, lengthwise into 5- to 6-cm cylindrical pieces. Quarter the cylinders. Lay one of the quarters lengthwise with the rounded surface facing you. From the right edge, cut into slices about 1.5 mm thick.
2. Align the slices so they are slightly overlapping, stacked slightly higher to the left. Slice them vertically from the right into 1.5-mm-wide strips.
3. Align the strip ends and lengths and turn 90 degrees to the right. Cut into uniform 1.5-mm cubes.

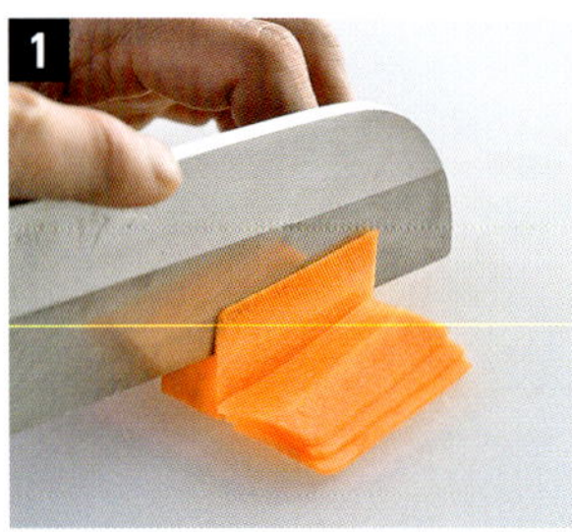

1

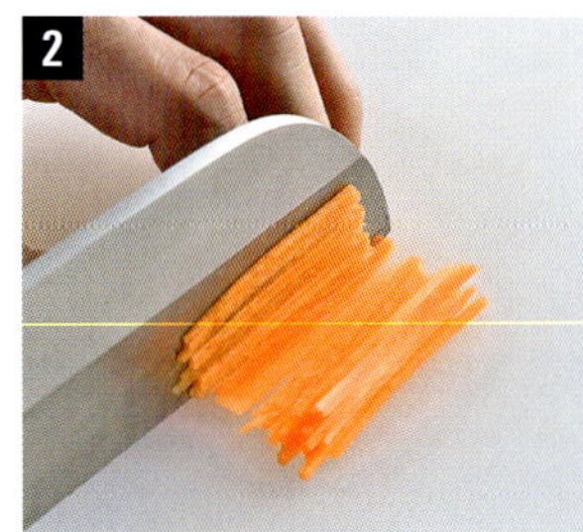

2

3

Wagiri Rounds

This method is for cutting vegetables crosswise into rounds used in simmered dishes. The diameter and thickness of the rounds vary according to the dish.

1 Cut the vegetable lengthwise into 5- to 6-cm (2¼-in.) cylindrical pieces and peel by the *katsuramuki* rotary technique. Place lengthwise on the cutting board. Insert the tip of the knife about 5 mm (¼ in.) from the right end and push forward along about half of the blade.

2 Draw the knife toward you and down, completing the cut. Inserting the knife, cutting down halfway, and drawing the blade toward you should be one motion. Cutting only with the part of blade near the tip assures that the ingredients will keep their shape in cooking.

Hangetsugiri "Half-moon" cut (half rounds)

Method for cutting half-round pieces. Cutting the cylinder in half first makes it quicker to make the half-moons and assure uniformity of shape.

1 As in *wagiri* (rounds) step **1**, cut the vegetable into cylinder-shaped pieces and peel. Cut each cylinder in half along the vertical axis.

2 As in the case of cutting rounds, using the tip of the blade, move the knife forward to cut part way and then pull back toward you to slice through; cut slices about 5 mm thick from the right end of each half cylinder.

Ichogiri "Ginkgo-leaf" cut (quarters)

This method is for cutting quarter rounds. The name comes from the resemblance of the cut to the shape of a ginkgo leaf. Usually done in thin slices that are used for garnishing (*ashirai*) of clear soup dishes and the like.

1. As in *wagiri* step 1, cut the vegetable into cylindrical pieces and peel. Cut the cylinders in half through the vertical axis and then each half in half again.
2. Place one of the quartered pieces lengthwise in front of you and cut, following the same motion as described for cutting *wagiri*, using the tip of the blade, moving the knife forward to cut part way down and drawing it back toward you to slice through. Cut from the right in slices about 2 mm thick.

Shikishigiri "*Shikishi* card" cut (thin squares)

This method is for cutting thin squares, the size of which will depend upon the dish and the serving vessel. Colorful carrot and daikon *shikishi*-cut pieces are often used for clear soup dishes.

1. Cut the vegetable lengthwise into 5- to 6-cm (2¼-in.) cylinders. Peel off the outer layer of each cylinder. Cut off about 1 cm from each cylinder on four sides to form a square in cross section.
2. Place the block lengthwise in front of you. Insert the tip of the knife about 3 mm from the right end and push forward along about half the length of the blade. Draw the knife toward you and down, completing the cut.

Tanzakugiri "Rectangular strip" cut

Pieces cut into thin rectangles are used for decorative purposes for clear soup dishes, soups, and for dressed foods and other dishes.

1. Cut the vegetable into 4- to 5-cm (about 2-in.) lengths and peel by the *katsuramuki* rotary technique. Cut into a block about 1 cm x 1 cm x 4 to 5 cm.
2. Using the tip of the blade, slice the block lengthwise, parallel to the fiber, from the right end in 1-mm-thick slices.

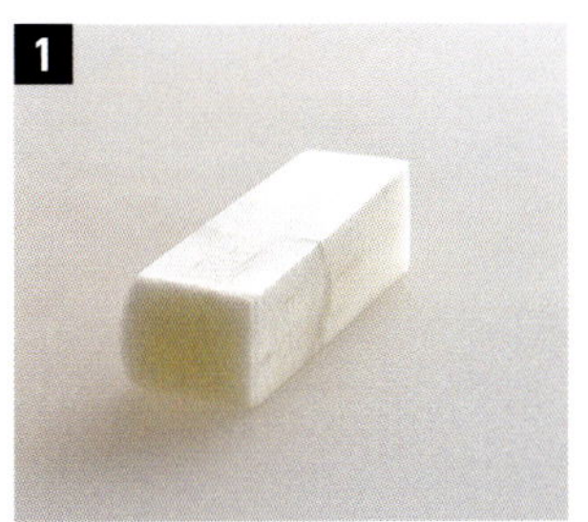

Hyoshigi-giri "Clapper" cut (rectangular blocks)

Slim blocks are widely used for dressed foods and simmered dishes. Uniformity of thickness and length is desired.

1. Cut the vegetable lengthwise into 4- to 5-cm cylinders and peel by the *katsuramuki* rotary technique. Cut off about 1 cm from each cylinder on four sides to form a square in cross section. Lay the piece lengthwise in front of you and cut 1-cm-wide slabs from the right side, parallel with the fiber.
2. Lay each slab flat and, using the tip of the blade, cut from the right side into 1-cm (½-in.)-wide rectangular blocks.

Sainomegiri "Dice" cut (cubing)

This technique is for making cubes by cutting aligned rectangular blocks. Vegetables are cubed mainly for simmered dishes. For smaller-scale cubing, see *araregiri* and *mijingiri*.

1. Cut the vegetable into rectangular blocks 1 cm (½ in.) thick and 1 cm (½ in.) wide.
2. Align the blocks lengthwise in front of you. Cut 1-cm (½ in.)-wide cubes from the right side.

Rangiri Irregular cut

This method is for cutting ingredients in random shapes, mainly for simmered dishes. The cut side is continually turned upward and the knife inserted at an angle (as shown). This technique increases the area of cut surfaces, allowing seasonings to penetrate thoroughly. Long, thin vegetables like burdock (*gobo*) are cut, rolled over, and cut again.

1. Scrub the burdock carefully to remove soil (the skin contains aroma and flavor, so do not peel). Place the burdock on the cutting board lying at an angle down to the right. Starting from the thick end, cut at an angle from the end.
2. With the left hand, roll the root toward you 90 degrees so that the cut side faces upward (the angle of the knife does not change) and cut diagonally as before, so that the pieces are about the same size.

Sasagaki "Bamboo leaf" cut (whittling)

This technique is mainly used with burdock. The long, thin vegetable is rotated and whittled or shaved like a pencil. Vegetables shaved by this technique are used in *aemono* dressed foods, *yanagawa* (*dojo*) hot pot made with loaches and burdock, and other dishes.

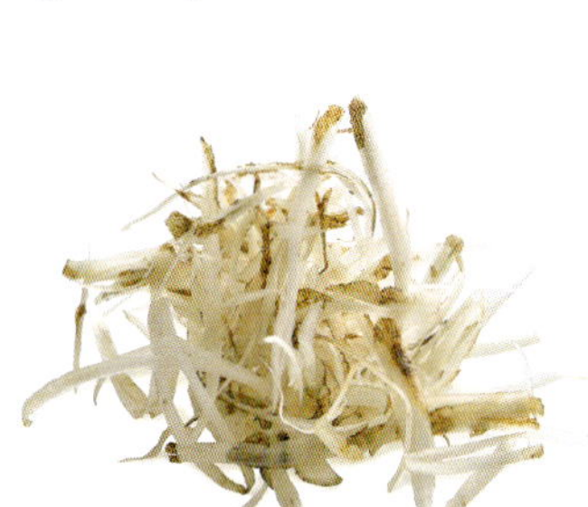

1. Cut off the ends of the burdock. Place the root lengthwise with the thin end to the right. Rotating the root with the left hand and holding the knife with the blade facing right (*sakasabocho*), use short, quick motions just grazing the surface to shave off flakes about 1 mm thick, as shown.
2. Where it is very thick, make several shallow cuts lengthwise around the root, as shown.
3. After making the incisions, continue whittling as shown in step 1.

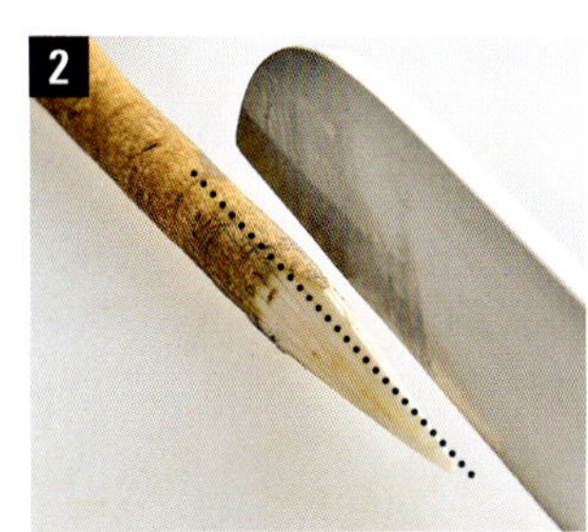

Koguchigiri "Small end" cut

This technique is for making uniformly thin crosscut slices of vegetables that are small in diameter such as long onions (*naganegi*) and Japanese cucumbers. The thickness of the slices will vary according to the dish.

Align a bunch of several *negi* long onions lengthwise and, steadying them with the left hand, cut 1-mm slices from the right end of the bunch.

Harigiri "Needle" cut

Slicing lengths of onion along the grain into extremely fine strips, this standard cutting technique for *ashirai* garnishes is the *harigiri* or "needle cut." In addition to long onions (*harinegi*), it is often used for cutting ginger root (*harishoga*) and yuzu peel (*hariyuzu*). When only the white part of the long onion (*naganegi*) is used, the needle strips are called *shiraga-negi* ("white hair *negi*"), but when white long onion and green onion are mixed, they are called *harinegi*.

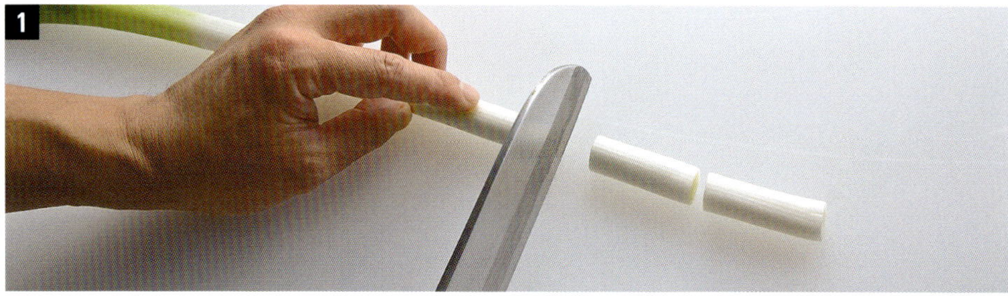

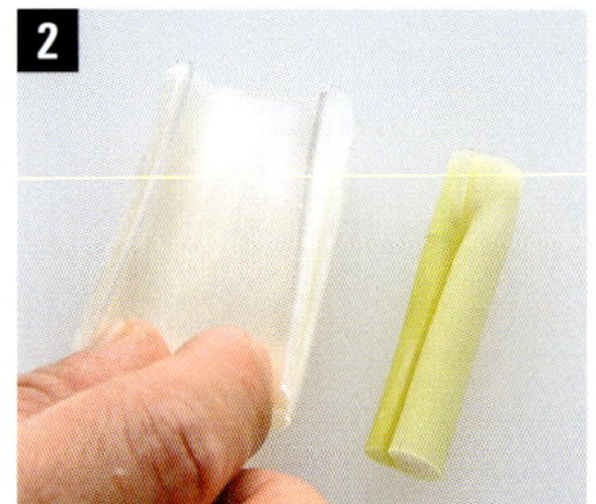

White and green strips can be mixed attractively by placing them together in water.

1. After cutting off about 1 cm from the root end of the long onion, cut the white part into 4- to 5-cm (about 2-in.) lengths.
2. Place one of the pieces vertically. Score the piece halfway through and remove the greenish center core.
3. Stack a few of the separated outside white "sheets" produced in step 2 and lay them lengthwise. Placing the inside down will keep the sheets from curving too much and also make them easier to cut.
4. Holding the sheets with the left hand, slice them along the grain into about 1-mm strips.
5. Soak in water for about 5 minutes (this removes the harshness and restores crispness).

Simmered Pork Belly *Buta Kaku-ni*

To survive the enervating effects of the intense heat of summer in Kyoto, a favored dish is simmered pork. The meat is simmered briefly to drain out the fat, and the dense umami and slight astringency of the *hatcho* miso as well as the richness of the dark sugar permeates deeply into the meat in the simmering process. The *harigiri*-cut long onion (also called *arai-negi*) added as a garnish provides a pleasant crunchy contrast to the soft texture of the meat.

Serves 4 or 5

1.5 kg (3⅓ lbs.) pork belly

15 cm (6 in.) white portion of long onion (*naganegi*)

Cooking liquid

- 540 ml (2¼ cups) sake
- 540 ml (2¼ cups) water
- 4⅔ Tbsp. unrefined sugar (*kurozato*)
- 4 Tbsp. *hatcho* miso
- 1 Tbsp. plus 2 tsp. shoyu

1. Cut the meat into blocks and brown them on all sides (do not use oil in the pan). Simmer for 15–16 hours in water saved from washing rice (*togijiru*) (if liquid decreases while simmering, add additional hot water). Rinse in cold water. Put meat and water in a pot and bring to a boil again. After water boils, remove the meat, rinse in cold water again, and cool. Place in a perforated tray and steam over high heat for 10 minutes, then allow excess moisture to evaporate while cooling.
2. Place ingredients for the cooking liquid in a pot, mix, and place over high heat. When liquid comes to a boil, lower heat to medium and add the meat prepared in step 1. Cover with a drop lid (*otoshibuta*) and simmer for 30 to 40 minutes.
3. Cut *naganegi* in the *harigiri* needle cut (facing page) and blot away excess moisture. Cut pieces of simmered pork into 5-cm (about 2-in.) cubes and re-warm before arranging in a dish. Pour over a little of the cooking liquid (about 2 Tbsp. per serving) and top with the *harigiri* long-onion garnish.

Simmered Pork Belly

arai-negi

Peeling and Decorative Carving

Peeling and decorate carving techniques that highlight the colors of the vegetables not only make dishes more attractive but express a sense of the season. Peeling methods such as hexagonal paring (*roppomuki*) also help ingredients keep their shape during cooking.

Katsuramuki

Basic to good peeling technique, regardless of the ingredient, is that the knife held in one hand and the ingredient held in the other move simultaneously. When the movement is coordinated, the cut surface will be smooth. The key point in the *katsuramuki* rotary cut technique is to clasp and steady the blade with the right thumb and forefinger.

To make the shredded daikon or other vegetable garnish—called *ken*—that serves as a bed for sashimi, cut thin layers made by the *katsuramuki* rotary technique into pieces about 5 cm wide, stack them, and cut very thin strips from the right edge. *Ken* strips may be either *tate ken*, cut along the grain of the fiber, or *yoko ken*, cut across the grain of the fiber. When used as a garnish, *tate ken* is stronger and will stand up higher and more crisply because more of the long fibers remain intact, so it is often used for dishes served on celebratory occasions.

The *katsuramuki* rotary technique results in a thin, virtually transparent layer of even thickness.

PREPARATION

Cut a piece of daikon (unpeeled) about 12–13 cm (about 5 in.) long. Hold the daikon in the left hand and lay the knife down along its length. Cut horizontally under the surface of the skin with the knife held nearly flat. With the left thumb lightly pressing both daikon and cutting edge and the right hand moving the knife up and down without changing the angle, use the left hand to rotate the daikon and peel off a layer somewhat thickly (this is because the flesh near the skin contains rather tough fibers).

TECHNIQUE FOR MAKING PAPER-THIN SHEETS

Holding the peeled daikon with the left hand, cut under the surface with the blade lying nearly flat. In order to peel a uniform thickness, place the left thumb at the center of the daikon cylinder, lightly pressing down on the blade. As when peeling off the skin, rotate the daikon against the knife as it moves up and down, cutting a paper-thin, continuous sheet until the daikon is pared down to a cylinder about the diameter of the thumb. The speed with which the left hand turns the daikon and the motion of the right hand should be coordinated.

Roppomuki Hexagonal paring

This method of paring away the skin of vegetables so that the ends form hexagons is often used for *satoimo* tubers. The shape holds well for simmered dishes because it does not have sharp corners.

1 Place a small to medium *satoimo* tuber on its side and cut off both ends.

2 The *satoimo* with both ends sliced off.

3 Holding the *satoimo* between the fingers of the left hand, hold the knife with the same grip as used for the *katsuramuki* rotary cut. Moving the blade upward and running over the bulging side of the tuber, pare off one side in a width of about one-sixth the circumference, judging by eye.

4 Pare the other side of the tuber using the same motion as described in step **3**. Rotating the *satoimo* with the left hand as with the *katsuramuki* technique, cut the other five sides.

Pare the *satoimo* on six sides as shown by the dotted line in the photograph.

Yorininjin Carrot curls

Yori means "spiral twist." This decorative cut applies the *katsuramuki* rotary technique. A layer of the vegetable is cut slightly thicker than is usual with *katsuramuki*. The peel is then cut into strips on the diagonal and shaped. Intended to express ocean waves, these decorative curls made with mainly with *udo* (aralia), daikon, carrot, and cucumber are used as garnishes with sashimi.

Udo and carrot curls, representing the auspicious red and white colors, make a festive garnish

1. Cut a cylinder of carrot and peel off the outer yellowish layer (fibrous part) using the *katsuramuki* rotary technique. Then peel the cylinder into a sheet about 0.8 mm thick
2. Spread out the sheet and lay it on a slant, top to the left, bottom to the right. Cut off the square end at an angle. Lift the edge slightly and, using the tip of the blade, cut diagonally across the grain to make strips about 5 mm (¼ in.) wide, sliding the knife tip from the far edge toward you.
3. Place in a bowl of chilled water for 20–30 minutes (soaking causes the strips to curl); wrap around a cooking chopstick and press lightly into the palm to form an attractive spiral shape.

Shobu-udo Iris-shaped *udo* cut

This decorative cut in the shape of an iris blossom is usually made with a slice of *udo* (aralia) stalk. Iris blooms in May, so it is often used for garnishes on sashimi or clear soup dishes served around that season of the year.

1. Peel a stalk of *udo* and cut into 3- to 4-cm (1¼-in.) lengths. Trim off the sides to form a rectangular block. Holding the block with the left hand, slice from the center of one end in an arc extending about two-thirds the length of the block toward the other end, as shown in the diagram ①②. Cut in an arc on the opposite side of the block as well.
2. Repeat to form two sets of "petals" (diagram: ③④). Cut a v-shaped notch just above the center as shown in the diagram ⑤.
3. Cut the block into 1-mm-thick slices.
4. Soak in water until the petals of the flower open slightly.

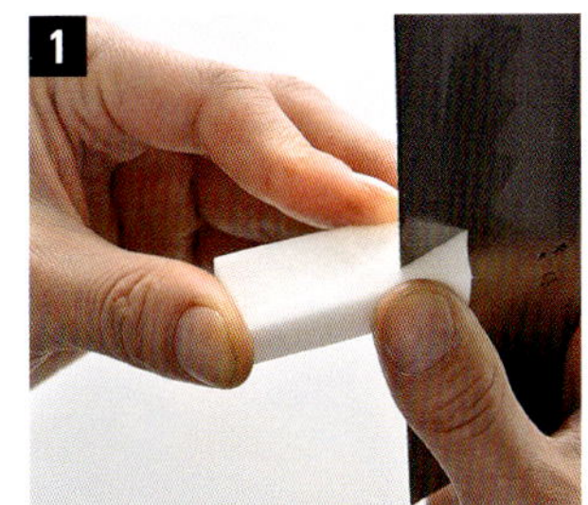

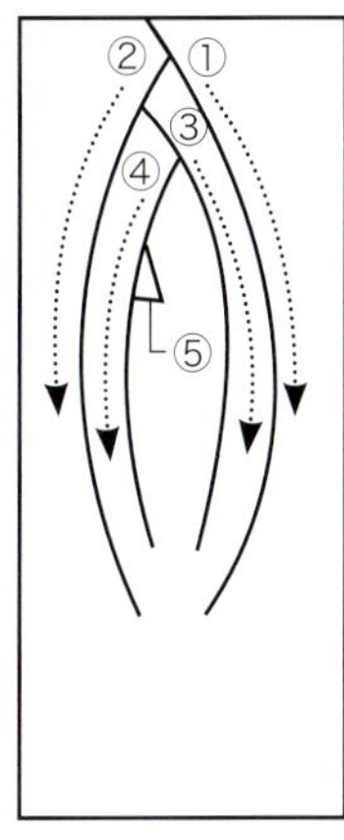

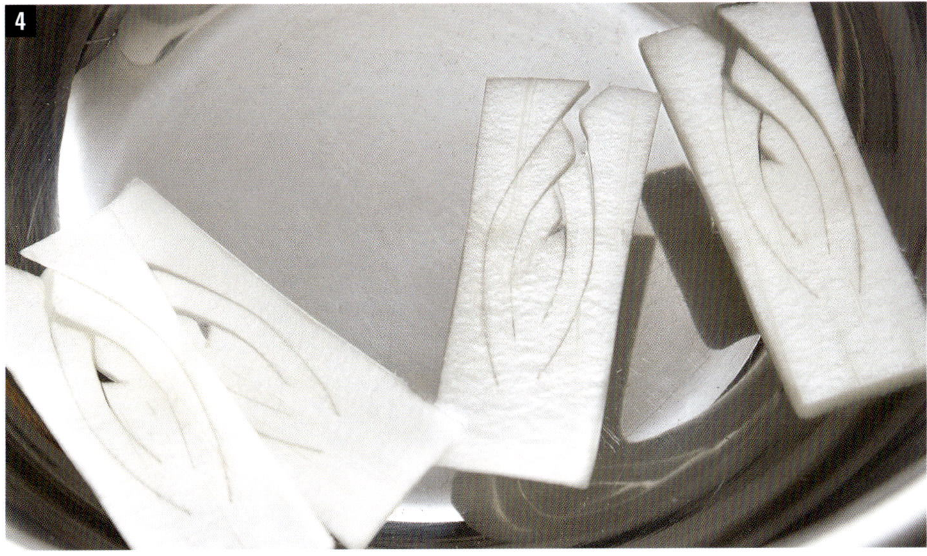

Baika-ninjin "Plum blossom" carrot

To peel a vegetable in a "plum blossom" shape, a cylinder is first cut into a pentagon shape, and then the sides rounded to form the petals. In order to make an attractive flower shape, it is crucial to cut a well-balanced pentagon. A variation of the same cutting technique is used for a cherry blossom shape.

Carrot and daikon plum blossom shapes form an auspicious "red and white" combination suitable for clear soup dishes for the early spring season.

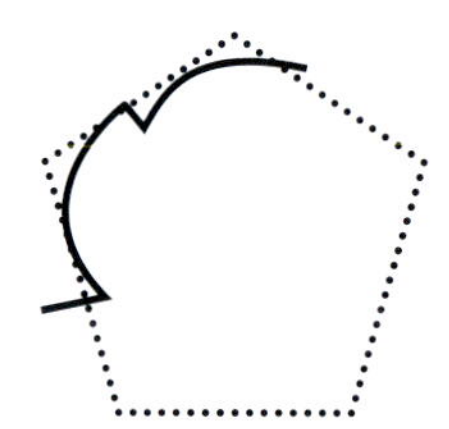

1. Peel the skin off a carrot and cut it into 5 to 8 cm cylinders. Lay the cylinder down and cut straight down to form one side; rolling the cylinder over, cut on four more sides to form a well-balanced pentagon.
2. Make a 2-to-3-cm (1¼-in.) deep incision both at one of the points of the pentagon and at the center of the side immediately to the right (see illustration). With the knife parallel to the length of the pentagon, insert the knife to the right of one point and round off the point in the direction of the incision to its left, as shown by the black line in the illustration.
3. Shows the piece after two of the points have been rounded off.
4. Repeating step 2, insert an incision between the other points and round off each point from the right to the incision.
5. Reverse the direction of the carrot end to end, and round off the points neatly to a clean curve.
6. Cut the plum-blossom-shaped cylinder into 8-mm (⅓-in.) slices.

To cut a cherry blossom, insert the blade to the left of one of the points of the pentagon and cut a gentle convex arc ending at the center of one side of the pentagon about 2–3 mm below the surface. Repeat cuts from each point, and reverse direction to round off opposite sides from each point. Finish by notching the tip of each point for the cherry blossom petal shape.

Nejiri-ume "Twisting" plum-blossom

Diagonal incisions are made on the petals for this variation of the plum-blossom cut, producing a more three-dimensional shape. Used for clear soup dishes, simmered dishes, and the like (*osechi* New Year's dishes, etc.), these floral tidbits add color and gaiety to the table.

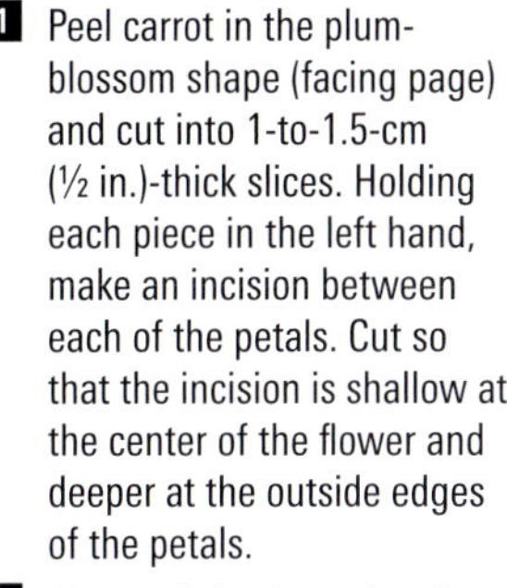

1 Peel carrot in the plum-blossom shape (facing page) and cut into 1-to-1.5-cm (½ in.)-thick slices. Holding each piece in the left hand, make an incision between each of the petals. Cut so that the incision is shallow at the center of the flower and deeper at the outside edges of the petals.

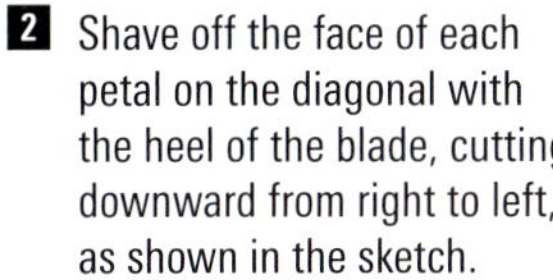

2 Shave off the face of each petal on the diagonal with the heel of the blade, cutting downward from right to left, as shown in the sketch.

view from top of the block

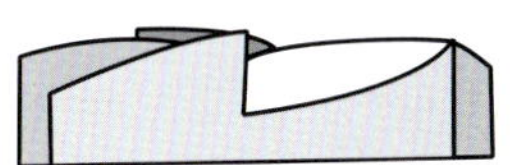

View from the side

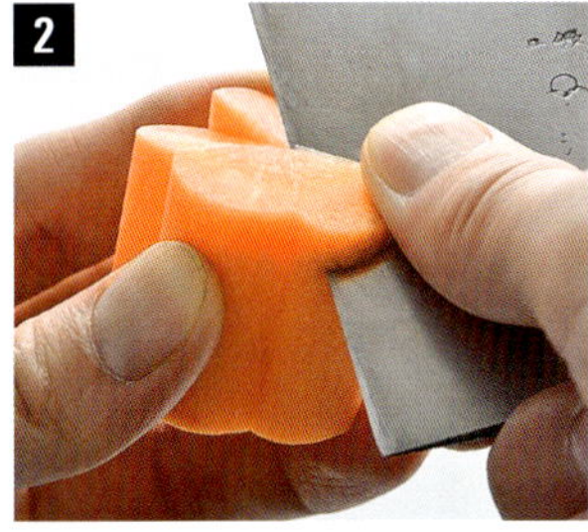

Hanabira-ninjin "Petal" carrot

This decorative cut is made to produce a flower petal shape. When notched at one end, it represents a cherry blossom petal. Petal cuts are made with *udo* (aralia), lily bulb, daikon, and ginger root and used as garnishes to highlight the season.

view from top of the block

①

view from the side of the block

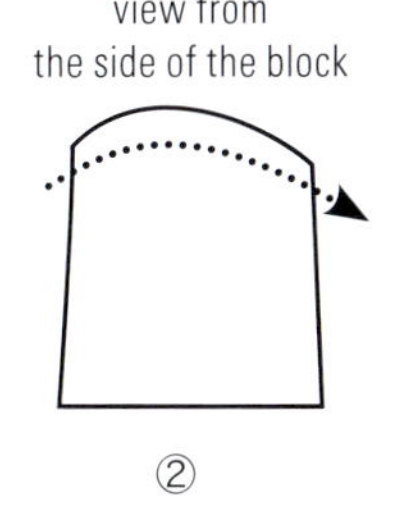

②

1 Cut a 3-to-5-cm (1¼-in.-to-2-in.) length of carrot and, using the *katsuramuki* rotary technique, peel and cut the block to form an elliptical shape in cross-section (as shown in drawing ①). Peel the other side to form the other side of the ellipse.

2 Holding the block in the left hand, use the heel of the blade to peel off a 2-mm-thick slice, carving it off in a rounded contour (as shown in drawing ②).

3 To represent a cherry blossom petal, make a small v-shaped notch in one end of the petal.

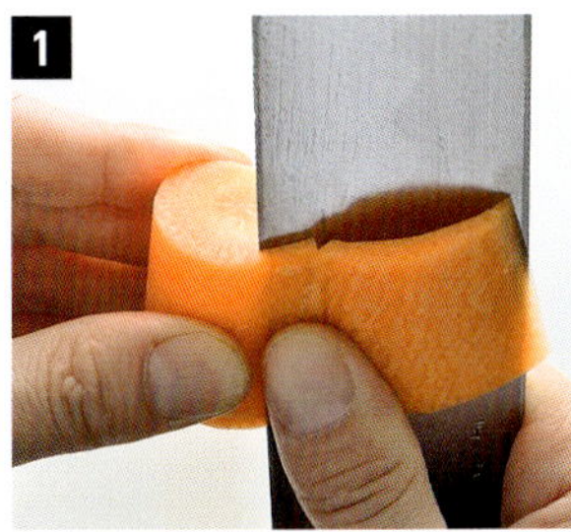

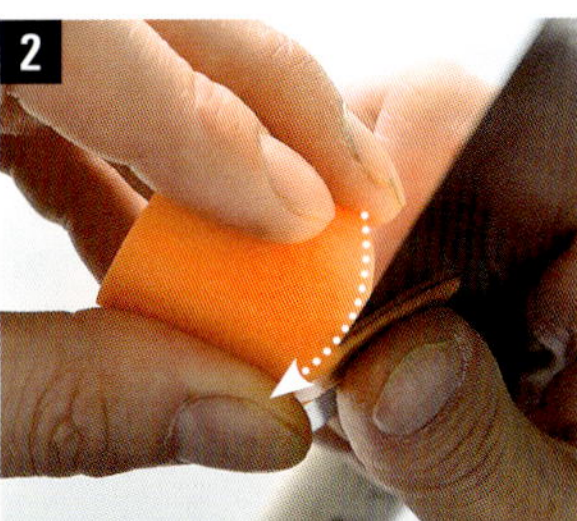

Kikka-kabura "Chrysanthemum-cut" turnip

This decorative turnip cut represents a chrysanthemum floweret. The flowerets are marinated in a sweet vinegar (*ama-zu*; p. 245) sauce and used as a garnish for grilled dishes and servings for special occasions.

1. Leaving the skin intact, cut a turnip in 2-cm (about 1-in.)-thick rounds (a number of flowerets can be made simultaneously from a large turnip).
2. Peel a thick slab from the circumference using the *katsuramuki* technique, removing the tough, fibrous layer on the outside.
3. Score at about 1-mm intervals down to about two-thirds of the thickness of the round.
4. Turn 90 degrees to the right and cut the slab again at about 1-mm intervals to the same depth.
5. Turn the cross-scored turnip slab upside down. Cut off the rough edges and cut into 1.5-to-2-cm (about 1-in.)-wide strips.
6. Turn 90 degrees to the right and cut into 1.5-to-2-cm squares.

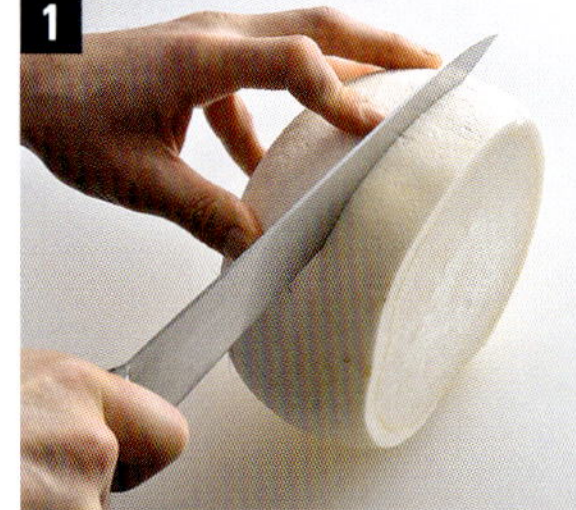
1

2

3

4

5

6

Sweet Vinegar Marinade

Place the squares in a 0.8 percent salt water bath; when the petals grow soft and open up, remove from salt water and squeeze out moisture. Marinate in *ama-zu* for two hours. Drain off *ama-zu*; open out the petals in a floral shape and place a round-cut piece of red pepper in the middle before adding as garnish.

Yuga-Style Grilled Butterfish

Managatsuo Yuga-yaki

Yuga-yaki is grilled fish that has been marinated in a sauce flavored with yuzu zest, the zest adding a tasty aroma to the fish. Here the fatty butterfish is marinated in a white miso sauce. The turnip cut in the chrysanthemum-cut (facing page) is a seasonal touch, evoking the simple *yugagiku* aster flower of autumn.

Serves 3

3 pieces butterfish, each weighing 70 g (2⅓ oz.)

3 2-cm (about 1-in.) cubes of *kabu* turnip

100 ml *ama-zu* (p. 245)

3 1-mm circles of red pepper

2 chrysanthemum leaves

Marinade (easy-to-use quantity)

- 1 kg (2¼ lbs.) white miso
- 180 ml (¾ cup) sake
- 180 ml (¾ cup) water
- 90 ml (generous ⅓ cup) mirin
- 2 Tbsp. *koikuchi* shoyu
- 1 Tbsp. *usukuchi* shoyu
- yuzu zest (from half a yuzu + from one quarter of a yuzu)

1. Make the marinade. Mix sake, water, mirin, and both kinds of shoyu in a pot and place over high heat. When liquid comes to a boil, remove from heat and cool. When cooled, mix in the white miso and add the yuzu peel from half a yuzu.
2. Fillet the butterfish and prepare pieces of about 70 g (2⅓ oz.) each. Marinate for 12 hours. After removing from marinade, wash away the miso and skewer in a "wave" shape, as shown.
3. Grill over medium heat starting with the top surface. When fish is well browned, turn over and grill for about 5 minutes on the other side. After grilling, remove the skewers and dust tops of "waves" with fine gratings of yuzu peel as shown.
4. Make the chrysanthemum-cut *kabu* turnips. Cut the turnip into 2-cm (about 1-in.) x 2-cm (about 1-in.) blocks. Score the blocks about 1.5 cm (½ in.) down, turn 90 degrees and score across, as shown on p. 238. Soak the blocks for an hour in water containing 3 percent salt by weight. Lightly squeeze out the water, then marinate for 2–3 hours in the *ama-zu*. Open out scored turnip pieces to look like a flower and put a circle of red pepper in the center of each "flower." Arrange the butterfish in a dish and add the turnip as garnish.

Yuga-Style Grilled Butterfish

Chrysanthemum-cut turnip

Chrysanthemum leaves

Kikka-renkon "Chrysanthemum-cut" lotus root

Using the *katsuramuki* rotary peeling technique, the lotus root is cut into a shape resembling a flower. Thin slices, flavored with vinegar, are used as a garnish with grilled dishes.

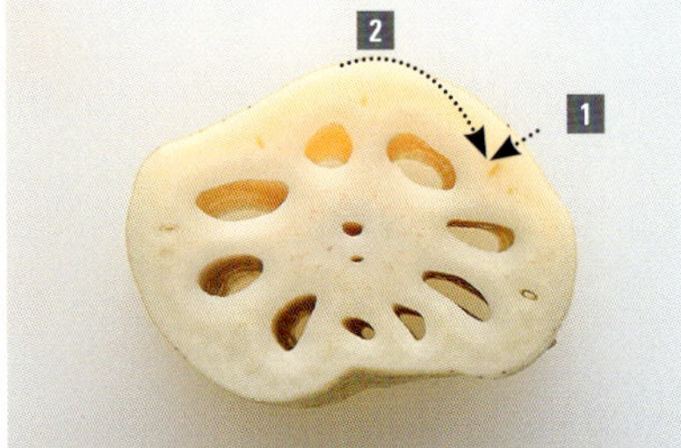

1 Cut the lotus root into pieces about 5 cm (about 2 in.) long, leaving the skin on. Holding the piece in the left hand, make a 2-to-3-mm incision in the spaces between all the holes around the perimeter of the root.

2 Peel off a layer of half of the root following the contours of the surface and connecting the incisions made in step 1. Reverse the direction of the block and connect the incisions on the other side. Turn the piece over vertically and connect the incisions while peeling off a layer as done previously.

Cut the piece of root into thin slices about 1 to 2 mm thick.

1

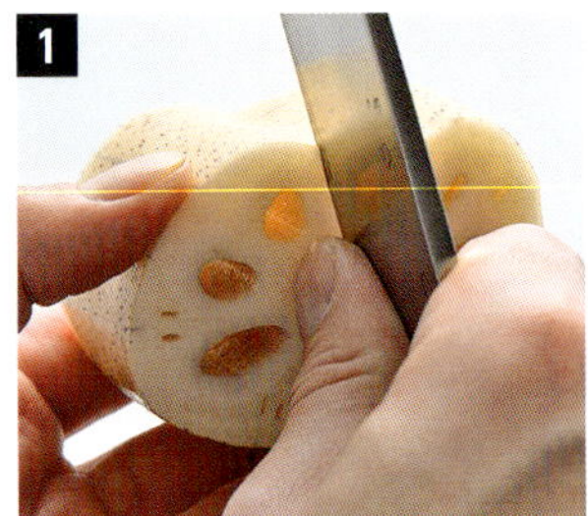

2

Konoha-kabocha "Tree leaf" squash

Used mainly for simmered dishes, this technique is for decorating chunks of squash with a "tree leaf" pattern cut into the green skin.

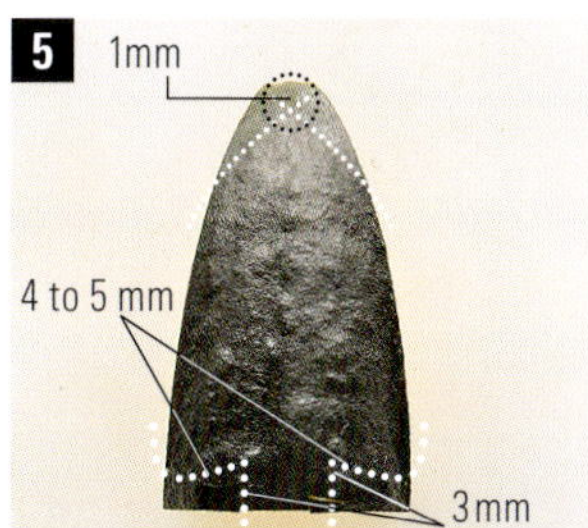

1 Cut a *kabocha* squash in half and, with the open side down, cut radially into three or four crescent-shaped (in Japanese *kushigata*, or "comb-shaped") sections.

2 Place one of the sections on its side and chop in half through the thickest part.

3 Remove the pithy inside part.

4 One bite-sized piece of squash, ready for decoration with the "tree leaf" pattern.

5 Place the piece with the skin side up. In the center of the wide end, cut in about 3 mm and notch on both sides (as shown) to form the "stem." Pare off the tip of the piece, removing about 5 mm (1/4 in.) from both sides of the tip (as shown; crossing about 1 mm below tip end).

6 Round off the sides as shown.

7 Cut the "tree leaf" pattern. Placing the heel of the blade in the center of the piece, cut a slender V-shaped notch representing the central leaf vein.

8 Using the heel of the blade, cut short notches on either side of the central vein cut in step 7.

9 Cut three or four branch veins on either side of the central vein notch.

Jabara-kyuri "Serpent-belly" cut cucumber

The slender Japanese cucumber cut halfway through on the diagonal in slender slices is likened to the appearance of a snake's belly and has an accordion-like stretch ability. *Jabara-kyuri* is used as a garnish with sashimi and in vinegared dishes.

1

2

3

4

1. Sprinkle cucumber with salt and work it in by rolling the cucumber on the cutting board (*itazuri*; p. 249). Plunge into boiling water for 3 seconds; transfer to ice water. Cut away about 1 cm (½ in.) at the stem end, which is bitter-tasting. Steadying the cucumber with the left hand, slit the cucumber from the right end, cutting through about two-thirds in 2-mm-thick intervals.
2. Turn the cucumber over and likewise slit in fine intervals from the opposite side.
3. Shows the cucumber slit from both sides. Slitting from both sides keeps the slices from detaching, and creates the snake-like texture.
4. Divide the cucumber into pieces about 1.5 cm (about ½ in.) in length. After cutting, soak for 2 or 3 hours in a 3 percent salt solution. This helps drain off excess moisture, giving it a crunchy texture and a light salty taste. The flavor will be further enhanced if kombu is added to the salt water. Drain and squeeze out the moisture after soaking. Display the serpent-belly texture by lightly pressing down on the sections.

APPENDIX

BASIC RECIPES

Ichiban Dashi

[pp. 141, 180]

Yields about 5.5 L (5.7 qt.)

7.2 L (7.2 qt.) water

120 g (4 oz.) Rishiri kombu

200 g (about 7 oz.) katsuobushi (*honkarebushi*) flakes

Place water and kombu in a large pot. Heat over low heat, slowly raising temperature to 140°F (60°C). Once liquid has reached 140°F (60°C), simmer for 1 hour, adjusting heat to maintain even temperature. This step brings out maximum umami.

Remove kombu and raise temperature to 185°F (85°C) over high heat. When temperature reaches 185°F (85°C), remove pot from heat and add katsuobushi flakes. Wait for the katsuobushi flakes to thoroughly soak up water. 10 seconds later, strain liquid through a fine-mesh cloth and leave to drain naturally, without squeezing the cloth.

Warijoyu

[pp. 69, 133]

Yields about 120 ml (½ cup)

100 ml (scant ½ cup) *ichiban* dashi

2 Tbsp. plus 1 tsp. *tosajoyu* (see below)

3 g katsuobushi flakes

Place dashi and *tosajoyu* (below) in pan and heat over high heat. When it boils, remove from heat and add katsuobushi. Strain after cooling.

Tosajoyu

Yields about 400 ml (1⅔ cups)

100 ml (scant ½ cup) de-alcoholized sake

200 ml (scant 1 cup) *koikuchi* shoyu

100 ml (scant ½ cup) *tamari* shoyu

Dash of mirin

20 g (⅔ oz.) katsuobushi flakes

10 g (⅓ oz.) kombu

Combine all ingredients except katsuobushi in pan and place over low heat. When liquid boils, remove from heat and add katsuobushi. Cool, then strain, squeezing liquid out of katsuobushi.

Grilling Sauce

[p. 68]

Yields about 3.5 L (3.7 qt.)

175 g (about 6 oz.) eel head and bones (grilled)

1.5 L (1.6 qt.) sake

2 L (2.2 qt.) mirin

1 L (1.1 qt.) *koikuchi* shoyu

150 ml (scant ⅔ cup) *tamari* shoyu

About 7 Tbsp. glucose syrup (*mizuame*)

Wash blood and debris from the eel head and bones, blot away excess moisture with a cloth, and roast well until crisp.

Place sake and mirin in a pot and heat over high heat. After liquid comes to a boil, lower heat to medium and simmer until reduced by 20–30 percent. Add the glucose syrup and increase to high heat; add the roasted eel head and bones. Bring to a boil once more; reduce to low heat and add the *koikuchi* shoyu and *tamari* shoyu. Taking care not to scorch the mixture, cook until thickened. Strain while the mixture is still warm.

CONVERSIONS

Measurements in this book are given in accordance with the metric system; conversions using standard U.S. measures are given in parentheses.

1 cup = 240 ml (rounded up from 236.59 ml)
1 ounce = 30 g (rounded up from 28.349 g)

Please use the conversion table below as a guide.

Volume	
Metric	**USA**
5 ml	1 teaspoon
15 ml	1 tablespoon
50 ml	3 tablespoons + 1 teaspoon
60 ml	¼ U.S. cup
80 ml	⅓ U.S. cup
100 ml	⅓ U.S. cup + 4 teaspoons
240 ml	U.S. 1 cup
400 ml	U.S. 1⅔ cups
480 ml	U.S. 2 cups = 1 pint
1000 ml (1 L)	U.S. 4 cups = 2 pints = 1 quart

Basic Vinegar Flavoring (*Kagen-su*)

[p. 133, 140]

Yields about 720 ml (about 3 cups)

400 ml (1⅔ cups) *ichiban* dashi
4 Tbsp. plus 1 tsp. *usukuchi* shoyu
2 Tbsp. plus 1 tsp. *koikuchi* shoyu
juice from 8 large *sudachi* and 2 yuzu

Place all ingredients in a bowl and blend.

Tosa-zu

[p. 153]

Yields about 880 ml (scant 4 cups)

600 ml (2½ cups) *ichiban* dashi
200 ml (scant 1 cup) rice vinegar
4 Tbsp. plus 1tsp. *usukuchi* shoyu
1 tsp. sugar
5 g kombu
20 g (⅔ oz.) katsuobushi

Place all ingredients except katsuobushi in a pan and heat over high heat. Add katsuobushi just before the mixture boils and remove from heat. Strain after cooling.

Pon-zu

[p. 56]

Yields 850 ml (about 3½ cups)

100 ml (scant ½ cup) sake
100 ml (scant ½ cup) mirin
420 ml (about 1⅔ cups) shoyu
2 Tbsp. water
360 ml (1½ cups) juice of two or more citrus like yuzu or lemon.

Heat sake and mirin to evaporate alcohol. Add shoyu and water and boil mixture briefly. Add citrus juice and store in refrigerator for 2 days to allow flavors to blend. Strain and refrigerate.

Kimi-zu

[p. 153]

Yields about 130 ml (about ½ cup)

5 egg yolks
50 ml (scant ¼ cup) rice vinegar
1 Tbsp. sugar

Place all ingredients in a bowl and mix well. Place bowl over in boiling water (340°F /170°C) and mix well until thickened. When thickened, remove from heat, press through a sieve, and cool.

Ama-zu

[pp. 45, 238, 239]

Yields about 850 ml (about 3½ cups)

200 ml (scant 1 cup) rice vinegar
600 ml (2½ cups) water
80 g (2⅔ oz.) sugar
7 g kombu

Mix vinegar, water, and sugar. Place kombu in mixture and let sit for one day.
Place ingredients in a pan and heat; remove from heat when it boils. Remove kombu after mixture has cooled.

Sushi-zu

Yields about 180 ml (¾ cup)

120 ml (½ cup) rice vinegar
1 Tbsp. plus 1 tsp. sea salt
75 g (2½ oz.) sugar

Combine all ingredients in a pan and bring to a boil. Mix well, and when salt and sugar dissolve, remove from heat.

Sushi Rice

[pp. 45, 57]

Yields about 450 g (2½ cups)

210 g (generous 1 cup) rice
1 cup plus 2 Tbsp. water
2.5 cm (1 in.) square kombu
2 Tbsp. *sushi-zu* (recipe above)

Wash rice in two or three changes of cold water and let drain in a sieve 30 minutes before cooking. Combine kombu, water, and rice in a rice cooker and cook. Let the just-cooked rice rest for 10 minutes and transfer to a sushi tub. Pour the *sushi-zu* over the rice and mix using a rice paddle in a gentle slicing and tossing motion.

Length	
Metric	USA
3 mm	⅛ inch
6 mm	¼ inch
1.25 cm	½ inch
2.5 cm	1 inch
5 cm	2 inches
6.25 cm	2½ inches
7.5 cm	3 inches
10 cm	4 inches

Weight	
Grams	USA
10 g	⅓ ounce
15 g	½ ounce
20 g	⅔ ounce
30 g	1 ounce
50 g	1⅔ ounces
100 g	3⅓ ounces
150 g	5 ounces
200 g	7 ounces

Temperature	
Celsius (°C)	Fahrenheit (°F)
100°C	210°F
120°C	250°F
130°C	270°F
150°C	300°F
160°C	325°F
170°C	340°F
180°C	350°F
190°C	375°F
200°C	390°F

Japanese Kitchen Utensils

The cutting techniques for the fish in this volume (horse mackerel and sardines) call for scaling using the *deba* knife, but since the fish scaler is often used for scaling large fish, we include it here for reference.

Fish scaler

Uroko-tori

Utensils for removing fish scales allow a quicker, more efficient job than a knife and are also easy to use on large fish. Removing scales is difficult if the surface of the fish is dry, so it should be wetted first.

Wire for neural spiking

Shinkeijime waiya

This wire is used for severing the spinal cord in order to best preserve the freshness of fish. The wires are available in various lengths and thicknesses depending on the shape of the fish. A wire long enough to firmly spike the fish to be used for cooking should be selected.

Bamboo brush

Sasara

This cleaning utensil is made from narrow bamboo splints bundled to form a brush. Used for clearing blood and debris left after fish has been cleaned, the *sasara* has bristles that can reach every crevice without damaging the flesh. Bamboo is not moisture resistant, so the brush should be thoroughly cleaned and dried after use.

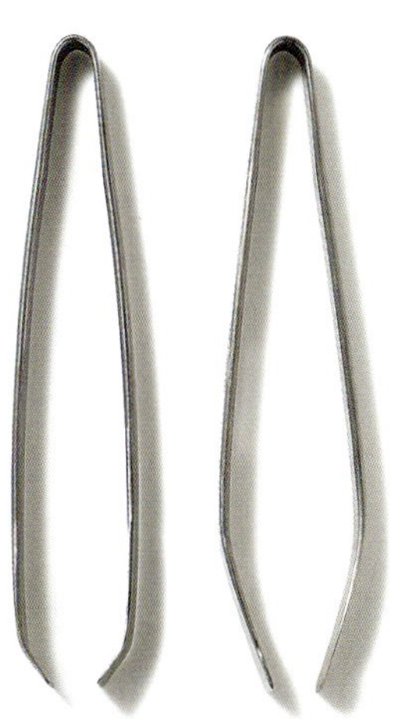

Fish-bone tweezers

Hone-nuki

Tweezers for kitchen use with a strong grasp that facilitates deboning fish, whether the bones are large or small. Come in various shapes and sizes, and different ones are used depending on the size of the fish.

Grater and brush

Oroshigane, burashi

Although graters can also be made of ceramic or glass, this one of metal, with tiny raised metal teeth is a standard grater in Japanese kitchens. A special grater-cleaning brush makes it easy to remove lingering bits remaining in the teeth. Such brushes are usually made of bamboo.

Wasabi grater

Samegawa-oroshi

This grater, consisting of a piece of sharkskin (*samegawa*) glued onto a wooden base, is used mainly for grating wasabi into a fine paste. Grating wasabi against the textured sharkskin gives the paste a mellow tang and a fine aroma. The wasabi root top (not the bottom) should be held vertically against the grater and grated slowly in a circular motion.

GLOSSARY

Aka-oroshi
Grated radish mixed with chili powder. Grated carrot is sometimes added to further enhance the color. Also called *momiji-oroshi*.

Ara
Head, central bones, collar, tail, and other bones remaining from the filleting of fish. Rich in umami, *ara* are sprinkled with salt and eaten grilled, or simmered, or used to make soup broth.

Arai
Method of removing excess moisture, fat, and strong odors from fish by thoroughly washing sashimi of very fresh fish such as sea bream or carp in ice water. The procedure gives the flesh a crisp and crunchy texture.

Arai-negi
Garnish made by chopping long onions (*naganegi*) or green onions (*aonegi*) in thin rounds, wrapping loosely in cheesecloth, and swishing in water to rinse away sliminess; the cheesecloth should be gently wrung.

Ashirai
Garnishes added to enhance the flavors of the main ingredients as well as the color and aroma of a dish. Applies to daikon beds for sashimi, condiments like wasabi, and accents such as green ingredients of soups.

Chiai
Dark meat specific to fish, found in abundance especially in migratory fish that are very active. The dark meat is rich in iron and other nutrients but tends to have a strong odor. Its freshness decreases quickly, so it is usually removed from fish to be used for sashimi. The term *chiai* is also used for the area where blood collects along the central bones of the fish.

Engawa
Muscle along the base of the dorsal and anal fins of flounder (*hirame* or *karei*). The muscle of the *engawa* is succulent and fatty and, since the amount found on one fish is small, is considered a sashimi and sushi delicacy. The name derives from its structural resemblance to the veranda (*engawa*) of a house. The fringe of tough tissue around the body of abalone or *tokobushi* abalone is also called *engawa*.

Empera
The wide side fins (also called *mimi*) of squid.

Fundoshi
Apron. Also called *maekake* or *hakama*, it is the soft part of the undershell of the crab. In male crabs, it is triangular in shape, while in female crabs the upper part is rounded.

Gani
Sponge-like tissue on the inside of the crab's carapace that functions like the gills of fish. The *gani* decays quickly and often harbors parasites, so it is best not to eat it.

Gara
Bones remaining after removing flesh from poultry such as chicken or duck. Used mainly for making soup stock or broth.

Gari
Pickled ginger, made with thin slices of gingerroot rubbed with salt. May be blanched in boiling water to remove bitterness and then pickled in *ama-zu* (see p. 245).

Geso
Literally "lower legs," this is the term for the "arms" surrounding the head in the class Cephalopoda ("head"+"foot"), including various kinds of squid and octopus.

Hamabofu
A plant of the same family as *seri* (water dropwort), but with slender reddish stems and green leaves, which grows along the seashore. It is used as a garnish with sashimi for its distinctive aroma and slight astringency.

Hana sansho
Flowers of the male **sansho** plant.

Hana yurine (lily bulb "flower" garnish)
For this garnish served mostly with grilled dishes, the tips of the lily bulb corms are notched to form a floral shape resembling a peony and then the whole is steamed with salt.

Hanamaru kyuri
A slender, small (about 10 cm) cucumber. Often used to fashion garnishes for sashimi or grilled dishes.

Himo
The mantle around the main body of such shellfish as scallops or Broughton's ribbed ark shell. Also called *kai-himo*. In addition to being served with sashimi or in *aemono* salads, it is a delicacy in its dried form as well.

Honekiri
Cutting technique for finely scoring the flesh of pike conger (*hamo*) and other fish with fine bones too numerous to remove. Practice is needed to master the skill of making very fine incisions in the flesh without cutting through the skin.

Ikejime
Method of spiking a fish after capture; spiking the brain and spinal cord slows the stiffening of the muscles and maintains the quality and freshness of the flesh until the fish arrives in the kitchen.

Itazuri
Sprinkling a vegetable with salt and rolling on the cutting board. The rolling promotes permeation of salt and helps in removing bitterness as well as bringing up the color of the vegetable. Method used frequently with cucumbers (p. 242) and butterbur (*fuki*).

Ji
Dashi seasoned with salt, soy sauce, and other ingredients. Varieties include *suiji*, which is used for thin soups, and *happoji* (versatile base), which contains dashi, sake, mirin, or other ingredients and is used in preparing a wide variety of dishes. Marinating ingredients in a seasoned liquid like this is called *jizuke*.

Kagen-su
A basic vinegar flavoring, a combination of vinegar, *ichiban* dashi, and seasonings. Made mild enough even to drink. Used to dress *sunomono*, *aemono*, as well as kombu-cured sashimi.

Kama
Collar. Arc-shaped area behind the gill cover, the area to which the pectoral and ventral fins are attached, often carries ample fat.

Kani miso
Crab "butter." The paste-like substance attached to the inside of the crab's upper carapace. Color and shape differ with the species of crab and with size. The texture is rich and creamy.

Kanokobocho
Square- or diagonal-grid scoring of ingredients. The basic procedure is scoring the ingredient lengthwise. When the scoring is on the diagonal, the effect is called *matsukasabocho* ("pine cone" cut).

Katsuramuki
A 6-to-7 cm cylindrical section of a vegetable—usually a *daikon*—peeled while rotating into a thin continuous sheet. This sheet may then be cut into long threads or into decorative forms.

Ken
Thinly cut strands of vegetable, usually daikon or carrot, used as a garnish or cushion for sashimi. Strands cut with the grain, called *tate ken*, are used for mounded garnishes, and strands cut against the grain, called *yoko ken*, are used as a bed on which sashimi is laid.

Kesho-jio (decorative salt)
Salt applied to fish or other ingredients immediately prior to grilling to give them an attractive appearance. The areas where the salt is applied will stand out with a whitish tinge, and a generous amount of salt on the tail and fins inhibits scorching.

Kikka-kabura
This decorative turnip cut evokes the shape of a chrysanthemum flower. It is marinated in *ama-zu* (p. 245) and used as a garnish for grilled and other dishes.

Kimo
Generally referring to the liver in fish, *kimo* is a choice delicacy for its rich flavor. Especially prized are the liver of *anko* (monkfish), known as *ankimo*, as well of *okoze* (devil stinger), and *kawahagi* (filefish). If very fresh, liver may be eaten raw or salted, but cooking is recommended. *Kimojoyu*, made by boiling *kimo*, pressing it through a sieve and softening it with shoyu and sake, is a sashimi dipping sauce. In some fish and shellfish, the term *kimo* may be used to refer to the internal organs (including the liver), or to the reproductive glands, or to the intestinal tract.

Kobujime
This is a technique of curing whereby the umami of kombu is transferred to other ingredients such as white-fleshed fish (sea bream, flounder, etc.) by sandwiching or rolling up salted fish in strips of kombu.

Komi
Another name for *yakumi*, the term for garnishes used with sashimi to provide a refreshing piquancy or spice and bring out the flavor of the fish. Includes wasabi, grated daikon, and **arai-negi.**

Kosode-zushi
This type of molded sushi—so named because the cross-section of a piece evokes the sleeve of a kimono (*kosode*)—is smaller than the usual molded sushi.

Kushiuchi
Skewering technique(s) with bamboo or metal skewers for grilling ingredients over direct heat. Allows appropriate adjustment of distance from the fire and helps maintain the shape of the ingredients while grilling.

Kuzu

A thickening starch made from the root of the kuzu vine, it is often used in Japanese cuisine because it does not change the taste or coloring of the food.

Mimi (see Empera)

Moromi

The fermentation mash prepared in the process of making sake or shoyu. The solids remaining after pressing out the liquid from sake *moromi* are sake lees (*sakekasu*). The solids remaining from making shoyu can be eaten as is or used as a seasoning.

Mukimono

Carving vegetables for decorative effect or to make them easier to cook; the leading techniques are **katsuramuki** rotary peeling, flower-cut carrots, and the *roppo-muki* method of hexagonal paring of *imo* tubers.

Ore-matsuba

This is a decorative trimming usually made with yuzu peel after removing the white spongy inner peel, which is bitter. The *matsuba* (pine-needle) shape (p. 173) is made by slitting a long slender strip of yuzu peel down the center, leaving about 5 mm connected at one end. The *ore-matsuba* decorative cut, made by cutting the strip in thirds from opposite directions, imitates the look of two pine needles joined together.

Otoshi

One method of preparing pike conger (*hamo*) by plunging 3-cm pieces into boiling water until the flesh opens out like a flower and then curing in ice water to remove excess fat and tighten the flesh. (See also **yubiki** and **shimofuri**)

Sakasabocho

Cutting with the knife blade facing upward or to the right. This technique is used when cutting fish, for example, in removing belly bones.

Sakutori

Preparing blocks of fish to make sashimi by trimming the flesh and removing the **chiai**, belly bones, and skin. The blocks are called *saku*.

Sanmai oroshi

Literally, "three-piece cutting," *sanmai oroshi* is the most basic of fish-dressing techniques. The head is removed and the body filleted, slicing off the "top fillet" (*uwami*) and the "lower fillet" (*shitami*), leaving the central bones (backbone and tail) as the third piece.

Sansho

Japanese pepper (*Zanthoxylum piperitum*). The dried seeds have the sharpness of pepper and leave a tingling sensation that lingers on the tongue. The young leaves, called *kinome*, are used as an aromatic garnish. The flowers of the male plant are also a favored garnish.

Sasami

Tenderloin (or tender) of chicken breast or other fowl, named after the shape, which resembles the leaf of broad-leaf bamboo (*sasa*). The texture is tender, with little fat, and the flavor is light.

Sazanami-zukuri

Slicing the tough flesh of abalone, octopus, and other shellfish tipping the blade up and down in a waving motion, to create a somewhat uneven surface—like waves on a beach (*sazanami*)—to make the morsels easier to eat.

Shimofuri

Scalding fish or meat by plunging briefly in boiling water, then immediately cooling in cold water so that the surface turns white, leaving a pattern resembling frost (*shimo*). *Shimofuri* removes fishy or fatty smells and seals in the food's umami (see also **yubiki**).

Shiomigaki

Method of cleaning the suction-cup side of abalone and other shellfish by rubbing with salt before scrubbing with a brush to remove grime and sliminess (p. 155).

Shiraga-negi

A garnish used for grilled dishes and "soups" made by cutting the outer white part of the long onion (*naganegi*) using the *hari-giri* (needle cut) technique and soaking the slices in water.

Shiroita kombu

Kombu kelp from which the surface has been planed to form thin, translucent sheets. Used in making *saba* (mackerel) sushi, *battera* sushi, and other preparations (see p. 45).

Shitami

Lower fillet. Flesh of the fish on the lower side when it is placed with the head to the left and the belly facing you (see **uwami**).

Sotoko

Fertilized crab eggs attached under the apron of the female crab. *Sotoko* have a crunchy texture (see also **uchiko**, **fundoshi**).

Tade

An annual herb, also called *yanagitade*, with a distinctive aroma in its leaves and stems. There are red and green varieties. A common condiment for *ayu* (sweetfish) is a mixture of ground green *tade* leaves and **tosa-zu** vinegar. Red *tade* (*benitade*) leaves are a frequent garnish for sashimi.

Tasuki-otoshi

Method of removing the head from a fish leaving the collar (*kama*) in place by cutting in a deep v-shape so as to minimize amount of flesh adhering to the head.

Tataki

Method of preparing sashimi by searing the surface of the block briefly over a strong fire and then cooling in ice water. Often used with bonito (*katsuo*), known as *Tosa-zukuri*. The term is also used for dicing up the flesh of fish, such as horse mackerel, into small pieces.

Tebiraki

After removing the head and internal organs, the fish is opened up and the central bones removed using the fingers rather than a knife. This method is adopted for sardines and other small fish with very soft flesh and numerous small bones.

Tosa-zu

A vinegar mixture made by mixing dashi, *usukuchi* shoyu, and mirin, heating, then adding *oigatsuo* to deepen the umami. With this richer umami, it makes a suitable dressing for salads containing light-tasting seafood.

Tsukejoyu

Shoyu prepared for dipping sashimi. Shoyu alone can be too strong, so restaurants may have a recipe for their dipping shoyu made by adding seasonings and dashi.

Tsukuri

Sliced sashimi. The term may also be used to denote the method of cutting *usu-zukuri* or *hoso-zukuri*.

Tsuma

One of the garnishes served with sashimi. The significance of the *tsuma* is primarily decorative and usually added to evoke the season. Examples are curled vegetable strips, shiso leaves, **hamabofu** sprigs.

Tsuyu-shoga

The juice of grated raw ginger.

Uchiko

Unfertilized eggs found inside the abdomen of the female crab. The season for harvesting snow crab lasts only about two months, so the rich-flavored *uchiko* is a particularly prized delicacy (see also **sotoko** and **fundoshi**).

Udo

Aralia cordata. The stalk and young leaves of this indigenous mountain vegetable have a crisp texture and a flavor resembling that of asparagus or celery with a faint licorice overtone.

Umami

Along with sweet, sour, salty, and bitter, umami is considered one of the five basic tastes, resulting largely from the presence of glutamic acid, inosinic acid, and other umami substances.

Uwami

Upper fillet; the flesh of the fish on the upper side when the fish is lying with its head to the left and the belly facing you. The upper fillet may be used for sashimi and the lower fillet for simmered or grilled dishes (see also **shitami**). The same characters are also read *jomi*, which refers to the choicest parts of fish after bones and inedible parts have been removed.

Warijoyu

Shoyu that has been flavored with dashi and other seasonings. Used for dipping sashimi. See **tsukejoyu**.

Yakishimo

Seared sashimi. The block is seared on the skin side briefly over a strong fire and transferred to ice water to serve rare. The searing not only gives the sashimi a toasty aroma but draws out the umami of the fat. This technique is often used for sea bream, bonito, pike conger, and other fish with umami in their skins.

Yori

Literally "strings," these are spirals made by cutting vegetables in the **katsuramuki** peeling technique then cutting the slices on the diagonal and soaking them in water until they curl up. Curled daikon, carrot, and *udo* are frequently used as decorative garnishes with sashimi.

Yubiki

Scalding of fish, a technique used in preparing sashimi. The fillets are briefly plunged into boiling water and then transferred to cold water to remove unpleasant odors and excess fat. Often used for *anago* (conger eel) and octopus. This is an alternative term for **shimofuri**.

Zeigo

Hard scales of horse mackerel found in a line from the tail along the sides of the fish. Generally they are sliced away before further preparation.

INDEX

Page numbers in *italics* refer to a recipe.
Titles of a dish are also in *italics*.

Publication Committee Chairperson: Nakata Masahiro, Japanese Culinary Academy
Art Direction and Design: Miki Kazuhiko and Hayashi Miyoko, Ampersand Works
Editing: Kawakami Junko, Letras
Writing: Kawakami Junko and Kitagawa Yoshiko
Translation: Center for Intercultural Communication
Copyediting: Kim Schuefftan
Proofreading: Center for Intercultural Communication

PHOTO CREDITS
Saito Akira: pp. 11, 13–27, 30–71, 75–87, 89–242
Yamagata Shuichi: pp. 8–9, 74, 243, 246–247
Kuma Masashi: Jacket

COOPERATION
The publisher thanks the following individuals and institutions for cooperation with photography for this book:
pp. 28–29: New World Transparent Specimens/Tomita Iori; pp. 72–73: A and Z Co., Ltd

CONTRIBUTORS
Nakata Masahiro, specialist in Japanese cuisine: The Hygiene for Food Eaten Raw (p. 10); Knives in the Japanese Kitchen (p. 12)

英文版 日本料理大全 向板Ⅱ
切る技法 魚介類、鳥類、野菜

2025年4月6日発行

監　　修	特定非営利活動法人 日本料理アカデミー 村田吉弘
出版委員長	仲田雅博
発 行 者	栗栖正博
制作責任	築地　正
発 行 所	特定非営利活動法人 日本料理アカデミー 〒604-8187 京都府京都市中京区東洞院通御池下ル 笹屋町436番地 office@culinary-academy.jp https://culinary-academy.jp/ Tel 075-241-4163／Fax 075-241-4168
印刷・製本	大日本印刷株式会社

ISBN 978-4-911188-07-1 C3077